Collins Children's Thesaurus

Published by Collins
An imprint of HarperCollins Publishers
Westerhill Road, Bishopbriggs, Glasgow G64 2QT

HarperCollins Publishers
1st Floor, Watermarque Building, Ringsend Road,
Dublin 4, Ireland

First Edition 2018

10 9 8 7 6 5

ISBN 978-0-00-827118-3

www.collins.co.uk/dictionaries

Typeset by QBS Learning

Printed in India by Replika Press Pvt. Ltd.

A catalogue record for this book is available from the British Library.

If you would like to comment on any aspect of this book, please contact us at the given address or e-mail dictionaries@harpercollins.co.uk.

Acknowledgements
We would like to thank those authors and publishers who kindly gave permission for copyright material to be used in the Collins Corpus. We would also like to thank Times Newspapers Ltd for providing valuable data.

Managing Editors:
Maree Airlie
Mary O'Neill

Contributors:
Anna Osborn
Lynne Tarvit

Artwork and Design:
Maria Herbert-Liew

For the Publisher:
Kerry Ferguson
Michelle Fullerton
Laura Waddell

FSC
www.fsc.org
MIX
Paper from responsible sources
FSC™ C007454

This book is produced from independently certified FSC™ paper to ensure responsible forest management.

For more information visit: www.harpercollins.co.uk/green

Contents

How to use this thesaurus

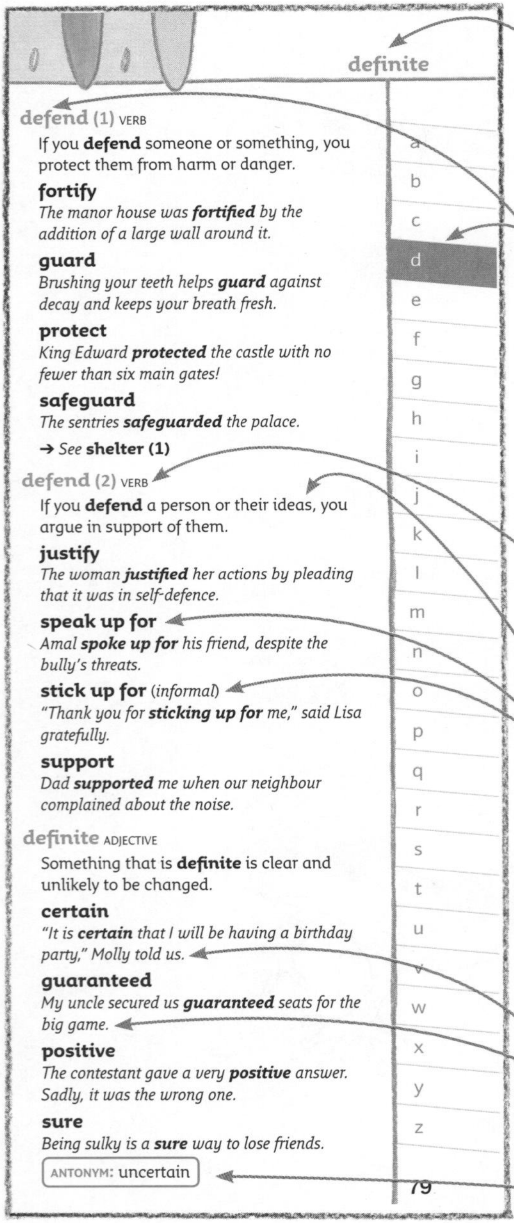

definite

defend (1) VERB

If you **defend** someone or something, you protect them from harm or danger.

fortify
*The manor house was **fortified** by the addition of a large wall around it.*

guard
*Brushing your teeth helps **guard** against decay and keeps your breath fresh.*

protect
*King Edward **protected** the castle with no fewer than six main gates!*

safeguard
*The sentries **safeguarded** the palace.*

→ *See* **shelter (1)**

defend (2) VERB

If you **defend** a person or their ideas, you argue in support of them.

justify
*The woman **justified** her actions by pleading that it was in self-defence.*

speak up for
*Amal **spoke up for** his friend, despite the bully's threats.*

stick up for (informal)
*"Thank you for **sticking up for** me," said Lisa gratefully.*

support
*Dad **supported** me when our neighbour complained about the noise.*

definite ADJECTIVE

Something that is **definite** is clear and unlikely to be changed.

certain
*"It is **certain** that I will be having a birthday party," Molly told us.*

guaranteed
*My uncle secured us **guaranteed** seats for the big game.*

positive
*The contestant gave a very **positive** answer. Sadly, it was the wrong one.*

sure
*Being sulky is a **sure** way to lose friends.*

ANTONYM: uncertain

a b c d e f g h i j k l m n o p q r s t u v w x y z

79

1. The **guide word** on a left-hand page tells you the first word you will find on the page. On a right-hand page, the guide word tells you the last word on the page.
2. The **alphabet line** shows you which letter you are in.
3. The **headword** is the word in blue, listed in alphabetical order. Some headwords have a number in brackets. This tells you that this headword can have different meanings, so you need to find the right one.
4. The **word class** tells you if the headword is, for example, a noun, verb, adjective, adverb or pronoun.
5. The **definition** tells you what the word means.
6. **Synonyms** are words that you can use instead of the headword. Sometimes synonyms have a label, for example, *formal* or *informal*. *Formal* tells you that a word is used in serious writing and speech. *Informal* tells you that a word is used between family and friends. The most informal words are marked *slang*.
7. Each synonym has an **example** to show how the word is used.
8. You will find **antonyms**, which are words that have the opposite meaning, for some words.

9 **Blue boxes** contain words for different 'types of' something, or more specific words for certain things.

10 Sometimes **illustrations** are included to show you different types of something. These appear throughout the thesaurus so that you can compare things which are similar but not quite the same. This will help you to extend your vocabulary and choose the most appropriate word for what you want to say.

11 A **language tip** helps you with the spelling of words or the way they are used. A **pronunciation tip** shows you how to say a difficult word.

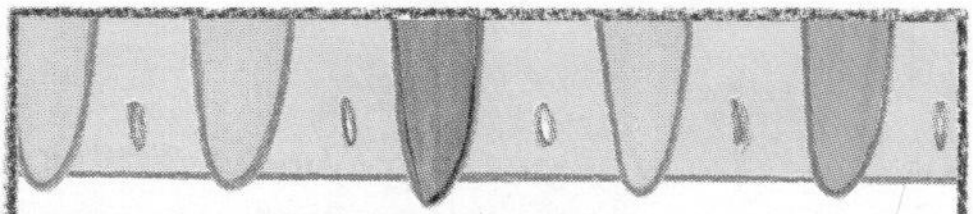

Shades of blue:

aquamarine	azure	indigo
navy	sky blue	turquoise

boast VERB

If you **boast**, you talk proudly about what you have or what you can do.

brag
*Alison couldn't resist **bragging** about her new DVD player.*

blow your own trumpet
*I prefer modest people to those who **blow their own trumpet**.*

crow
*Paulo was so busy **crowing** about his marks, that he didn't see Mrs Walker behind him.*

show off
*Brian is always **showing off** about the amount of pocket money he gets.*

boat NOUN

A **boat** is a floating vehicle for travelling across water.

craft
*At that distance, it was hard for the coastguard to identify the **craft**.*

ship
*Sir Francis Drake sailed in a **ship** he named the Golden Hind.*

vessel
*The tiny tug was nevertheless a sturdy **vessel**, capable of pulling much larger boats.*

➔ Have a look at the **Illustration** page!

body NOUN

Your **body** is all of you, from your head to your feet.

build
*Although flyweight boxers only have a slight **build**, they are powerful for their size.*

figure
*My sister maintains her **figure** by practising yoga regularly.*

form
*A shadowy **form** hovered at the end of Nikki's bed, but it was only her mum, tucking her in!*

physique
*Most sportspeople lift weights in the gym to improve their **physique**.*

LANGUAGE TIP
The upper body is the **trunk** or **torso**.

Word Power

There are special pages throughout this thesaurus called **Word Power**. These pages help you find more precise or interesting words to replace words that are used too often.

Imagine, for example, that you want to say *We had a nice day*, but you don't want to use the word 'nice' too often, or you just want to use a better word!

Look at the **Word Power** page for 'nice'. You will find it in its alphabetical position in letter N.

As you would with any entry, use the word class and definition to help you choose exactly which meaning of 'nice' you want:

> **(2)** ADJECTIVE A **nice** event is pleasant and enjoyable.
>
> **delightful**
> *"What a **delightful** evening," said Pete.*
>
> **enjoyable**
> *We spent an **enjoyable** hour chatting on the phone.*
>
> **pleasant**
> *The sun shone and the whole barbecue was a **pleasant** event.*

Then you can choose a synonym from the list to use instead of 'nice':

We had an enjoyable day.

There are **Word Power** pages for these over-used words:

bad	**eat**	**laugh**	**sad**
big	**good**	**look**	**say**
cold	**happy**	**nice**	**small**
cry	**hot**	**run**	**walk**

Aa

ability NOUN

If you have **ability**, you have the intelligence and skill to do things.

competence
*Sunita showed **competence** in most school subjects, particularly science.*

gift
*Jack had a **gift** for remembering long and complicated equations.*

skill
*Brackford United played with enthusiasm but little **skill** in Saturday's match.*

talent
*Seamus has a **talent** for cooking delicious seafood dishes.*

ANTONYM: inability

able ADJECTIVE

If you are **able** to do something, you can do it.

allowed
*"I'm **allowed** to play for half an hour, but then I have to go home," Ron complained.*

available
*Rhys said he was **available** to swim for the team on Saturday.*

capable
*Mrs Diss said that my twin brother was a **capable** pupil, but rather lazy.*

free
*My big sister is **free** to take me bowling now.*

ANTONYM: unable

about (1) PREPOSITION

If you talk or write **about** a particular thing, you say things that are to do with that subject.

concerning
*The police interviewed the bank manager **concerning** the robbery.*

regarding
*Parents were sent a letter **regarding** half term.*

to do with
*Mum had a long phone conversation **to do with** our holiday plans.*

about (2) ADVERB

You say **about** in front of a number to show it is not exact.

approximately
*The theatre held **approximately** 800 people.*

around
***Around** 50 000 people attended the big game.*

in the region of
*The bike cost **in the region of** £100.*

more or less
*Each jar holds **more or less** five litres.*

roughly
*We had to wait for **roughly** three hours.*

about (3) ADVERB

About can mean in different directions.

around
*"Stop dancing **around** while I'm talking to you," Mum said irritably.*

here and there
*My sister's clothes were scattered **here and there** in her room.*

hither and thither (*old-fashioned*)
*The bee flew **hither and thither** collecting pollen from the flowers.*

about to PREPOSITION

If you are **about to** do something, you are just going to do it.

on the point of
*I was **on the point of** closing the front door, when the phone rang.*

ready to
*The pilot was **ready to** turn back, when he saw the missing boat.*

above (1) PREPOSITION

If one thing is **above** another, it is directly over or higher than it.

on top of
*Ali balanced the bag of flour **on top of** the door, so that it would fall on Craig when he came in.*

over
*A cloud of smoke hung ominously **over** the grumbling volcano.*

ANTONYM: below

A B C D E F G H I J K L M N O P Q R S T U V W X Y Z

above (2) PREPOSITION

Above can mean greater than something in level or amount.

beyond
*The dancer's skill was **beyond** anything we could have imagined.*

greater than
*The number of visitors to the museum this year is **greater than** last year.*

higher than
*The cost of the repairs was **higher than** Mum had expected.*

ANTONYM: below

absolutely ADVERB

If you are **absolutely** sure about something, you are completely sure of it.

completely
*Anoop was **completely** satisfied with his new computer.*

thoroughly
*We were **thoroughly** fed up of waiting for the train to arrive.*

totally
*We sat **totally** enthralled by the magician's amazing tricks.*

utterly
*The instructions to the board game left me **utterly** confused.*

abuse (1) NOUN

Abuse is the cruel treatment of someone.

cruelty
*Sadly, many animals are injured through **cruelty** or neglect.*

harm
*Fortunately, the two lost children were found with no **harm** done to them.*

ill-treatment
*Oliver Twist suffered much **ill-treatment** in the workhouse.*

PRONUNCIATION TIP
When it is a noun, **abuse** is pronounced ab-**yooss**.

abuse (2) VERB

To **abuse** someone is to treat them cruelly.

harm
*Now the animal was at the rescue kennels, no one could **harm** it any more.*

ill-treat
*People who **ill-treat** their animals should face heavy fines.*

mistreat
*Cinderella was constantly **mistreated** by her two ugly sisters.*

misuse
*The dictator **misused** his power by giving jobs to his relatives.*

PRONUNCIATION TIP
When it is a verb, **abuse** is pronounced ab-**yooz**.

accident NOUN

An **accident** is something that happens suddenly or unexpectedly, causing people to be hurt or killed.

collision
*Eight vehicles were involved in a **collision** during the heavy rain.*

crash
*The police advised that the airport should be closed because of the plane **crash**.*

mishap
*Falling off my bike was a minor **mishap**, but luckily I wasn't hurt.*

→ *See* **disaster**

accidental ADJECTIVE

Something that is **accidental** has not been planned.

unexpected
*The sail's tearing in the wind was a totally **unexpected** problem.*

unintentional
*"I didn't mean to stand on the flowers. It was quite **unintentional**," I apologised.*

unplanned
*Although our beach volleyball tournament was **unplanned**, it was a great success.*

ANTONYM: deliberate

accurate ADJECTIVE

If something is **accurate**, it is absolutely correct.

exact
*In order to set my watch, I need to know the **exact** time.*

factual
*Non-fiction books are **factual** accounts of real people and events.*

faithful
*The French version of the book is a **faithful** translation of the English original.*

precise
*Tightrope walkers must be very **precise** in their movements.*

spot-on (*informal*)
*Your guess about the train's arrival time was **spot-on**.*

true
*"Is this statement a **true** record of where you were?" queried the police officer.*

ANTONYM: inaccurate

ache VERB

If a part of your body **aches**, you feel a continuous, dull pain there.

be sore
*Jane's leg muscles **were sore** after aerobics.*

hurt
*"Ouch!" said Devendra as the nurse cleaned his cut knee. "That **hurts**!"*

throb
*My knee really **throbbed** after I fell over on the uneven pavement.*

action (1) NOUN

An **action** is something you do for a particular purpose.

act
*Rescuing the baby from the burning house was an **act** of great courage.*

deed
*Theseus's bravest **deed** was the slaying of the dreaded Minotaur.*

exploit
*The explorer, Sir Archie Pounder, told the school of his **exploits** in the jungle.*

feat
*To build Stonehenge without modern equipment was a great **feat**.*

move
*I think resting after dinner is a sensible **move**.*

action (2) NOUN

An **action** is a physical movement, such as jumping.

activity
*Our classroom was a hive of **activity** as we got ready for the concert.*

motion
*The up-and-down **motion** of the boat made me feel queasy.*

movement
*The **movements** of the conductor's baton guided the orchestra.*

actual ADJECTIVE

Actual can mean something is real, rather than imaginary or guessed at.

genuine
*"This table is a **genuine** antique," said Gran.*

real
*The film is based on a **real** story.*

true
*"Is this a **true** record of what you said?" the judge demanded to know.*

very
*The guide told us Ann Boleyn was beheaded on the **very** spot where we stood.*

add (1) VERB

If you **add** something to a number of things, you put it with those things.

combine
*Orange juice **combined** with lemonade makes a refreshing drink.*

include
*"Don't forget to **include** a sentence about what your friends think," Mr Bishop reminded us.*

LANGUAGE TIP
Remember that you add something **to** something else, but combine something **with** something else.

add (2) VERB

If you **add** numbers together, or **add** them up, you work out the total.

count up
*I **counted up** the spoons, and found there were three missing.*

total
*Miss Dobson told us to **total** the figures at the bottom of each column.*

tot up (*informal*)
*It took me ages to **tot up** how many hours I had worked that week.*

ANTONYM: subtract

A B C D E F G H I J K L M N O P Q R S T U V W X Y Z

adjust VERB

If you **adjust** something, you change its position or alter it in some other way.

change
*I **changed** the time on my new watch so that it was correct.*

correct
*Fortunately, the pilot **corrected** the plane's course before it hit the storm clouds.*

modify
*The racing car's tyres had been specially **modified** for wet weather.*

tune
*Dad **tuned** the radio to a different station.*

tweak (*informal*)
*Mrs Tordoff asked me to **tweak** my story to include more dialogue.*

admit VERB

If you **admit** something, you agree that it is true.

acknowledge
*Good drivers **acknowledge** when they have made a mistake.*

confess
*The prisoner **confessed** that she had lied.*

grant
*"I **grant** that it's not a great meal," my brother said, "but at least I cooked it myself."*

own up
*The head teacher asked whoever had broken the window to **own up** to it.*

adult ADJECTIVE

An **adult** is a mature and fully developed person.

grown-up
*Dad asked another **grown-up** for directions.*

man
*Jim is now a **man** of 42.*

woman
*A **woman** was seen leaving the building.*

adventure NOUN

An **adventure** is something that is exciting, and perhaps even dangerous.

escapade
*Entering the Sheriff of Nottingham's chamber was perhaps Robin Hood's boldest **escapade**.*

exploit
*Several films have been made of the brave **exploits** of the Three Musketeers.*

feat
*To abseil down a skyscraper would certainly be a daring **feat**.*

venture
*The expedition proved a dangerous **venture**.*

advice NOUN

Advice is a suggestion from someone about what you should do.

guidance
*Larissa needed **guidance** from her teachers about which college to apply for.*

recommendation
*Mum followed the doctor's **recommendation**, and gave up smoking.*

suggestion
*My friend's **suggestion** was to do our work first and play later.*

tip (*informal*)
*A good **tip** is to test the water with your toe before you jump in.*

advise VERB

If you **advise** someone to do something, you tell them you think they should do it.

recommend
*Mrs Singh **recommended** that I should sit nearer the front of the classroom.*

suggest
*"I **suggest** we go home," said Mum.*

urge
*In his speech, the MP **urged** people to vote for him in the election.*

affect VERB

If something **affects** someone or something else, it influences or changes them.

concern
*The issue of global warming **concerns** everybody on the planet.*

have an effect on
*The moon's gravity **has an effect on** the oceans, creating high and low tides.*

influence
*The judge's sentence was **influenced** by the prisoner's previous good behaviour.*

involve
*The accident happened nearby, but fortunately our car was not **involved**.*

LANGUAGE TIP

Be careful not to confuse the verb **affect** with the noun **effect**.

---

afraid ADJECTIVE

If you are **afraid**, you are frightened.

alarmed
*"Don't be **alarmed**," Mum said calmly. "It's only the wind rattling the windows."*

anxious
*As I had not revised my spellings, I was **anxious** about the test the next morning.*

fearful
*Faiza is **fearful** of the dark.*

frightened
*"Don't be **frightened**," said the giant. "I won't hurt you."*

nervous
*Alim was **nervous** before his driving test.*

petrified
*My brother is **petrified** of going to the dentist.*

scared
*I told my brother there was nothing to be **scared** of.*

terrified
*I used to be **terrified** of injections, but now that I've had one I'm not scared any more.*

timid
*I was quite **timid** on my first day at school.*

ANTONYM: unafraid

LANGUAGE TIP
To be afraid of something is to **fear** or **dread** it.

after (1) ADVERB

After can mean later than a particular time, date or event.

afterwards
*We had our lunch and **afterwards** went out to the school field.*

following
***Following** the professor's talk on birds, we had the chance to ask her questions.*

later than
*It was **later than** six o'clock when we finally finished shopping.*

subsequently
*The injured driver was taken to hospital, but was allowed to go home **subsequently**.*

ANTONYM: before

after (2) PREPOSITION

If you come **after** someone or something, you are behind them and following them.

behind
***Behind** the royal procession came the jester, prancing about and waving some sort of wand.*

following
*Off went the removal van, with Dad **following** it at a distance.*

again ADVERB

Again can mean happening one more time.

afresh
*The couple moved abroad to start life **afresh**.*

a second time
*The traveller waited before knocking at the door **a second time**.*

once more
***Once more** Dad tried to put up the deckchair, and **once more** it collapsed.*

against PREPOSITION

Something that is **against** something else is in opposition to it.

anti (*informal*)
*Our entire family is **anti** hunting. We think it's cruel.*

opposed to
*I was **opposed to** the idea of moving house.*

versus
*In our playground game, it was Rachel and me **versus** the rest of the class.*

LANGUAGE TIP
If something is against the law, it is **illegal**.

aim (1) VERB

If you **aim** to do something, you are planning to do it.

intend
*One day, I **intend** to own a chocolate factory.*

mean
*The player **meant** to hit the ball down the line, but it flew into the crowd.*

plan
*Dad had **planned** to work abroad, but then he was offered a job in Britain.*

propose
*Mr Potter **proposes** to put on a school play this year.*

A
B
C
D
E
F
G
H
I
J
K
L
M
N
O
P
Q
R
S
T
U
V
W
X
Y
Z

set your sights on
*Louis had **set his sights on** becoming an artist, but became a photographer instead.*

aim (2) NOUN

Your **aim** is what you intend to achieve.

goal
*Cassandra's **goal** is to make a million pounds before she is 25.*

object
*The **object** of the game is to throw the ball in your opponents' basket.*

objective
*"Men," barked the Major, "our **objective** is to cross that river before the enemy sees us."*

purpose
*The **purpose** of the meeting was to decide what our class would do for the school concert.*

target
*The **target** for this year's bring-and-buy sale is to raise a thousand pounds.*

aircraft NOUN

An **aircraft** is any vehicle that can fly.

→ Have a look at the **Illustration** page!

alike ADJECTIVE

Things that are **alike** are very similar in some way.

comparable
*The two boys had had **comparable** experiences at primary school.*

identical
*The twins were **identical** except for the way they styled their hair.*

indistinguishable
*The forgery and the original painting were **indistinguishable**.*

similar
*Phoebe's house is like ours, and Justin's is **similar** too.*

ANTONYMS: different, unlike

all right (1) ADJECTIVE

If something is **all right**, it is satisfactory, but not especially good.

acceptable
*Your work is **acceptable**, Watts, but by no means outstanding.*

adequate
*The nurse thought her temporary bandage would be **adequate** to stop the bleeding.*

average
*"My exam marks were **average**, but I'm sure I can do better," said Ron.*

fair
*Leo made a **fair** attempt at the test, considering he had felt so ill earlier.*

satisfactory
*The car was in a **satisfactory** condition to pass the safety test.*

all right (2) ADJECTIVE

If someone is **all right**, they are safe and not harmed.

safe
*"You'll be quite **safe** provided that you wait here," the police officer said.*

unharmed
*After getting lost in the hills, the boys were returned **unharmed** to their parents.*

unhurt
*The stunt rider escaped **unhurt** after his bike cartwheeled into the air.*

uninjured
*I was shaken but **uninjured** after falling during the race.*

almost ADVERB

Almost can mean very nearly.

just about
*We were **just about** ready to go, when Mum's phone bleeped.*

nearly
*It was **nearly** five years since Hanif had seen his aunt and uncle.*

not quite
*I had **not quite** finished the test when Mr Halliday said the time was up.*

practically
***Practically** all the sandwiches had been eaten.*

virtually
*Despite having **virtually** no time to practise, Darius played the piano piece perfectly.*

alone (1) ADJECTIVE

Someone or something that is **alone** is not with other people or things.

detached
*The elephant was **detached** from the herd.*

isolated
*The old man lived in a cottage on the cliff top. He felt quite **isolated**.*

AIRCRAFT

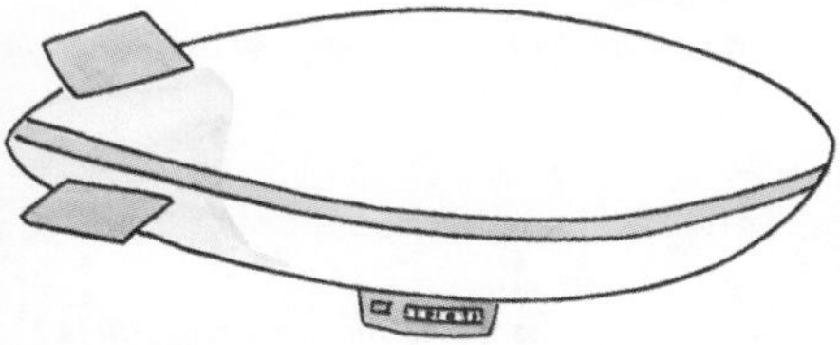

airship

hang-glider

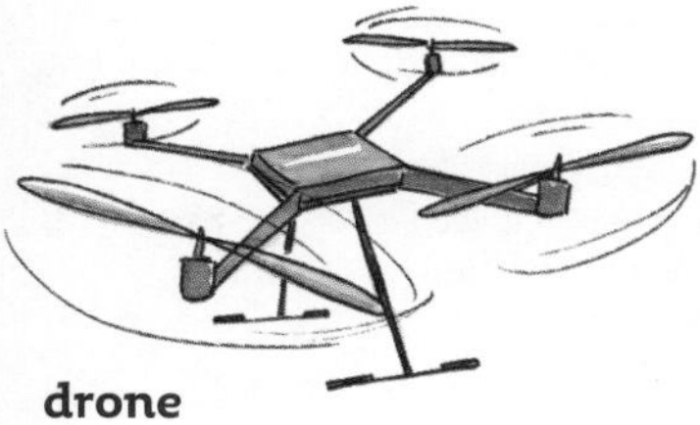

drone

microlite

helicopter

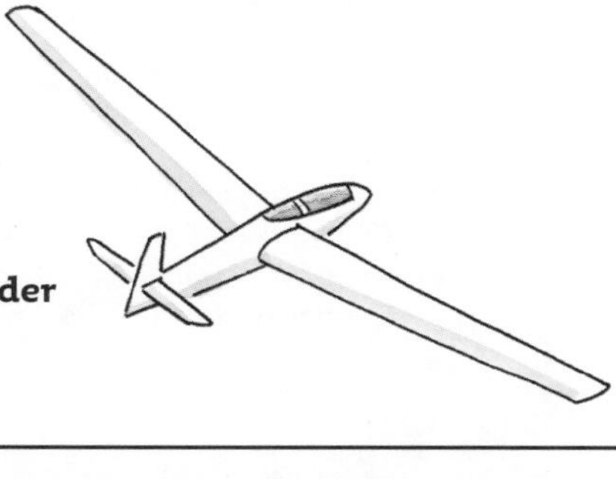

glider

hot-air balloon

Some other types of aircraft:

aeroplane	biplane	blimp	dirigible
jumbo jet	propeller plane	sea plane	quadcopter

A B C D E F G H I J K L M N O P Q R S T U V W X Y Z

solitary
*Robinson Crusoe was **solitary** on his desert island home.*

alone (2) ADVERB

Something that happens **alone**, happens without other people or things.

independently
*Sian did her homework **independently**.*

separately
*The teachers came with us on the bus, except for the head who came later, **separately**.*

solo (*informal*)
*The pilot now flew **solo** for the first time.*

also ADVERB

Also can mean in addition to something that has just been mentioned.

as well
*Ella had just bought the lettuce when she remembered to get some tomatoes **as well**.*

besides
*The competition winner received a sports bag, and a signed bat to go in it **besides**.*

furthermore (*formal*)
*"You've worked well," the teacher said, "and **furthermore** you've worked quietly."*

in addition
*My prize was free tickets to the show. **In addition**, it included a meal afterwards.*

moreover (*formal*)
*It was cold, and **moreover** it was getting dark.*

too
*William is nine, and Rina is **too**.*

although CONJUNCTION

Although can mean in spite of the fact that.

even though
*Jessica managed to win the marathon, **even though** she'd had flu earlier that week.*

while
***While** the work on an oil rig is tough, the pay is good.*

altogether ADVERB

Altogether can mean in total and is used when talking about amounts.

all told
*There were over two thousand people at the show, **all told**.*

everything included
***Everything included**, the fête raised enough money for the new equipment.*

in total
***In total**, the auction raised well over five thousand pounds.*

always (1) ADVERB

Always can mean all the time.

consistently
*Andy is **consistently** the best player on our hockey team.*

constantly
*We are **constantly** receiving junk emails.*

continually
*My sister is **continually** nagging me to keep my half of the room tidy.*

continuously
*The generator chugged away **continuously** throughout the night.*

invariably
*Aissa is **invariably** late for school.*

regularly
*Stars are **regularly** asked for their autographs.*

repeatedly
*"I'm **repeatedly** telling you not to speak with your mouth full!" Dad said crossly.*

time after time
***Time after time**, my little brother asked me to play with him.*

ANTONYM: never

always (2) ADVERB

Always can mean forever.

endlessly
*I shall be **endlessly** grateful to the woman who saved my life.*

forever
*"Madam, I am **forever** in your debt," the musketeer said as he swept from the room.*

perpetually
*He seems **perpetually** in a hurry.*

ANTONYM: never

amazing ADJECTIVE

If something is **amazing**, it is very surprising.

astonishing
*It is **astonishing** that we breathe, on average, 500 million times in our lives.*

astounding
*The marathon runner kept up an **astounding** pace for the whole 26 miles.*

breathtaking
*Seeing Niagara Falls was a **breathtaking** experience.*

sensational
*The show was **sensational**, with superb music and dancing.*

staggering
*It is **staggering** to realize that 60 per cent of our body is water.*

among; also **amongst** PREPOSITION

Among or **amongst** can mean surrounded by.

amid
*They lived **amid** the chaos while builders worked round them.*

amidst
***Amidst** all the weeds, a single rose bloomed.*

in the middle of
***In the middle of** the herd of cows was a newborn calf.*

surrounded by
*Mum and I found ourselves **surrounded by** inquisitive sheep.*

LANGUAGE TIP

If there are more than two things, you should use **among(st)**. If there are only two things, you should use **between**.

---

amount NOUN

An **amount** is how much there is of something.

mass
*There was a great **mass** of tadpoles in our garden pond.*

quantity
*"For sale: a **quantity** of unused garden tools," read the advert.*

sum
*The house was sold for an undisclosed **sum** of money.*

total
*Our little sideshow raised quite a **total** at our school fête.*

volume
*A huge **volume** of water cascades over the waterfall every minute.*

amphibian NOUN

An **amphibian** is one of a group of animals that live both on land and in water.

➔ Have a look at the **Illustration** page!

anger NOUN

Anger is the strong feeling you get about something unfair or cruel.

annoyance
*You could see the **annoyance** on the little boy's face when he couldn't have any sweets.*

fury
*Her face purple with **fury**, the reporter stormed from the room.*

indignation
*My sister stared in **indignation** as I ate the last biscuit.*

irritation
*Sissy stormed out in **irritation**.*

rage
*I flew into a **rage** and slammed the door.*

temper
*In a fit of **temper**, I flung my sister's hairbrush into the garden.*

wrath
*The player incurred the **wrath** of the referee for committing a foul.*

angry ADJECTIVE

Someone who is **angry** is very annoyed.

annoyed
*Mr Danesh was **annoyed** that Anna hadn't handed in her homework.*

cross
*The shopkeeper could tell the customer was **cross**. His forehead had turned red and wrinkly.*

displeased
*"Smithers, I'm **displeased** with the poor spelling in this report," Sir Hector boomed.*

enraged
*The bull, **enraged**, came charging, head down, towards them.*

fuming
*I was **fuming** that he was late.*

furious
***Furious** at such a messy piece of work, Mr Ross flung my book back on my desk.*

indignant
*You could see by her face that our cousin, Tess, was **indignant** that we had left her behind.*

a b c d e f g h i j k l m n o p q r s t u v w x y z

AMPHIBIANS

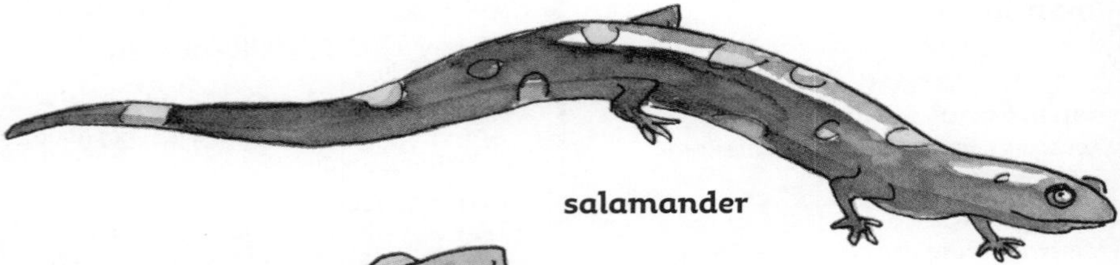

salamander

frog

toad

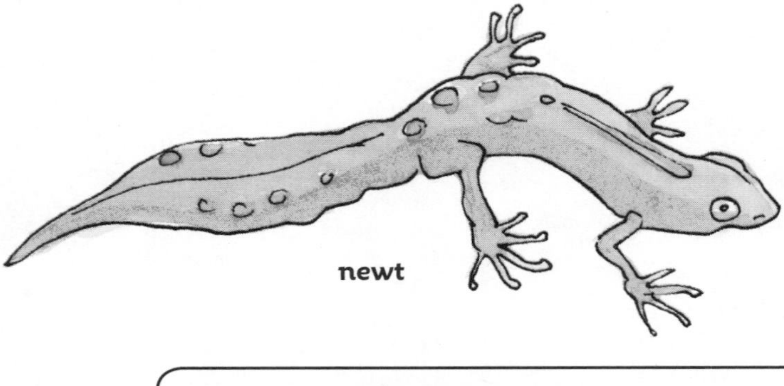

newt

Some other types of amphibian:

American bullfrog

great crested newt

tiger salamander

yellow-bellied toad

infuriated
*The stressed commuter was **infuriated** to find out that the train had left seconds earlier.*

irate
*It made Mrs Mawdsley **irate** to find the staffroom key missing.*

irritated
*I was **irritated** to discover that Alex had borrowed my pencil.*

livid
*Father was **livid** that I had broken his favourite fishing rod.*

outraged
*Many townsfolk were **outraged** that the lovely old cinema was to be torn down.*

seething
*I knew from his gritted teeth that the boss was **seething**.*

Try these lively words and phrases:

apoplectic
*The team manager was **apoplectic**, dancing with rage when the referee disallowed the goal.*

ballistic
*He went **ballistic** at the mess.*

beside yourself
*The teacher was **beside herself** when the money was stolen.*

hot under the collar (*informal*)
*Many motorists were getting **hot under the collar** as the traffic jam built up.*

animal NOUN

An **animal** is any living being that is not a plant.

beast
*The thoroughbred horse was a beautiful but temperamental **beast**.*

creature
*The platypus is a strange-looking **creature**.*

→ *See* **group** and **sound** and **young**

LANGUAGE TIP

General names for animals are **fauna** and **wildlife**.

Types of animal:

amphibian	bird	fish
insect	mammal	reptile

annoy VERB

If someone or something **annoys** you, they make you angry or impatient.

aggravate
*My gran is often **aggravated** by noisy motorbikes late at night.*

bother
*"Please don't **bother** me now. I'm really very busy," said Dad.*

harass
*Many famous people are **harassed** by reporters and photographers.*

irritate
*My mum was **irritated** by the constant dripping of the tap in the night.*

needle (*informal*)
*The soccer player tried to **needle** his opponent by muttering insults.*

provoke
*My sister **provoked** me into an argument by saying I was no good at singing.*

Try these lively words and phrases:

drive someone crazy
*It's a catchy song but it **drives me crazy**.*

drive someone round the bend
*Our constant chatting drove our teacher **round the bend**.*

drive someone up the wall (*informal*)
*"Some of these stupid TV adverts **drive me up the wall**!" said Grandad.*

get on someone's nerves (*informal*)
*Mitchi's whiny voice really **gets on my nerves**.*

answer (1) VERB

If you **answer** someone, you reply to them in speech or writing.

answer back
*When spoken to by the judge, the defendant was foolish enough to **answer back** rudely.*

reply
*If you receive an invitation, it's polite to **reply** promptly.*

respond
*The captain asked for volunteers, and two crewmen **responded**.*

retort
*"I'd love to go to the ball," said Cinderella. "No chance!" **retorted** her ugly sister.*

A B C D E F G H I J K L M N O P Q R S T U V W X Y Z

return
"Yes, I'd love to come to the theatre," Genevieve ***returned****.*

answer (2) NOUN
An **answer** is the reply you give when you answer someone.

acknowledgment
The palace sent a brief letter as an ***acknowledgment*** *to my request.*

reaction
The mayor received an angry ***reaction*** *to his scheme to sell off the sports field.*

reply
The salesman rang the door bell, but there was no ***reply****.*

response
There was a terrific ***response*** *to the famine appeal.*

retort
"Ouch, that hurt!" I said. "Serves you right!" came the ***retort****.*

appear VERB
When something **appears**, it moves from somewhere you could not see it to somewhere you can see it.

come into sight
A woolly mammoth ***came into sight****, lumbering from behind the rock.*

come into view
A triceratops ***came into view****, its serrated back appearing over the ridge.*

emerge
Emerging *from his bedroom, my lazy brother rubbed his eyes.*

loom
The gigantic airship blotted out the sun as it ***loomed*** *nearer.*

→ *See* **arrive**

area (1) NOUN
An **area** is a particular part of a place, country or the world.

community
We live in a friendly ***community****, with lots going on.*

district
It was a poor ***district****, where litter and street crime were a problem.*

neighbourhood
In our ***neighbourhood****, everybody helps one another.*

region
This ***region*** *of Italy is famous for its pizzas.*

zone
That ***zone*** *is open only to airport staff.*

area (2) NOUN
Area can mean the measurement of a flat surface.

extent
From the top of the tower, Jamie could see the ***extent*** *of the city.*

size
"What ***size*** *of paper shall I use?" Dani asked.*

area (3) NOUN
The **area** of a piece of ground or surface is the amount of space it covers.

expanse
When Noah looked from his ark, all he saw was a huge ***expanse*** *of water.*

patch (*informal*)
The police officer said he would miss the people in his ***patch*** *when he retired.*

plot
My parents bought a ***plot*** *of land, hoping to build a house there.*

stretch
You can see otters on this ***stretch*** *of the river.*

argue (1) VERB
If you **argue** with someone about something, you disagree with them about it, sometimes in an angry way.

bicker
My sisters are always ***bickering*** *at the table.*

disagree
Simon and Sanjiv ***disagreed*** *passionately about which team would win.*

fall out
Hazel and I ***fell out*** *when she broke her promise to keep my secret.*

have a difference of opinion
The two neighbours ***had a difference of opinion*** *over who owned the fence.*

have an argument
Dad and Mum ***had an argument*** *about whose turn it was to get up and see to the baby.*

quarrel
Jack and Wilbur ***quarrelled*** *over land, and their two families have not spoken since.*

row
*The couple next door were always **rowing**. Now they've gone we'll get some peace!*

squabble
*"Stop **squabbling**, you two!" Mum said, exasperated. "You'll both get a turn."*

argue (2) VERB

If you **argue** that something is true, you give reasons why you think that it is.

assert
*The prisoner continues to **assert** his innocence.*

claim
*Mervyn **claimed** he was the lost King of Albania, but nobody believed him.*

debate
*"I think we'll be **debating** this issue forever!" joked Mrs Evans.*

hold
*Before 1492, many people **held** that the earth was flat.*

maintain
*Columbus always **maintained** that the earth was round, and proceeded to prove it.*

put the case
*In the debate, Scarlet **put the case** for hunting and I opposed it.*

reason
*Mum tried to **reason** with my little brother, but it was a waste of time.*

argument (1) NOUN

An **argument** is a talk between people who do not agree.

barney (*informal*)
*Kayla and I had a bit of a **barney**, but we soon made up.*

difference of opinion
*Panna and Liz had a **difference of opinion** over which team would win.*

disagreement
*The tennis players had a **disagreement** about whether the service was in or out.*

dispute
*The long-running **dispute** between the two neighbours ended in a court case.*

feud
*Occasionally, the **feud** between the Campbell clan and the MacDonald clan erupted into violence.*

fight
*Two girls in our class got into a **fight** over a missing purse.*

quarrel
*The **quarrel** started when Colin was left out of the team in favour of Barry.*

row
*I was upstairs in my room when the **row** between Dad and Grandad started.*

squabble
*It was a silly **squabble** over who would sleep in the top bunk.*

LANGUAGE TIP
A formal talk between people who do not agree is a **debate**.

---

argument (2) NOUN

An **argument** is a point or set of reasons you use to convince people about something.

case
*The barrister set out the **case** for the prosecution.*

grounds
*The judge decided there were no **grounds** on which to find the defendant guilty.*

reason
*Guy Fawkes was asked to give his **reasons** for wishing to blow up Parliament.*

army NOUN

An **army** is a large group of soldiers who are trained to fight on land.

LANGUAGE TIP
Military means "connected with an army".

Some words to do with the armed forces:

air force	artillery	battalion
brigade	cavalry	commando
company	garrison	infantry
legion	marine	navy
paratrooper	platoon	regiment
reinforcements	squad	squadron
troops		

around (1) PREPOSITION

You can use **around** when something is surrounding or encircling a place or object.

on all sides of
***On all sides of** the camp, a barbed-wire fence rose menacingly towards grim watchtowers.*

on every side of
*The word "Fragile" was written **on every side of** the box.*

around (2) PREPOSITION

Around can mean at approximately the time or place mentioned.

about
*"I'll meet you at **about** three o'clock," Kamilah whispered.*

approximately
*"The train will be **approximately** five minutes late," said the announcer.*

in the region of
*The government spent **in the region of** 30 billion pounds on new roads.*

roughly
*The new garage will be **roughly** ten metres in length.*

around (3) ADVERB

You say **around** when things are in various places.

all over
*Papers were scattered **all over** Mum's office.*

everywhere
*In the wind, fallen leaves flew **everywhere**.*

here and there
*"I always find the odd bargain **here and there**," said Gran cheerfully.*

arrange (1) VERB

If you **arrange** to do something, or arrange something for someone, you make plans for it or make it possible.

fix
*Mr Pearson **fixed** our soccer game for next Tuesday afternoon.*

organise
*Mum said she would **organise** a trip to the zoo during the holidays.*

plan
*Dad **planned** a secret birthday surprise for Mum.*

prepare
*Most good chefs **prepare** their menu well in advance.*

settle
*The old lady **settled** her affairs before she left town.*

arrange (2) VERB

If you **arrange** objects, you set them out in a particular way.

group
*For the photograph, all the wedding guests were **grouped** in front of the hall door.*

organise
*For the tournament, players were **organised** into teams of five.*

place
*The artist carefully **placed** the objects she was going to paint.*

position
*Guards were **positioned** outside the palace.*

arrest VERB

If the police **arrest** someone, they take them to a police station because they believe they may have committed a crime.

capture
*A search party **captured** the escaped prisoner in an isolated shack.*

nick (*slang*)
*The bloke next door got **nicked** for burglary the other day.*

take someone into custody
*Police officers cautioned the suspect and **took her into custody**.*

arrive VERB

When you **arrive** at a place, you reach it at the end of your journey.

appear
*The film star finally **appeared**, an hour late.*

show up (*informal*)
*Jeremy **showed up** just in time.*

turn up
*"If you **turn up** late, the coach will have gone," warned the driver.*

ANTONYM: depart

ashamed ADJECTIVE

If you are **ashamed**, you feel embarrassed or guilty.

embarrassed
*Karen was **embarrassed** to find that the rain had streaked her make-up.*

guilty
*I hadn't done anything, but I still felt **guilty** about the missing money.*

humiliated
*Jade felt **humiliated** after the coach had publicly blamed her for losing the game.*

sorry
*Misha was **sorry** that his stupid comment had caused so much upset.*

ask (1) VERB

If you **ask** someone something, you put a question to them.

enquire or **inquire**
*"If you want more information, **enquire** at the desk over there," the woman said.*

interrogate
*Secret police **interrogated** the spy about his mission, but he told them nothing.*

query
*Mr Blake **queried** the bill, saying he'd been overcharged.*

question
*The suspicious-looking stranger was stopped and **questioned** about what she was doing.*

quiz
*My mum **quizzed** me about where I was going, and who with.*

ask (2) VERB

If you **ask** for something, you say you would like to have it.

appeal
*Our church **appealed** for money to help repair the roof.*

apply
*If you are travelling abroad, you must **apply** for a passport.*

beg
*I **begged** Mum to let me go to the party, and eventually she said yes.*

beseech
*"Have mercy on me, I **beseech** you!" the frog prince cried to the princess.*

demand
*The angry diner **demanded** to know what a beetle was doing in his pudding.*

implore
*"I **implore** you to think twice before running away," said Emma.*

plead
*Holly **pleaded** to be allowed to stay up late and read her book.*

request
*The soccer player **requested** a transfer to another club.*

ask (3) VERB

If you **ask** someone to come or go somewhere, you invite them there.

ask someone round
*The vicar **asked us round** for a cup of tea.*

bid (*old-fashioned*)
*His lordship **bade** me enter and enquired if I would drink wine with him.*

invite
*Whoopee! Della has **invited** me to her party.*

summon
*King Arthur **summoned** his knights to an assembly at the Round Table.*

asleep ADJECTIVE

If you are **asleep**, your eyes are closed and your whole body is resting.

fast asleep
*The dog was **fast asleep** with his legs in the air.*

sound asleep
*I was so **sound asleep** that my little brother had to sit on me to wake me up.*

Try these lively words and phrases:

dead to the world (*informal*)
*Dad was **dead to the world** in the armchair.*

out for the count (*informal*)
*She was **out for the count** as soon as she got into bed.*

ANTONYM: awake

→ *See* **sleep (1)**

LANGUAGE TIP

Animals that **hibernate** spend the winter in a state like a deep sleep.

attack (1) VERB

If a person or an animal **attacks** another person or animal, they use violence in order to hurt or kill them.

assault
*The muggers **assaulted** the man, then tried to steal his wallet.*

charge
*The troops **charged** the enemy's guns at full tilt.*

mug
*Unfortunately, some people are **mugged** on dark city streets.*

raid
*Police **raided** the house where the escaped criminal was living.*

A B C D E F G H I J K L M N O P Q R S T U V W X Y Z

storm
*Troops **stormed** the cliffs and succeeded in silencing the machine guns above.*

ANTONYM: defend

LANGUAGE TIP
In sport, to attack is to **move forward**.

attack (2) NOUN

An **attack** is a violent, physical action against someone or something.

assault
*"This was a serious **assault**, for which you must pay," said the judge grimly.*

charge
*The Light Brigade's **charge** was brave but doomed.*

invasion
*The landings in France were part of the biggest **invasion** in world history.*

raid
*The air **raids** continued night after night.*

strike
*The missile **strike** destroyed the buildings.*

ANTONYM: defence

attractive ADJECTIVE

If someone or something is **attractive**, they are nice to look at.

beautiful
*The car stopped and a **beautiful** woman got out.*

charming
*We had tea in the garden of a **charming** little cottage.*

handsome
*"I'll turn into a **handsome** prince if you kiss me," said the frog.*

lovely
*There was a **lovely** view from the window.*

pretty
*On the way, we passed through several **pretty** villages.*

automatic ADJECTIVE

An **automatic** machine is programmed to do a task without needing a person to operate it.

automated
*The new **automated** answering service kept Dad waiting for half an hour.*

computerised
*Most photocopiers are **computerised** these days.*

robotic
*In car factories, **robotic** arms put most of the parts together.*

self-propelling
*My **self-propelling** model glider worked by twisting an elastic band.*

avoid (1) VERB

If you **avoid** someone or something, you keep away from them.

dodge
*We **dodged** our nosy neighbour by hiding behind a tree as she went past.*

elude
*By going out of the back door, the celebrity **eluded** the photographers.*

evade
*The criminal managed to **evade** the police for several days, but was eventually caught.*

shun
*The shy film star **shunned** publicity, preferring a quiet family life.*

steer clear of (*informal*)
*"If I were you I'd **steer clear of** that quarry," my dad said sternly.*

avoid (2) VERB

If you **avoid** doing something, you make an effort not to do it.

dodge (*informal*)
*My lazy brother tried to **dodge** cleaning the car, but Dad made him do it.*

duck out of (*informal*)
*I tried to **duck out of** unpacking the dishwasher, with no success.*

escape
*The prisoner tried to **escape**, but the police officer stopped him.*

get out of
*"It's no use trying to **get out of** it. You'll have to mow the lawn," said Dad.*

shirk
*The farmer tried to **shirk** responsibility for the pollution in the river.*

away ADVERB

If you are **away** from somewhere, you are not in that place.

absent
*With such a high temperature, Edward was forced to be **absent** from school.*

elsewhere
I searched the house for my gran, but she was obviously ***elsewhere****.*

on holiday
Our family is going ***on holiday*** *to Florida this summer.*

LANGUAGE TIP
To be away from school when you should be there is to **play truant**.

awful ADJECTIVE

Something **awful** is very unpleasant or very bad.

appalling
The karaoke singer's voice was ***appalling*** *– he sounded like a dog howling!*

dreadful
We had a ***dreadful*** *time in Venice. All the streets were flooded.*

fearful (*informal*)
Mr Bellamy had a ***fearful*** *cold and sneezed all the way to London.*

frightful
The house was in a ***frightful*** *state after it had been burgled.*

ghastly (*informal*)
The chef made a ***ghastly*** *mistake, and put salt in the cake mixture instead of sugar.*

gruesome
Greg told a rather ***gruesome*** *ghost story.*

harrowing
The film was ***harrowing*** *to watch.*

hideous
The monster's head was truly ***hideous****: bloated, scarred and covered in scales.*

horrendous
It was a ***horrendous*** *meal, with half of the food burnt and the other half undercooked.*

horrible
For one ***horrible*** *moment, I thought my wallet had been stolen.*

horrid
"William, that was a ***horrid*** *thing to say," said Mrs Brown.*

horrific
"Unless this fog goes, I'm afraid there'll be a ***horrific*** *accident," the police officer said.*

shocking
"I think it's ***shocking****," put in Dad, "that those refugees should be left without shelter."*

terrible
The sun rose on the scene of the earthquake, a ***terrible*** *sight to behold.*

unpleasant
Shingles is a very ***unpleasant*** *disease to have.*

ANTONYM: lovely

awkward (1) ADJECTIVE

If a situation is **awkward**, it is difficult to deal with.

delicate
It was a ***delicate*** *situation: to ask Julie about her exams or not to mention the subject.*

embarrassing
It was very ***embarrassing*** *to be stuck outside in my pyjamas in the pouring rain!*

tricky
"Now this bit could be ***tricky****," muttered Bond coolly. "Which wire should I cut?"*

uncomfortable
The spy had an ***uncomfortable*** *moment when the guards stared in through the car window.*

awkward (2) ADJECTIVE

If a person or animal is **awkward**, they are difficult to deal with.

hard to handle
Donkeys have a reputation for being ***hard to handle****.*

stubborn
My brother can be very ***stubborn*** *when it comes to helping me wash up.*

troublesome
On the journey to Scotland, the car proved ***troublesome****, but eventually we got there.*

uncooperative
The lady at the enquiries desk was ***uncooperative*** *and didn't help at all.*

a b c d e f g h i j k l m n o p q r s t u v w x y z

A B C D E F G H I J K L M N O P Q R S T U V W X Y Z

Bb

baby NOUN

A **baby** is a child in the first year or two of its life.

infant
The shepherds found the ***infant*** *in a stable, lying in a manger.*

newborn child
The mother proudly gazed at her tiny ***newborn child****.*

toddler
Waddling on bandy legs, the ***toddler*** *was off round the corner in a flash.*

tot (*informal*)
"Don't tease your brother," said Mum. "He's only a ***tot****."*

LANGUAGE TIP
The babies of animals are their **young** and the babies of humans are their **offspring**. Together, the babies of an animal are sometimes called a **litter**.

back NOUN

The **back** of something is the part behind the front.

end
At the ***end*** *of the queue, people were setting up tents for the night.*

rear
I could see smoke coming from the ***rear*** *of the vehicle in front.*

reverse
Genevieve wrote her answers on the ***reverse*** *of the worksheet.*

ANTONYM: front

LANGUAGE TIP
The back part of an animal is its **rear**, **rump** or **hindquarters**. The back end of a ship is the **stern**.

bad

→ Look at the **Word Power** page!

badly (1) ADVERB

If you do something **badly**, you do it in an inferior way.

inadequately
He had been ***inadequately*** *trained for the job.*

poorly
The event was ***poorly*** *organised.*

shoddily
This house has been ***shoddily*** *built.*

unsatisfactorily
I feel the whole business has been handled ***unsatisfactorily****.*

ANTONYM: well

badly (2) ADVERB

If something affects you **badly**, it affects you in a serious way.

deeply
I am ***deeply*** *hurt by these remarks.*

gravely
He was ***gravely*** *ill following a heart operation.*

seriously
Four people have been ***seriously*** *injured.*

bad-mannered ADJECTIVE

Bad-mannered people are rude and thoughtless.

disrespectful
It is ***disrespectful*** *to interrupt people when they are speaking.*

inconsiderate
It was ***inconsiderate*** *of Meg to take a second helping when others had not had their first.*

rude
We decided not to leave a tip for the ***rude*** *waiter.*

bad-tempered ADJECTIVE

Bad-tempered people often lose their temper.

grumpy
Dad is always cheerful in the mornings. It's me that is ***grumpy****.*

irritable
Some people get ***irritable*** *when you read over their shoulder.*

moody
When people are ***moody****, you never quite know how they will greet you.*

quarrelsome
*The two **quarrelsome** brothers were always looking for a fight.*

sulky
*"If you're going to be **sulky**, miss, you can go to your room," Dad replied.*

sullen
*The **sullen** waiter snatched my plate and stalked off to the kitchen.*

bag NOUN

A **bag** is a container for carrying things in.

→ Have a look at the **Illustration** page!

ban VERB

If you **ban** something, you forbid it to be done.

make illegal
*The government proposes to **make illegal** the sale of imitation guns.*

prohibit
*The landowner put up a sign **prohibiting** walkers from crossing his land.*

band (1) NOUN

A **band** is a small number of people, like a group of musicians.

group
*Five of us have formed a pop **group**.*

orchestra
*Our school has its own **orchestra**.*

band (2) NOUN

A **band** can be a strip of material such as iron, cloth or rubber.

hoop
*Metal **hoops** held the barrel together.*

strap
*Strong **straps** keep the luggage safe on the roof rack.*

strip
***Strips** of gold round the sailor's sleeve showed he was in charge.*

bang (1) NOUN

A **bang** is a hard, painful bump against something.

blow
*Kirstin suffered a **blow** to her head when the door opened suddenly.*

knock
*When I slipped on the stairs, I got a sharp **knock** on my funny bone.*

bang (2) NOUN

A **bang** is a sudden, short, loud noise.

blast
*The **blast** echoed round the quarry.*

thud
*With a **thud**, the encyclopedia hit the floor.*

bare (1) ADJECTIVE

If your body is **bare**, it is not covered by any clothing.

in your birthday suit (*informal*)
*I dreamt I was walking down the high street **in my birthday suit**.*

naked
*Lady Godiva rode **naked** on a horse through the middle of town.*

nude
*For many centuries, the **nude** body has been a popular subject for artists.*

undressed
*The nurse asked me to get **undressed**, ready for the medical examination.*

without a stitch on (*informal*)
*"And there I was, **without a stitch on**," Mrs Lee, our neighbour, told me.*

bare (2) ADJECTIVE

If something is **bare**, it is not covered with anything.

barren
*The Grand Canyon, although magnificent, is a **barren** wilderness.*

bleak
*The Brontë sisters lived on the edge of a **bleak**, windswept moor.*

desolate
*The abandoned town was **desolate**.*

→ *See* **empty (1)**

barrier NOUN

A **barrier** is a fence or wall that prevents people or animals getting from one area to another.

barricade
*The protesters erected a **barricade** across the main street.*

obstacle
*There are lots of **obstacles** to get over and under in an obstacle race.*

obstruction
*The roadworks were an **obstruction** and drivers had to be diverted around them.*

a b c d e f g h i j k l m n o p q r s t u v w x y z

bad

(1) ADJECTIVE **Bad** things are harmful or upsetting.

appalling
The weather for our sports day was ***appalling****.*

damaging
Car fumes can be highly ***damaging*** *to the environment.*

dangerous
Building sites are ***dangerous*** *places.*

distressing
Melinda found it ***distressing*** *to see pictures of abandoned animals.*

dreadful
It was a ***dreadful*** *shame that the weather was so bad for the party.*

grave
A spokesperson announced the ***grave*** *news that the king was dying.*

serious
The artist's illness was too ***serious*** *for him to continue painting.*

terrible
Our team was ***terrible*** *today. We lost by four goals!*

(2) ADJECTIVE **Bad** can also mean of poor quality.

abysmal
"Such ***abysmal*** *work will have to be redone," said Mr Malone severely.*

atrocious
The reporter admitted that his spelling was ***atrocious****.*

faulty
Engineers soon fixed the ***faulty*** *telephone line.*

inferior
The paint Dad bought was of ***inferior*** *quality and didn't last very long.*

shoddy
Owing to ***shoddy*** *workmanship, the house had to be redecorated.*

unsatisfactory
The teacher wrote that my school report was ***unsatisfactory****.*

bad

(3) ADJECTIVE A **bad** person is naughty or unkind.

corrupt
*The **corrupt** politician had taken money from all sorts of people.*

cruel
*I can't stand people being **cruel** to children or animals.*

disobedient
*The **disobedient** boy ignored the warning notice and fell into the quarry.*

evil
*The **evil** villain plotted how to ensnare the handsome knight.*

mischievous
*Tying Kerry's shoelaces together was a **mischievous** prank.*

naughty
*"You're a **naughty** girl, Cassandra," said her mother angrily.*

unkind
*It was **unkind** to go without asking her.*

wicked
*The **wicked** witch lived alone.*

(4) ADJECTIVE If you are **bad** at something, you cannot do it very well.

incompetent
*The person who dealt with our complaint was completely **incompetent**.*

rubbish (*informal*)
*I have always been **rubbish** at remembering people's birthdays.*

useless
*After that last mistake, it was obvious that he was **useless** at his job.*

Names for bad people include **rogue**, **villain** and **scoundrel**.

→ Also have a look at the **Word Power** page for **good**!

A B C D E F G H I J K L M N O P Q R S T U V W X Y Z

BAGS

handbag

toilet bag

rucksack

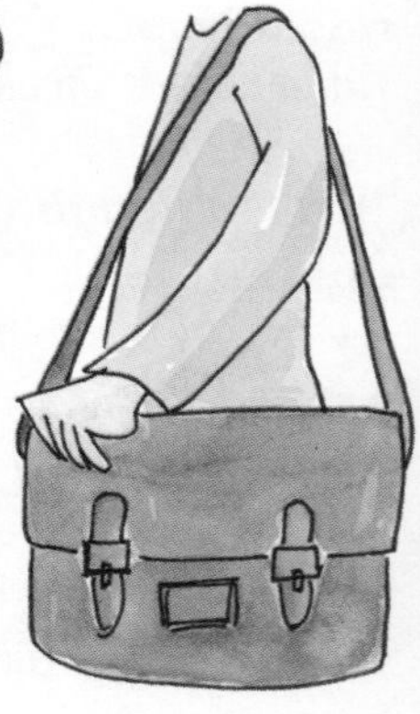

satchel

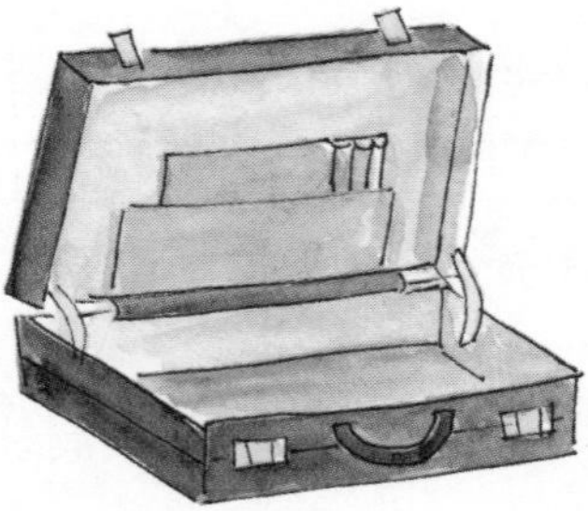

briefcase

suitcase

holdall

Some other types of bag:

backpack	carrier bag	duffel bag	laptop bag	makeup bag
phone case	sack	shopping bag	shoulder bag	sponge bag

base (1) NOUN

The **base** is the lowest part of something.

bottom
*The lost cat mewed at the **bottom** of the well.*

foot
*"Please would you stand on the **foot** of my ladder to stop it slipping?" Dad asked.*

foundation
*The **foundations** of New York's skyscrapers rest on solid rock.*

base (2) NOUN

A **base** is the headquarters of an organisation.

centre
*A humble office in a run-down district was the unlikely **centre** of a huge corporation.*

head office
*If you want to make a reservation, please contact the **head office**.*

headquarters
*We arranged to meet at our scout **headquarters** at four o'clock.*

HQ
*"**HQ** calling Tank 5," the colonel snapped.*

basic ADJECTIVE

Basic means the simplest things you need, or need to know.

chief
*The **chief** thing to remember when hiking is to shut gates behind you.*

essential
*Water is an **essential** requirement for all living creatures.*

important
*An **important** rule is to check the traffic before you cross a road.*

main
*The **main** thing is not to panic if the fire alarm goes off.*

standard
*Our car is a **standard** model.*

bat NOUN

A **bat** is a specially shaped piece of wood with a handle, used for hitting a ball in some games.

→ Have a look at the **Illustration** page!

battle NOUN

A **battle** is a fight between armed forces, or a struggle between two people or groups with different aims.

action
*It was the first time that the young soldier had seen **action**.*

conflict
*There was a **conflict** of opinions: the red party on one side, the greens on the other.*

struggle
*The **struggle** for power between the king and the government was a long one.*

beach NOUN

The **beach** is an area of sand or pebbles beside the sea.

sands
*The lifeguards sprinted down the **sands** and plunged into the waves.*

seashore
*After the tanker disaster, much of the **seashore** was coated in an oily sludge.*

seaside
*Aaron loved to spend his holidays at the **seaside**.*

shore
*We walked along the **shore**, looking for attractive shells.*

water's edge
*The **water's edge** was a seething mass of turtles.*

beat (1) VERB

If someone or something **beats** someone or something else, they hit them hard and repeatedly.

batter
*The burglar had **battered** down the door.*

flog
*In Nelson's day, sailors who stole would be **flogged** with a whip called a cat-o'-nine-tails.*

pound
*Waves **pounded** the shore as the wind rose to screaming pitch.*

thrash
*The bully threatened, "Tom Brown, I shall **thrash** the living daylights out of you."*

BATS, STICKS AND RACKETS

hockey stick

cricket bat

golf club

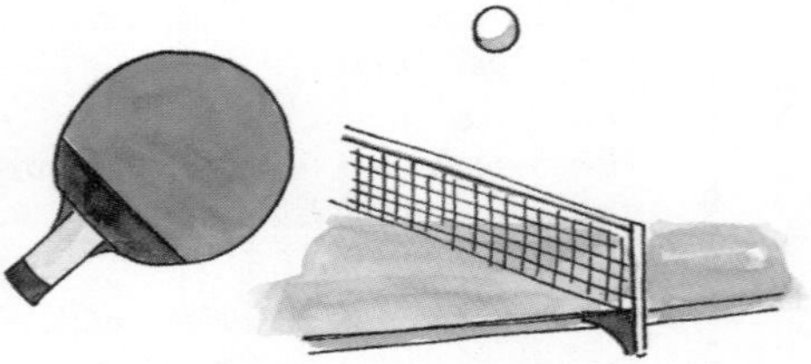

table tennis bat

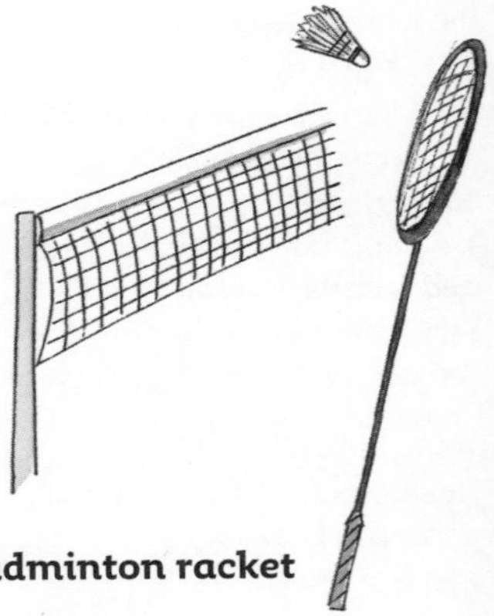

badminton racket

tennis racket

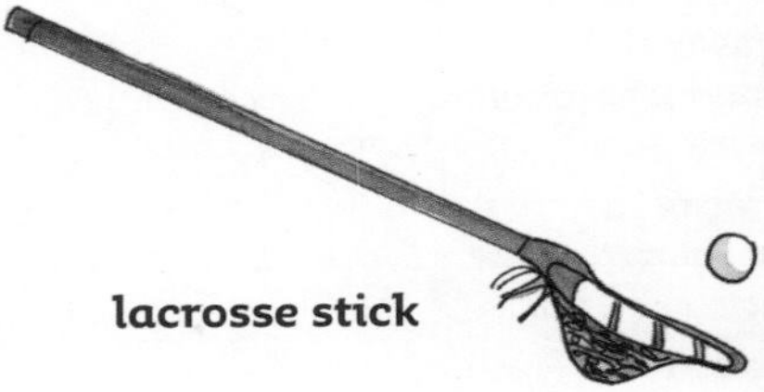

lacrosse stick

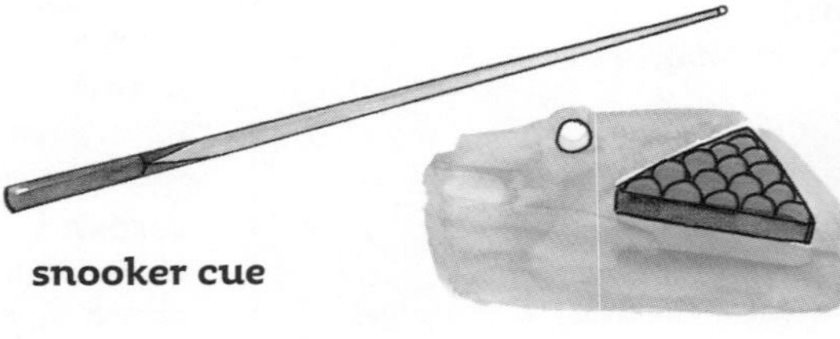

snooker cue

beat (2) VERB

If you **beat** someone in a race or game, you defeat them or do better than them.

conquer
*William, Duke of Normandy, **conquered** England in 1066.*

lick (*informal*)
*Abdel really **licked** me in the 100 metres sprint race.*

run rings round (*informal*)
*Our speedy attackers **ran rings round** their lumbering defenders.*

thrash (*informal*)
*"It's a safe bet that we'll get **thrashed** when we play you," said Tim.*

wipe the floor with (*informal*)
*Our school team **wiped the floor with** kids much bigger than they were.*

beautiful ADJECTIVE

You say someone or something is **beautiful** if they are very pleasing to look at.

attractive
*People say my sister is **attractive**.*

gorgeous
*I overheard Dad telling Mum she looked **gorgeous**.*

lovely
*The photograph, I had to admit, even made my aunt look **lovely**.*

pretty
*Even some garden weeds can look **pretty** at certain times.*

stunning (*informal*)
*The sunset over the mountains was nothing less than **stunning**.*

ANTONYMS: ugly, unattractive

beauty (1) NOUN

If a person has **beauty**, they have the quality of being beautiful.

elegance
*Every movement the duchess made had an **elegance** about it.*

good looks
*The actor possessed rugged **good looks**.*

loveliness
*The opera singer's **loveliness** was not matched by her selfish behaviour.*

beauty (2) NOUN

If a place has **beauty**, it has the quality of being beautiful.

charm
*This country cottage has tremendous **charm** and character.*

loveliness
*I think the **loveliness** of Athens is somewhat spoilt by the pollution.*

splendour
*Rome is famous for the **splendour** of its ancient buildings.*

ANTONYM: ugliness

because CONJUNCTION

Because is used with other words to give a reason for something.

as
***As** you've been so helpful, I'll treat you to an ice cream.*

owing to
***Owing to** work on the track this Sunday, trains will be delayed.*

since
*"**Since** Fred is here, why don't we build a tree house?" my sister suggested.*

thanks to
*I got no pocket money, **thanks to** my brother telling tales on me.*

bed NOUN

A **bed** is a piece of furniture that you lie on when you sleep.

Some types of bed:		
bunk beds	cot	cradle
double bed	futon	hammock
inflatable bed	single bed	sofa bed
water bed		

before ADVERB

If something happens **before**, it happens earlier than something else.

formerly
***Formerly**, Mrs Patterson was a teacher at my dad's old school.*

previously
***Previously**, Mr Cruickshank had always let us off homework, but not today.*

a b c d e f g h i j k l m n o p q r s t u v w x y z

sooner
*If I had got the invitation **sooner**, I would have come to the party.*

LANGUAGE TIP
Something that goes before something else **precedes** it.

begin VERB
If you **begin** something, you start it.

commence
*The king shouted "Let battle **commence**!" and the two knights thundered towards each other.*

embark on
*As soon as we'd **embarked on** our journey to the park, it started to rain.*

set about
*We **set about** digging the vegetable garden.*

start
*Dad told me to **start** my homework soon.*

ANTONYM: end

beginner NOUN
A **beginner** is someone who has just started to learn something.

learner
*Swimmers use the big pool, while **learners** use the shallower pool.*

novice
*Although a complete **novice**, Britney showed a flair for ski jumping.*

ANTONYM: veteran

beginning NOUN
The **beginning** of something is when or where it starts.

introduction
*In the **introduction**, the author explains how she came to write the book.*

opening
*The band played at the **opening** of the fête.*

origin
*The **origin** of the universe is still a mystery.*

ANTONYM: end

behave VERB
If you **behave** in a particular way, you act that way.

act
*Emir is **acting** like a spoilt child.*

function
*"The girls are finally **functioning** as a team!" exclaimed the coach.*

operate
*Sally **operates** in a certain way to get what she wants.*

work
*Anoup **worked** methodically in order to get the work done.*

believe (1) VERB
If you **believe** someone, you accept that they are telling the truth.

accept
*It took some people a long time to **accept** that the world was round.*

be certain of
*"We have to **be certain of** your story before we can take action," warned the sergeant.*

have faith in
*It is important to **have faith in** your own ability, Grandad says.*

trust
*I **trust** my sister, even if she is rotten to me sometimes.*

ANTONYMS: disbelieve, doubt

LANGUAGE TIP
Something that you cannot believe is **unbelievable** or **incredible**.

believe (2) VERB
If you **believe** that something is true, you think that it is true.

feel
*"How do you **feel** the match will go?" asked the interviewer.*

presume
*Mr Jackson said, "I **presume** you will all be handing in your homework tomorrow."*

suppose
*I **suppose** that the school sports day will be in July as usual.*

belongings NOUN
Your **belongings** are all the things that you own.

possessions
*Almost all their **possessions** were destroyed in the fire.*

property
*"Make sure your **property** is labelled," insisted Miss Carter.*

stuff
*The firefighters grabbed their **stuff** and jumped in the cab.*

below PREPOSITION

If something is **below** something else, it is in a lower position.

beneath
***Beneath** the trees, bluebells were waving in the breeze.*

under
*With the help of a torch, I could read secretly **under** my duvet.*

underneath
***Underneath** the streets are hundreds of miles of sewers.*

ANTONYM: above

bend (1) VERB

When something **bends**, it becomes curved or crooked.

buckle
*The car **buckled** when the elephant sat on it.*

curve
*After the village, the road **curves** to the left.*

twist
*The ornament was made of glass **twisted** into patterns.*

warp
*My DVD **warped** when I left it in the sun.*

ANTONYM: straighten

bend (2) VERB

When you **bend**, you move your head and shoulders forwards and downwards.

crouch
*Lyra **crouched** behind the bushes, waiting for the police officer to turn away.*

duck
***Duck**, or you'll hit your head on the beam!*

stoop
*Farouk **stooped** to pick up a coin from the path.*

beside PREPOSITION

If one thing is **beside** another, it is next to it.

adjacent to
***Adjacent to** the station was an old signal box.*

alongside
*The lifeboat rowed up **alongside** the stricken yacht, and the crew jumped across.*

next to
*The boy sitting **next to** me kept prodding me with a ruler.*

besides PREPOSITION

Besides can mean in addition to.

apart from
***Apart from** some shorts and a T-shirt, I'm taking very little with me.*

other than
***Other than** our family, there was hardly anybody on the beach.*

best ADJECTIVE

Best is the superlative of good and well.

finest
*Wuffles is the **finest** pet food money can buy.*

leading
*The operation will be performed by the world's **leading** surgeon.*

outstanding
*Our birthday presents from Grandma are always **outstanding**.*

supreme
*The judges thought that our Shetland pony was the **supreme** entrant in the competition.*

ANTONYM: worst

better (1) ADJECTIVE

Better is the comparative of good and well.

higher quality
*Steak is usually **higher quality** than other cuts of meat.*

more suitable
*The lightweight tent proved **more suitable** for the expedition.*

preferable
*Of the two designs, I think the red is **preferable**.*

superior
*Usually, **superior** products cost more than inferior ones.*

ANTONYM: worse

better (2) ADJECTIVE

If you are **better** after an illness, you are no longer ill.

healed
*The doctor told Sheila that her broken leg was completely **healed**.*

improved
*Gran was much **improved** after her operation.*

A B C D E F G H I J K L M N O P Q R S T U V W X Y Z

recovered
*Ali is now **recovered** after a bout of flu.*

beware VERB

If you tell someone to **beware** of something, you are warning them that it might be dangerous or harmful.

be careful
*"**Be careful**, child, for there are wolves in the forest!" said Red Riding Hood's mother.*

guard against
*With exams, it's important to **guard against** being over-confident.*

look out
***Look out**! Here comes another big wave.*

watch out
***Watch out**, or that sail will hit you when the boat turns!*

big

→ Look at the **Word Power** page!

bit NOUN

A **bit** of something is a small amount of it.

chunk
*Sam broke off a **chunk** of chocolate and gobbled it up.*

fraction
*I arrived a **fraction** of a moment too late. The bus was just leaving.*

fragment
***Fragments** of the wrecked aircraft were found all over the field.*

morsel
*"Kind sir, please spare me a **morsel** of food," begged Oliver.*

part
*A **part** of me wanted to stay and yet I was also desperate to leave.*

piece
*Marina cut the cake into **pieces** and took the largest one for herself.*

scrap
*My dad writes reminders to himself on **scraps** of paper.*

bite VERB

If you **bite** something, you use your teeth to hold, cut or tear it.

champ
*The horse **champed** at the bit as it waited impatiently for the race to begin.*

chomp
*Dad says that I **chomp** my food like a waste-disposal unit.*

gnaw
*Mice had **gnawed** through the electric wires.*

nibble
*Some creature had **nibbled** at the chair leg.*

bitter ADJECTIVE

A **bitter** taste is sharp and unpleasant.

sour
*If you leave milk in the sun, it turns **sour**.*

tart
*The lemon cake was slightly **tart**.*

blame VERB

If someone **blames** a person for something bad that has happened, they believe that person caused it to happen.

accuse
*The woman was **accused** of breaking the law.*

charge
*Police **charged** the man with being drunk and disorderly.*

hold responsible
*At the enquiry, the bus company was **held responsible** for the accident.*

block (1) VERB

If someone or something **blocks** a road or channel, they put something across it so that nothing can get through.

bar
*Access to the back road was **barred** by a police checkpoint.*

bung up (*informal*)
*I could hardly breathe, my nose was so **bunged up**.*

choke
*The traffic jam **choked** the road into town for many hours.*

clog up
*Don't pour liquid fat down the sink as it **clogs up** the drains when it sets.*

dam
*Beavers **dam** streams with logs to create a pool which will not freeze solid in winter.*

obstruct
*Uncle Pete tried to **obstruct** the door as I went through, but I ducked under his arm!*

big

(1) ADJECTIVE Something or someone **big** is large in size.

colossal
*To an ant, an elephant must seem **colossal**.*

enormous
*She was presented with an **enormous** bunch of flowers.*

giant
*My mum buys the **giant** packs of toilet rolls.*

gigantic
*The section of bridge required a **gigantic** crane to lift it.*

huge
*Gran gave me a **huge** hug.*

immense
*The floods had covered an **immense** area of the county.*

large
*We have a **large** hole in our kitchen ceiling.*

massive
*"We believe a **massive** asteroid is heading for Earth," she said.*

vast
*The Sahara Desert is a **vast** area of rolling sand dunes.*

(2) ADJECTIVE Something **big** has a lot of space.

roomy
*"You'll find this is a **roomy** loft," the estate agent said.*

sizable
*Our house has a **sizable** garden.*

spacious
*The living room is **spacious**, but the kitchen is cramped.*

(3) ADJECTIVE Something **big** is important.

important
*It was an **important** day in Sophie's life – her first at her new school.*

momentous
*The Prime Minister made the **momentous** decision to declare war.*

significant
*Carrying rucksacks made a **significant** difference to their progress.*

→ Also have a look at the **Word Power** page for **small**!

Try these lively words and phrases!

gargantuan *Some of these **gargantuan** spiders have a poisonous bite.*
mammoth *The **mammoth** circus had two separate rings.*

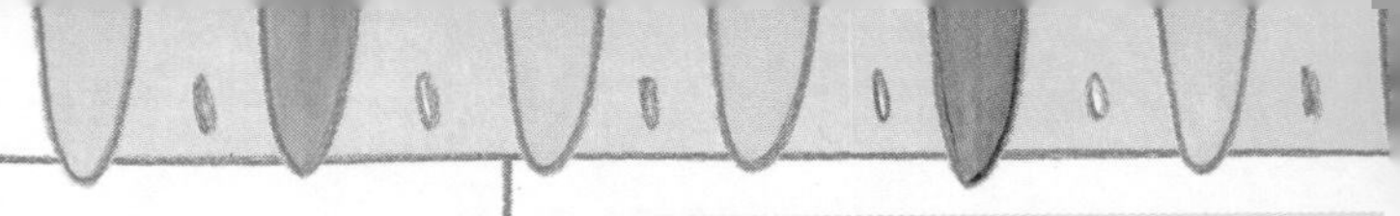

A B C D E F G H I J K L M N O P Q R S T U V W X Y Z

block (2) VERB

If someone tries to **block** something, they try to stop it happening.

hinder
*It is said that flourescent lighting **hinders** concentration.*

impede
*The walkers' progress was **impeded** by an angry goat on the path.*

obstruct
*The protesters were arrested for **obstructing** the police.*

prevent
*Residents **prevented** a nightclub from being built near their houses.*

thwart
*The wicked baron was **thwarted** in his evil plans by a quick-thinking boy.*

block (3) NOUN

A **block** is something put across a road or channel so that nothing can get through.

barrier
*For the parade, **barriers** were erected to keep the crowds back.*

blockage
*"There's a **blockage** in the drain under the sink," the plumber said.*

obstacle
*Alpa had to overcome many **obstacles** on his road to success.*

obstruction
*If you swallow chewing gum, it may cause an **obstruction** in your stomach.*

block (4) NOUN

A **block** is a large, rectangular, three-dimensional piece of something.

bar
*The robbers put the gold **bars** in the back of the getaway van.*

chunk
*A **chunk** of metal fell off the back of the truck as it left the scrap yard.*

lump
*With the help of a wheel, the potter formed the shapeless **lump** of clay into a vase.*

blue ADJECTIVE

If something is **blue**, it has the colour of the sky on a sunny day.

Shades of blue:

aquamarine	azure	indigo
navy	sky blue	turquoise

boast VERB

If you **boast**, you talk proudly about what you have or what you can do.

brag
*Alison couldn't resist **bragging** about her new DVD player.*

blow your own trumpet
*I prefer modest people to those who **blow their own trumpet**.*

crow
*Paulo was so busy **crowing** about his marks, that he didn't see Mrs Walker behind him.*

show off
*Brian is always **showing off** about the amount of pocket money he gets.*

boat NOUN

A **boat** is a floating vehicle for travelling across water.

craft
*At that distance, it was hard for the coastguard to identify the **craft**.*

ship
*Sir Francis Drake sailed in a **ship** he named the Golden Hind.*

vessel
*The tiny tug was nevertheless a sturdy **vessel**, capable of pulling much larger boats.*

→ Have a look at the **Illustration** page!

body NOUN

Your **body** is all of you, from your head to your feet.

build
*Although flyweight boxers only have a slight **build**, they are powerful for their size.*

figure
*My sister maintains her **figure** by practising yoga regularly.*

form
*A shadowy **form** hovered at the end of Nikki's bed, but it was only her mum, tucking her in!*

physique
*Most sportspeople lift weights in the gym to improve their **physique**.*

LANGUAGE TIP
The upper body is the **trunk** or **torso**.

BOATS

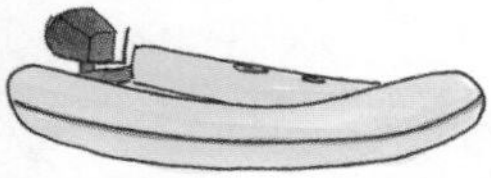

dinghy

galleon

hovercraft

speedboat

yacht

tug

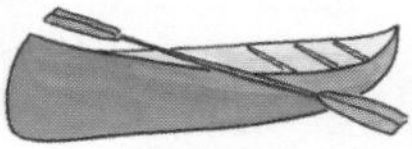

canoe

submarine

longship

aircraft carrier

Some other types of boat:

Leisure boats:	catamaran	cruise ship	kayak	pedalo
	raft	rowing boat	sailing boat	
Working boats:	barge	destroyer	ferry	frigate
	paddle boat	steamboat	tanker	trawler

A B C D E F G H I J K L M N O P Q R S T U V W X Y Z

bog NOUN

A **bog** is an area of land that is always wet and spongy.

marsh
*The **marsh** is full of wild flowers at this time of year.*

morass
*After the agricultural show had finished, the field was a **morass**.*

quagmire
*Thanks to the pouring rain, the fairground became a **quagmire**.*

swamp
*"Be careful of that **swamp**," Holmes warned.*

boil VERB

When a liquid **boils**, or when you **boil** it, it starts to bubble and give off steam.

bubble
*The witch cackled as she stirred the potion **bubbling** in the cauldron.*

steam
*The geyser **steamed** for an hour before erupting violently.*

book NOUN

A **book** is a number of pages held together inside a cover.

LANGUAGE TIP
A word for all books is **literature**.

Some types of book:

address book	album	annual
anthology	atlas	brochure
catalogue	cookbook	diary
dictionary	directory	encyclopedia
exercise book	guidebook	hymnbook
jotter	manual	notebook
novel	reference book	scrapbook
storybook	textbook	thesaurus

boring ADJECTIVE

Something **boring** is dull and uninteresting.

dreary
*"That's a **dreary** picture," said Dad. "Who painted it?"*

monotonous
*The professor's **monotonous** voice droned on through the hot afternoon.*

tedious
*Waiting in traffic jams is a **tedious** business.*

Try these lively words and phrases:

ho-hum
*The group released a **ho-hum** third album.*

mind-numbing
*Doing constant laps of the racetrack was **mind-numbing**.*

ANTONYM: interesting

boss NOUN

Someone's **boss** is the person in charge of the place where they work.

employer
*My Dad's **employer** is an American.*

head
*The shop assistant worked so hard, she soon became **head** of her department.*

leader
*The party **leader** hoped one day to be elected Prime Minister.*

manager
*Dad is the **manager** of a supermarket.*

supervisor
*Carol's **supervisor** let her have the afternoon off work to go to the doctor.*

bossy ADJECTIVE

If you are **bossy**, you like to order other people around.

arrogant
*The **arrogant** young man had a rather unfriendly management style.*

domineering
*The timid salesman had a **domineering** wife.*

overbearing
*My Uncle Ted can be **overbearing**.*

bother (1) NOUN

A **bother** is a trouble, fuss or difficulty.

inconvenience
*We apologise for any **inconvenience** our repair work may cause you.*

nuisance
*"Toddlers can be a real **nuisance** – always getting in the way!" said Nurse Adams.*

trouble
*Miss Pollard apologised on arrival. "I don't want to be any **trouble** to you," she said.*

bother (2) VERB

If something **bothers** you, you are worried about it.

concern
*The pilot was clearly **concerned** about the poor weather.*

disturb
*The Kemps were **disturbed** by the disappearance of their rabbit.*

fluster
*My sister is easily **flustered**, especially if she's in a hurry.*

trouble
*This latest news from Egypt **troubles** me greatly.*

worry
*"Don't **worry**, you won't forget your lines," said Ajay.*

bottom (1) NOUN

The **bottom** of something is the lowest part of it.

base
*The **base** of the iceberg is hidden beneath the surface of the water.*

foot
*The chest of gold lay at the **foot** of a long, winding flight of stairs.*

ANTONYM: top

bottom (2) NOUN

The **bottom** is the lowest part of an ocean, sea or river.

bed
*To his utter delight, the prospector saw gold nuggets glinting on the river **bed**.*

depths
*The **depths** of the ocean are darker than we can imagine.*

floor
*The Titanic lay unseen and undisturbed on the sea **floor** for 70 years.*

ANTONYM: surface

bottom (3) NOUN

Your **bottom** is the part of your body that you sit on.

backside
*"Ashraf, get off your **backside** and give me a hand!" Dad said.*

behind
*My **behind** ached for days after the injection.*

buttocks
*Horse riding develops the muscles in one's **buttocks** and thighs.*

posterior
*The toddler fell on his **posterior**.*

rear end
*"Get lost, Alfie!" said Olly, and aimed a tennis ball at Alfie's **rear end**.*

bounce VERB

When an object **bounces**, it springs back from something after hitting it.

rebound
*The ball **rebounded** off the post, straight into the goalkeeper's hands.*

ricochet
*During the gun battle, bullets **ricocheted** off the walls in a terrifying fashion.*

box NOUN

A **box** is a container with a firm base and sides, and usually a lid.

LANGUAGE TIP
A box in which a dead body is buried or cremated is a **coffin**.

Some types of box:

carton	case	casket
chest	container	crate
package	packet	trunk

brainy ADJECTIVE (*informal*)

Someone who is **brainy** is clever and good at learning things.

bright
*"We're looking for someone **bright** for the job," the interviewer said.*

brilliant
*You could tell Narinder was **brilliant** from the start. He could read fluently at the age of two.*

intelligent
*Air-traffic controllers have to be **intelligent** and alert.*

smart
*"As you're so **smart**, Rumpold, I'm promoting you!" the manager said.*

brave ADJECTIVE

A **brave** person is willing to do dangerous things and does not show any fear.

bold
*I'm not **bold** enough to ride that rollercoaster.*

courageous
*Many ordinary situations demand **courageous** behaviour.*

daring
*The **daring** stuntwoman jumped across ten cars on her motorbike.*

fearless
*The **fearless** St George rode straight towards the dragon.*

intrepid
*The **intrepid** explorer risked death to reach the Pole.*

break (1) VERB

When an object **breaks**, or when it is **broken**, it becomes damaged or separates into pieces.

crack
*The giant egg **cracked**, and a pink beak pushed its way out.*

fracture
*"You have **fractured** your leg in three places," said the doctor.*

shatter
*The windscreen **shattered** as the car careered into the barrier.*

smash
*At the fête, there's a chance to **smash** plates by throwing balls at them.*

snap
*Sanjiv **snapped** the bar of chocolate in half and gave some to Kelly.*

splinter
*The boat's hull **splintered** as the novice yachtsman rammed the pier.*

break (2) NOUN

A **break** is a short period during which you rest or do something different.

breather (*informal*)
*"Let's stop for a **breather**," suggested Josie.*

interval
*Between the two acts of the play there will be an **interval** of 15 minutes.*

pause
*There was a **pause** of several seconds before the audience started to applaud.*

rest
*"What you need is a long **rest**," said the doctor.*

breakable ADJECTIVE

Something that is **breakable** is easy to break.

brittle
*Dry earth is **brittle** and crumbles easily.*

delicate
*"Handle that antique vase gently. It's **delicate**," the auctioneer shouted.*

easily broken
*Pottery is **easily broken**.*

flimsy
*The fence suddenly seemed very thin and very **flimsy**.*

fragile
*The label on the box read "**Fragile**", but the camera within was damaged beyond repair.*

break down VERB

When a machine or a vehicle **breaks down**, it stops working.

conk out (*informal*)
*The motorcyclist looked helpless. "Give us a push please, mate. My bike's **conked out**."*

fail
*When the steam train **failed**, a diesel had to tow it back to the depot.*

go wrong
*"I just knew that fancy juicer would **go wrong**," Mum sighed.*

seize up
*Our lawn mower **seized up** when a twig got jammed in the blades.*

LANGUAGE TIP
If someone's car has a **breakdown**, it stops working during a journey.

break up VERB

If something **breaks up**, it comes apart.

disintegrate
*Meteors burn up and **disintegrate** when they enter the atmosphere.*

fall apart
*My wonderful go-kart **fell apart** during its maiden trip.*

LANGUAGE TIP
When a married couple break up, they **separate** or get a **divorce**.

breathless ADJECTIVE

If you are **breathless**, you are breathing very fast or with difficulty.

gasping
*By the time we reached the ridge of the hill, we were **gasping**.*

A B C D E F G H I J K L M N O P Q R S T U V W X Y Z

out of breath
*My gran gets **out of breath** even when she bends down.*

puffed out (*informal*)
*After running for the train I was **puffed out**.*

puffing and panting (*informal*)
*By the end of the fathers' race Dad was **puffing and panting**.*

wheezing
*The poor asthmatic girl was still **wheezing** even after using her inhaler.*

bright (1) ADJECTIVE

Bright colours or things are strong and startling.

brilliant
*The **brilliant** diamond glittered in the light.*

dazzling
*We stepped out into **dazzling** sunshine.*

gleaming
*I polished the car until it was **gleaming**.*

glistening
*The **glistening** dewdrop sat like a jewel on the leaf.*

glittering
*For the show, Mum made me a **glittering** dress with sequins all over.*

glowing
*The **glowing** fire lit the old cottage kitchen far into the night.*

shimmering
*The sun rose as the ship sailed out onto the **shimmering** sea.*

shining
*The **shining** stars lit up the night.*

twinkling
*From the opposite shore we could see the **twinkling** lights of the town.*

vivid
*The parrot's feathers were **vivid** shades of red, green and blue.*

ANTONYMS: dim, dull

bright (2) ADJECTIVE

Someone who is **bright** is clever.

clever
*My aunt is **clever**. At antique fairs, she never misses a bargain.*

intelligent
*Collies are **intelligent** dogs and can understand many commands.*

quick-witted
*Reginald's **quick-witted** action saved his house from burning down.*

smart
*People say I'm **smart** because I'm as quick as lightning at identifying pop songs.*

bright (3) ADJECTIVE

Someone who is **bright** is cheerful.

cheerful
*A **cheerful** manner is important if you are dealing with the public.*

jolly
*My grandpa is a **jolly** man who always seems to be smiling.*

light-hearted
*In our class, discussions are always **light-hearted**, never too serious.*

lively
*Mrs Fenkle is a **lively** teacher, who always makes lessons interesting.*

brilliant (1) ADJECTIVE

A **brilliant** colour or light is extremely bright.

bright
*The dentist shone a **bright** light into my mouth so he could see my teeth clearly.*

dazzling
*The magnificent ruby was a **dazzling** red.*

sparkling
*As the plane came in to land, we could see the **sparkling** city lights below.*

brilliant (2) ADJECTIVE

Someone who is **brilliant** is extremely clever or skilful.

exceptional
*Parvinder is an **exceptional** pupil and is certain to go to university.*

gifted
*The Russian was a **gifted** pianist before he became a conductor.*

talented
*Nicole is a **talented** actress who would like to go to stage school.*

bring VERB

If you **bring** something with you when you go to a place, you take it with you.

carry
*A hotel porter's job is to **carry** people's luggage to their rooms.*

A B C D E F G H I J K L M N O P Q R S T U V W X Y Z

convey
*The minibus **conveyed** people out to the waiting aircraft.*

transport
*Cable cars **transport** sightseers to the top of the mountain.*

bubbles PLURAL NOUN

Bubbles are balls of gas in a liquid.

fizz
*"My cola has lost its **fizz**," Wayne complained.*

foam
*As the tap kept running, the **foam** spilt over the sides of the bath.*

froth
*As we added the lemonade to the orange juice, **froth** started to appear on top.*

suds
*The washing-up bowl was full of **suds**.*

bug NOUN (*informal*)

A **bug** is an infection or virus that makes you ill.

disease
*The **disease** spread rapidly, and soon thousands were infected.*

germ
*Teachers tend to pick up all sorts of **germs** from the children.*

infection
*Hospitals have to fight a constant battle against **infection**.*

virus
*Antibiotics are not effective in curing a **virus**.*

build VERB

If you **build** something, you make it from all its parts.

assemble
*"**Assembling** a bookcase from a kit is easy," Dad said. Ours collapsed two days later.*

construct
*Grandad helped me **construct** a tree house in our back garden.*

erect
*The monument was **erected** within a week.*

ANTONYM: demolish

building NOUN

A **building** is a structure with walls and a roof.

construction
*The huge **construction** on the edge of town is going to be the new sports centre.*

structure
*The Eiffel Tower in Paris is perhaps the world's best-known **structure**.*

build up VERB

If something **builds up**, it becomes greater.

accumulate
*Snow **accumulated** on the snowball as it rolled downhill.*

amass
*Old Mr Godber **amassed** a fortune through dealing in scrap metal.*

collect
*A layer of dust and dead flies had **collected** on top of my wardrobe.*

bully VERB

If someone **bullies** you into doing something, they make you do it by using force or threats.

frighten
*The boys who **frightened** me by calling me names got into trouble.*

intimidate
*"Don't try to **intimidate** me," the old lady called. "I'm not afraid of you!"*

terrorise
*Some fanatics try to **terrorise** others by setting off bombs.*

threaten
*When the bully **threatened** me, I used my judo skills to stop him in his tracks.*

bump (1) VERB

If you **bump** into something, you knock into it accidentally.

collide with
*My bike **collided with** a tree at top speed.*

knock
*Julian **knocked** his knee against the table leg.*

strike
*Allegra fell downstairs, **striking** her head on the banister.*

LANGUAGE TIP
To **bump into someone** is to meet them by chance.

bump (2) NOUN

A **bump** is a sound like something knocking into something else.

thud
*I heard a **thud** from upstairs – my sister had fallen out of bed.*

thump
*The apple landed with a **thump** on the ground beneath the tree.*

bump (3) NOUN

A **bump** is a raised, uneven part of a surface.

bulge
*The **bulge** under the shoplifter's coat proved to be a clock radio.*

lump
*I couldn't sleep last night because of a **lump** in my mattress.*

swelling
*When I banged my head I got a **swelling** over my eye, but it soon went down.*

bumpy ADJECTIVE

Something that is **bumpy** has a rough, uneven surface.

rough
*The pirate's chin was **rough**, as though he had shaved with a knife and fork.*

uneven
*Our soccer pitch is **uneven**, which makes the ball's bounce unpredictable.*

bunch (1) NOUN

A **bunch** is a group of things together.

bundle
*The servant gathered a **bundle** of twigs.*

cluster
***Clusters** of grapes hung from the vine.*

LANGUAGE TIP
A bunch of flowers is a **bouquet**, **posy** or **spray**. A bunch of flowers for a funeral is a **wreath**.

---

bunch (2) NOUN

A **bunch** is a group of people.

crowd
*The **crowd** grew restless as the floodlights stayed off.*

gang
*In the old days, **gangs** of sailors would use force to persuade men to join the navy.*

party
*A **party** of people from each school turned up for the tug-of-war.*

bundle NOUN

A **bundle** is a number of small things gathered together.

batch
*The first **batch** of letters arrived next day.*

collection
*We put a **collection** of newspapers out for recycling.*

heap
*On the table was a **heap** of clothes for the charity shop.*

pile
*A **pile** of dirty washing was waiting to go to the launderette.*

burglar NOUN

A **burglar** is someone who breaks into buildings and steals things.

intruder
*Dad woke up and realised that there was an **intruder** downstairs.*

robber
*The traveller was set upon by **robbers**, who stole his money.*

thief
***Thieves** broke into the warehouse and stole 100 televisions.*

burn (1) VERB

If something is **burning**, it is on fire.

be alight
*The stove **was** still **alight** when we came down in the morning.*

blaze
*A fire **blazed** merrily in Mole's sitting room.*

flame
*The barbecue **flamed** up around the burgers.*

flicker
*The fire **flickered** and crackled.*

LANGUAGE TIP
Something burning is said to be **ablaze**.

---

burn (2) VERB

To **burn** something can mean to damage or destroy it with fire.

char
*The barbecue was too hot and **charred** the sausages.*

A B C D E F G H I J K L M N O P Q R S T U V W X Y Z

scorch
*The baking sun had **scorched** the dry grass on the prairies.*

shrivel
*The heat of the desert had **shrivelled** even the toughest of the plants.*

singe
*I leaned too close to the candle and **singed** my hair.*

burst VERB

When something **bursts**, or you **burst** it, it splits open suddenly.

break
*The coffin **broke** open and the zombie's hands grasped the fractured lid.*

explode
*Shells were **exploding** just behind the enemy trenches.*

rupture
*A water pipe had **ruptured**.*

split
*With the force of the player's shot, the leather ball had **split**.*

bury VERB

If something is **buried** under something, it is covered by it.

conceal
*The secret door was **concealed** behind the bookshelves in the library.*

cover
*I couldn't find my homework as I had accidentally **covered** it with my dirty socks!*

hide
*Her mother used to **hide** biscuits at the back of the cupboard.*

secrete
*The thief **secreted** the stolen jewels in a box under the floorboards.*

→ *See* **hide (2)**

business (1) NOUN

A **business** is an organisation that produces or sells goods, or provides a service.

company
*My mum runs her own **company**.*

corporation
*Whizzo Fireworks is part of a big **corporation** making flares and explosives for quarries.*

firm
*My uncle's **firm** deals in electrical supplies.*

organisation
*"Grappo Inc," boasted the president, "is a big **organisation** full of high achievers."*

business (2) NOUN

Business is work relating to buying and selling goods and services.

industry
*The steel **industry** requires plenty of water for cooling the metal.*

trade
*The clothing business is sometimes called the rag **trade**.*

business (3) NOUN

Business is a general word for any event, situation or activity.

affair
*"That Baskerville murder was a strange **affair**," said Sherlock Holmes.*

issue
*Who owned the buried treasure? It was a complex **issue**!*

matter
*"Stop waffling and stick to the **matter** in hand," the chairman cut in.*

busy (1) ADJECTIVE

If you are **busy**, you are doing something.

employed
*Amal would clearly be **employed** for the next half hour, dealing with a difficult customer.*

hard at work
*My brother was **hard at work** revising when his friends came round.*

occupied
*I was **occupied** looking after my baby brother.*

working
*I was **working** on my school project when I was interrupted by the phone ringing.*

ANTONYMS: idle, unoccupied

busy (2) ADJECTIVE

A **busy** place is full of people doing things or moving about.

bustling
*Trafalgar Square is the **bustling** heart of London.*

hectic
*The streets of Rome were **hectic** and noisy.*

lively
*There is a **lively** market in the town centre every Saturday.*

but CONJUNCTION

But is used to introduce an idea that is opposite to what has gone before.

however
The games were about to start. ***However****, I felt poorly and sat in the corner.*

nevertheless
In my opinion, Sunita had the best fancy dress. ***Nevertheless****, Emma got the prize.*

on the other hand
My sister said she'd had a good time. ***On the other hand****, she always says things like that.*

yet
It was time to go to bed, ***yet*** *I wasn't really tired.*

buy VERB

If you **buy** something, you get it by paying money for it.

acquire
The school ***acquired*** *a piece of land to extend the playing field.*

obtain
Dad ***obtained*** *tickets for the concert.*

pay for
We saved up our pocket money and used it to ***pay for*** *a new CD player.*

purchase
"My good man, where in your emporium can I ***purchase*** *a handbag?" sniffed Lady Bracknell.*

Cc

café NOUN

A **café** is a place where you can buy light meals and drinks.

coffee shop
My sister took me into her favourite ***coffee shop*** *for a treat.*

snack bar
Dad remembers when that expensive restaurant was a simple ***snack bar****.*

teashop
On holiday, we had tea and scones in an old-fashioned ***teashop****.*

Different places to eat:

canteen	coffee shop	diner
dining room	refectory	restaurant
snack bar		

call (1) VERB

If you **call** someone or something a particular name, that is their name.

christen
My mum has ***christened*** *her little soft-top car William.*

name
My parents wanted to ***name*** *me Humphrey, but changed their minds.*

call (2) VERB

If you **call** someone, you telephone them.

phone
"Dad just ***phoned*** *to say he'll be home shortly," I told Mum.*

ring
Lisa ***rang*** *the hospital to see how her brother was doing.*

telephone
"If you ***telephone*** *between twelve and one o'clock, you'll catch me," the salesman said.*

A B C D E F G H I J K L M N O P Q R S T U V W X Y Z

call off VERB

If something is **called off**, it is cancelled.

abandon
When the heavy rain turned to snow, the referee decided that the match should be ***abandoned****.*

cancel
Owing to lack of support, the dance had to be ***cancelled****.*

postpone
Because of building repairs, our bowling is being ***postponed*** *until Tuesday.*

calm (1) ADJECTIVE

Someone who is **calm** is quiet and does not show any worry or excitement.

composed
Mrs Yamamoto is a very ***composed****, businesslike woman.*

level-headed
Sanjay is a ***level-headed*** *individual who would never panic in a crisis.*

relaxed
Cameron was so ***relaxed*** *about his exam, he fell asleep on the first page.*

unflappable (*informal*)
The lifeboat crew were selected for being ***unflappable*** *as well as skilled sailors.*

ANTONYM: excitable

calm (2) ADJECTIVE

If the sea is **calm**, the water is not moving very much.

peaceful
The sea was ***peaceful*** *as we walked along the beach in the early morning.*

quiet
After the storm the sea became ***quiet*** *again.*

still
The lake was absolutely ***still****, reflecting the mountains behind.*

tranquil
It was a hot, sunny day and the children enjoyed swimming in the ***tranquil*** *bay.*

ANTONYM: rough

calm down VERB

If you **calm** someone **down**, you help make them less upset or excited.

quieten
A lollipop helped to ***quieten*** *the squealing toddler.*

soothe
Some farmers turn on the radio to ***soothe*** *pigs in their pens.*

cancel VERB

If you **cancel** something that has been arranged, you stop it from happening.

abandon
The match was ***abandoned*** *at half-time when the floodlights failed.*

abort
Mission Control decided to ***abort*** *the mission and bring the shuttle back.*

call off
When I caught chickenpox, Mum and Dad ***called off*** *the party.*

scrap (*informal*)
"Let's ***scrap*** *the idea of Paris, and go to Rome instead," Dad suggested.*

capable ADJECTIVE

Someone who is **capable** is able to do something well.

able
Mr. Johnstone is an ***able*** *businessman.*

accomplished
Rajesh is one of our most ***accomplished*** *violinists.*

competent
Sir Winston Churchill was a surprisingly ***competent*** *artist.*

efficient
Mrs Kemp was very ***efficient****; everything was done to a tight schedule.*

skilful
My sister is a ***skilful*** *horsewoman, with several medals to her name.*

ANTONYM: incompetent

captain NOUN

A **captain** is the officer in charge of a ship or aeroplane.

commander
Uncertain what to do, Lieutenant Zarg called the spacecraft ***commander*** *to the bridge.*

master
The ***master*** *of the oil tanker reluctantly gave the order to abandon ship.*

pilot
"It looks as if we're in for some turbulence," the ***pilot*** *announced.*

skipper
*Trawler **skippers** and their crews have to endure awful weather conditions.*

capture VERB

If someone **captures** someone or something, they take them prisoner.

arrest
*Police **arrested** the woman on suspicion of blackmail.*

kidnap
*The villains **kidnapped** the wealthy businessman's son and held him hostage.*

nab (*informal*)
*Sergeant Philpot **nabbed** the burglar as he tried to make his escape.*

take captive
*After being **taken captive**, the explorer was imprisoned in a hut.*

ANTONYM: release

car NOUN

A **car** is a four-wheeled road vehicle with an engine and room to carry a few passengers.

automobile
*"This motorcar," boasted Mr Toad, "is the finest **automobile** ever built."*

banger (*informal*)
*Our new teacher drives a real old **banger**.*

motorcar
*The sign read, "This road is unsuitable for **motorcars**".*

LANGUAGE TIP
The word **vehicle** can be used for a car, but also for other forms of transport, especially those with wheels.

care (1) VERB

If you **care** about something or someone, you are concerned about them and interested in them.

be concerned
*Yolanda doesn't seem to **be concerned** about next week's test.*

bother
*"If you're not **bothered** about the state of your room, why should I be?" snapped mother.*

mind
*Graham didn't **mind** if Sanjiv borrowed some of his pens.*

care (2) NOUN

A **care** is a worry or trouble.

anxiety
*The twins hadn't returned, and their father was showing signs of **anxiety**.*

concern
*Our **concern** is that Midori will miss too much school while she's off with mumps.*

trouble
*I don't like to burden other people with my **troubles**.*

worry
*One **worry** for the head teacher was what to do if several teachers were ill at once.*

care (3) NOUN

If you do something with **care**, you concentrate very hard on it so that you don't make any mistakes.

attention
***Attention** to detail is an important aspect of an architect's work.*

caution
*You must always exercise **caution** when you cross a road.*

ANTONYM: carelessness

care for VERB

If you **care for** a person or animal, you look after them.

look after
*Connor and I **looked after** Mum when she was ill.*

nurse
*Mrs Nelson **nursed** her sick husband for some months before he recovered.*

tend
*We take it in turns to **tend** the three class guinea pigs.*

ANTONYM: neglect

careful (1) ADJECTIVE

If someone is **careful**, they act sensibly and with care.

alert
*"Be **alert** at all times," the major warned. "You don't know who's out there!"*

attentive
*The nurse was very **attentive** when she stitched up Paul's cut forehead.*

a b c d e f g h i j k l m n o p q r s t u v w x y z

cautious
*I have learnt always to be **cautious** about so-called "free" offers.*

sensible
*My gran is very **sensible** and always takes a coat if the weather looks doubtful.*

wary
*The barons were right to be **wary** of King John's cunning schemes.*

careful (2) ADJECTIVE

Something that is **careful** shows a concern for detail.

accurate
*If you work in a shop, it's important to be **accurate** in giving change.*

meticulous
*Alyssa produces **meticulous** work. She gets very upset if the slightest detail is wrong.*

painstaking
*I admired Nicholas for his **painstaking** work. His painting took weeks to finish.*

precise
*"Be very **precise** in your workings," said Mr Matthews, our maths teacher.*

thorough
*Mrs Chan is very **thorough**; she always cleans behind her furniture.*

ANTONYM: careless

careful (3) ADJECTIVE

If you are **careful** in what you say, you think before you speak.

discreet
*Jamila was **discreet** in not mentioning the party, in case Tanya hadn't been invited.*

tactful
*Shopkeepers have to be **tactful**, as some customers are easily offended.*

ANTONYM: careless

careless ADJECTIVE

If you are **careless**, you do not pay enough attention to what you are doing.

inaccurate
*The clerk's **inaccurate** adding up cost the company thousands of pounds.*

slapdash
*"This is **slapdash** work, Rachel," snapped Miss Greer. "Do it again slowly!"*

slipshod
***Slipshod** tiling by the builders caused our roof to leak.*

sloppy (*informal*)
*Mr Ismail told me off for my **sloppy** handwriting.*

ANTONYM: careful

carry VERB

When you **carry** something, you hold it and take it somewhere.

convey
*The robot arm **conveyed** the large nut to the bolt, and screwed them together.*

lug
*It was hard work **lugging** the case upstairs.*

transport
*Mrs Bartlett **transported** the table to her home by car.*

carry on VERB

If you **carry on** with something, you continue doing it.

continue
*"Please **continue** with what you were doing," the head teacher said when she came in.*

persevere
*It pays off, in the end, to **persevere** with a job.*

persist
*"If you **persist** in talking, you'll lose your playtime," Mrs Rasheed warned.*

proceed
*Grandad took a sip of his tea and then **proceeded** with his story.*

castle NOUN

A **castle** is a large building with walls or ditches round it to protect it from attack.

fort
*The cavalry rode out from their **fort**, trumpets blaring and guns blazing.*

fortress
*On the very peak of the mountain stood the enemy **fortress**.*

stronghold
*King Edward I built **strongholds** in Wales.*

cat NOUN

A **cat** is a small animal covered with fur that people in some countries keep as a pet.

→ Have a look at the **Illustration** page!

BIG CATS

tiger

puma/cougar/
mountain lion

cheetah

panther

lion

snow leopard

jaguar

Some other types of big cat:

Bengal tiger	caracal	clouded leopard
Eurasian lynx	leopard	Siberian tiger

catch (1) VERB

If you **catch** a person or animal, you capture them.

arrest
*Navy police **arrested** the drunken sailor.*

capture
*Luckily, the cowboys managed to **capture** the runaway horse.*

ensnare
*The unfortunate trespasser found herself **ensnared** in barbed wire.*

trap
*In the forests of Russia, hunters **trap** animals for their skins.*

catch (2) NOUN

A **catch** is a hidden difficulty.

disadvantage
*One of the **disadvantages** of having long hair is that it can get very tangled.*

drawback
*There is a **drawback** to eating too much chocolate. It can make you feel sick!*

snag
*When putting the shelves up we came across a **snag** – we didn't have enough screws.*

cause (1) VERB

If someone or something **causes** something, they make it happen.

bring about
*The curse of the Baskervilles **brought about** the family's downfall.*

create
*Last night some noisy party-goers **created** a disturbance in our street.*

lead to
*More police officers on the beat **led to** a drop in the crime rate.*

produce
*Who would have thought that a small baby would **produce** so much noise?*

cause (2) NOUN

The **cause** of something is the thing that makes it happen.

origin
*The **origin** of the tradition was a mystery.*

source
*Gambling was the **source** of all Matt's troubles.*

cautious ADJECTIVE

Someone who is **cautious** acts carefully to avoid possible danger or disappointment.

careful
*Ashley was **careful** about handling the precious eggs.*

wary
*The sparrows were **wary** of the nearby cat.*

ANTONYM: reckless

celebration NOUN

A **celebration** is an occasion to mark a happy day or event.

Some types of celebration:

banquet	carnival	feast
festival	fête	gala
jubilee	party	reunion
wedding		

centre NOUN

The **centre** of an object or area is the middle of it.

core
*The earth's **core** consists of molten rock.*

heart
*In the **heart** of the city, a musician played on a street corner.*

hub
*At the **hub** of operations was my brother, with his walkie-talkie set.*

middle
*The bull's-eye is in the **middle** of a dartboard.*

certain (1) ADJECTIVE

If you are **certain** about something, you are sure it is true.

confident
*Shula was **confident** that the rumour she had heard was true.*

convinced
*Al was **convinced** that he would pass his exam.*

positive
*"Are you **positive** that's what you want for your birthday?" Mum asked.*

sure
*"I'm **sure** I put my homework in my bag, but I can't find it," I said.*

ANTONYM: uncertain

certain (2) ADJECTIVE

If something is **certain** to happen, it is likely to happen.

inevitable
*It was **inevitable** that the bully would meet his match before long.*

likely
*According to the weather forecast, it's **likely** to be a sunny afternoon.*

unavoidable
*When the cars' brakes failed, a collision was **unavoidable**.*

ANTONYM: unlikely

certainly ADVERB

Certainly can mean without any doubt.

definitely
*"Put me down for a ticket," Dad said. "I'm **definitely** going to the game."*

undoubtedly
*The horse was **undoubtedly** the fastest that Jo had ridden.*

without doubt
***Without doubt**, geography was John's favourite subject.*

chance (1) NOUN

If there is a **chance** that something will happen, it might happen.

danger
*At oil refineries, there is always a **danger** of fire breaking out.*

likelihood
*With those clouds, there was a **likelihood** of rain before long.*

possibility
*"Is there any **possibility** of a lift, please?" Hamal asked.*

probability
*It is a **probability** that humans will one day walk on Mars.*

chance (2) NOUN

Something that happens by **chance** happens unexpectedly, without being planned.

accident
*It was totally by **accident** that Mum bumped into her old friend.*

coincidence
*"What a **coincidence**!" Robin gasped. "I went to that school too!"*

fortune
*By good **fortune**, a passer-by heard the calls of the stricken climber.*

luck
*The tennis player's injury was just bad **luck**.*

stroke of luck
*By a **stroke of luck**, the massive doors were unguarded.*

change (1) VERB

When something **changes**, or you **change** it, it becomes different.

alter
*The colour of Gavin's hair has **altered** since he was a baby.*

convert
*Dad **converted** the old shed into a play hut.*

mutate
*Before Kirk's eyes, the handsome crewman **mutated** into a fanged, drooling monster.*

transform
*Bond's car **transformed** into a boat.*

change (2) VERB

If you **change** something, you swap or replace it.

exchange
*We had to take my new shoes back and **exchange** them for a larger size.*

replace
*Today Mr Woo **replaced** his old banger with a smooth sports car.*

substitute
*"What happens if you **substitute** milk for water?" the teacher asked.*

swap
*Dylan **swapped** his cards for Salman's.*

trade in
*Mum joked that she wanted to **trade** my dad **in** for a newer model!*

change (3) NOUN

A **change** is a difference or alteration in something.

difference
*Mum and I noticed the **difference** in Gran after her illness.*

metamorphosis
*Caterpillars undergo an amazing **metamorphosis** into butterflies.*

transformation
*We gasped at the **transformation** when Iris emerged from the hairdresser's.*

character NOUN

Someone's **character** is all the qualities which combine to form their personality.

nature
*It was not in Abigail's **nature** to be rude.*

personality
*Gran had a bubbly **personality** and was always making friends.*

temperament
*A dog's **temperament** depends largely on how it is treated.*

charge VERB

If something or someone **charges**, they rush forward.

attack
*The infantry **attacked** the fortress at dawn.*

rampage
*Boadicea's angry tribesmen **rampaged** through the streets, yelling and whooping.*

run wild
*Leaving their longships, the Viking marauders **ran wild** in the Saxon village.*

rush
*When the bell went, Boris **rushed** for the door, only to be hauled back.*

storm
*On D-Day 1944, Allied troops **stormed** the beaches and cliffs of Normandy.*

chase VERB

If you **chase** someone, you run after them or follow them in order to catch them.

follow
*Fans **followed** the pop idol wherever he went.*

hound
*Reporters **hounded** the star until she gave them an interview.*

hunt
*Lions **hunt** antelope as their prey.*

pursue
*Detectives **pursued** the gangster to South America.*

track
*Sniffer dogs **tracked** the thief to a disused dockside warehouse.*

cheap ADJECTIVE

Something that is **cheap** costs very little money.

bargain
*My **bargain** laptop computer cost half of what most people pay.*

economical
*That car is very **economical** on fuel, but it'll cost more in repairs.*

inexpensive
*The jacket was **inexpensive** but looked very smart.*

reasonable
*Mum thought that it was a **reasonable** price for a second-hand mountain bike.*

cheat (1) VERB

If someone **cheats**, they lie or do unfair things to win or get what they want.

con (*informal*)
*The thief **conned** his way into the old woman's house by asking if he could use her phone for an emergency.*

deceive
*"It's no good trying to **deceive** me," Mum said. "I know you're up to something!"*

double-cross (*informal*)
*The thief **double-crossed** his accomplice and took all the cash.*

dupe
*The stamp collectors were **duped** into buying some very convincing fakes.*

rip off (*informal*)
*"We were **ripped off** there!" snorted my brother disgustedly, as we left the burger bar.*

swindle
*The cashier had systematically **swindled** the bank for years before she was caught.*

trick
*Trying to **trick** his pursuers, the getaway driver doubled back.*

cheat (2) NOUN

A **cheat** is a person who lies or does unfair things to win or get what they want.

con man (*informal*)
*There's a **con man** about, pretending to be from the electricity company.*

double-crosser
*The gangster snarled "You dirty **double-crosser**!" and sped away.*

swindler
*The **swindler** sold villas to his clients which did not really exist.*

check (1) VERB

If you **check** something, you examine it to make sure that everything is all right.

assess
*Miss Connolly will **assess** our term's work before writing her report.*

examine
*Sherlock Holmes picked up the knife and **examined** it.*

inspect
*The council team **inspect** the food cupboards carefully.*

test
*To **test** our multiplication tables, Mr Murphy fires questions at us.*

check (2) NOUN

A **check** is an inspection to make sure that everything is all right.

assessment
*Every soldier has to do his PFA, or Physical Fitness **Assessment**.*

check-up
*After his fall, Grandad had to visit the doctor's for a **check-up**.*

examination
*Detectives carried out a minute **examination** of the crime scene.*

inspection
*Even the best schools are subject to regular **inspections**.*

test
*Older vehicles have to go through a safety **test** to ensure that they are roadworthy.*

cheeky ADJECTIVE

Someone who is **cheeky** is rude and disrespectful, often in an amusing way.

disrespectful
*It's unacceptable to be **disrespectful** to teachers.*

impertinent
*What an **impertinent** thing to say to someone who has helped you!*

impudent
*The **impudent** waiter said the cheekiest things to his customers.*

rude
*"Try not to be **rude** to people, even if they are unpleasant to you," said Mum.*

ANTONYMS: respectful, polite

cheerful ADJECTIVE

A **cheerful** person is happy.

bright
*I'm quite **bright** in the morning.*

cheery
*The postman gave us a **cheery** wave.*

chirpy (*informal*)
*Despite her aches, Gran is always **chirpy**.*

jolly
*They could hear the sounds of a rather **jolly** baby.*

light-hearted
*Holly was bubbly, **light-hearted**, and ambitious.*

merry
*They were feeling quite **merry** by the time they arrived.*

chew VERB

When you **chew** something, you use your teeth to break it up in your mouth before swallowing it.

chomp
*The horse **chomped** its way through several carrots.*

crunch
*Some people **crunch** their lollipops. Others suck them.*

gnaw
*Beavers had **gnawed** away the bark of the tree.*

munch
*Lucy and Megan happily **munched** their cheeseburgers and chatted about school.*

child NOUN

A **child** is a young person who is not yet an adult.

juvenile
*In the eyes of the law, anyone under 18 is a **juvenile**.*

kid (*informal*)
*Mum takes several **kids** to school, not just us.*

nipper (*informal*)
*"When I was a **nipper**," Grandad said, "I used to climb that oak tree."*

youngster
*The **youngster** ran out into the road without even looking.*

→ *See* **baby**

LANGUAGE TIP
A child whose parents are dead is an **orphan**.

A B C D E F G H I J K L M N O P Q R S T U V W X Y Z

childish ADJECTIVE

If someone is **childish**, they are not acting in an adult way.

immature
To lark around like that was ***immature*** *for a man of his age.*

infantile
Jafar's temper tantrum was ***infantile****.*

juvenile
"Such ***juvenile*** *behaviour must be punished," the head teacher said grimly.*

choice (1) NOUN

A **choice** is a range of different things that are available to choose from.

selection
What a ***selection*** *of chocolates greeted my eyes when I opened the box!*

variety
There was a ***variety*** *of films to choose from on the plane.*

choice (2) NOUN

A **choice** is something that you choose.

option
We had no ***option*** *but to accept a refund when our flights were cancelled.*

preference
My ***preference*** *is action movies rather than romances.*

selection
To her disgust, the judges' ***selection*** *did not include Mrs Whipple's fairy cakes.*

LANGUAGE TIP
If you have a choice whether or not to do something, it is **optional**.

choose VERB

If you **choose** something, you decide to have it or do it.

opt for
We couldn't decide which holiday to ***opt for****: Florida or France.*

pick
My mean sister always ***picks*** *the chocolates that I want.*

select
The archer ***selected*** *an arrow.*

single out
The judge ***singled*** *her* ***out*** *as being especially intelligent.*

circle VERB

If someone or something **circles** an object, they move around it in a circle.

lap
The cyclist ***lapped*** *the track for the final time.*

orbit
The earth takes around 365 days, or one year, to ***orbit*** *the sun.*

→ *See* **go round (1)**

LANGUAGE TIP
To sail round the world is to **circumnavigate** it.

circumstances NOUN

The **circumstances** of a situation or event are the conditions that affect what happens.

background
Our history teacher explained the ***background*** *of the American Civil War.*

context
The police had to consider the ***context*** *of the accident.*

situation
The ***situation*** *was difficult for everyone.*

claim VERB

If you **claim** that something is the case, you say that it is so.

allege
The witness ***alleged*** *that Jones had threatened several people.*

argue
The boss ***argued*** *that it was fair to sack someone who worked slowly.*

declare
The smuggler ***declared*** *that he had nothing illegal in his case.*

insist
The arrested woman ***insisted*** *that the officer had made a mistake.*

maintain
Hal ***maintained*** *that only Leroy was better than him at basketball.*

class (1) NOUN

A **class** is a group of pupils or students who are taught together.

group
Mum's drama ***group*** *meets on Tuesday.*

set
Ahmed is in the top maths ***set****.*

stream
*At the grammar school, children were put in **streams** according to their ability.*

tutor group
*Jennifer is in Mrs Burton's **tutor group**.*

class (2) NOUN
A **class** of people or things is a group of them that are alike in some way.

category
*Nitesh entered the junior **category** of the poetry competition.*

kind
*Beavenutti is the best restaurant of its **kind** in the area.*

sort
*"What is your favourite **sort** of music?" Carly asked.*

type
*The market stall sold lots of different **types** of vegetables and fruits.*

clean (1) ADJECTIVE
If something is **clean**, it is free from dirt or unwanted marks.

immaculate
*The car was **immaculate** when Leo bought it, but filthy two days later.*

spotless
*"I want this cabin **spotless**," rasped the captain, "or you're for the high jump!"*

ANTONYM: dirty

clean (2) VERB
If you **clean** something, you remove dirt from it.

Some ways to clean:

bathe	brush	dry-clean
dust	hoover	launder
mop	polish	rinse
scour	scrub	shampoo
sponge	sweep	swill
vacuum	wash	wipe

clear (1) ADJECTIVE
If something is **clear**, it is easy to understand, see or hear.

apparent
*It was **apparent** we were going to lose, right from the start of the match.*

definite
*There were **definite** indications that the swallows were nesting in the eaves.*

distinct
*We could hear the **distinct** sound of church bells in the distance.*

evident
*It was **evident** from the wet roads that it had been raining.*

obvious
*The man showed **obvious** signs of having been in a fight.*

plain
*"It's **plain** to see that you have learnt very little," the head teacher said.*

ANTONYM: unclear

clear (2) ADJECTIVE
A **clear** sky has no clouds in it.

bright
*A very **bright** morning can mean rain later.*

cloudless
*Skylarks sang high in the **cloudless** sky.*

moonlit
*The UFO slid silently across the **moonlit** sky.*

starlit
*On that **starlit** night, I could have stayed for hours by the shore.*

ANTONYM: cloudy

clear (3) ADJECTIVE
If something is **clear**, it is easy to see through.

see-through
*My mum has a **see-through** plastic coat.*

translucent
*The dragonfly's **translucent** wings beat against the sky.*

transparent
*Scott covered his book with **transparent** sticky-backed plastic.*

ANTONYMS: murky, opaque

clever ADJECTIVE
Someone who is **clever** is intelligent and quick to understand things.

brainy
*My **brainy** brother came top of his class.*

bright
*Jim was only three, but he was **bright** enough to understand what was going on.*

intelligent
*"It's no good just being **intelligent**. You have to work hard too," said my English teacher.*

A B C D E F G H I J K L M N O P Q R S T U V W X Y Z

smart
*He's far too **smart** to get mixed up in anything illegal.*

ANTONYM: unintelligent

climb VERB
When you **climb**, you move upwards.

ascend
*Alice **ascended** the stairs, carrying a candle.*

clamber up
*Having locked himself out, Dad had to **clamber up** the drainpipe to an open window.*

scale
*The climber had to **scale** the overhanging rockface.*

clock NOUN
A **clock** is an instrument that measures and shows the time.

→ Have a look at the **Illustration** page!

close (1) VERB
If you **close** something, you move it so that it is no longer open.

seal
*The crewman **sealed** the hatch and the submarine was ready to dive.*

secure
*"Make sure you **secure** all the bolts on that cage," the zookeeper warned.*

shut
*"**Shut** the door behind you, but first check you've got your key," said Mum.*

ANTONYM: open

PRONUNCIATION TIP
When it is a verb, **close** is pronounced **klohz**.

close (2) ADJECTIVE
If something is **close** to something else, it is near to it.

adjacent
*The amusement arcade was **adjacent** to the holiday camp.*

handy
*Our chalet was **handy** for the camp shop.*

nearby
*Grabbing a towel that was **nearby**, Jacinth soaked it and threw it over the flaming pan.*

neighbouring
*The **neighbouring** woods are full of bluebells.*

ANTONYM: far

PRONUNCIATION TIP
When it is an adjective, **close** is pronounced **klohss**.

cloth NOUN
Cloth is fabric made by a process such as weaving.

fabric
*"This **fabric** will make lovely curtains for the spare room," said Gran.*

material
*The tailor used only the best **material** for the suits he made.*

textiles
*Natural **textiles** such as wool are warmer than man-made ones.*

Some types of cloth:

corduroy	cotton	denim
felt	lace	Lycra™
nylon	satin	silk
tweed	velvet	wool

clothes PLURAL NOUN
Clothes are the things people wear on their bodies.

clothing
*"My son is in the **clothing** trade," Manny told everyone proudly.*

costume
*At the open-air museum, the guides wore period **costume**.*

dress
*"Shorts and trainers are hardly suitable **dress** for a wedding," Lady Etherington said.*

garments
*The notice read: "To try **garments** on, please use the changing room".*

gear (*informal*)
*As the forecast was poor, Kayla took her wet weather **gear** with her.*

cloudy (1) ADJECTIVE
If the sky is **cloudy**, it is full of clouds.

dull
*The weather was **dull**, but there was some sunshine forecast for later.*

gloomy
*It was a **gloomy** day for the start of our holiday.*

CLOCKS

digital clock

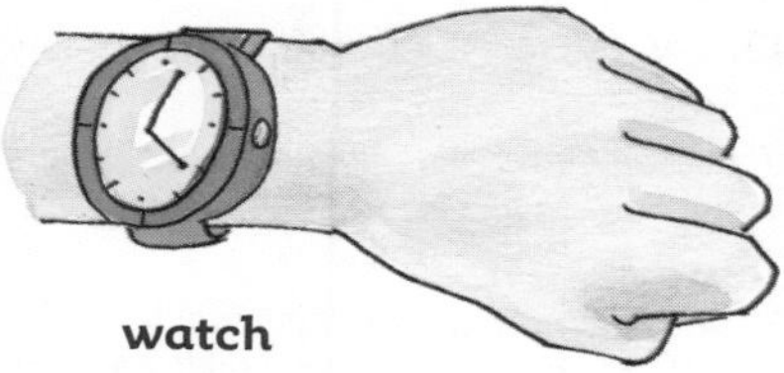

watch

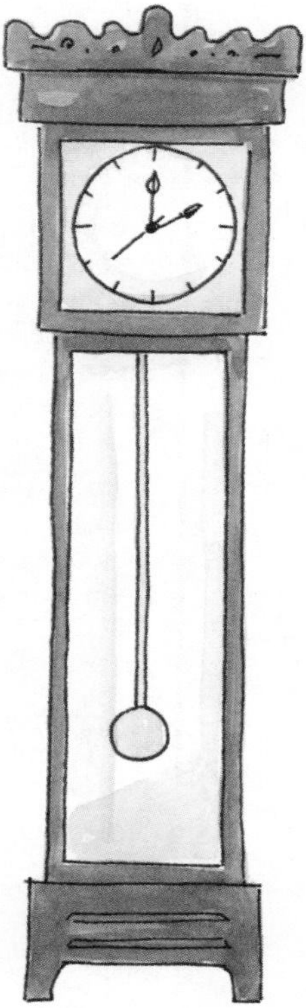

grandfather clock

phone

stopwatch

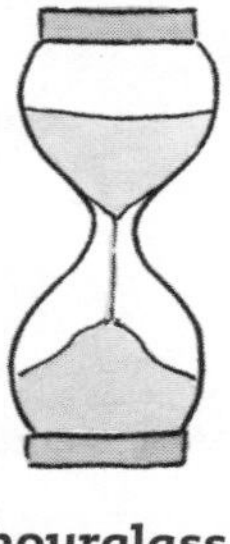

hourglass

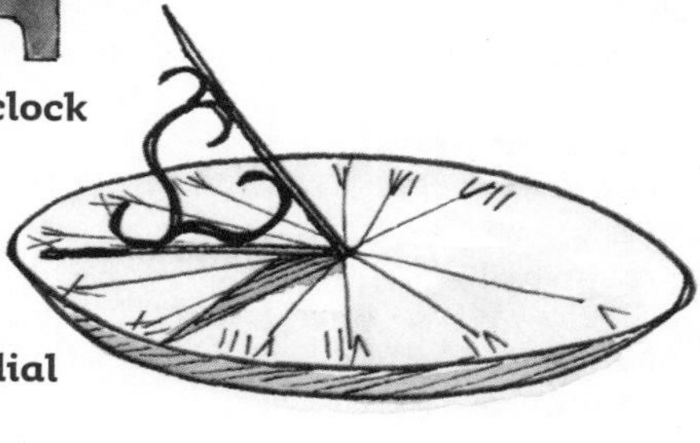

sundial

Some other types of clock:
alarm clock   cuckoo clock   egg timer   timer

overcast
*The sky was **overcast** when the plane took off.*

cloudy (2) ADJECTIVE

Cloudy can mean difficult to see through.

muddy
*The scuba divers could not find the shipwreck in the **muddy** water.*

murky
*The travellers could see a faint light shining through the **murky** evening – shelter at last!*

opaque
*The bottle was made of **opaque** glass, so we could not see clearly what was in it.*

club (1) NOUN

A **club** is an organisation of people with a particular interest, who meet regularly.

association
*Grandad belongs to an ex-servicemen's **association**.*

group
*Mr Fanshaw runs a local pottery **group**.*

society
*Maya is a member of a **society** for the protection of wildlife.*

club (2) NOUN

A **club** is a thick, heavy stick used as a weapon.

baton
*Police carry **batons** in case they need to defend themselves.*

truncheon
*In Grandad's day, all police officers were issued with **truncheons**.*

clumsy ADJECTIVE

Someone who is **clumsy** moves awkwardly and carelessly.

accident-prone
*Matt is **accident-prone**; he's always hurting himself somehow.*

awkward
*There's something **awkward** about the way Indira holds her cutlery.*

blundering
*The **blundering** chef clattered about in the kitchen.*

butterfingered *(informal)*
***Butterfingered** people should not work in china shops!*

lumbering
*Giant Grumbleweed was a **lumbering** hulk with a knack for breaking things.*

uncoordinated
*Karim is a very **uncoordinated** dancer.*

coat (1) NOUN

An animal's **coat** is the fur or hair on its body.

fleece
*In a blur of movement, the shearer had the sheep's **fleece** off in seconds.*

fur
*Stephanie sobbed into her kitten's **fur**.*

hide
*The **hide** of cows is treated to make leather.*

LANGUAGE TIP
The fur from certain dead animals is called a **pelt**.

coat (2) NOUN

A **coat** is a piece of clothing with long sleeves, that you wear over other clothes.

LANGUAGE TIP
A **waistcoat** is a sleeveless piece of clothing, often worn under a suit or jacket, which buttons up at the front.

Some types of coat:

anorak	blazer	bomber jacket
duffel coat	jacket	kagoul
mackintosh	overcoat	raincoat
trench coat	waterproof	

cold

➔ Look at the **Word Power** page!

collapse (1) VERB

If something such as a building **collapses**, it falls down suddenly.

cave in
*The miners were trapped when the roof of the passage **caved in**.*

crumple
*As the charges exploded, the walls **crumpled** to the ground.*

give way
*In 1879, the poorly built Tay Bridge in Scotland **gave way** in a storm.*

collapse (2) VERB

If a person **collapses**, they fall down suddenly because they are ill.

A B C D E F G H I J K L M N O P Q R S T U V W X Y Z

faint
*I cut my knee and nearly **fainted** when I saw the blood.*

pass out
*The parade ground was so hot that several soldiers **passed out**.*

collect VERB

If you **collect** things, you gather them together for a special reason.

assemble
*For the exhibition, the gallery **assembled** paintings from all over the world.*

cluster
*Interested buyers **clustered** around the beautiful bronze statue.*

compile
*The editor **compiled** an anthology of poems.*

gather
*"**Gather** your tools up before you run off," Dad reminded me.*

collection NOUN

A **collection** is a group of things brought together over a period of time.

array
*The shelf held a dazzling **array** of trophies.*

compilation
*The book is a **compilation** of short stories by famous writers.*

LANGUAGE TIP
A collection of poems is an **anthology**.

---

come VERB

If you **come** to a place, you move there or arrive there.

arrive
*As soon as we **arrived**, my auntie started hugging people.*

materialise
*In no time at all, thanks to Ratty, a splendid tea had **materialised**.*

show up (*informal*)
*Josh **showed up** at the very last minute, just when we had started to panic.*

turn up
*Sarah and I weren't expecting Faith to **turn up**, but she did.*

come about VERB

If something **comes about**, it happens.

happen
*Mr Abiola was walking past the shop when the robbery **happened**.*

occur
*The incident **occurred** at the swimming pool.*

take place
*The party will **take place** from three to five o'clock on Saturday afternoon.*

comfortable (1) ADJECTIVE

Something that is **comfortable** makes you feel relaxed.

comfy (*informal*)
*He settled himself into a **comfy** seat.*

cosy
*Mark felt very **cosy** under the duvet.*

relaxing
*On holiday, Mum loves a **relaxing** sauna.*

restful
*The seaside resort had a **restful** atmosphere.*

comfortable (2) ADJECTIVE

If you are **comfortable**, you are at ease and relaxed.

at ease
*Sir George was the sort of person to make you feel **at ease** straight away.*

contented
*Gran was **contented** in her little flat.*

relaxed
*After a week of her holiday, Mrs Archer felt completely **relaxed**.*

ANTONYM: uncomfortable

common ADJECTIVE

Something that is **common** exists in large numbers or happens often.

average
*The **average** person doesn't know much about nuclear physics.*

everyday
*In a quarry, explosions are an **everyday** occurrence.*

normal
*It was **normal** for Harry to take his granny up a morning cup of tea.*

ordinary
*It started off like any **ordinary** day at work.*

A B C D E F G H I J K L M N O P Q R S T U V W X Y Z

cold

ADJECTIVE If something is **cold**, it has a very low temperature.

Very cold weather:

arctic (*informal*)
The toilet block had no heating and was positively ***arctic****.*

baltic (*informal*)
The main problem is that the flat is ***baltic*** *in winter and absolutely boiling in summer.*

biting
The ***biting*** *wind seemed to go right through my thin jacket.*

bitter
A ***bitter*** *east wind was accompanied by flurries of snow.*

freezing
Many people had to spend the whole night in their cars in ***freezing*** *temperatures.*

frosty
It was a bright ***frosty*** *morning when we set off.*

harsh
As we went further and further north, the weather grew ***harsh*** *and unpredictable.*

icy
An ***icy*** *wind blew across the playground.*

perishing
It was ***perishing*** *and we had no choice but to invest in moon boots and ski jackets.*

raw
The funeral took place on a ***raw*** *December morning.*

snowy
On a cold ***snowy*** *day in mid-February I eventually married my childhood sweetheart.*

cold

Slightly cold weather:

bleak
*The weather can be quite **bleak** on the coast.*

chilly
*It was an especially **chilly** afternoon and the fire did little to warm the room.*

cool
*Anna took a breath of the **cool** morning air.*

nippy
*There was a **nippy** wind blowing under the door.*

wintry
*It was a grey **wintry** day when we set off.*

Feeling cold:

freezing
*Even with the extra blanket, I was absolutely **freezing**.*

frozen
*I tried to warm my **frozen** hands at the fire.*

perished
*I was **perished** – my own fault for not taking a jacket.*

shaking with cold
*She was **shaking with cold** as she stood at the side of the pool.*

shivering
*He threw his jacket around her shoulders to try and stop her **shivering**.*

Try these lively words and phrases!

chilled to the bone	*We were **chilled to the bone** as we waited for the bus.*
freeze your backside off *(informal)*	*We were **freezing our backsides off** standing in the rain.*
frozen to the marrow	*Marie was **frozen to the marrow** and desperate to go home.*
get goosebumps	*Sitting in the shade, she started to **get goosebumps**.*

→ Also have a look at the **Word Power** page for **hot**!

A B C D E F G H I J K L M N O P Q R S T U V W X Y Z

standard
*"A **standard**-class ticket, please," I said to the train guard.*

usual
*The **usual** lunch on Friday is fish.*

ANTONYM: uncommon

company NOUN

A **company** is a business that sells goods or provides a service.

business
*My father runs an electrical **business**.*

corporation
*Mrs Fletcher's tiny company belongs to a huge global **corporation**.*

firm
*Mum's **firm** is paying for her to go on a management course.*

competition NOUN

A **competition** is an event in which people take part to find out who is the best at something.

championship
*Wimbledon is a famous tennis **championship**.*

contest
*The two villages faced each other in a tug-of-war **contest**.*

event
*The Commonwealth Games is a great sporting **event**.*

tournament
*Our school entered two teams in the Under-11 netball **tournament**.*

complain VERB

If you **complain**, you say that you are not happy about something.

bleat
*Sam kept **bleating** that he had lost his pen.*

fuss
*The customer was **fussing** over a minute mark on the desk.*

grouse
*"It's no good **grousing** now. You had your chance and didn't take it," she said.*

grumble
*The next day it was raining and I **grumbled** about the weather.*

moan
*All my big sister ever does is **moan**!*

whinge
*The millionaire rock star was always **whingeing** about how unfair life is.*

complete (1) ADJECTIVE

If something is **complete**, none of it is missing.

entire
*At the end, the **entire** cast took a bow.*

full
*"Pay me the **full** amount now," the landlord insisted.*

whole
*"I swear to tell the **whole** truth," the witness declared to the court.*

complete (2) ADJECTIVE

Complete can mean to the greatest degree possible.

absolute
*"You're talking **absolute** rubbish," the major replied.*

sheer
*The winning jockey leapt off his horse in **sheer** joy.*

thorough
*The disobedient little girl made a **thorough** nuisance of herself.*

utter
*Chander felt an **utter** fool dressed as a clown.*

complete (3) VERB

If you **complete** something, you finish it.

conclude
*Professor Jones **concluded** his talk and then asked if there were any questions.*

end
*The crowd was in tears as he **ended** his speech.*

finalise
*The airline staff **finalised** arrangements for the plane to take off.*

finish
*When Gran had **finished** her tea she turned on the radio.*

round off
*We **rounded off** our day out with a delicious meal in a steakhouse.*

wrap up *(informal)*
*"OK, darlings, we'll **wrap** it **up** for today," the film director announced.*

ANTONYM: begin

completely ADVERB

Completely can mean totally, absolutely and utterly.

absolutely
By the end of the sponsored swim, Kalil was ***absolutely*** *exhausted.*

entirely
"I ***entirely*** *agree with you," put in Kaylee.*

fully
The new manager said he was ***fully*** *committed to the club and the team.*

totally
Fire ***totally*** *destroyed the pier buildings.*

utterly
You could see by the expression on her face that Isha was ***utterly*** *fed up.*

complicated ADJECTIVE

Something that is **complicated** has so many parts or aspects that it is difficult to understand or deal with.

complex
It was a ***complex*** *engine, which my brother struggled to understand.*

elaborate
They had an ***elaborate*** *plan to build their dream home.*

intricate
Clock mechanisms are too ***intricate*** *for you or me to tamper with.*

ANTONYMS: simple, straightforward

concentrate VERB

If you **concentrate** on something, you give it all your attention.

apply yourself to
Previously lazy, Watkins now ***applied himself to*** *his work and did well in the exam.*

be engrossed in
My sister ***was*** *so* ***engrossed in*** *a TV programme, she failed to see me sneaking up.*

focus on
"Today, we are going to ***focus on*** *fractions," Mrs Abrahams said, to a chorus of groans.*

pay attention to
*"****Pay attention to*** *what I'm saying, Jamie," said Dani. "It's important."*

condition NOUN

The **condition** of someone or something is the state they are in.

fitness
Army doctors examine the ***fitness*** *of soldiers each year.*

order
The television was in good working ***order*** *when we sold it.*

shape
Mr Singh is in pretty good ***shape*** *for a man of 75 – he still goes for a run every morning.*

state
"Just look at the ***state*** *of your trousers!" my stepmum sighed.*

confess VERB

If you **confess** to something, you admit that you did it.

admit
After questioning, the suspect ***admitted*** *she had stolen the bag.*

come clean (*informal*)
"Now ***come clean****, David," Auntie Julie said. "I know you've been at the chocolates."*

own up
The head teacher demanded that the person responsible for the damage should ***own up****.*

confused ADJECTIVE

If you are **confused**, you are uncertain about what is happening or what to do.

baffled
Lyra was ***baffled****. What on earth was the significance of the dust?*

bewildered
Bewildered *by his sudden fame, Robbie went completely off the rails.*

muddled
The useless new parking scheme was a prime example of ***muddled*** *thinking.*

perplexed
Frank stood at the crossroads, totally ***perplexed*** *by the map he'd been given.*

puzzled
"Then I'm ***puzzled****," Mum said. "How did the biscuit tin fly to your room?"*

confusing ADJECTIVE

If something is **confusing**, it makes you uncertain about what is happening or what to do.

baffling
No body. No weapon. No witnesses. The whole thing was ***baffling****.*

bewildering
There was a ***bewildering*** *choice of stereos.*

perplexing
*The mystery got more **perplexing**. Where on earth had the shoe gone?*

puzzling
*Sergeant Assad found it **puzzling** that everyone had volunteered for the job.*

connect (1) VERB

If you **connect** two things, you join them together.

attach
*When Mum receives nice postcards, she **attaches** them to the fridge with magnets.*

couple
*The man in the overalls dropped from the platform to **couple** the engine to the coaches.*

fasten
*Phil **fastened** the papers together with a clip.*

join
*The plumber **joined** the two pipes underneath the sink.*

link
*"This deal," said the chairman, "will **link** two fine companies."*

unite
*On their wedding day, the couple were **united** in marriage.*

connect (2) VERB

If one thing or person is **connected** with another, there is a link between them.

associate
*He claims that he no longer **associates** with any of those people.*

relate
*In good non-fiction writing, each sentence should **relate** to the one before.*

connection NOUN

A **connection** is a link or relationship between two things.

association
*Dad has always had a close **association** with the school. He attended as a pupil when he was a boy and is now a governor.*

bond
*There was a **bond** between the two brothers that could not be broken.*

link
*There are strong historical **links** between Britain and India.*

relationship
*Luis' **relationship** with his stepfather was not always an easy one.*

contact VERB

If you **contact** someone, you telephone them or write to them.

communicate with
*Television reporters often **communicate with** the studio by satellite phone.*

get in touch with
*Message for Mr Sample: please urgently **get in touch with** your son.*

make contact
*Joe wants me to **make contact** when I arrive in New York.*

contain VERB

The things that something **contains** are the things in it.

accommodate
*The narrowboat could **accommodate** up to nine people.*

comprise
*Our cottage **comprises** six rooms: three upstairs and three down.*

consist of
*Pancake mix mainly **consists of** flour, eggs and milk.*

hold
*An average household bucket will **hold** ten litres of liquid.*

include
*The holiday package **includes** all flights, accommodation and meals.*

container NOUN

A **container** is something that you keep things in, such as a box or a jar.

receptacle
*"What we need," said Mr Vanstone, "is some sort of **receptacle** for these tadpoles."*

vessel
*A pitcher is a **vessel** for carrying liquids.*

contest NOUN

A **contest** is a competition or game.

battle
*The Cup Final was a **battle** between the two top clubs.*

bout
*The wrestling announcer began, "This is a **bout** of eight rounds of three minutes each."*

competition
*Sheila is a fanatic for entering **competitions**.*

head-to-head (*informal*)
*The finish of the sack race was a close-run **head-to-head** between Mrs Robinson and Miss Penn.*

match
*The **match** against Holcombe was played in pouring rain.*

tournament
*The chess **tournament** featured players from all over the country.*

continue VERB

If you **continue** to do something, you keep doing it.

carry on
*"If you **carry on** prodding me, I'll prod you back," I said to Barry.*

keep on
*"If you **keep on** forgetting your homework, you'll get detention," I told Anita.*

persevere
*Although she was tired, Jamilah **persevered** with her drawing.*

persist
*Although I hate it, Dad **persists** in calling me by my nickname.*

continuous ADJECTIVE

Something that is **continuous** goes on without stopping.

ceaseless
*The **ceaseless** noise of drilling was driving me mad.*

constant
*Bill and Ben were **constant** companions. You never saw them apart.*

incessant
*After a few minutes, Mrs Snell's **incessant** chatter became annoying.*

nonstop
*The disco played **nonstop** music throughout the evening.*

uninterrupted
*Good weather meant **uninterrupted** play at Wimbledon for the whole fortnight.*

→ *See* **endless**

control (1) VERB

To **control** something is to have power over it.

be in charge of
*Our teacher **is in charge of** our local Under-11s soccer team.*

command
*Captain Hardy **commanded** HMS Victory, the flagship of Admiral Lord Nelson.*

direct
*The fire chief **directed** operations from a mobile control centre.*

manage
*Mum's sister **manages** a supermarket down the road.*

control (2) NOUN

Control is the power over something.

authority
*The mayor had **authority** over the city's transport system.*

command
*Luckily, he was in complete **command** of the situation.*

direction
*The team is playing well under the **direction** of the new manager.*

power
*"The Wizard of Oz has the **power** to give you courage, Lion," said Dorothy.*

convenient (1) ADJECTIVE

If a time to do a particular thing is **convenient**, it is suitable for those concerned.

agreeable
*"Is three o'clock **agreeable** to you, Mrs Williams?" the receptionist enquired.*

appropriate
*Max felt it was an **appropriate** moment to ask the question.*

suitable
*"Eight o'clock would be a **suitable** time for me to pick you up," my stepdad said.*

ANTONYM: inconvenient

convenient (2) ADJECTIVE

If something is **convenient**, it is easy to use, do or go to.

handy
*The store is really **handy** for Grandma to pop down to.*

helpful
*Mrs Hakim handed out a **helpful** fact sheet at the end of the lesson.*

A B C D E F G H I J K L M N O P Q R S T U V W X Y Z

useful
*Tin-openers are a **useful** invention which we couldn't do without!*

ANTONYM: inconvenient

conversation NOUN

When people have a **conversation**, they talk to each other.

chat
*Auntie Doris often pops in for a **chat** on her way home from work.*

dialogue
*The opening scene of Macbeth consists of a **dialogue** between three witches.*

discussion
*Our **discussion** centred on whether to play indoors or outdoors.*

cook VERB

When you **cook** food, you prepare it for eating by boiling, baking or frying it.

Some ways to cook:

bake	barbecue	blanch
boil	braise	fry
grill	microwave	poach
roast	simmer	steam
stew	stir-fry	toast

cool (1) ADJECTIVE

Something **cool** has a low temperature but is not cold.

chilly
*It was **chilly** outside, so we stayed by the fire.*

fresh
*A **fresh** breeze blew off the estuary, flapping the flag on the church tower.*

nippy
*"It's rather **nippy**," Nan said. "I'd take a pullover if I were you."*

refreshing
*In summer there's nothing to beat **refreshing** orange juice.*

ANTONYM: warm

→ *See* **cold**

cool (2) ADJECTIVE

If you are **cool** in a difficult situation, you stay calm.

calm
*"Now everybody keep **calm**," the captain said. "There is no need for panic."*

laid back (*informal*)
*My friend Chris was totally **laid back** about the exam. "If I fail, I fail," he said.*

relaxed
*Despite the tension in those around him, the sub's commander looked **relaxed**.*

ANTONYM: nervous

cope VERB

If you **cope** with a task or problem, you deal with it successfully.

carry on
*Despite the rain, the team **carried on** and eventually won the game.*

get by
*Although money was tight, Mona **got by** doing all sorts of odd jobs for people.*

manage
*"That piano's heavy. Can you **manage**?" a kind passer-by enquired.*

survive
*During the exams, Liam **survived** by drinking cups of coffee and going to bed early.*

cope with VERB

If you have to **cope with** a difficult situation, you have to deal with it.

contend with
*Apart from blizzards, Captain Scott had to **contend with** a growing shortage of food.*

deal with
*I don't know how teachers **deal with** 30 kids like my little brother.*

copy (1) NOUN

A **copy** is something made to look like something else.

duplicate
*As the new car came with only one key, Dad had a **duplicate** made.*

forgery
*The banknotes were such good **forgeries** that only an expert could tell they weren't real.*

imitation
*"If that diamond is an **imitation**, it's very like the real thing," I thought.*

replica
*The miniature locomotive was an exact **replica** of the real train.*

reproduction
*As the real painting is worth millions, our family was quite happy with a **reproduction**.*

ANTONYM: original

copy (2) VERB

If you **copy** what someone does, you do the same thing.

follow
*If you set a good example, others may **follow**.*

imitate
*Jordan sits behind me, **imitating** Mr Heaney's funny voice.*

impersonate
*To gain access to the jewels, the thief **impersonated** the head porter.*

copy (3) VERB

If you **copy** something, you make a copy of it.

counterfeit
*The criminals tried to **counterfeit** passports with false names.*

duplicate
*Before you mail the completed form, **duplicate** it so we have a copy for the files.*

forge
*The couple **forged** tickets and then tried to sell them outside the stadium.*

replicate
*The artist **replicated** paintings and passed them off as originals.*

correct ADJECTIVE

Something that is **correct** is true and has no mistakes.

accurate
*Make sure that your measurements are **accurate**, or the pieces will not fit together.*

exact
*It's no good guessing the amount of flour you need, it must be **exact**.*

precise
*"It's very important that the details you give are **precise**," said the police officer.*

right
*In the test, all his answers were **right**.*

true
*"Your report may be exciting," said her teacher, "but is it **true**?"*

cost NOUN

The **cost** is the amount of money needed to buy, do or make something.

charge
*"You know, sir, there'll be a **charge** for any phone calls," the hotel clerk said smoothly.*

expense
*My father didn't want the **expense** of a new roof, but the leaks changed his mind.*

price
*The money I made from errands was just about the **price** of the model I wanted.*

LANGUAGE TIP
The cost of travelling on transport is the **fare**.

cosy ADJECTIVE

Somewhere **cosy** is warm and comfortable.

comfortable
*Gramps finds his new reclining armchair very **comfortable**.*

comfy (informal)
*I was very **comfy** in my little room right up in the loft.*

snug
*The blanket kept the baby **snug** in her pram.*

ANTONYM: uncomfortable

count (1) VERB

If you **count**, or count up, all the things in a group, you add them up to see how many there are.

add up
*Irina **added up** the number of times Mr Reid clapped his hands.*

calculate
*The salesman **calculated** the money he would make that week.*

reckon up
*If you **reckon up** the rainy days we've had recently, you'll get a surprise.*

tot up (informal)
*My friend Ainsley and I **totted up** the number of cakes our dads had eaten.*

count (2) VERB

If something **counts** in a situation, it is important or valuable.

carry weight
*The politician assured people that their opinions did **carry weight**.*

make a difference
*The crook's previous crimes certainly **made a difference** to the length of his jail sentence.*

matter
*The goals you scored before don't **matter**. It's the ones you get now that are important.*

count (3) VERB

If you can **count** on someone or something, you can rely on them.

bank
*We were **banking** on good weather for the school fête.*

depend
*"I'm **depending** on you, Smithers. Don't let me down," the lieutenant said.*

rely
*"Can I **rely** on you to check that all doors are locked?" my mother asked.*

country (1) NOUN

A **country** is one of the political areas the world is divided into.

kingdom
*Beyond the barren plains of Kremmen lay the **kingdom** of the Wargs.*

land
*"We're very proud of our **land**," said the Welshman.*

nation
*Napoleon once said that England was a **nation** of shopkeepers.*

state
*After the war a new **state** was created which united the people.*

country (2) NOUN

The **country** is land away from towns and cities.

bush
*The Pritchards' farm is right out in the **bush**.*

countryside
*The **countryside** was a patchwork of fields.*

outback
*A lot of the **outback** in Australia is really very wild.*

wilds
*The gamekeeper lived out in the **wilds** in a small cottage.*

LANGUAGE TIP

The word **bush** is used in Australia, New Zealand and Africa. The **outback** is found in Australia and New Zealand.

---

courage NOUN

Courage is the quality shown by people who do things that they know are dangerous or difficult.

bravery
*His **bravery** in saving the child brought him letters from all over the world.*

daring
*The **daring** of King Arthur's knights is recorded in legend.*

guts (*informal*)
*The timid girl showed real **guts** when she went down the rope slide.*

heroism
*For her **heroism** in an enemy country, the undercover agent received a secret award.*

ANTONYM: cowardice

course NOUN

A **course** is the route something such as an aircraft, river or ship takes.

path
*The plane's flight **path** brought it close to the enemy coast.*

route
*Our quickest **route** to the Far East is, surprisingly, over the North Pole.*

trajectory
*The stone's **trajectory** was a graceful arc from my catapult to our greenhouse.*

way
*"Which **way** do you go home?" I asked Sunil.*

of course PHRASE

If you say **of course**, you are showing that you are absolutely sure about something.

certainly
*School meals are **certainly** tastier than they used to be.*

definitely
*"I'm **definitely** coming to camp," Vadim confirmed.*

undoubtedly
*I bragged that my team was **undoubtedly** the best in the world.*

cover VERB

If you **cover** something, you put something else over it to protect or hide it.

cloak
*Mist **cloaked** the mountain top, making it too dangerous to climb.*

conceal
*The boy **concealed** his work with his hand.*

hide
*During winter a blanket of snow **hid** the lawn and flowerbeds.*

mask
*Edmund **masked** his feeling of dismay with a smile.*

crack NOUN

A **crack** is a narrow gap.

crevice
*Climbers use **crevices** in the rock to hold the pieces of equipment that support them.*

nook
*The birds lay their eggs in **nooks** in the sheer cliffs above the sea.*

crafty ADJECTIVE

Someone who is **crafty** gets what they want by tricking people in a clever way.

cunning
*Bond's **cunning** trick was to hide above the door.*

sly
*The **sly** fox hid behind the henhouse.*

wily
*The **wily** coyote was no match for the even cleverer roadrunner.*

crash (1) NOUN

A **crash** is an accident in which a moving vehicle hits something and is damaged.

accident
*Queues built up, as the **accident** had blocked both sides of the road.*

collision
*The **collision** took place at a busy road intersection.*

pile-up
***Pile-ups** often occur during fog, when vehicles collide with one another.*

smash
*It was a bad **smash**, with two people injured.*

crash (2) VERB

If a vehicle **crashes**, it hits something and is badly damaged.

bump
*The motorbike **bumped** into the back of the car.*

collide
*The sports car **collided** with a quarry truck on a narrow bend.*

plough into
*The runaway lorry **ploughed into** the wall.*

crazy (1) ADJECTIVE (*informal*)

Someone or something **crazy** is very strange or foolish.

absurd
*How **absurd** that you should think that baked beans grow on trees!*

bizarre
*To see my brother on a bike dressed as a teddy bear was a **bizarre** experience.*

insane
*I reckon that bungee jumping is an **insane** thing to do.*

outrageous
*Uncle Will is aways doing **outrageous** things.*

ridiculous
*Papa thought the idea was **ridiculous**.*

strange
*The cowboy had a **strange** look in his eye.*

creep VERB

If you **creep** somewhere, you move there quietly and slowly.

edge
*I **edged** towards the door, hoping that no one would notice me leave.*

slink
*"Don't try to **slink** off. I haven't finished yet!" snapped the irritable countess.*

sneak
*The cat **sneaked** up the fire escape and crept in through the back door.*

tiptoe
*I heard my big brother **tiptoe** past my room.*

creepy ADJECTIVE

Someone or something **creepy** is strange and frightening.

eerie
***Eerie** noises floated down from the moor.*

mysterious
*The **mysterious** stranger disappeared into the mist with a flourish of his cloak.*

sinister
*With his eyepatch and wooden leg, Long John looked a truly **sinister** character.*

spooky (*informal*)
*The film was so **spooky** Hailey had to cover her eyes.*

criminal NOUN

A **criminal** is someone who has committed a crime.

crook *(informal)*
*Two **crooks** called at our door pretending to be from the water company.*

offender
*As a young **offender**, the 15-year-old was not sent to prison.*

villain
*"Have nothing to do with him. He's a total **villain**," PC Phillips warned.*

Types of criminal:

assassin	bandit	blackmailer
burglar	cybercriminal	gangster
hacker	highwayman	hijacker
kidnapper	mugger	murderer
pickpocket	pirate	robber
shoplifter	smuggler	terrorist
thief	vandal	

crisp ADJECTIVE

Food that is **crisp** is pleasantly fresh and firm.

crispy
*To really be enjoyed, lettuce needs to be fresh and **crispy**.*

crunchy
*The apples were **crunchy** and juicy.*

ANTONYM: soft

criticise VERB

If you **criticise** someone or something, you say what you think is wrong with them.

disapprove of
*My parents **disapprove of** expensive fast food which is full of chemicals.*

find fault with
*The duchess managed to **find fault with** everyone in the room.*

crooked (1) ADJECTIVE

Something that is **crooked** is bent or twisted.

deformed
*Grandma's hands are **deformed** with arthritis.*

distorted
*The **distorted** shape of the trees was caused by the onshore wind.*

twisted
*The wreckage of the car was **twisted** beyond all recognition.*

ANTONYM: straight

crooked (2) ADJECTIVE

A **crooked** person is dishonest.

corrupt
*The **corrupt** police officer accepted bribes.*

criminal
*"You have committed a **criminal** offence," intoned the judge.*

dishonest
*Something made me suspect that the salesman was **dishonest**.*

shady *(informal)*
*"He looks a **shady** customer," said Carlos, nodding towards a surly man across the street.*

ANTONYMS: law-abiding, honest

cross ADJECTIVE

Someone who is **cross** is rather angry.

angry
*My friend Anna was rather **angry** when I lost her favourite CD.*

annoyed
*Dad was **annoyed** that I hadn't washed up as I'd promised.*

cantankerous
*The **cantankerous** old farmer used to shout at anyone who walked past his farm.*

crotchety
*Gran sometimes gets **crotchety** when her arthritis is painful.*

grumpy
*My brother is always **grumpy** when it comes to having a bath.*

irritable
*Mum was rather **irritable** because she had a bad headache.*

snappy
*"There's no need to get **snappy**," Lynn retorted. "Here's your wretched comb."*

crowd (1) NOUN

A **crowd** is a large group of people gathered together.

mass
*The whole square was a seething **mass** of red, white and blue flags.*

mob
*Enraged, the **mob** surged through the streets like a human tide.*

multitude
*The prophet spoke to the **multitude**, foretelling the great events to come.*

swarm
*A **swarm** of demonstrators headed for the parliament building.*

crowd (2) NOUN

A **crowd** is a large number of people watching an event.

audience
*The concert **audience** clapped when the conductor took the stage.*

spectators
***Spectators** cheered on competitors as they sprinted to the finish line.*

cruel ADJECTIVE

Cruel people deliberately cause pain or distress to other people or to animals.

callous
*The **callous** emperor made his slaves work their fingers to the bone.*

hard-hearted
*Even **hard-hearted** Barry couldn't bring himself to kill a spider.*

heartless
*The **heartless** landlord threw the poor widow into the street.*

merciless
*He was **merciless** if they broke his strict rules.*

ruthless
*Anyone who disagreed with the **ruthless** dictator disappeared.*

vicious
*The **vicious** crocodile clamped its jaws on the unfortunate bird.*

crumble VERB

When something **crumbles**, or you **crumble** it, it breaks into small pieces.

collapse
*Weak foundations caused the apartment block to **collapse**.*

decay
*The beam had **decayed**, bringing the floor above it crashing down.*

decompose
*The vegetable peelings were **decomposing** on the compost heap.*

disintegrate
*The old newspaper just **disintegrated** in his hands.*

crush VERB

To **crush** something is to destroy its shape by squeezing it.

flatten
*They **flattened** the soft drink cans before recycling them.*

screw up
*She **screwed up** the letter into a ball and threw it into the fire.*

squash
*I dropped the shopping bag and **squashed** the tomatoes.*

cry

→ Look at the **Word Power** page!

cure NOUN

A **cure** is something that heals or helps someone to get better.

antidote
*There is no known **antidote** to the bite of that particular snake.*

medicine
*Dad took some **medicine** for his stomach ache.*

remedy
*The **remedy** for boredom is simple. You need to get out more!*

treatment
*Fortunately, the **treatment** helped and my ankle soon felt better.*

curious ADJECTIVE

Someone who is **curious** wants to know more about something.

inquiring
*"Dad, it said on my report that I've an **inquiring** mind. What does that mean?"*

inquisitive
***Inquisitive** about anything mechanical, Fiona dismantled the cuckoo clock.*

interested
*If it's anything about trains, then my brother is **interested**.*

nosy
*Our **nosy** neighbour was anxious to hear any gossip she could.*

A
B
C
D
E
F
G
H
I
J
K
L
M
N
O
P
Q
R
S
T
U
V
W
X
Y
Z

cry

(1) VERB When you **cry**, tears come from your eyes because you are unhappy or hurt.

bawl
*The moment the baby saw me, it stopped **bawling**.*

blubber
*After losing his dummy, the toddler **blubbered** for the next half hour.*

shed tears
*Dad's advice is not to **shed tears** over something that is in the past.*

snivel
*"Stop **snivelling** and you might get a lolly," the girl's mother snapped.*

sob
*Milly **sobbed** her heart out when her best friend moved away.*

weep
*After her sisters went out, Cinderella **wept** silently.*

whimper
*The baby started to **whimper** in his cot, hungry for his next feed.*

(2) VERB If you **cry** something, you shout it or say it loudly.

bawl
*Everyone came running when the camp cook **bawled** "Dinner's ready!"*

bellow
*"Time for school," Dad **bellowed** up the stairs.*

boom
*"Attention!" **boomed** the sergeant major to the new recruits.*

call
*When I saw my friend on the other side of the street I **called** out her name.*

shout
*Ben **shouted** for help when he saw the child fall into the pond.*

yell
*"Watch out!" **yelled** Yanni as the tennis ball flew in Aidan's direction.*

cry

(3) NOUN A **cry** is a shout or other sound made with your voice.

bellow
We started to run as a loud ***bellow*** *came from the bull at the end of the field.*

howl
The wolf let out a ***howl*** *as he prowled through the moonlit night.*

shout
The crowd gave a ***shout*** *of joy as another goal hit the back of the net in the very last minute.*

shriek
My silly brother gave a ***shriek*** *when he saw the spider in the bath.*

yell
With a ***yell****, Oscar jumped out of the way of the speeding cricket ball.*

Try these lively words and phrases!

break down	*He was being so kind that I just* ***broke down*** *and cried.*
burst into tears	*He immediately* ***burst into tears*** *and ran from the kitchen.*
cry your eyes out	*I came in to find Lisa* ***crying her eyes out*** *over the news of his death.*
to cry...	
bitterly	*He says he cried* ***bitterly*** *when his father died last year.*
hysterically	*Many people sobbed while others cried* ***hysterically****.*
pitifully	*Terrified, he cried* ***pitifully*** *throughout the firework display.*

→ Also have a look at the **Word Power** page for **laugh**!

A B C D E F G H I J K L M N O P Q R S T U V W X Y Z

curl VERB

If something **curls**, it moves in a curve or spiral.

coil
*The boa constrictor **coiled** its body slowly round its prey.*

entwine
*Climbing clematis plants **entwined** themselves with the telephone wire.*

spiral
*Smoke **spiralled** up from the cottage chimney.*

twist
*The string from the kite **twisted** as it came tumbling down.*

wind
*The country road **wound** round in a series of bends.*

curly ADJECTIVE

Curly hair has many curls in it.

curled
*My sister's hair was all **curled** when she came out of the hairdresser's.*

frizzy
*Her **frizzy** hair was tied with a white and pink striped ribbon.*

kinky
*If your hair is naturally straight, you can make it **kinky** by having it permed.*

wavy
*I would love to have **wavy** hair, but mine's dead straight.*

cut (1) NOUN

A **cut** is a mark made with a knife or other sharp tool.

gash
*The nasty **gash** in Billy's knee needed to have several stitches.*

groove
*Uncle Ken chiselled a **groove** in the shelf for plates to stand up in.*

nick
*I was clumsy with the knife and made a **nick** in the desk.*

slit
*To make the pocket, Mandy cut a **slit** in the fabric.*

cut (2) VERB

If you **cut** something, you use a pair of scissors, a knife or another sharp tool to mark it or remove parts of it.

cut a little:

chip
*When she fell, Vanessa **chipped** her tooth.*

chisel
*I tried to **chisel** out a hole for the lock, but I split the wood.*

clip
*Ross **clipped** the hedge for his auntie.*

prune
*When you **prune** roses in winter, you cut them right back near the base.*

shave
*Kay **shaved** a little off the shelf to make it fit.*

snip
*For a practical joke, I **snipped** a bit off Dad's tie, but he didn't find it funny.*

trim
*Grandad has his hair **trimmed** each month – what's left of it, that is.*

cut hard at something:

chop
*The karate expert **chopped** the brick in half with a single blow.*

hack
***Hacking** her way through the jungle, the botanist searched for the rare plant.*

slash
*Bluebeard **slashed** downward with his cutlass, through the rope.*

cut something down:

chop
*Dad had to **chop** the old tree down after it was damaged in the storm.*

fell
*The stupid lumberjack proceeded to **fell** the wrong tree.*

mow
*It's useless to **mow** the lawn in wet weather.*

cut something in two:

bisect
*With one swing of the axe the man **bisected** the thick log.*

divide
*Using a sharp knife, Mum **divided** the last piece of pie for my brother and me.*

halve
*"If I **halve** this apple, will you share it with me?" I asked Helen.*

Dd

damage (1) VERB

If you **damage** something, you harm or spoil it.

deface
*The teacher was annoyed when she saw Craig had **defaced** his language book.*

harm
*Fortunately, no one was **harmed** in the crash.*

spoil
*My painting was **spoilt** when I spilt water on it.*

vandalise
*It's very sad when people **vandalise** buildings.*

→ *See* **destroy**

LANGUAGE TIP
Someone who damages something useful or beautiful on purpose and for no good reason is a **vandal**.

damage (2) NOUN

Damage is injury or harm done to something.

destruction
*"The **destruction** of rainforests should worry everyone on earth," Lisa said.*

harm
*The stolen painting was returned with no **harm** done to it.*

vandalism
*Owing to **vandalism**, the public lavatory had to be closed.*

damp ADJECTIVE

Something that is **damp** is slightly wet.

clammy
*Beneath her jungle gear, the explorer's skin felt **clammy**.*

drizzly
*All day the weather had been dull and **drizzly**.*

humid
*In tropical places, the weather is hot and **humid**.*

moist
*As its soil was still **moist**, Sophie didn't water the plant.*

muggy
*We all expected thunder as the air was **muggy**.*

dance VERB

When you **dance**, you move around in time to music.

caper
*The children **capered** about to the music.*

jig
*Guests bopped and **jigged** the night away to the music.*

danger NOUN

Danger is the possibility that someone may be harmed or killed.

hazard
*That raised paving stone is a **hazard**. Someone might trip over it.*

menace
*Pollution from farm fertilisers is a **menace** to fish in the rivers.*

peril
*Ivan put himself in **peril** by walking near the cliff edge.*

risk
*Despite the **risks**, the medic crawled out to help the wounded soldier.*

threat
*The prime minister tried to avert the **threat** of war by having meetings with other leaders.*

ANTONYM: safety

dangerous ADJECTIVE

If something is **dangerous**, it is likely to cause hurt or harm.

hazardous
*Road tankers have signs to show if their liquid cargo is **hazardous**.*

perilous
*Captain Scott set out on his **perilous** trek to the South Pole.*

risky
*Jenny knew that climbing the cliff was **risky**, but she had to escape the waves.*

a b c d e f g h i j k l m n o p q r s t u v w x y z

A B C D E F G H I J K L M N O P Q R S T U V W X Y Z

treacherous
*"Keep away from those mud flats. They're **treacherous**," warned the boatman.*

unsafe
*The derelict buildings were **unsafe**, and about to be demolished.*

ANTONYMS: safe, harmless

dare (1) VERB

If you **dare** to do something, you have the courage to do it.

brave
*Ray decided to **brave** a visit to the dentist's.*

have the courage
*The airman **had the courage** to go back to the burning plane.*

risk
*The athlete was not willing to **risk** getting an injury.*

venture
*Alek **ventured** to ask his boss for a pay rise.*

dare (2) VERB

If you **dare** someone to do something, you challenge them to do it.

challenge
*Yoshi **challenged** Tim to climb the wall.*

defy
*She **defied** me to come up with a better idea.*

daring ADJECTIVE

A **daring** person is bold and willing to take risks.

adventurous
*"Rihana is the **adventurous** type," her dad said. "She's always getting into scrapes."*

brave
*It was a **brave** and unexpected move by the submarine captain.*

fearless
*Even as a young midshipman, Nelson displayed a **fearless** character.*

dark (1) ADJECTIVE

If it is **dark**, there is not enough light to see properly.

dim
*In the **dim** light of the cave, Crusoe could make out a heap of bones.*

dingy
*With the shutters closed, the villa was **dingy** after the bright sunlight outside.*

gloomy
*On every **gloomy** landing, paintings of the earl's ancestors stared out from the walls.*

murky
*The divers could not see anything in the **murky** depths of the lake.*

shadowy
*A sinister figure appeared from a **shadowy** side street.*

ANTONYM: light

dark (2) NOUN

The **dark** is the lack of light in a place.

dusk
*Street lights began to twinkle in the **dusk**.*

gloom
*In the **gloom** of the attic, Nathan made out two staring eyes.*

murk
*Zora wished she was on the beach, not in the **murk** of a Manchester night.*

ANTONYM: light

dawn NOUN

Dawn is the time in the morning when light first appears in the sky.

break of day
*A chorus of hungry birds started up at the **break of day**.*

daybreak
*Even now he's retired, he still rises at **daybreak** every morning.*

sunrise
*By **sunrise**, the diver and his team were already at the pier.*

ANTONYM: dusk

dazed ADJECTIVE

If you are **dazed**, you are confused and bewildered.

bewildered
*Mum was **bewildered** by the huge range of mobile phones on offer.*

confused
*Old people sometimes get **confused** and say odd things.*

light-headed
*The paint smell was so strong that I began to feel **light-headed**.*

shocked
*After the explosion, **shocked**, dusty people wandered hopelessly around.*

stunned
*I felt **stunned** when I heard about James's accident.*

dead ADJECTIVE

A person, animal or plant that is **dead** is no longer alive.

deceased
*It was thought that the **deceased** man came originally from Ireland.*

extinct
*The **extinct** moa of New Zealand was a flightless bird like an ostrich.*

late
*Many people paid tribute to Mrs Suleiman's **late** husband.*

ANTONYM: alive

LANGUAGE TIP
A dead body is called a **corpse** or the **remains**. A person who has recently died is often referred to as the **deceased**.

deadly ADJECTIVE

Something **deadly** is likely or able to cause death.

lethal
*The chemicals were **lethal** to fish and other aquatic mammals.*

mortal
*Frodo suddenly came face to face with his **mortal** enemy.*

deal NOUN

A **deal** is an agreement or arrangement, especially in business.

agreement
*The countries formed an **agreement** about imports and exports.*

arrangement
*Dad made an **arrangement** to pick the car up on Tuesday.*

contract
*The player's **contract** with his club will expire in a year's time.*

deal with VERB

If you **deal with** something, you do what is necessary to sort it out.

attend to
*The receptionist has promised to **attend to** me in a moment.*

handle
*Mum **handled** all the holiday arrangements.*

see to
*"Please would you **see to** that customer," the manager asked the sales assistant.*

sort out
*Thank heavens Mrs Ito was there to **sort out** the problem.*

take care of
*"I'll **take care of** the flowers if you buy the chocolates," my sister suggested.*

➔ *See* **cope with**

dear (1) ADJECTIVE

Something or someone **dear** is much loved.

beloved
*The card read, "To my **beloved** wife".*

cherished
*Grandad has **cherished** memories of his time in Italy.*

treasured
*The old rocking chair was a **treasured** possession.*

dear (2) ADJECTIVE

Something that is **dear** is very expensive.

costly
*The furniture was **costly** but superbly made.*

pricey (*informal*)
*"That computer game's a bit **pricey**," my friend Sean muttered.*

ANTONYM: cheap

decay VERB

When things **decay**, they rot or go bad.

biodegrade
*Most plastic does not **biodegrade**, which is a problem for the environment.*

decompose
*I had a sinking feeling that my sandwiches were **decomposing** in my locker.*

perish
*The hot-water bottle leaked, as its rubber stopper had **perished**.*

rot
*Most softwood will **rot** if it is not painted.*

A B C D E F G H I J K L M N O P Q R S T U V W X Y Z

decide VERB

If you **decide** to do something, you choose to do it, usually after thinking about it carefully.

commit yourself
*In signing up for the course, my brother **committed himself** to do a year's study.*

make a decision
*The teacher **made a decision** to give out homework.*

make up your mind
*"Ted, will you **make up your mind**?" Dad demanded impatiently.*

reach a decision
*My parents **reached a decision**: we were going to move house.*

decision NOUN

A **decision** is a choice or judgment that is made about something.

choice
*Daniel faced a **choice** – to continue and risk getting lost, or to go back the way he had come.*

conclusion
*I came to the **conclusion** that I hadn't been working hard enough.*

judgment
*The panel's **judgment** was that Mrs Flaherty had been fairly treated.*

verdict
*The courtroom fell silent as the jury's **verdict** was announced.*

decorate VERB

If you **decorate** something, you make it more attractive by adding things to it.

adorn
*For the wedding, the gate to the churchyard was **adorned** with flowers.*

festoon
*The whole of Wall Street was **festooned** with tickertape streamers.*

trim
*The Christmas tree was **trimmed** with tinsel.*

decrease VERB

If something **decreases**, or if you **decrease** it, it becomes less.

decline
*Bird-lovers are worried that the number of house sparrows is **declining**.*

diminish
*The glow from the fire **diminished** as the night wore on.*

dwindle
*Once the mines closed, the valley population began to **dwindle**.*

lessen
*Getting immunised will **lessen** the risk of serious illness.*

reduce
***Reducing** your salt intake will help you to stay healthy.*

ANTONYM: increase

deep (1) ADJECTIVE

If something is **deep**, it goes a long way down from the surface.

bottomless
*"The way you spend, you must think I've got **bottomless** pockets!" Dad grumbled.*

yawning
*The earth shook violently, and a **yawning** hole opened up in the street.*

ANTONYM: shallow

deep (2) ADJECTIVE

Deep can mean great or intense.

intense
*Van Gogh painted vibrant pictures with **intense** colour.*

profound
*The discovery of penicillin had a **profound** effect on medicine.*

strong
*A **strong** wind blew the sailing boat off course.*

deep (3) ADJECTIVE

A **deep** sound is a low one.

bass
*The **bass** sound of the foghorn echoed through the mist.*

low
*Mrs Quail's voice is so **low** that she is sometimes difficult to understand on the telephone.*

ANTONYM: high

defeat (1) VERB

If you **defeat** someone or something, you win a victory over them, or cause them to fail.

beat
*"I hope my team **beats** yours," Pete said cheekily to Smithy.*

conquer
*To **conquer** Wales was King Edward's lifelong wish.*

overcome
*The girl **overcame** her disability to become a great champion.*

overpower
*Legions of screeching auks **overpowered** the tiny band of travellers.*

rout
*The forces of evil in Narnia were **routed** in the last battle.*

defeat (2) NOUN

A **defeat** is the state of being beaten or of failing.

beating
*Class 3a were delighted that the team from 3b had taken a **beating**.*

conquest
*The **conquest** of England by the Normans in 1066 was a turning point in history.*

downfall
*The dictator's **downfall** was sudden and spectacular.*

trouncing (*informal*)
*"What a **trouncing**," Mitch moaned.*

ANTONYM: victory

defence NOUN

Defence is the action that is taken to protect someone or something against attack.

immunity
*The nurse assured me that the vaccination would give **immunity** against measles.*

protection
*"Our paint offers ten-year **protection** against frost" the advert boasted.*

resistance
*"**Resistance** is useless. Come out with your hands up!" he shouted.*

safeguard
*Taking out insurance acts as a **safeguard** against misfortune.*

LANGUAGE TIP
A country's **defences** are its armed forces and its weapons.

defend (1) VERB

If you **defend** someone or something, you protect them from harm or danger.

fortify
*The manor house was **fortified** by the addition of a large wall around it.*

guard
*Brushing your teeth helps **guard** against decay and keeps your breath fresh.*

protect
*King Edward **protected** the castle with no fewer than six main gates!*

safeguard
*The sentries **safeguarded** the palace.*

→ *See* **shelter (1)**

defend (2) VERB

If you **defend** a person or their ideas, you argue in support of them.

justify
*The woman **justified** her actions by pleading that it was in self-defence.*

speak up for
*Amal **spoke up for** his friend, despite the bully's threats.*

stick up for (*informal*)
*"Thank you for **sticking up for** me," said Lisa gratefully.*

support
*Dad **supported** me when our neighbour complained about the noise.*

definite ADJECTIVE

Something that is **definite** is clear and unlikely to be changed.

certain
*"It is **certain** that I will be having a birthday party," Molly told us.*

guaranteed
*My uncle secured us **guaranteed** seats for the big game.*

positive
*The contestant gave a very **positive** answer. Sadly, it was the wrong one.*

sure
*Being sulky is a **sure** way to lose friends.*

ANTONYM: uncertain

definitely ADVERB

Definitely can mean certainly and without doubt.

absolutely
*Deepak is **absolutely** right.*

beyond any doubt
***Beyond any doubt**, the German was the best racing driver in the world.*

certainly
*The coach admitted, "We've **certainly** got a good team this year."*

plainly
*The witness was **plainly** going to say nothing.*

unquestionably
*The banquet was **unquestionably** the largest meal he had ever eaten.*

delay (1) NOUN

If there is a **delay**, something does not happen until later than planned or expected.

hold-up
*At the last minute, there was a **hold-up** in the live TV broadcast.*

pause
*After a **pause**, the mayor continued his speech.*

postponement
*Owing to the storms, there was a 24-hour **postponement** in the rocket launch.*

setback
*There were a few minor **setbacks** before the house was built.*

wait
*We had a slight **wait** before being ushered in to meet the prince.*

delay (2) VERB

If something **delays** you, it makes you late or slows you down.

hinder
*My baby brother did his best to **hinder** Mum from getting to work on time.*

hold up
*Traffic was **held up** by a burst water main.*

slow down
*Our progress was **slowed down** by a crawling tractor in front.*

deliberate ADJECTIVE

If you do something that is **deliberate**, you do it on purpose.

calculated
*The head teacher took a **calculated** risk and told staff to put the stalls outdoors.*

conscious
*"I want you to make a **conscious** effort to get to school on time," Mrs Lenster said.*

intentional
*The referee decided that the dangerous tackle was **intentional**, and sent the player off.*

ANTONYM: unintentional

delicious ADJECTIVE

Delicious food or drink tastes very nice.

appetising
*The waiter brought round all sorts of **appetising** titbits.*

delectable
*"Thank you, that was a **delectable** meal, Mrs Kean," Marie said politely.*

scrumptious (*informal*)
*I think meringues are **scrumptious**. My sister hates them.*

tasty
*Some cheese is **tasty**. Some seems to taste like rubber.*

ANTONYM: horrible

demonstrate (1) VERB

If someone **demonstrates** something, they show you how to do it.

explain
*Jamie **explained** how to separate the yolks and whites of eggs.*

illustrate
*Our music teacher **illustrated** how to play the violin.*

demonstrate (2) VERB

If people **demonstrate**, they hold a public meeting or march to show they are strongly for or against something.

march
*Sometimes thousands of people **march** in the capital to make their feelings known to the government.*

protest
*The students were **protesting** at the cost of accommodation.*

depend (1) VERB

If you **depend** on someone or something, you trust them and rely on them.

bank on
*Mr Marshall said he was **banking on** me to score a few goals.*

count on
*I was **counting on** Dennis to give me some good passes.*

rely on
*Lyra knew she could **rely on** her big sister to come to her aid.*

trust
*The owners **trusted** you to put the correct money in the box.*

depend (2) VERB

If one thing **depends** on another, it is influenced by it.

be based on
*"Our firm's success **is based on** the hard work of the staff," the boss stated.*

hinge on
*The battle **hinged on** whether the cavalry could break through the enemy line.*

describe VERB

If you **describe** someone or something, you say what they are like.

define
*The supply teacher asked me to **define** what a hexagon is.*

explain
*Beatrice **explained** what she had done and her reasons for doing it.*

relate
*My pal Vadim was bursting to **relate** what had happened on the way to school.*

report
*On Monday, I was expected to **report** on our weekend camping trip.*

description NOUN

A **description** is an account or picture of something in words.

account
*The witness gave his **account** of the incident.*

profile
*Police assembled a **profile** of the burglar, making him easy to identify.*

report
*Class 6 gave a **report** on all the activities they had taken part in.*

deserted ADJECTIVE

If a place is **deserted**, there are no people there.

abandoned
*In the middle of the wood, the boys came upon an **abandoned** cottage.*

empty
*They saw a farmhouse and ran towards it to ask for water, but it was **empty**.*

deserve VERB

If you **deserve** something, you earn it or have a right to it.

be worthy of
*The girl's bravery **was worthy of** the highest possible honour.*

earn
*The president's forgiveness of his kidnappers **earned** him the respect of the world.*

justify
*The boy's terrific courage **justified** his award.*

merit
*Her excellent exam results **merited** a celebratory meal.*

despair NOUN

Despair is a total loss of hope.

desperation
*In **desperation**, the pilot ejected.*

gloom
*The team had been relegated and **gloom** filled the dressing room.*

hopelessness
*The **hopelessness** of the situation made the reporter weep.*

desperate ADJECTIVE

A **desperate** situation is extremely dangerous or serious.

critical
*The sick woman's condition was **critical**.*

drastic
*Sealing the city was a **drastic** action, but it stopped the spread of the plague.*

grave
*"We are in a **grave** predicament," said the king. "We must fight for our lives."*

hopeless
*The situation of the soldiers seemed **hopeless**.*

despite PREPOSITION

If you do something **despite** some difficulty, you manage to do it anyway.

in spite of
***In spite of** her age, Granny is very fit.*

regardless of
***Regardless of** the danger, the medic carried the injured man to safety.*

a b c d e f g h i j k l m n o p q r s t u v w x y z

destroy VERB

If you **destroy** something, you damage it so much that it is completely ruined.

annihilate
*Scientists think that changes in the climate may have **annihilated** the dinosaurs.*

demolish
*Workmen **demolished** the disused factory.*

devastate
*In 1945, two Japanese cities were utterly **devastated** by atom bombs.*

ruin
*"They've **ruined** that park by chopping those trees down," Grandad grumbled.*

wreck
*A lifetime playing loud music **wrecked** the guitarist's hearing.*

determination NOUN

Determination is a great strength and will to do something.

dedication
*The nurse's **dedication** earned her the thanks of all the soldiers.*

drive
*To get to the top, businesspeople need **drive** and imagination.*

perseverance
*The tortoise's **perseverance** helped him beat the foolish hare in the race.*

will
*Matthew's **will** to win saw him achieve a gold medal.*

determined ADJECTIVE

If you are **determined** to do something, you will not let anything stop you from doing it.

intent
*She was so **intent** on doing well, she made herself ill with worry.*

persistent
*The salesman was so **persistent** that Mum shut the door on him.*

single-minded
*Sometimes you have to be **single-minded** to do a job properly.*

die (1) VERB

When a person, animal or plant **dies**, they stop living.

expire
*Tragically, the old man **expired** from the effort of the hill climb.*

pass away
*In memory of John Silver, who **passed away** this day in 1792.*

perish
*Around 700 seamen **perished** when the Mary Rose went down.*

die (2) VERB

When something **dies**, **dies away** or **dies down**, it becomes less intense and disappears.

dwindle
*Support for the team **dwindled** when they were relegated.*

fade
*Slowly, the desperate hammering **faded** to a faint knocking.*

peter out
*Just before the finish line, the old car's engine **petered out**.*

difference NOUN

The **difference** between two things is the way in which they are unlike each other.

contrast
*Although they look similar, there is a big **contrast** in the characters of the twins.*

distinction
*Colour-blind people often cannot see a **distinction** between red and green.*

variation
*We noticed a terrific **variation** in price between one shop and another.*

ANTONYM: similarity

different (1) ADJECTIVE

If one thing is **different** from another, it is not like it.

contrasting
*In the story, honest Cinderella is a **contrasting** character to her scheming stepsisters.*

distinct
*The taste of blue cheese is quite **distinct** from ordinary cheese.*

opposed
*The couple's viewpoints were **opposed**.*

ANTONYMS: similar, identical

LANGUAGE TIP
One thing is **different from** another thing. Some people think that **different to** is wrong. **Different than** is used in American English.

different (2) ADJECTIVE

If several things are **different** from each other, they are not the same.

assorted
*My pockets contained **assorted** coins, sweet wrappers, paperclips and fluff.*

varied
*The plants were of **varied** colours, including some lovely reds and purples.*

ANTONYMS: similar, identical

LANGUAGE TIP
If something is different from everything else in the world, it is **unique**.

difficult (1) ADJECTIVE

Difficult things are not easy to do, understand or solve.

difficult to work out or deal with:

awkward
*The tap was in an **awkward** place for the plumber to get at.*

challenging
*"It's the most **challenging** operation I've ever tackled," the surgeon admitted.*

demanding
*Sarah had a **demanding** week at work.*

formidable
*Rescuing thousands from the earthquake rubble was a **formidable** task.*

knotty
*It was a **knotty** problem: to cross the deep river without a bridge!*

puzzling
*Zara is **puzzling**. One minute she's pleasant, the next she's horrid.*

tricky
*The climbers were in a **tricky** situation, stuck on the ledge as night drew in.*

physically difficult:

backbreaking
*He had to do many of the **backbreaking** jobs around the farm.*

laborious
*Archaeology is **laborious** work, digging slowly and sifting carefully.*

strenuous
*Marathon running is a **strenuous** business.*

difficult (2) ADJECTIVE

Someone who is **difficult** behaves in an unreasonable way.

awkward
*"That horse is **awkward**," said the cowboy, "but I'll ride him eventually."*

troublesome
*The **troublesome** twins made their teacher's life a hard one.*

trying
*Mrs Kray had a **trying** time with Class 6 and their spellings.*

uncooperative
***Uncooperative** people never work well in a team.*

difficulty NOUN

A **difficulty** is a problem.

complication
*The biggest **complication** for the engineer was that his tunnel kept flooding.*

dilemma
*Karen faced a **dilemma**. Should she play with her friends or help her mum?*

hitch
*After a **hitch** with the curtains, the play began five minutes late.*

obstacle
*The star encountered many **obstacles** on the road to fame.*

plight
*"Your **plight** is indeed a sorry one," said the knight to the damsel in the tower.*

snag
*Progress on the house was smooth, until they hit a **snag** when they found a hole in the roof.*

dig VERB

If you **dig**, you make a hole in earth or sand, especially with a spade or shovel.

burrow
*Rabbits create warrens by **burrowing** into hillsides.*

delve
*The men **delved** deeper, looking for a glimmer of gold.*

excavate
*Rescue workers **excavated** the rubble to free the trapped people.*

hollow out
*We **hollowed out** a dip in the sand in which to build our camp fire.*

scoop out
*The squirrel **scooped out** a hole in the early snow to reach the acorns beneath.*

dim ADJECTIVE

Something that is **dim** is lacking in brightness and badly lit.

faint
*As they neared Mordor, **faint** lights shone in the hills beyond.*

gloomy
*The **gloomy** passages of the castle were lit by flaming torches on the walls.*

shadowy
*I had trouble finding my way across the **shadowy** room to reach the light switch.*

vague
*Ben Nevis was just a **vague** outline seen through the morning mist.*

ANTONYM: bright

dinosaur NOUN

Dinosaurs are large animals that lived millions of years ago.

→ Have a look at the **Illustration** page!

dirt NOUN

Dirt is any unclean substance such as dust, mud or stains.

filth
*Below the sink, the shelf was caked with **filth**.*

grime
***Grime** from a thousand mill chimneys had blackened the local buildings.*

muck
*It took me hours to clean the **muck** from the wheels of my bike.*

dirty (1) ADJECTIVE

Something that is **dirty** is marked or covered with dirt.

filthy
*"Get rid of that **filthy** rag," my dad ordered.*

grimy
*The windows were so **grimy** we could barely see out of them.*

grubby
*Mum suggested my little brother wash his **grubby** hands.*

mucky
*The children enjoy **mucky** jobs like gardening.*

mud-caked
*She wiped her brow with **mud-caked** hands.*

soiled
*The sign said, "Please place **soiled** nappies in the bin provided".*

stained
*The penny was badly **stained**, but came up shining after it was polished.*

ANTONYM: clean

dirty (2) ADJECTIVE

Water that is **dirty** is made unclean by poisonous substances.

contaminated
*The **contaminated** stream was an ominous red colour.*

polluted
***Polluted** lakes and waterways cannot support any wildlife.*

dirty (3) ADJECTIVE

Dirty language is unpleasant and offensive.

crude
*"That joke is very **crude** and not funny at all," the girl snapped.*

foul
*The player was sent off for using **foul** language.*

rude
***Rude** words offend many people.*

vulgar
*"There's no need to be **vulgar**," Mum told my big sister.*

disadvantage NOUN

A **disadvantage** is something that makes things difficult.

drawback
*The **drawback** of being late for the party was that I missed out on all the birthday cake.*

handicap
*Roddy's broken leg was a **handicap** to him for a couple of months.*

DINOSAURS

pterodactyl

diplodocus

triceratops

tyrannosaurus

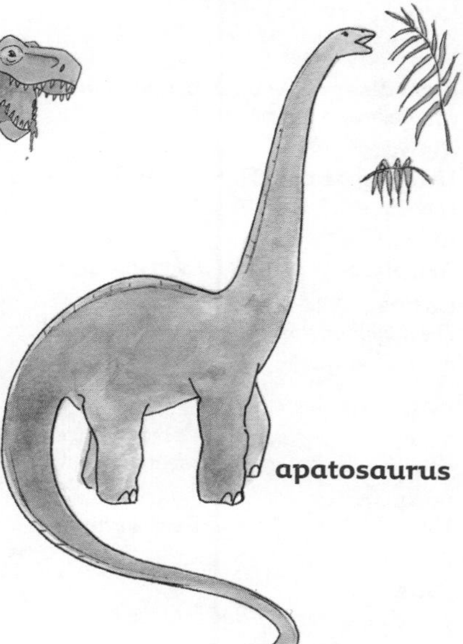

apatosaurus

iguanodon

stegosaurus

velociraptor

Some other types of dinosaur:

allosaurus
archaeopteryx
brachiosaurus
gallimimus
oviraptor
protoceratops
pterosaur
spinosaurus

inconvenience
*Mum doesn't find walking to work an **inconvenience**. It helps keep her healthy.*

snag
*The only **snag** with the hotel was that it was a long way from the beach.*

ANTONYM: advantage

disagree (1) VERB

If you **disagree** with someone, you have a different opinion or view from them.

argue with
*"If you **argue with** me," she said stiffly, "you will go to the head-teacher!"*

differ
*Dad and Mum **differed** in their attitude to bedtimes.*

disagree (2) VERB

If you **disagree** with an action or proposal, you believe it is wrong.

dispute
*The player **disputed** the umpire's decision and was disqualified.*

object to
*Fran **objected to** what I'd said about her.*

oppose
*The mayor **opposed** the government's policy on city traffic.*

disappear VERB

If someone or something **disappears**, they go where they cannot be seen or found.

evaporate
*The wizard uttered his spell and **evaporated** into thin air.*

fade
*The flight of geese **faded** into the twilight.*

melt away
*The crowd **melted away**, taking their memories of the music with them.*

vanish
*Without a second thought, Hermione made herself **vanish** in an instant.*

ANTONYMS: appear, reappear

disaster NOUN

A **disaster** is a very bad accident, such as an earthquake or a plane crash.

calamity
*Mr and Mrs Hassan suffered a **calamity** when they lost all their savings.*

catastrophe
*The earthquake killed 1500 people – a **catastrophe** on a huge scale.*

tragedy
*The fire in the old couple's home was a **tragedy**.*

discover VERB

When you **discover** something, you find it or find out about it.

find
*My brother has **found** a good way to train the new puppy.*

uncover
*Mehmet lifted some papers and **uncovered** a book he'd thought was lost.*

unearth
*Kylie was digging a hole in the garden and **unearthed** an old pot.*

ANTONYM: hide

discuss VERB

When people **discuss** something, they talk about it in detail.

chat about
*Lisa and I **chatted about** our favourite movie.*

debate
*"I'm not willing to **debate** the matter. Go to bed!" said my big sister.*

exchange views on
*The two presidents **exchanged views on** a possible agreement.*

disease NOUN

A **disease** is an illness that affects human beings, other animals or plants.

ailment
*Grandma was feeling ill, but the doctor wasn't sure what **ailment** she was suffering from.*

complaint
*She has to put cream on every day because she has an itchy skin **complaint**.*

illness
*Grandad had suffered from various **illnesses** in the last two years.*

sickness
*Passengers fell victim to a strange **sickness**.*

disgrace NOUN

Disgrace is the state you are in when othe people disapprove of what you have done.

embarrassment
*My dad suffered the **embarrassment** of coming last in the fathers' race.*

humiliation
*I felt nothing but **humiliation** at what I had done.*

shame
*The politician suffered the **shame** of being sent to prison.*

disguise VERB

If you **disguise** something, you change it so that people do not recognise it.

camouflage
*The army **camouflages** tanks to hide them from aircraft.*

conceal
*She tried to **conceal** the spot on her chin.*

cover
*He **covered** his hair with a black wig.*

dress up
*Murray **dressed up** as his father for the party.*

mask
*Dark sunglasses **masked** the expression in his eyes.*

disgusting ADJECTIVE

Something **disgusting** is very unpleasant and makes people feel a strong sense of dislike.

foul
*A **foul** smell emanated from the drain.*

loathsome
*Gollum was a **loathsome**, slimy creature.*

obnoxious
*That **obnoxious** woman is always causing trouble in the village.*

revolting
*I made a chocolate cake for Mum's birthday, but it tasted **revolting**.*

sickening
*It was **sickening** to read of children being used as cheap labour.*

vile
*"The whole **vile** trade in fur ought to be stopped," my aunt declared.*

dishonest ADJECTIVE

If someone is **dishonest**, they are not truthful and not to be trusted.

corrupt
*There will be an investigation to discover if the businessman is **corrupt**.*

crooked
*The **crooked** bank clerk embezzled thousands of pounds before she was caught.*

deceitful
*"You **deceitful** girl!" Mrs Flemming exploded. "How dare you tell me lies!"*

ANTONYM: honest

dislike VERB

If you **dislike** something or someone, you think they are unpleasant.

detest
*Mum **detests** people who promise lots but do very little.*

disapprove of
*My gran **disapproves of** any modern music.*

have no time for
*"**I have no time for** people who boast," Mr MacCuish said, looking at me.*

loathe
*The two men **loathe** each other.*

not be able to bear
*Mrs Arbuthnot **couldn't bear** anybody who didn't like hunting.*

ANTONYM: like

➔ *See* **hate**

disobedient ADJECTIVE

If someone is **disobedient**, they refuse deliberately to do what they are told.

mutinous
*Captain Bligh saw that the ship's mate had a **mutinous** look in his eye.*

rebellious
***Rebellious** troops in the west rose up against the king.*

ANTONYM: obedient

display (1) NOUN

A **display** is an arrangement of things designed to attract people's attention.

demonstration
*Mrs Paulin gave a falconry **demonstration** with her falcon, Kraa.*

exhibition
*An **exhibition** of Mum's paintings was very successful.*

parade
*The fancy-dress **parade** was bright and lively.*

A B C D E F G H I J K L M N O P Q R S T U V W X Y Z

presentation
*In assembly, we did a **presentation** on what our class had been studying during the term.*

display (2) VERB

If you **display** something, you show it to people.

demonstrate
*Mum **demonstrated** how to start the new lawn mower.*

exhibit
*The dog **exhibited** signs of some sort of rash.*

parade
*Nazim **paraded** his new motorbike outside our house.*

put on show
*The winning entries were **put on show** in the school hall.*

district NOUN

A **district** is an area of a town or country.

area
*This **area** is dotted with farms and villages.*

locality
*"We're building in your **locality** soon," the salesman announced.*

neighbourhood
*Our **neighbourhood** is busy by day, but very quiet at night.*

region
*The Champagne **region** of France is famous for its sparkling wine.*

disturb (1) VERB

If you **disturb** someone, you interrupt their peace or privacy.

bother
*"I'm sorry to **bother** you," our neighbour said, "but have you seen Tibbles?"*

interrupt
*My baby brother kept **interrupting** me while I was trying to read.*

intrude on
*Mrs Mosely said she didn't want to **intrude on** us, but that's just what she was doing.*

disturb (2) VERB

If something **disturbs** you, it makes you feel upset or worried.

concern
*I was **concerned** that the toddler was playing very near the busy road.*

trouble
*You could tell that my parents were **troubled** by the anxious look they both wore.*

unsettle
*Thunder and lightning always **unsettle** our parrot.*

worry
*"We'll be quite safe. You mustn't let it **worry** you," I reassured Sara.*

disused ADJECTIVE

Something **disused** is neglected or no longer used.

abandoned
*The **abandoned** mine was dangerous to explore, though it was an exciting find.*

derelict
*The tramp slept in the **derelict** warehouse.*

deserted
*The old air base was **deserted** except for some cats living in a hangar.*

dive VERB

To **dive** is to move suddenly and quickly, often downwards.

plummet
*The rocket soared upwards, only to **plummet** back down seconds later.*

plunge
*Holden **plunged** into the cool water of the mountain stream.*

pounce
*From behind the acacia tree, the cheetah suddenly **pounced** on its prey.*

swoop
*The kestrel hovered above, then **swooped** on the unsuspecting vole.*

divide VERB

When you **divide** something, or when it **divides**, it is separated into two or more parts.

segregate
*In South Africa's past, different races were **segregated**.*

separate
*It took courage on the part of the police officer to **separate** the fighting dogs.*

split
*The thieves had just **split** the banknotes when there was an almighty knock on the door and the police came charging in.*

ANTONYM: unite

dizzy ADJECTIVE

If you feel **dizzy**, you feel that you are losing your balance and are about to fall.

dazed
*The dog was **dazed** after the collision and wandered about, whining.*

faint
*Gran said she felt **faint**, so we sat her down and brought her some water.*

giddy
*Looking down from the skyscraper roof made me feel **giddy**.*

light-headed
*With all the excitement of the party, I felt quite **light-headed**.*

do VERB

Do has many meanings, some of which are listed below.

to carry out a task:

carry out
*After the fire, Dad asked the builders to **carry out** repairs.*

perform
*The children **performed** miracles in transforming the derelict shed into a den.*

tackle
*"How would you like to **tackle** a bigger slope?" the instructor asked.*

to complete something:

accomplish
*The hobbits **accomplished** things that stronger people could not.*

achieve
***Achieving** what you set out to do is always satisfying.*

complete
*My friend Ali **completed** the tables test in three minutes!*

finish
*It took me about ten minutes to **finish** the washing up.*

to be enough:

be adequate
*"Ten pounds ought to **be adequate** reward," said Dad.*

be enough
*"That will **be enough**, thank you," I said to Mrs Lampard, as she ladled out the soup.*

be sufficient
*"Will that bread **be sufficient** for all those in camp?" the head teacher enquired.*

to work something out:

figure out
*In the maths test, it took me a while to **figure out** the answers.*

solve
*Gran is good at **solving** crossword puzzles.*

work out
*Mrs Faisal **worked out** our schedule for the coming week.*

dodge VERB

If you **dodge** something, you move suddenly to avoid being seen, hit or caught.

avoid
*The driver **avoided** hitting the pedestrian by only a few inches.*

evade
*Trying to **evade** capture, the criminal climbed up the fire escape.*

sidestep
***Sidestepping** one defender, the forward ran smack into the next.*

swerve round
*The car **swerved round** the injured deer as it lay in the road.*

doubt (1) NOUN

A **doubt** is a feeling of uncertainty as to whether something is true or possible.

distrust
*As he handed the ransom over, you could see the **distrust** in his eyes.*

suspicion
*Lyra had a **suspicion** that Mrs Coulter was not all she seemed to be.*

uncertainty
*As he waited for news of the battle, Will found the **uncertainty** hard to bear.*

doubt (2) VERB

If you **doubt** something, you think that it is probably not true or possible.

distrust
*You could see that the Roho brothers **distrusted**, even feared, the tall stranger who rode into town.*

A B C D E F G H I J K L M N O P Q R S T U V W X Y Z

query
*"Are you **querying** my authority?" the teacher asked.*

question
*She started **questioning** her ability to do the job.*

suspect
*The thief knew the others had no reason to **suspect** him.*

ANTONYM: trust

doubtful (1) ADJECTIVE

If you are **doubtful** about something, you are not sure about it.

distrustful
*Zoe was immediately **distrustful** of the salesman.*

hesitant
*Despite her cruel father, Jayni was **hesitant** about leaving home.*

in two minds (*informal*)
*Legolas was **in two minds** whether to press on or to camp for the night.*

sceptical
*They were confident about United's chances in the final, whereas I was **sceptical**.*

suspicious
*The police were **suspicious** of the woman's alibi for the time of the crime.*

uncertain
*When the shop had to close, we faced an **uncertain** future.*

unsure
*At first she was **unsure** whether she had heard him correctly or not.*

ANTONYM: sure

doubtful (2) ADJECTIVE

If something is **doubtful**, it is uncertain or unlikely.

debatable
*My sister told Mum and Dad that it was **debatable** whether I would pass the test, but I was determined to prove her wrong.*

dubious
*The email contained a **dubious** story about a man who was desperate for money.*

questionable
*The judge warned the jury that the witness's honesty was **questionable**.*

drag VERB

If you **drag** a heavy object somewhere, you pull it there slowly and with difficulty.

haul
*The lifeboat crew **hauled** the last of the injured seamen aboard.*

heave
*When the cox gave the word, the eight rowers **heaved** on their oars together.*

lug
*We had to **lug** our heavy suitcases up three flights of stairs at the hotel.*

draw VERB

When you **draw** something, you use a pen or pencil to make a picture of it.

doodle
*Mrs Wilson caught me **doodling** during her history lesson.*

sketch
*Artists usually **sketch** the outlines of a picture before they paint it.*

trace
*I like **tracing** pictures from my storybook.*

drawing NOUN

A **drawing** is a picture made with a pencil, pen or crayon.

Some types of drawing:

cartoon	diagram	doodle
illustration	landscape	map
plan	portrait	sketch

dreadful ADJECTIVE

Something that is **dreadful** is very bad or unpleasant.

atrocious
*For our entire holiday, the weather was absolutely **atrocious**.*

awful
*India felt **awful** after speaking to her father like that.*

frightful
*"Darling, the whole thing was a **frightful** mess," the actress said, very loudly.*

ghastly
*The detective realised that it had all been a **ghastly** mistake.*

shocking
*The drunken driver's **shocking** conduct could have cost lives.*

terrible
Faith knew instantly that she had made a ***terrible*** *mistake.*

dream (1) NOUN

Your **dream** is a hope or ambition that you often think about because you would very much like it to happen.

ambition
It was Will's ***ambition*** *to find the truth about his father.*

fantasy
Madaleine's ***fantasy*** *was to meet her favourite pop group.*

dream (2) VERB

When you **dream**, you see events in your mind, often while you are asleep.

daydream
During maths I ***daydreamed*** *of far-off mountains topped by lonely castles.*

imagine
Kesia was staring out of the window, ***imagining*** *what it would be like to be famous.*

drill NOUN

A **drill** is a routine exercise or routine training.

exercise
The commando unit built a dummy village for their ***exercises****.*

procedure
In case of fire, it's important to follow the correct ***procedure****.*

drink VERB

When you **drink** a liquid, you take it into your mouth and swallow it.

gulp
Camels ***gulp*** *a lot of water and then store it in their humps.*

guzzle
I didn't notice that my brother was ***guzzling*** *all the lemonade.*

sip
Sipping *her tea, the countess gazed through the window.*

swig
The outlaw drew the cork out with his teeth and ***swigged*** *from the bottle.*

LANGUAGE TIP
When animals drink using their tongue, they **lap**.

drip VERB

When liquid **drips**, it falls in small drops.

dribble
Water from the hose ***dribbled*** *into the soil.*

plop
I could hear raindrops steadily ***plopping*** *into the gutter outside.*

splash
The clumsy artist accidentally ***splashed*** *paint on her canvas. It sold for lots of money.*

trickle
In the baking depths of the canyon, the river ***trickled*** *where it had previously gushed.*

drive VERB

If someone **drives** a vehicle, they operate it and control its movements.

control
Raoul ***controlled*** *his go-kart well, cornering at high speed.*

handle
"Ah, but could you ***handle*** *a Formula One racing car?" the instructor asked.*

droop VERB

If something **droops**, it hangs or sags downwards with no strength or firmness.

flop
Gavin's hair always ***flops*** *into his eyes.*

sag
The guesthouse bed ***sagged*** *unpleasantly in the middle.*

wilt
If you put bluebells in a vase, they ***wilt*** *after a few hours.*

drop (1) VERB

If something **drops**, it falls straight down.

descend
To her alarm, the parachute jumper ***descended*** *faster than she expected.*

plummet
The stricken Spitfire ***plummeted*** *into the sea.*

plunge
I watched my brother fasten his harness, then ***plunge*** *towards the river below.*

drop (2) NOUN

A **drop** is a very small quantity of liquid.

bead
After the race the athlete had ***beads*** *of sweat on her forehead.*

A B C D E F G H I J K L M N O P Q R S T U V W X Y Z

dash
"Just a ***dash*** *of vinegar, please," I said to the man serving the chips.*

drip
Drips *of water continued to fall from the trees after the rain had stopped.*

droplet
As the rain fell, ***droplets*** *of water trickled off my nose.*

dry ADJECTIVE

If ground is **dry**, it is not wet and contains no water.

arid
That desert is an ***arid*** *but beautiful region of rolling sand hills.*

barren
Wind blew uninterrupted across the ***barren****, treeless landscape.*

parched
The river bed was ***parched*** *and cracked where once torrents of water had flowed.*

LANGUAGE TIP
If your throat is dry, you may be **dehydrated** and need to drink fluid.

duck VERB

If you **duck**, you move your head quickly downwards in order to avoid being hit by something.

bob down
Dad kept ***bobbing down*** *behind the sofa, making her laugh.*

crouch
To avoid the gunfire, the soldier ***crouched*** *behind the fence.*

stoop
Tom had to ***stoop*** *to get through the door.*

dull (1) ADJECTIVE

If the weather is **dull**, the sky is not bright.

cloudy
The clear sky became more and more ***cloudy****.*

dismal
The weather was ***dismal*** *and the birds, for once, were silent.*

overcast
Despite the ***overcast*** *sky, the rain held off until the match was over.*

ANTONYM: bright

dull (2) ADJECTIVE

If something is **dull**, it has no bright colours.

drab
It was a ***drab*** *room, without picture or ornament.*

dreary
Heathcliff gazed through the raindrops at the ***dreary*** *landscape beyond.*

gloomy
There were ***gloomy*** *paintings of the earl's ancestors hanging on many of the castle walls.*

ANTONYM: bright

dull (3) ADJECTIVE

Someone or something that is **dull** is not interesting.

boring
Don't write ***boring*** *stories. Fill them with life!*

tedious
"I do find long speeches ***tedious****," my uncle whispered.*

uninteresting
Somehow, my photos always manage to look ***uninteresting****.*

ANTONYM: interesting

dull (4) ADJECTIVE

A **dull** sound is low-pitched and difficult to hear.

indistinct
Although the sound was ***indistinct****, the rescue team definitely heard something.*

muffled
A ***muffled*** *explosion came from deep within the mine.*

ANTONYM: clear

dumb ADJECTIVE (*informal*)

Dumb can mean stupid.

dim
Although Tim was rather ***dim****, his heart was made of gold.*

slow
The cat ran playfully around the ***slow*** *dog.*

unintelligent
"That was a pretty ***unintelligent*** *thing to say," said my brother.*

dummy NOUN

A **dummy** is an imitation or model of something which is used for display.

imitation

*I couldn't believe that the cake in the shop was an **imitation**. It looked so delicious!*

model

*In St Paul's Cathedral, London, you can see the architect's original **model**.*

dump VERB

If something is **dumped** somewhere, it is put there because it is no longer wanted.

dispose of

*Because of the gases inside them, fridges are not always easy to **dispose of**.*

jettison

*To maintain height, the balloon pilot **jettisoned** everything he could spare.*

throw away

*We had to **throw away** some of the fruit as it had gone bad.*

Ee

eager ADJECTIVE

If you are **eager**, you very much want to do or have something.

enthusiastic

*There were plenty of **enthusiastic** volunteers to help plan the school garden.*

impatient

*Mark was **impatient** to get back to school after the holidays.*

keen

*Brownie was **keen** to enter the competition.*

longing

*Rachel was **longing** to see her newborn baby brother.*

early (1) ADVERB

If something happens **early**, it happens before the arranged or expected time.

ahead of schedule

*Contractors completed the bridge three months **ahead of schedule**.*

ahead of time

*"As we're running **ahead of time**," Mum said as she drove, "let's stop for a coffee."*

in advance

*We bought our tickets for the show **in advance**.*

in good time

*Our coach arrived **in good time** to catch the cross-Channel ferry.*

ANTONYM: late

early (2) ADJECTIVE

Early relates to something that happened in a period far back in time.

ancient

***Ancient** man was a hunter gatherer: hunting animals and gathering fruits and nuts.*

first

*The **first** type of bicycle, known as a "penny-farthing", had a huge front wheel.*

A B C D E F G H I J K L M N O P Q R S T U V W X Y Z

primitive
*In **primitive** societies sugar was only consumed occasionally as honey.*

ANTONYMS: modern, recent

earth (1) NOUN

The **earth** is the planet we live on.

globe
*In 1961, Yuri Gagarin became the first astronaut to orbit the **globe**.*

planet
*The water in the seas and oceans covers the majority of the **planet**.*

world
*My big sister took a year off to travel around the **world**.*

earth (2) NOUN

Earth is another word for soil.

ground
*The **ground** arrived much sooner than the parachute jumper expected it.*

land
*"The **land** here is good for animals but poor for crops," the farmer said.*

soil
*Between my sister and me, we moved three tonnes of **soil**.*

easily ADVERB

If you do something **easily**, you do it without difficulty.

comfortably
*Iain was **comfortably** the winner in the 100 metres race.*

effortlessly
*The superhero's jet-powered car cruised **effortlessly** at 300 miles per hour.*

simply
*Border collie dogs are **simply** trained because they are intelligent and keen to work.*

with ease
*My brother bragged that he would pass his driving test **with ease**. How wrong he was!*

without difficulty
*The expedition reached 27 000 feet **without difficulty**, but then the storms came.*

ANTONYM: with difficulty

easy (1) ADJECTIVE

If something is **easy**, you can do it without difficulty.

a piece of cake (*informal*)
*"Anyone could do that!" my brother crowed. "It's **a piece of cake**!"*

effortless
*With her loping stride, the athlete made marathon running look **effortless**.*

no trouble
*Despite their size, it was **no trouble** for them to open the huge iron gates.*

simple
*For once, our maths homework was **simple**.*

straightforward
*The route is fairly **straightforward**, so we shouldn't need a map.*

ANTONYM: difficult

easy (2) ADJECTIVE

An **easy** life is comfortable and without problems.

carefree
*The two cats lived a **carefree** life, eating and sleeping.*

comfortable
*Flying first class is **comfortable** but boy, is it expensive!*

leisurely
*I spotted Mum and Dad taking a **leisurely** stroll on the seafront.*

relaxed
*Felicity spent a **relaxed** morning reading in the sun lounge.*

ANTONYM: hard

eat

→ Look at the **Word Power** page!

ecstasy NOUN

Ecstasy is a feeling of extreme happiness.

bliss
*They lived together in **bliss** and harmony.*

delight
*He squealed with **delight** when we told him.*

elation
*There were scenes of **elation** after the victory.*

joy
*I was full of **joy** when I found the kitten.*

ANTONYM: despair

→ *See* **happiness**

eat

VERB When you **eat** food, you chew it and swallow it.

eat normally:

consume
*For lunch I **consumed** a banana sandwich.*

dine
*We **dined** at a smart restaurant.*

feed
*It looked like the newborn lamb still wasn't **feeding** properly.*

eat greedily:

devour
*Christopher **devoured** his food greedily.*

gobble
*"Don't **gobble** your food – you'll get hiccups," my mother warned.*

gorge
*Ella **gorged** herself on chocolate, then began to feel ill.*

scoff (*informal*)
*"Oy! You've **scoffed** my ice cream!" my brother yelled angrily.*

tuck in (*informal*)
*"**Tuck in**, there's plenty for everyone!" she said.*

eat noisily:

chomp
*She began to **chomp** on her celery.*

munch
*All I could hear was my sister **munching** her apple.*

eat in small amounts:

nibble
*Still feeling poorly, Hakim could only **nibble** at dry biscuits.*

pick
*I could tell she was upset by the way she was **picking** at her food.*

taste
*The competition judges merely **tasted** the food.*

eat formally:

banquet
*The King's court **banqueted** on pheasant and quail.*

feast
*Minstrels played while the nobles **feasted**.*

Try these lively words and phrases!

polish off (*informal*) — *I **polished off** the last piece of cake.*
stuff your face (*informal*) — *He sat down and began to **stuff his face**.*
wolf down (*informal*) — *Ivan **wolfed down** five chocolate biscuits.*

a b c d e f g h i j k l m n o p q r s t u v w x y z

A B C D E F G H I J K L M N O P Q R S T U V W X Y Z

edge NOUN

The **edge** is the part along the side or end of something.

The edge of...
a circle is the **circumference**.
a city are the **outskirts** or **suburbs**.
a country is the **border** or **coast**.
a pavement is the **kerb**.
a picture is the **frame**.
a piece of land is the **boundary** or **perimeter**.
a piece of paper is the **border** or **margin**.
a shape is the **perimeter**.

effect (1) NOUN

An **effect** is something that happens as a result of something else.

consequence
*The day after the storm the **consequences** could be seen everywhere.*

outcome
*The **outcome** of Dad stopping for petrol was that I was late for school!*

result
*David worked hard for his exam, and was promoted as a **result**.*

effect (2) NOUN

An **effect** is the impression something makes.

impact
*Winning the lottery had a big **impact** on our neighbours' life.*

impression
*Hearing a real orchestra play made a huge **impression** on Carla.*

influence
*Under the **influence** of the anaesthetic, Craig had some strange dreams.*

LANGUAGE TIP
Do not confuse the noun **effect** with the verb **affect**.

effort NOUN

Effort is the energy needed to do something.

energy
*It took a huge amount of **energy** to climb to the top of the hill.*

force
*With great **force**, the giant pushed a boulder from the mouth of the cave.*

struggle
*The boys found it a **struggle** to drag the heavy sack.*

work
*"They have put a lot of **work** into this project," said the teacher.*

emphasise VERB

If you **emphasise** something, you make it look or sound more important than the things around it.

focus on
*The newspaper article **focused on** where to look for antiques.*

highlight
*In his speech, the minister **highlighted** the need for a good railway network.*

stress
*In the word "telephone", you should **stress** the first syllable.*

empty (1) ADJECTIVE

Something that is **empty** has no people or things in it.

bare
*Wandering round the **bare** rooms, I said goodbye to the house I had always lived in and still loved.*

deserted
*From within the **deserted** warehouse came a muffled bark.*

unfurnished
*My big sister rented an **unfurnished** flat, so our parents lent her lots of household stuff.*

uninhabited
*The film star's mansion looked **uninhabited**.*

unoccupied
*Before they were due to be demolished, the houses were left **unoccupied** for some weeks.*

vacant
*Luckily, the hotel had several **vacant** rooms that night.*

ANTONYMS: full, occupied

LANGUAGE TIP
The antonym **full** is used to describe things and the antonym **occupied** is used to describe places.

empty (2) VERB

If you **empty** something, you remove the contents.

drain
Drain *the boiling water from the pan before you serve the vegetables.*

pour out
I ***poured*** *the cold tea* ***out*** *of my cup.*

unload
It was Tariq's job to ***unload*** *the truck.*

ANTONYM: fill

empty (3) VERB

If a building is **emptied**, everybody in it has to go outside.

clear
The bomb squad ***cleared*** *the building.*

evacuate
For our fire practice, the teachers had to ***evacuate*** *the school.*

encourage (1) VERB

If you **encourage** someone, you give them the confidence to do something.

inspire
Inspired *by the example of Shackleton, Rupert resolved to become a polar explorer.*

motivate
The instructor ***motivated*** *us to have a go at abseiling.*

urge
"Ladies and gentlemen, I ***urge*** *you to vote for me!" the politician shouted.*

encourage (2) VERB

If you **encourage** someone, you support them.

boost
Winning the cup ***boosted*** *the team's confidence.*

foster
Mrs Ali's sense of humour ***fostered*** *a terrific relationship with her pupils.*

further
The new library was added to ***further*** *children's interest in reading.*

promote
Adverts were no longer allowed to ***promote*** *cigarette smoking.*

support
Dad ***supported*** *my idea about joining the hockey team.*

end (1) NOUN

The **end** of an event is the last part of it.

close
At the ***close*** *of play today, Australia had scored 452 runs.*

conclusion
In the ***conclusion*** *of her speech, Mrs Abrahams said how much she would miss us.*

ending
Every story needs an interesting ***ending****.*

finale
For the show's ***finale****, all the dancers came on stage in a spectacular jazz number.*

finish
At the ***finish****, three horses were neck and neck.*

ANTONYMS: beginning, start

end (2) NOUN

The **end** of something is the furthest point of it.

boundary
In cricket, if the ball goes over the ***boundary****, four runs are scored.*

edge
When I got to the ***edge*** *of the diving board, I was shaking with nerves.*

limit
Something was moving, right at the ***limit*** *of her vision.*

end (3) VERB

When something **ends**, it finishes.

conclude
The evening ***concluded*** *with a vote of thanks to the school choir.*

culminate
The fireworks display ***culminated*** *in a huge explosion of colour and noise.*

terminate
For his bad behaviour, the club ***terminated*** *the player's contract.*

ending NOUN

The **ending** of something is when it finishes.

climax
For the ***climax****, the lion tamer put her head inside the great beast's mouth.*

culmination
As a ***culmination*** *to the week's events, Saturday's grand parade took some beating.*

finale
*Our grand **finale** involved the whole school.*

ANTONYMS: beginning, start

endless ADJECTIVE

Something that is **endless** has, or seems to have, no end.

continual
*Our **continual** arguing was driving Mum mad.*

continuous
*Day and night, the **continuous** throb of the generator echoed through the woods.*

everlasting
*The couple knew their love was **everlasting**.*

perpetual
*"That **perpetual** din is driving me crackers!" complained the neighbour from downstairs.*

LANGUAGE TIP
The word **continual** describes things which happen again and again, but not constantly. **Continuous** actions happen without stopping.

endure VERB

If you **endure** someone or something unpleasant, you put up with them.

bear
*For the swordsman, mortally wounded, the pain was hard to **bear**.*

brave
*Grace **braved** the wind and the waves to rescue her drowning brother.*

cope with
*Sometimes my mum finds her teenager's moods difficult to **cope with**.*

experience
*The refugees **experienced** great hardship on their trek to freedom.*

stand
*I don't know how the people who live near the sewage works **stand** the smell.*

suffer
*Malik has **suffered** years of pain from arthritis.*

undergo
*Dad had to **undergo** surgery on his knee.*

enemy NOUN

Your **enemy** is someone who is very much against you and may wish to harm you.

adversary
*Finally, King Harold faced his **adversary**, William of Normandy.*

foe
*At Agincourt, the French **foe** were defeated by English archers.*

opponent
*Early on, the **opponents** had the upper hand, but our team had more stamina.*

rival
*The evil sheriff was Robin Hood's **rival** for the hand of Maid Marion.*

ANTONYMS: friend, ally

energetic ADJECTIVE

Someone who is **energetic** is full of energy.

active
*Even though he is in his 70s, Grandpa is still very **active**, especially in his garden.*

lively
*My **lively** baby brother likes to jump on my bed in the morning.*

vigorous
*Apparently, **vigorous** exercise is the best way to stay healthy.*

ANTONYM: lethargic

energy NOUN

Energy is the physical strength you need to do active things.

drive
*My big brother's **drive** and ambition earned him the top sales award.*

get-up-and-go (*informal*)
*My mum has more **get-up-and-go** than I do! She's always busy.*

stamina
*To survive a marathon run, you need **stamina** more than speed.*

vigour
*We laughed at the **vigour** with which our head teacher strutted up and down.*

vitality
*Uncle Archie is full of **vitality**; he plays squash, hockey and golf.*

enormous ADJECTIVE

Something that is **enormous** is very large in size or amount.

colossal
*My greedy brother grabbed a **colossal** helping of pudding.*

gargantuan
*After a sea trip, the fisherman's appetite was **gargantuan**.*

gigantic
*The tidal wave formed a **gigantic** wall, visible for miles out to sea.*

huge
*It was a **huge** relief to pass my exams.*

massive
*In one **massive** surge, the surfer was swept towards the shore at 80 miles an hour.*

vast
*The Sahara desert covers a **vast** area of northern Africa.*

enough ADJECTIVE

Enough can mean as much or as many as is necessary.

adequate
*I wasn't sure if my knowledge was **adequate** to pass the test.*

ample
*We had **ample** time to study for the test.*

sufficient
*"Have you all got **sufficient** wet weather gear?" Miss Perkins asked.*

entertain VERB

If you **entertain** somebody, you do something they enjoy and find amusing.

amuse
*Our baby is very easy to **amuse**, unless he's hungry or tired.*

delight
*The conjuror **delighted** everybody with his magical tricks.*

occupy
*Can you think of something to **occupy** the children while they are waiting?*

please
*She made a list of party games that would **please** her friends.*

enthusiasm NOUN

If you show **enthusiasm** for something, you show much interest and excitement.

excitement
*You could feel the **excitement** in the school as Christmas approached.*

interest
*Grandad has always had an **interest** in trains.*

passion
*Olga's **passion** for horses rules her life.*

zeal
*My mum plays tennis with **zeal**.*

enthusiastic ADJECTIVE

If you are **enthusiastic** about something, you show great excitement, eagerness and approval for it.

ardent
*As an **ardent** Reds fan, my friend wore as much red clothing as he could find.*

eager
*Janet was so **eager** to get to the food, she tripped and fell headfirst into the trifle.*

keen
*When it comes to fishing, Mr Hayles is as **keen** as anyone.*

passionate
*Jill is a **passionate** believer in green issues and often goes on protest marches.*

wholehearted
*Crudsea Town Council gave its **wholehearted** support to our club's plan.*

ANTONYM: unenthusiastic

envious ADJECTIVE

If you are **envious**, you wish you could have what someone else has.

green with envy
*The wicked witch was **green with envy** that her good sister was liked by everybody.*

jealous
*My sister gets **jealous** if I get more attention than she does.*

envy VERB

If you **envy** someone, you wish you had what they have.

begrudge
*Scrooge **begrudged** every penny that he paid his poor clerk.*

be jealous
*Several of the others **were jealous** of Lyra's skill and intelligence.*

covet
*You could tell from his envious glances that my brother **coveted** my bike.*

resent
*Because she was unsuccessful herself, the artist **resented** the success of other painters.*

a b c d e f g h i j k l m n o p q r s t u v w x y z

A B C D E F G H I J K L M N O P Q R S T U V W X Y Z

equal (1) ADJECTIVE

If two things are **equal**, they are the same in size, number or amount.

balanced
*Our attack and defence were **balanced** in size and ability.*

equivalent
*A hundred centimetres are **equivalent** to one metre.*

equal (2) VERB

If something **equals** something else, it is equivalent to it.

be equal to
*In soccer, two yellow cards **are equal to** one red card, and the player is sent off.*

match
*Caroline's skill at multiplication **matched** my skill at spelling.*

equipment NOUN

Equipment is all the things that are needed or used for a particular job or activity.

apparatus
*I love gymnastics, especially when we use all of the **apparatus**.*

gear
*Dave the mechanic has all the **gear** for welding metal.*

paraphernalia
*Granny would insist on taking all her **paraphernalia** with her on holiday.*

tackle
*Dad keeps all his fishing **tackle** in the garage.*

tool
*My brother keeps his plumbing **tools** in a huge expanding box.*

escape VERB

If you **escape** from someone or something, you succeed in getting away from them.

break free
*Frightened by the storm, the horse **broke free** from its stable.*

break out
*Prisoners planned to **break out** with the aid of a helicopter.*

flee
*When they heard the police siren, the vandals tried to **flee** the scene.*

make a getaway
*The robbers **made a getaway** in a stolen van.*

make your escape
*After an hour of boredom, the twins **made their escape** through a back door.*

especially ADVERB

You say **especially** to show that somethin applies more to one thing, person or situation than to others.

in particular
*Krim, the alien, liked all earthlings, but Sean i **particular**.*

particularly
*"I **particularly** fancy that lampshade," Mum said thoughtfully.*

specifically
*Dad said any colour of front door would do, while Mum **specifically** wanted blue.*

essential ADJECTIVE

Something that is **essential** is absolutely necessary.

crucial
*Food and other supplies are **crucial** to any expedition's success.*

indispensable
*Florence and her nursing team proved **indispensable** to the hospital's doctors.*

key
*"Listen up. This is **key** to the whole operation!" the general barked.*

vital
*Before exams, it's **vital** to be well rested.*

ANTONYM: unnecessary

even (1) ADJECTIVE

An **even** surface is level, smooth and flat.

flat
*For a land speed record, the surface must be perfectly **flat**.*

level
*Builders always make sure that each layer of bricks is **level**.*

smooth
*After a bumpy journey, the aircraft made a **smooth** landing.*

ANTONYM: uneven

even (2) ADJECTIVE

An **even** measurement or rate stays at about the same level.

constant
*The temperature in the zoo is kept at a **constant** level.*

regular
*Outside my window, the trees kept up a **regular** tapping in the wind.*

steady
*Viking longships were rowed to the **steady** beat of a drum.*

ANTONYM: irregular

even (3) ADJECTIVE
Something that is **even** is equally balanced between two sides.

balanced
*The debate was **balanced** between the pros and the cons.*

equal
*Both players had an **equal** chance of winning the tennis match.*

level
*The two athletes were **level** as they came to the last hurdle.*

tied
*At full time, the scores were **tied**, so we took penalties to decide the winner.*

well-matched
*Our team and my sister's were **well-matched**, and we just scraped a win.*

Try these lively words and phrases:

all square
*We were **all square** in the match at 3–3.*

level pegging
*A poll of voters showed that the parties are **level pegging**.*

neck and neck
*The two runners were **neck and neck** in the race.*

evening NOUN
The **evening** is the part of the day between the end of the afternoon and the time you go to bed.

dusk
*As the **dusk** gathered, street lights flickered on.*

nightfall
*By **nightfall**, most creatures were asleep and the wood was silent.*

sunset
***Sunset** over the sea is a magical sight.*

twilight
*Angela started telling stupid stories about ghosts and zombies coming alive at **twilight**.*

event (1) NOUN
An **event** is something that happens, especially when it is unusual or important.

episode
*"The **episode** where my bicycle brakes failed is not one I want to repeat," Dad said.*

incident
*Police were called to an **incident** outside a bar. A woman was arrested.*

occurrence
*After the house shook, Gran remembered a similar **occurrence** over 20 years before.*

event (2) NOUN
An **event** is an organised activity, such as a sports match or a concert.

ceremony
*The wedding **ceremony** took place at the registry office.*

competition
*The first **competition** of the afternoon was the long jump.*

function
*Last night there was a very noisy **function** in the town hall.*

occasion
*"This christening is an **occasion** to remember!" announced Uncle George.*

evil (1) ADJECTIVE
Something or someone **evil** is very bad and causes harm to people.

nasty
*"I couldn't believe the **nasty** things she came out with," my mum said in dismay.*

vicious
*It was a **vicious** attack, causing the victim severe injuries.*

vile
*Von Hugo was a **vile** man who fully deserved his prison sentence.*

villainous
*The **villainous** Cruella plotted to capture the Dalmatian puppies.*

wicked
*The witch's **wicked** plans were thwarted by the good fairy.*

A B C D E F G H I J K L M N O P Q R S T U V W X Y Z

evil (2) NOUN

Evil is used to refer to all the wicked or bad things that happen in the world.

corruption
*"Where **corruption** exists, bribes are taken. Money, not honesty, is king," said Grandpa.*

wickedness
*The count was the soul of **wickedness**, enjoying the misery he inflicted.*

wrongdoing
*Towards the end of his life, the king repented of his lifetime of **wrongdoing**.*

exact ADJECTIVE

If something is **exact**, it is accurately measured or made.

accurate
*"Here's an **accurate** time check. Synchronise your watches," the colonel called.*

detailed
*Bonnie wrote down **detailed** notes of what she had witnessed.*

precise
*It's difficult to give a **precise** date for the painting.*

specific
*"Be **specific** about what equipment you need," said our science teacher.*

true
*The excellent new portrait was a **true** likeness of the queen.*

ANTONYM: inaccurate

exaggerate VERB

If you **exaggerate**, you make something seem better, worse, bigger or more important than it really is.

lay it on thick (*informal*)
*Nick was telling us of his exploits and **laying it on thick**.*

overdo
*That bit about wrestling the polar bear was **overdoing** it, I thought.*

overemphasize
*"I can't **overemphasise**," the skipper said, "the importance of life jackets."*

overstate
*In her concern for the children, Mrs Lucas had **overstated** the actual danger.*

examination (1) NOUN

If you take an **examination**, you take a test to find out how much you know about a subject.

assessment
*Many workers have to have a yearly **assessment** of their performance.*

exam
*"My next **exam** is on Wednesday," remarked my cousin gloomily.*

test
*Mr Ricketts' weekly Latin **test** was always a real killer.*

examination (2) NOUN

An **examination** is a close inspection of something.

analysis
*An **analysis** of the scene of the crime revealed no clues.*

check-up
*Uncle Steve had to go to the local hospital for a **check-up**.*

inspection
*Dad asked his friend to do an **inspection** of the second-hand car he wanted to buy.*

investigation
*Detectives conducted an **investigation** into the theft.*

study
*A **study** of the ancient axe proved it was of Viking origin.*

survey
*Our class conducted a **survey** on children's heroes and heroines.*

examine VERB

If you **examine** something, you inspect it carefully.

analyse
*"When you **analyse** what went wrong, the causes are plain," the scientist said.*

check
*Mrs Knox tells us to **check** our work, then check it again.*

inspect
*Scientists in radiation suits **inspected** the shattered reactor.*

investigate
*Dogs like to **investigate** every interesting smell along the road.*

scrutinise
*An official **scrutinised** the trials results to make sure every rider had been fairly treated.*

study
*For some time, my parents **studied** the menu on the restaurant window.*

example NOUN

An **example** is something that is typical of a particular group of things.

illustration
*"This is an **illustration** of the kind of work I'd like to see," said Mrs Clarke.*

instance
*"In this **instance** you should contact your doctor," advised the leaflet.*

sample
*Mum brought home a **sample** of the carpet, to check for colour.*

specimen
*To give the pupil a guide, some books have **specimen** answers to exam questions.*

excellent ADJECTIVE

Something that is **excellent** is very good indeed.

first-class
*I thought the acting was **first-class**, even if the singing was not as good.*

first-rate
*Becky gave a **first-rate** talk about her trip to Australia.*

outstanding
*Mrs Burton is an **outstanding** head teacher.*

superb
*"That was a **superb** meal, thank you," said Natalie, rubbing her tummy.*

ANTONYM: terrible

except PREPOSITION

Except can mean apart from or not including.

apart from
***Apart from** London, which other European cities have royal palaces?*

besides
***Besides** Ashley, everyone was going to the school camp.*

excluding
*The whole team got a medal, **excluding** poor Eric, who missed the final.*

with the exception of
***With the exception of** my brother, the whole family went to the beach.*

excited ADJECTIVE

If you are **excited** about something, it makes you feel very happy and enthusiastic.

enthusiastic
*Greg was very **enthusiastic** about anything to do with tennis.*

thrilled
*All the class were **thrilled** to take part in the television quiz.*

ANTONYM: unexcited

excitement NOUN

Excitement is the feeling of being excited.

eagerness
*The kids were all full of **eagerness** to be off on the school trip.*

enthusiasm
*I love the bubbly **enthusiasm** which my sister puts into her dancing lessons.*

passion
*My dad has a **passion** for fishing, but I think it's boring.*

thrill
*Lots of people love the **thrill** of horse racing, especially my Uncle Rupert.*

exciting ADJECTIVE

Something **exciting** makes you feel very happy and enthusiastic.

dramatic
*It was a **dramatic** scene, with ambulances and police cars all over the place.*

enthralling
*To watch such a spectacular show was an **enthralling** experience.*

inspiring
*Seeing those children and what they could do was absolutely **inspiring**.*

stirring
*The **stirring** sound of the bagpipes caused many Scots' hearts to quicken.*

thrilling
*The marathon race was **thrilling**, with the two athletes neck and neck for the last two miles.*

ANTONYM: unexciting

excuse NOUN

An **excuse** is a reason you give to explain why something has been done, has not been done, or will not be done.

explanation
*Serena came out with all sorts of **explanations** for her missing homework, but none of them were true.*

justification
*The judge declared that there could be no **justification** for such a wicked crime.*

reason
*"What possible **reason** can you have for borrowing my wetsuit?" Dad asked.*

PRONUNCIATION TIP
When it is a noun, **excuse** is pronounced ex-**kyooss**.

exercise (1) NOUN

Exercise is any activity that you do in order to improve at something, or to get fit and stay healthy.

activity
*One **activity** we did was to run up and down bouncing the ball.*

exertion
*Hassan was tired after the **exertion** of football practice.*

training
*For any type of sport, **training** is essential if you want to do well.*

exercise (2) VERB

When you **exercise**, you do activities that help you to get fit and stay healthy.

keep fit
*The prisoner **kept fit** by doing yoga regularly in her cell.*

train
*Every Wednesday, we had to **train** for Saturday's soccer match.*

expect (1) VERB

If you **expect** something to happen, you believe that it will happen.

anticipate
*For some months, Crusoe **anticipated** rescue, but eventually stopped thinking about it.*

believe
*Gita **believed** that she would fulfil her ambition to be a dancer.*

predict
*As Mum's teachers had all **predicted**, she did very well in her exams.*

expect (2) VERB

If you **expect** something, you believe that you ought to get or have it.

bank on
*"I was **banking on** you to remind me to do my homework," complained my sister.*

count on
*The injured climber was **counting on** his friend to get help.*

rely on
*"Can I **rely on** you to feed the dogs?" my brother asked, staring at me hard.*

expedition NOUN

An **expedition** is an organised journey made for a special purpose, often to explore.

mission
*Perhaps the most dangerous space **mission** will be to land on an outer planet of the galaxy.*

trek
*Shackleton's men were faced with an exhausting **trek** to the whaling station.*

expensive ADJECTIVE

If something is **expensive**, it costs a lot of money.

costly
*"Jewels that are **costly** are only for the rich," I agreed.*

exorbitant
*"But that's **exorbitant**!" my father burst out. "We can't afford that!"*

overpriced
*"It's my view that perfumes are grossly **overpriced**," said my grandmother.*

ANTONYMS: inexpensive, cheap

experience (1) NOUN

Experience is knowledge or skill in a particular job or activity, which you have gained from doing that job or activity.

expertise
*The expedition leader's medical **expertise** made the difference between life and death.*

know-how (*informal*)
*It was good of Mrs Flaherty to share her **know-how** with me.*

knowledge
*I was amazed by Gran's wide **knowledge** of computers.*

practice
*The old gardener had had many years' **practice** at growing plants from cuttings.*

understanding
*Gus's **understanding** of the area was useful on our treasure hunt.*

experience (2) NOUN

An **experience** is something that you do or something that happens to you, especially something new or unusual.

adventure
*For many children, a train trip is a real **adventure**.*

incident
*"I'll never forget the **incident** when your grandma lost her passport!" Grandpa told me.*

ordeal
*The hostage's **ordeal** was one that she never wanted to experience again.*

experienced ADJECTIVE

An **experienced** person has been doing a particular job or activity for a long time, and knows a lot about it.

accomplished
*My dad, an **accomplished** pianist, plays the organ in church.*

expert
*D'Artagnan was an **expert** swordsman and a reasonable shot with a pistol.*

practised
*The con man was a **practised** liar.*

skilful
*Already a **skilful** ice skater, Philip took to skiing like a veteran.*

ANTONYMS: inexperienced, novice

expert (1) NOUN

An **expert** is a person who is very skilled at something, or who knows a lot about a particular subject.

authority
*My dad is an **authority** on mice, and gives lectures on them.*

professional
*We saw our neighbour, a **professional** pianist, playing on TV the other day.*

specialist
*As the mechanic is a **specialist** in old cars, Grandad took his sports car to him.*

wizard (*informal*)
*One of my brothers is a computer **wizard**.*

expert (2) ADJECTIVE

If someone is **expert** at something, they are very skilled at it, or know a lot about it.

experienced
*My gran is an **experienced** cook who makes brilliant chocolate cake.*

knowledgeable
*Our teacher, Mrs Crowther, is very **knowledgeable** about local history.*

proficient
*Mrs Fiddis, our French teacher, is **proficient** in several languages.*

skilled
*The **skilled** photographer took some great photographs of the wedding.*

explain VERB

If you **explain** something, you give information about it or reasons for it so that it can be understood.

clarify
*I asked Mr Ledbetter to **clarify** what he meant by the word "hypothetical".*

give an explanation of
*"Now, Sian," Miss Cooke said, "**give** us **an explanation of** the water cycle."*

interpret
*"Can you **interpret** these instructions for me?" Dad asked Mum.*

make clear
*The instructions in the recipe book did not **make clear** what I should do next.*

→ *See* **describe**

explanation (1) NOUN

An **explanation** is something that helps people understand something.

clarification
*The minister requested **clarification** about certain parts of the proposed treaty.*

interpretation
*They put forward their own **interpretation** of the facts.*

a b c d e f g h i j k l m n o p q r s t u v w x y z

A
B
C
D
E
F
G
H
I
J
K
L
M
N
O
P
Q
R
S
T
U
V
W
X
Y
Z

explanation (2) NOUN

An **explanation** is something that explains why something happens.

excuse
*There was no **excuse** for the new system of parking machines being worse than the old.*

reason
*Robert's **reason** for being late was that the alarm didn't wake him up.*

explore VERB

If you **explore** a place, you travel around it to discover what it is like.

reconnoitre
*The captain sent two men to **reconnoitre** the machine-gun post.*

scout
*Graham **scouted** ahead to make sure no one was around, before he and Carl crept out.*

search
*"We **searched**, sir, but there's no sign of the enemy," Trooper Smith said.*

survey
*My brother and I **surveyed** the holiday camp eagerly.*

take a look around (*informal*)
*Tamara and Craig **took a look around** the garden of their new house.*

explosion NOUN

An **explosion** is a sudden violent burst of energy, for example one caused by a bomb.

blast
*The **blast** from the quarry echoed round the surrounding hillside.*

detonation
*When a car engine runs, a repeating series of small **detonations** takes place.*

expression NOUN

Your **expression** is the look on your face that shows what you are thinking or feeling.

a happy expresssion:

beam
*The hotel owner greeted us with a friendly **beam**.*

grin
*Her face broke into a broad **grin**.*

smile
*She gave the teacher a **smile**, then turned away.*

smirk
*He always had a sly look or a satisfied **smirk** on his face.*

a pained expresssion:

wince
*Gran pulled herself out of bed with a **wince**.*

a menacing expresssion:

glower
*My brother shot me a **glower** when I told mum what he'd done.*

leer
*The scarecrow had tiny eyes with a sinister **leer**.*

scowl
*From the angry **scowl** on her face, I knew she was not happy with me.*

sneer
*"Now, listen to me," he said, with an unpleasant **sneer**.*

a serious expresssion:

frown
*Sarah, a **frown** of concentration on her face, studied her maths book.*

grimace
*When he remembered the test, a **grimace** crossed his face.*

poker-face
*Rohan kept a **poker-face**, but was obviously hiding his delight.*

pout
*My cousin sighed and stuck his lower lip out in a **pout**.*

extra ADJECTIVE

You use **extra** to mean more than is usual, necessary or expected.

additional
*"I'll need **additional** time for this job," the writer said wearily.*

further
*The refugees received **further** aid in the form of tents and cooking equipment.*

supplementary
*Some people believe in taking **supplementary** vitamins, besides their normal diet.*

→ *See* **spare**

extraordinary ADJECTIVE

Someone or something that is **extraordinary** is very unusual or surprising.

amazing
*A volcano erupting is an **amazing** sight.*

remarkable
*"What a **remarkable** coincidence," exclaimed the old lady. "That's my name too!"*

surprising
*I found it **surprising** that no one besides me had heard of the explorer.*

unheard-of
*Everybody gasped. It was **unheard-of** for Martin to say more than a single word!*

unique
*The beautiful antique vase was **unique**.*

unusual
*It was **unusual** for my sister to wash up, but there she was at the sink!*

ANTONYM: ordinary

Ff

fabulous ADJECTIVE

Someone or something **fabulous** is wonderful or very impressive.

astounding
*The new drug for asthma sufferers achieved **astounding** results.*

marvellous
*"It's **marvellous** news that Colin is going on the school skiing trip!" Mrs Finch exclaimed.*

phenomenal
*To score that many home runs was a **phenomenal** achievement.*

superb
*The weather was **superb** and the picnic was quite delicious.*

wonderful
*We had a **wonderful** holiday in Cyprus.*

face NOUN

Your **face** is the front part of your head, from your chin to your forehead.

countenance
*Scrooge's **countenance** betrayed no emotion.*

features
*The film star's rugged **features** appeared in magazines throughout the world.*

fact NOUN

If something is a matter of **fact**, it is true.

certainty
*"Looking at this traffic jam, it is a **certainty** that we will miss the train," said Dad.*

reality
*Callum dreamt of being a superhero, although in **reality** he was just an everyday boy.*

truth
*The **truth** was that the climber was in danger.*

A
B
C
D
E
F
G
H
I
J
K
L
M
N
O
P
Q
R
S
T
U
V
W
X
Y
Z

fade VERB

If something such as light, colour or sound **fades**, it becomes less strong.

bleach
*"Be careful drying your jeans outside," said Granny. "The sun might **bleach** them."*

die away
*The sound of clapping **died away**.*

grow dim
*The light in the room **grew dim**.*

vanish
*The buzzing noise **vanished** as soon as we stepped outside.*

fail VERB

If someone or something **fails**, they do not succeed.

be unsuccessful
*At their first attempt to launch, the balloonists **were unsuccessful**.*

come to grief
*The sailing ship Hesperus **came to grief** on the rocks at Norman's Woe.*

fall through
*Our plans for a new hall **fell through** owing to lack of money.*

flop (*informal*)
*The Broadway show **flopped**, closing after only three nights.*

ANTONYM: succeed

failure NOUN

A **failure** is a lack of success in doing something.

breakdown
*There was a **breakdown** in communications between us, and Finn didn't turn up.*

defeat
*The Blues suffered a bad **defeat** to the Reds.*

disaster
*Our caravan holiday was a total **disaster**. Just about everything went wrong!*

lack of success
*My brother's **lack of success** in finding a job could be because he's very lazy.*

washout (*informal*)
*Sadly, because of the awful weather, the country show was a **washout**.*

ANTONYM: success

faint (1) ADJECTIVE

A **faint** sound is not loud and cannot be heard easily.

distant
*To her delight, Anastasia heard the **distant** tinkle of sleigh bells.*

dull
*There was a **dull** thud from upstairs. My sister had fallen out of bed.*

indistinct
*Throughout the wood was the **indistinct** murmur of a thousand animal voices.*

muffled
*From within the mine came a **muffled** cry.*

ANTONYM: loud

faint (2) ADJECTIVE

A **faint** light or colour is not strong or intense.

dim
*In the **dim** light of the evening, it was difficult to find the path off the hill.*

hazy
*A **hazy** sun shone through the skeletal branches of the trees.*

pale
*From the moorland cottage, the **pale** glow of a lamp shone into the night.*

subdued
*The lighting in the restaurant was **subdued**.*

ANTONYM: strong

faint (3) ADJECTIVE

If you feel **faint**, you feel dizzy and unsteady.

dizzy
*Gran felt **dizzy** and had to sit down.*

giddy
*Emily was almost **giddy** with excitement. A new pony!*

light-headed
*After hours writing sentences on the computer, John felt quite **light-headed**.*

unsteady
*The old man, a little **unsteady** at first, stood up and brushed the crumbs off his suit.*

→ *See* **weak (1)**

fair ADJECTIVE

Something that is **fair** seems reasonable to most people.

impartial
*It's important that umpires are **impartial**.*

just
*The judge's verdict was a **just** one, although the prisoner didn't see it that way.*

right
*Ami felt it only **right** that she should be paid for the hard work she did.*

unbiased
*We asked an outsider to give us her **unbiased** opinion on the argument.*

ANTONYM: unfair

fairly ADVERB

Fairly can mean quite or rather.

moderately
*Mum was **moderately** pleased with her painting, but felt she could do better.*

quite
*Marcel was **quite** happy to watch the game, rather than join in.*

rather
***Rather** worried by the black clouds, Dad brought the washing in.*

reasonably
*We were **reasonably** sure that this was the place we'd started from.*

somewhat
*"I was **somewhat** surprised, Potter," the principal said, "to find you missing."*

faithful ADJECTIVE

If you are **faithful** to someone or something, you are loyal and continue to support them.

dependable
*The **dependable** farm horse would plod up and down all day long.*

devoted
*The card with the flowers read, "To a **devoted** wife and mother".*

loyal
*Despite his low wages, the servant stayed **loyal** to his employers.*

staunch
*My pal Sanjay is a **staunch** City supporter.*

ANTONYM: unfaithful

fake (1) NOUN

A **fake** is an imitation of something, made to trick people into thinking that it is genuine.

copy
*The painting was clearly not an original, but merely a poor **copy**.*

forgery
*I handed over the banknote, not realising it was a **forgery**.*

imitation
*The diamonds were only **imitations**, but they fooled the thief.*

reproduction
*The gallery displayed a **reproduction** of the painting because the original was damaged.*

fake (2) ADJECTIVE

Something that is **fake** is an imitation and not genuine.

artificial
*There were **artificial** flowers in all the vases at the restaurant.*

bogus
*Beware of **bogus** callers who pretend to be from the electricity company.*

counterfeit
*The shop assistant accidentally accepted a **counterfeit** note from the forger.*

false
*The spy had a **false** passport to travel with.*

forged
*The cashier immediately spotted the **forged** signature on the cheque.*

imitation
*The wallpaper had an **imitation** brick design.*

phoney *(informal)*
*The count didn't fool anybody with his **phoney** French accent.*

ANTONYM: genuine

fake (3) VERB

If you **fake** a feeling, you pretend that you are experiencing it.

feign
*Avinash **feigned** happiness at being given socks as a gift.*

pretend
*I thought at first that my brother was angry, but he was only **pretending**.*

simulate
*To help the first-aiders practise for their test, some people **simulated** being ill.*

LANGUAGE TIP
A person who fakes the identity of another person is an **impostor**.

A B C D E F G H I J K L M N O P Q R S T U V W X Y Z

fall (1) VERB

When someone or something **falls**, or **falls over**, or **falls down**, they drop towards the ground.

collapse
*Exhausted, Della **collapsed** into a chair.*

keel over
*Several soldiers in the parade **keeled over** in the sweltering heat.*

topple
*As the angry crowd pulled and pushed, the dictator's statue **toppled** to the ground.*

tumble
*The toddler **tumbled** awkwardly, but soon picked herself up.*

> **Try these lively words and phrases:**
>
> **come a cropper**
> *He almost **came a cropper** tripping over Tom, who was sitting on the floor.*
>
> **drop like a stone**
> *The bag **dropped like a stone** into the depths of the river.*

fall (2) VERB

If something **falls**, it becomes less or lower.

decrease
*The number of people unemployed **decreased** this year.*

drop
*The cost of foreign holidays has **dropped** over the past five years.*

plummet
*The temperature could **plummet** to below freezing.*

tumble
*House prices **tumbled** last year.*

ANTONYM: rise

fall (3) NOUN

If there is a **fall** in the amount of something, it gets smaller.

decrease
*Bosses say that a **decrease** in orders is going to lead to a loss of jobs.*

reduction
*All over the store there was a 20 per cent **reduction** of prices.*

ANTONYM: rise

fall out VERB

If you **fall out** with someone, you disagree and quarrel with them.

quarrel
*Marsha and I **quarrelled** because she wouldn't let me have my turn.*

squabble
*I could hear my sister and brother **squabbling** over a game.*

false (1) ADJECTIVE

Something that is **false** is not real or genuine, but intended to seem real.

artificial
*Douglas Bader, a famous World War II pilot, had **artificial** legs and still managed to fly.*

bogus
*The couple put in a **bogus** claim to the insurance company.*

fake
*The **fake** painting fooled most people.*

forged
*Customs officers took one look at the **forged** passport and arrested its owner.*

false (2) ADJECTIVE

If something you say is **false**, it is untrue or incorrect.

deceptive
*The politician's answer was **deceptive**, as it only told half the truth.*

fictitious
*Sherlock Holmes's **fictitious** address was 221b Baker Street, London.*

untrue
*"It's quite **untrue** to say that money brings happiness," sighed the miserable millionaire.*

wrong
*Carruthers had the **wrong** idea, and was wasting his time.*

ANTONYM: true

famous ADJECTIVE

Someone or something **famous** is very well-known.

acclaimed
*Roald Dahl was the **acclaimed** author of many popular children's books.*

celebrated
*The programme was presented by a **celebrated** Italian chef.*

renowned
*Luigi's restaurant was **renowned** for its pasta.*

well-known
*My mum is **well-known** for her paintings.*

ANTONYM: unknown

LANGUAGE TIP
A person who is well-known for being bad or evil is **infamous**.

fan NOUN

If you are a **fan** of something or someone famous, you like them very much.

enthusiast
*My Grandad, being an ex-railwayman, was a great rail **enthusiast**.*

fiend (*informal*)
*Omar is a real go-kart **fiend**. He may well become a champion some day.*

supporter
*After the match, the team jogged round the pitch, waving to their **supporters**.*

fancy ADJECTIVE

Something that is **fancy** is highly decorated and special.

decorative
*Fiona added **decorative** sequins to her dress.*

elaborate
*The cathedral had **elaborate** carved wood choir stalls.*

ornate
*Around the ancient manor stretched **ornate** gardens with fountains.*

ANTONYM: plain

fantastic ADJECTIVE

Something **fantastic** is wonderful and very pleasing.

excellent
*At the zoo, you have an **excellent** underwater view of penguins swimming.*

out of this world (*informal*)
*The dress the film star wore to the premiere was **out of this world**.*

sensational
*Mum's chocolate cakes are always **sensational**.*

superb
*It was a **superb** day out: great weather and a beautiful beach.*

far (1) ADVERB

Far can mean a long distance away.

a great distance
*The sisters travelled **a great distance** from their homeland to help others.*

a long way
*We had to travel **a long way** before we found somewhere to spend the night.*

miles
*"You don't want to cycle there, it's **miles** away!" my friend scoffed.*

ANTONYMS: near, close

far (2) ADVERB

You can use **far** to mean very much or to a great extent.

considerably
*The trip cost **considerably** more than Dad had anticipated.*

decidedly
*Mum's cooking is **decidedly** more tasty than school dinners.*

much
*Mrs Cornelius said my handwriting was **much** neater than it was last year.*

far (3) ADJECTIVE

A **far** place is one that is very distant, or the more distant of two things.

distant
*Across the meadows, a **distant** bell tolled.*

faraway
*Isla dreamed of lying on a **faraway** beach by a clear turquoise sea.*

far-flung
*Dad's job took him to **far-flung** places.*

remote
*The **remote** villages of the rainforest are hundreds of miles from the nearest town.*

ANTONYMS: near, close

farm NOUN

A **farm** is an area of land and buildings used for growing crops or raising animals.

LANGUAGE TIP
Agriculture is a formal word for farming. A person who runs a farm is called a **farmer**.

fashion NOUN

A **fashion** is a style of dress or way of behaving that is popular at a particular time.

craze
*There seems to be a new **craze** for toys based on television characters.*

fad
*Dad's latest **fad** was for pasta dishes. Pasta was all we got for a month!*

style
*My sister's jeans were the latest **style**.*

trend
*Gran says she can't keep up with all the new **trends**.*

fast (1) ADJECTIVE

If something is **fast**, it is quick.

breakneck
*At **breakneck** speed, the ski jumper hurtled down the launch ramp.*

rapid
*With **rapid** thrusts of his sword, Athos tore his opponent's coat to ribbons.*

speedy
*After I'd finished my homework, I made a **speedy** exit and headed for the playground.*

swift
*With a few **swift** strokes of his brush, the artist had painted a beautiful yet simple picture.*

ANTONYM: slow

LANGUAGE TIP

Something that goes faster than the speed of sound is **supersonic**.

---

fast (2) ADVERB

Something that moves **fast**, moves quickly or with great speed.

quickly
*"If you don't come **quickly** we'll miss the bus," my sister shouted up the stairs.*

rapidly
*The magician **rapidly** slipped out of the handcuffs and dropped through the trapdoor.*

speedily
*Max **speedily** popped the sweet into his mouth before anyone could see.*

swiftly
*The stuntman rode **swiftly** towards the burning lorry.*

Try these lively words and phrases:

in a flash (*informal*)
*The rocket took off and, **in a flash**, was roaring away into the blue, many miles up.*

like a shot (*informal*)
***Like a shot**, the greyhounds were off round the track.*

quick as lightning
***Quick as lightning**, Magda caught the ball as it flew towards her.*

ANTONYM: slowly

fasten VERB

If you **fasten** something, you close it or attach it firmly to something else.

attach
*"Make sure you **attach** the label firmly to your luggage," advised Mum.*

connect
*To restore the power, the electrician had to **connect** the two cables.*

fix
*Dad **fixed** the shelf to the wall.*

join
*The two tins are **joined** by a long piece of string.*

fasten a door closed:

bolt
*Dancer's groom **bolted** the stable door and said goodnight to her horse.*

lock
*Make sure you **lock** the door when you leave.*

padlock
*As his tractor was in the field, Farmer Palfrey **padlocked** the gate.*

secure
*It's wise to **secure** all doors and windows before going away.*

fasten two surfaces together:

nail
*It was John's foolish idea to **nail** shut the door of the grandfather clock.*

screw
*The picture was firmly **screwed** to the wall.*

fasten metal together:

rivet
*The hulls of ships are made by **riveting** plates of steel together.*

solder
*Using a soldering iron, Don **soldered** the wires to their terminals.*

weld
*The process of **welding** melts and blends the edges of metal surfaces.*

fasten clothes or fabric:

button
*"**Button** your shirt," Mum suggested. "You don't want to look scruffy."*

tie
*"**Tie** your shoelaces before you trip up!" Mrs Akhbar said.*

zip
*The front of the tent **zipped** up to keep out the wind and rain.*

fasten paper:

clip
*The papers were **clipped** together in the correct order.*

pin
*Several notices had been **pinned** on the board.*

staple
*Miss Jeffers **staples** our best work onto a display board.*

fasten shoes:

buckle
*Gulliver **buckled** his shoes and crept away.*

lace
*The game stopped while a player **laced** his boots which had come undone.*

ANTONYM: unfasten

fat ADJECTIVE

Someone or something that is **fat** has a lot of flesh on their body.

chubby
*The pop star had become quite **chubby** since he stopped doing live shows.*

overweight
***Overweight** and unfit, the jockey knew he had work to do in the gym.*

plump
*Gran got quite thin when she was ill, but now she's pleasantly **plump** again.*

podgy
*"If you eat too much pudding, you'll get **podgy**!" my horrible brother called out.*

rotund
*A **rotund**, smiling, red-faced gentleman appeared.*

stout
*He was a tall, **stout** man with grey hair.*

ANTONYMS: slim, thin

fault NOUN

A **fault** is a mistake or something wrong with the way something is made.

defect
*A **defect** in the aerial cable meant that our television picture was fuzzy.*

flaw
*The crash was ultimately caused by a slight **flaw** in the metal of the wing.*

glitch (*informal*)
*A mystery **glitch** in the signalling system delayed several trains.*

problem
*Our boiler had a **problem**, so Mum sent for the engineer.*

favourite ADJECTIVE

Your **favourite** person or thing is the one you like best.

best-loved
*Gran had a CD called "Your Hundred **Best-Loved** Tunes". They certainly weren't my favourite tunes!*

favoured
*The big-headed prince was clearly the king's **favoured** son.*

preferred
*When you vote, you put a cross against your **preferred** candidate.*

fear NOUN

Fear is the feeling of worry you have when you think you are in danger or that something bad might happen.

alarm
*As the tide started to come in, Caitlin was filled with **alarm**.*

dread
*My sister has a **dread** of spiders.*

panic
*As the alarm sounded, the crowd began to flee in **panic**.*

terror
***Terror** was written all over the faces of the hostages.*

LANGUAGE TIP
A fear of a specific thing is a **phobia**.

A fear of...
enclosed spaces is called **claustrophobia**.
ghosts is called **phasmophobia**.
going out is called **agoraphobia**.
spiders is called **arachnophobia**.
thunder is called **brontophobia**.
water is called **hydrophobia**.

feel (1) VERB

If you **feel** something, you touch it.

feel with your hands:

finger
*In the dark, I **fingered** the light switch and finally switched it on.*

handle
*Kevin doesn't like buying vegetables that have been **handled** by others.*

touch
*"If you **touch** that paint, you're in trouble," Dad warned.*

feel in a loving way:

caress
*The mother **caressed** her newborn baby.*

fondle
*Tyrone made me laugh, the way he kept **fondling** his new watch.*

stroke
*Wuffles enjoys being **stroked**, especially on his tummy.*

feel roughly:

maul
*One man picked up a cabbage to inspect it and, having **mauled** it, put it back.*

paw
*I reckon that girl **pawed** every sweet in the pick 'n' mix.*

feel your way around in the dark:

fumble
*Mum **fumbled** for her car keys in her bag.*

grope
*Through the smoke, Rajesh managed to **grope** his way to the door.*

feel (2) VERB

If you **feel** an emotion or sensation, you experience it.

feel pain or pleasure:

experience
*After his accident, Dad **experienced** headaches for several weeks.*

have a sensation of
*When you get an electric shock, you **have a sensation of** lightning going through you.*

feel or be aware:

be aware
*In the dark, I **was aware** that something hairy was in the room.*

feel in your bones
*A storm was brewing – I could **feel it in my bones**.*

have a hunch
*I **had a hunch** that it was you on the phone!*

sense
***Sensing** she was cold, I gave her my jacket.*

suspect
*I would never have **suspected** that a dog could be so frightening.*

feeling (1) NOUN

If you have a **feeling** about something, you have thoughts about it without being certain.

idea
*Going shopping was Indira's **idea**.*

suspicion
*Emilia had a **suspicion** that the man loitering outside the shop was a thief.*

feeling (2) NOUN

A **feeling** is an emotion.

emotion
*Strong **emotions** were expressed by several people at the meeting.*

passion
*Mrs Kalim had a real **passion** for games, especially tennis.*

LANGUAGE TIP
A feeling of liking someone is **affection** or **fondness**. A feeling of worry is **anxiety** or **concern**.

fetch VERB

If you **fetch** something, you go to where it is and bring it back.

collect
*Mum sent me to **collect** a parcel that had been delivered next door.*

retrieve
*The dog is brilliant at **retrieving** a ball when you throw it for her.*

A B C D E F G H I J K L M N O P Q R S T U V W X Y Z

transport
*Dad was asked to **transport** some furniture for a school disco.*

few ADJECTIVE
Few can mean not many or a small number of things.

hardly any
***Hardly any** people returned the questionnaire I sent out.*

infrequent
*Ships made only **infrequent** visits to the remote Pacific islands.*

rare
*Visits to the studio were **rare**, and Monica jumped at the chance.*

ANTONYM: many

fiddle (1) VERB
If you **fiddle** with something, you keep touching it and playing with it in a restless way.

fidget
*"Stop **fidgeting** with your pencil!" Mrs O'Keefe ordered Christopher.*

twiddle
*Even after I had **twiddled** with all the knobs, the radio sounded no better, so then I fiddled with the aerial.*

fiddle (2) VERB (*informal*)
To **fiddle** can mean to swindle, or change something dishonestly for your own profit.

cheat
*The con man **cheated** an old couple out of their life savings.*

swindle
*A shop assistant was sacked for trying to **swindle** his employers.*

fidget VERB
If you **fidget**, you keep changing your position or making small restless movements because you are nervous or bored.

squirm
*Angela **squirmed** in her seat as she waited to go into the dentist's surgery.*

twitch
*Miss Westwood told Craig to stop **twitching** or go outside.*

wriggle
*Mum told me to stop **wriggling**, but speech day was lasting ages!*

field NOUN
A **field** is an area of land where crops are grown or animals are kept.

meadow
*Across the **meadows** lay the village and, beyond that, the sea.*

paddock
*The racehorses were kept in several large, fenced **paddocks**.*

pasture
*The land by the river was perfect **pasture** for cattle and sheep.*

LANGUAGE TIP
A general word for fields is **grassland**.

fierce (1) ADJECTIVE
A person or animal who is **fierce** is very aggressive.

dangerous
*Although the dog looked **dangerous**, it was really a big softy.*

ferocious
*The **ferocious** tiger sprang from the branch onto the antelope.*

savage
*Many dogs are only **savage** because they have been mistreated.*

fierce (2) ADJECTIVE
Someone or something that is **fierce** is very intense.

keen
*"There is always **keen** competition between these two athletes," said the commentator.*

relentless
*Rescue workers battled against **relentless** rain and strong gusts of wind.*

strong
*I've always had a **strong** dislike of any food with mushrooms in.*

fight (1) VERB
When people **fight**, they take part in a battle, a boxing match, or in some other attempt to hurt or kill someone.

battle
*In Roman times, gladiators **battled** with each other to entertain the crowds.*

come to blows
*The two women **came to blows** over a purse.*

exchange blows
*When Mr Rae arrived on the scene, the two boys were **exchanging blows**.*

scrap (*informal*)
*"I will not have anyone **scrapping** in this school," the head teacher thundered.*

struggle
*Pete and I **struggled** for a minute or two, then started laughing.*

wrestle
*The two athletes **wrestling** in the ring were both talented, but only one could win.*

fight (2) NOUN

A **fight** is a situation in which people hit or try to hurt each other.

battle
*The famous **battle** was fought not at Hastings, but several miles away.*

brawl
*When Lee insulted Jesse, a **brawl** began.*

combat
*Half of the aircraft are ready for immediate **combat**.*

conflict
*The **conflict** was ended by lack of food, diseases and bitter cold.*

scuffle
*Several protestors were involved in a **scuffle** outside Parliament.*

skirmish
*Two platoons met in a **skirmish** on the edge of the woods.*

tussle
*In summer, we have **tussles** on the grass.*

war
*The American Civil **War** lasted four years.*

warfare
*There was open **warfare** on the streets.*

> **A fight between...**
> two groups is a **feud**.
> two people with pistols or swords is a **duel**.
> two boxers or wrestlers is a **bout** or **contest**.

fill VERB

If you **fill** something, or if it **fills** up, it becomes full.

load
*We all helped **load** the car, then set off on our summer holidays.*

pack
*My brother foolishly **packed** his rucksack with his phone right at the bottom.*

replenish
*Mum sent me to **replenish** the water barrel at the campsite tap.*

stuff
*I **stuffed** my suitcase with presents for everyone back home.*

top up
*"Please would you **top up** my radiator water?" Dad asked the mechanic.*

fill in (1) VERB

If you **fill in** a form, you write information in the spaces on it.

complete
*Please **complete** the slip below and send it to us at this address.*

fill out
*I **filled out** the internet questionnaire, but the wretched thing wouldn't upload to the website.*

fill in (2) VERB

If you **fill in** for somebody, you take their place temporarily.

deputise
*I usually sort out the PE equipment. My assistant **deputises** for me if I am away.*

replace
*As Mrs Kirkpatrick was off sick, another teacher **replaced** her.*

stand in
*Mum sometimes **stands in** for her friend who drives people to hospital.*

substitute
*I had to **substitute** the team captain when she was poorly.*

find VERB

If you **find** someone or something, you see them or discover where they are.

come across
*In the loft we **came across** an old painting.*

discover
*I **discovered** my old diary under my bed.*

stumble upon
*Dad **stumbled upon** his old record collection.*

track down
*The police promised to **track down** whoever had left the box there.*

unearth
*After interviewing the criminal, the police **unearthed** the truth about the robbery.*

find out VERB

If you **find out** something, you learn or discover it.

become aware
*As I gazed at the stars, I **became aware** that one of them was moving.*

discover
*After a long search, Paula **discovered** where she had left her wallet.*

realise
*We were so busy we didn't **realise** the time.*

fine (1) ADJECTIVE

If something is **fine** it is satisfactory or suitable.

acceptable
*"Your homework is **acceptable**," Mr Hill said.*

satisfactory
*The fit of the shoes was **satisfactory**, so Mum bought them.*

suitable
*"Come round this afternoon, if that's **suitable**," Indira said.*

ANTONYMS: unsatisfactory, unacceptable

fine (2) ADJECTIVE

Fine material is thin and delicate.

delicate
*The bride's veil was made of a **delicate** gauze.*

flimsy
*The **flimsy** fishing line snapped.*

light
*In summer, people tend to wear **light** clothing.*

ANTONYMS: thick, heavy

LANGUAGE TIP
Fine sand or powder is made up of very small particles.

finish (1) VERB

When you **finish** something, you do the last part of it and complete it.

bring to a close
*A sudden thunderstorm **brought** the fête **to a close** rather early.*

complete
*Both my parents **completed** the marathon.*

ANTONYMS: begin, start

finish (2) NOUN

The **finish** of something is the last part of it.

completion
*The **completion** of the tunnel was delayed because of flooding.*

end
*A fight on stage meant the **end** for the band.*

termination
*The **termination** of the player's contract occurred last season.*

ANTONYMS: beginning, start

fire (1) NOUN

Fire is the flames produced when something burns.

blaze
*Firefighters put out the **blaze** in the heather.*

flames
*He dropped in on the ground and quickly stamped out the **flames**.*

inferno
*A helicopter airlifted them from the blazing **inferno**.*

on fire PHRASE

If something is **on fire**, it is burning.

ablaze
*By the time firefighters arrived, the house was **ablaze**.*

alight
*Although our campfire was **alight**, there was little heat coming from it.*

in flames
*After the air raid, the town was **in flames**.*

set on fire PHRASE

If something is **set on fire**, it starts burning.

ignite
*An accidental spark **ignited** the gunpowder.*

kindle
*We **kindle** our fire with rolled-up paper and small sticks.*

light
*Dad **lit** the firework and stood well back.*

set ablaze
*Sparks from the steam train **set ablaze** the dry summer grass.*

fire (2) VERB

If someone **fires** a gun, they shoot a bullet.

pull the trigger
*When the Ringo Kid made a move, the sheriff **pulled the trigger**.*

shoot
*The man accidentally **shot** himself in the foot while cleaning his gun.*

fire (3) VERB (*informal*)

If an employer **fires** someone, that person loses their job.

dismiss
*It was only a matter of time before the military commander was **dismissed**.*

sack
*It's unfair! Lily was **sacked** just because she overslept one day.*

> **Try these lively words and phrases:**
>
> **give someone their marching orders** (*informal*)
> *My brother's boss **gave him his marching orders** for being late too often.*
>
> **show someone the door** (*informal*)
> *The manager **showed Dad the door** when he asked for a pay rise.*

firm (1) ADJECTIVE

Something that is **firm** is fairly hard and does not move or change shape very much when it is pressed.

rigid
*"Make sure that tent pole is **rigid** before you crawl inside," said Dad.*

solid
*The plaster quickly set **solid** around Tristan's broken wrist.*

ANTONYM: soft

firm (2) ADJECTIVE

Something that is **firm** is fastened securely and is not movable.

fixed
*Once the concrete had set, the post was **fixed**.*

secure
*We thought the door was **secure**, but when he leant against it, it came off its hinges.*

stable
*Ships have special fixtures underwater to help keep them **stable** in rough weather.*

ANTONYMS: insecure, unsteady

firm (3) NOUN

A **firm** is a business that sells or produces something.

business
*Fujita's parents run an electronics **business**.*

company
*The **company** which Dad works for is building a new factory.*

first ADJECTIVE

The **first** of something happened, came or was done before all others.

earliest
*The **earliest** motorcars had to observe an eight miles per hour speed limit.*

oldest
*Remains of the **oldest** known humans are reputed to have been found in East Africa.*

original
*This picture is a print. The **original** painting hangs in a New York gallery.*

fit (1) VERB

If something **fits**, it is the right shape or size.

correspond
*One side of a reflection **corresponds** exactly with the other.*

match
*Leah **matched** the pegs with the holes.*

suit
*"Those jeans really **suit** you," my aunt said admiringly.*

fit (2) ADJECTIVE

Someone who is **fit** is healthy and physically strong.

healthy
*It is hard to stay **healthy** if you eat junk food.*

in good condition
*The player is **in good condition**.*

in good shape
*The boxer looked **in good shape** for his forthcoming title fight.*

ANTONYM: unfit

A B C D E F G H I J K L M N O P Q R S T U V W X Y Z

fit (3) ADJECTIVE

If you say someone or something is **fit** to do something, you mean they are suitable.

appropriate
*The mayor said my mum was a very **appropriate** person to be a councillor.*

suitable
*When Jade moved, her parents did not think her new school was **suitable**.*

worthy
*The mystery knight was a **worthy** opponent for Sir Bedivere.*

fix (1) VERB

If you **fix** something somewhere, you attach it there securely.

attach
*Mrs Archer **attached** an extra page to my school report.*

connect
*When the heating man **connected** the boiler to the gas pipes, it blew up.*

fasten
*Uncle Michael **fastened** the shelf to the living room wall.*

secure
*Gaby **secured** the mirror firmly above the hand basin with two strong nails.*

fix (2) VERB

If you **fix** something that is broken, you repair it.

mend
*Dad managed to **mend** the car without taking it to the garage.*

repair
*My grandad likes to **repair** things that are broken, rather than buy new ones.*

fizzy ADJECTIVE

A **fizzy** drink has a gas called carbon dioxide in it to make it bubbly.

bubbly
*Champagne is so **bubbly** it explodes out of the bottle if shaken up.*

effervescent
*The **effervescent** tablets fizzed as they dissolved in the water.*

foaming
*I watched in horror as my drink tipped over and lay **foaming** on my homework.*

frothy
*Carla put her straw through the **frothy** bit and sucked the milk shake beneath.*

sparkling
*I don't like **sparkling** water in bottles – it gives me hiccups.*

ANTONYMS: flat, still

flap VERB

Something that **flaps** moves quickly up and down or from side to side.

flail
*The sailor's arms **flailed** about helplessly as he tried to stay afloat.*

flutter
*In the marina, the sails on the boats **fluttered** in the sea breeze.*

wave
*The flags on the marquee **waved** in the gusty wind.*

flat ADJECTIVE

Something that is **flat** is level and smooth.

even
*For outdoor bowling, the grass needs to be **even** and well cut.*

horizontal
*Dad's wall looked vaguely **horizontal**, but his spirit level told a different story.*

level
*Despite the mountains around, the land in the valley was completely **level**.*

smooth
*Painters use sandpaper to make sure every coat of paint they put on is **smooth**.*

float VERB

Something that **floats** is supported by liquid or hangs in the air.

bob
*After the liner passed, the moored boats started **bobbing** up and down.*

drift
*The pilot of the rescue plane sighted a raft, **drifting** but empty.*

hover
*Dragonflies **hovered** above the pond.*

ANTONYM: sink

A B C D E F G H I J K L M N O P Q R S T U V W X Y Z

flood (1) VERB

If water **floods** an area that is usually dry, or if the area floods, it becomes covered with water.

inundate
When the bath upstairs overflowed, the ceiling came down and our kitchen was ***inundated****.*

submerge
The holed tanker was ***submerged*** *as the weight of water took it down.*

swamp
Massive waves ***swamped*** *the promenade.*

flood (2) NOUN

A **flood** of something is a large amount of it occurring suddenly.

deluge
A sudden ***deluge*** *of rain put a swift end to the school fête.*

torrent
The dam burst, and a ***torrent*** *of water swept down the narrow valley.*

flop VERB

If something or someone **flops**, they bend or fall loosely and heavily.

collapse
The runners ***collapsed*** *onto the grass at the end of the marathon.*

droop
Left unwatered, flowers will soon ***droop*** *in hot, dry weather.*

sag
The elderly peasant ***sagged*** *under the weight of his burden.*

slump
Disappointed with her game, the tennis player ***slumped*** *in a corner of the dressing room.*

flow (1) VERB

If something **flows** somewhere, it moves there in a steady and continuous manner.

pour
Water ***poured*** *over the waterfall into the pool.*

ripple
The ***rippling*** *stream sparkled in the sunshine.*

stream
Tears of relief ***streamed*** *down my dad's face, as he saw Mum was safe.*

surge
The torrent ***surged*** *down the hillside, taking boulders with it.*

sweep
As the river broke its banks, water ***swept*** *into nearby streets.*

flow (2) NOUN

A **flow** of something is a steady, continuous movement of it.

current
A ***current*** *of water flowed round the rocks.*

stream
The northern lights are caused by a ***stream*** *of electrical particles from the sun.*

tide
A ***tide*** *of people made its way to the stadium.*

fluffy ADJECTIVE

Something that is **fluffy** is very soft and light.

feathery
Snow fell in ***feathery*** *flakes, white against the dark sky.*

furry
Jamilla gently stroked the kitten's ***furry*** *black coat.*

light
Her angora jumper was wonderfully ***light*** *and warm.*

soft
The ***soft*** *white bread was still warm from the oven.*

fly VERB

When a bird, insect or aircraft **flies**, it moves through the air.

flit
In summer, bees ***flit*** *from flower to flower.*

glide
Against the sky, gannets ***glided*** *effortlessly, their wings hardly moving.*

soar
With a deafening roar, the plane ***soared*** *into the air.*

fog NOUN

Fog is a thick mist caused by tiny drops of water in the air.

mist
A cotton-wool ***mist*** *rolled in the valleys.*

murk
Through the ***murk****, the car headlights picked out a shadowy figure.*

fold VERB

If you **fold** something, you bend it so that one part lies over another.

bend
He wrote on the envelope, "Photographs. Please do not ***bend****."*

crease
The instructions told him to ***crease*** *along the dotted line.*

crumple
Ben ***crumpled*** *the note and put it away in his pocket.*

tuck
Mum showed me how to ***tuck*** *in the sheet.*

follow (1) VERB

If you **follow** someone or something, you move along behind them.

pursue
Pursued *by the hounds, the fox sought shelter in a barn.*

shadow
Unknown to the suspect, police were ***shadowing*** *her every move.*

stalk
Some celebrities are continually ***stalked*** *by newspaper photographers.*

tail
Looking in his mirror, the police officer saw a car ***tailing*** *him.*

track
Sniffer dogs ***tracked*** *the missing man to a hut in the woods.*

follow (2) VERB

If you **follow** instructions or advice, you do what you are told.

comply
If you don't ***comply*** *with the rules, you will be disqualified.*

conform
Pupils are expected to ***conform*** *to the rules about uniform.*

obey
The police officer signalled Mum to pull over, and she ***obeyed****.*

observe
In any country, it's important to ***observe*** *the code about driving behaviour.*

follow (3) VERB

If you **follow** an explanation or the plot of a story, you understand each stage of it.

grasp
Julian at last ***grasped*** *the plot of the film.*

understand
"Do you ***understand*** *what you have to do?" Mr Peabody enquired, scanning the room.*

fond ADJECTIVE

If someone treats you in a **fond** way, they show that they like you.

affectionate
Gran gave Mum an ***affectionate*** *hug.*

loving
The gravestone read, "In ***loving*** *memory of a dear father".*

tender
Most children are not keen on receiving ***tender*** *kisses from adoring aunties.*

food NOUN

Food is what people and other animals eat.

diet
It's important that your ***diet*** *includes fresh fruit and vegetables.*

nourishment
Babies need plenty of ***nourishment*** *to grow.*

nutrition
Good ***nutrition*** *is an important part of an athlete's performance.*

fool (1) VERB

If you **fool** someone, you deceive or trick them.

bamboozle (*informal*)
My pals ***bamboozled*** *me into believing their story about the aliens.*

deceive
We were all ***deceived*** *by Mike. He seemed so honest, yet he stole our money.*

hoodwink
The crooks were ***hoodwinked*** *into attending the party, which in fact was a trap.*

take in
"You really ***took*** *me* ***in*** *with that disguise!" Jessie gasped.*

trick
They ***tricked*** *me into phoning the zoo and asking for Mr C. Lyon.*

fool (2) NOUN

A **fool** is someone who is silly and is not sensible.

dimwit
What a ***dimwit****! I forgot my lunch money.*

A B C D E F G H I J K L M N O P Q R S T U V W X Y Z

idiot
*"What an **idiot**," the boss muttered, under his breath.*

foolish ADJECTIVE

A **foolish** idea is not sensible and shows poor judgment.

half-baked *(informal)*
*"Whose **half-baked** plan was this?" Aunt Vera demanded.*

hare-brained
*Building a canal on porous rock was a **hare-brained** scheme.*

ridiculous
*"What a **ridiculous** suggestion!" Dad laughed.*

silly
*It was a **silly** thing to say, and Keara was really upset.*

unwise
*Riding three on a bike was an extremely **unwise** idea.*

ANTONYM: sensible

foot NOUN

Your **foot** is the part of your body at the end of your leg.

The name for the foot of...

a bird is a **claw**.

a bird of prey, for example an eagle, is a **talon**.

a cat or dog is a **paw**.

a crab or lobster is a **claw**.

a horse, sheep or deer is a **hoof**.

a penguin is a **webbed foot**.

forbid VERB

If someone **forbids** you to do something, they order you not to do it.

ban
*Chewing gum had recently been **banned** at our school.*

outlaw
*Advertising cigarettes has been **outlawed** in some countries.*

prohibit
*From today, smoking is **prohibited** in all public areas.*

veto
*Dictators tend to **veto** anybody's decisions they do not like.*

ANTONYM: permit

force (1) VERB

If you **force** someone to do something, you make them do it.

compel
*All of my brother's classmates were **compelled** to do woodwork or metalwork.*

drive
*They are **driving** the engineering company into bankruptcy.*

order
*The sergeant **ordered** his troops to do another circuit of the parade ground.*

force (2) NOUN

Force can mean violence or great strength.

impact
*The **impact** of a meteorite is shown by the area of the crater.*

power
*All over the world, the **power** of water, wind and sun is being harnessed.*

strength
*He threw it forward with all his **strength**.*

forever ADVERB

Forever means eternally.

always
*I think I'll **always** like dogs.*

eternally
*The damsel vowed that she was **eternally** grateful to the knight who had saved her.*

forget VERB

If you **forget** something, you do not remember it.

omit
*I was so nervous that I **omitted** a whole section of the test!*

overlook
*Cassandra was so busy talking, she **overlooked** the time.*

LANGUAGE TIP
If you forget to do something, you can say that it **slipped your mind**.

forgive VERB

If you **forgive** someone who has done something wrong, you stop being angry with them.

excuse
*As Nori's tooth was so painful, we **excused** her for being rather snappy.*

pardon
*Hundreds of prisoners were **pardoned** and released.*

LANGUAGE TIP
A phrase for forgiving someone is to **let bygones be bygones**.

formal ADJECTIVE

Formal means official and correct.

correct
*The head teacher expects polite and **correct** behaviour.*

official
*The **official** results of the election were declared.*

precise
*The tourist spoke very **precise** English.*

smart
*My mum has to wear **smart** clothes to work.*

foul (1) ADJECTIVE

If something is **foul**, it is extremely unpleasant.

disgusting
*"What a **disgusting** mess!" was all Mum could say about my room.*

filthy
*Mice ran all over the place and every nook and cranny was **filthy**.*

offensive
*There was an **offensive** smell coming from the fields where the farmer had spread manure.*

repulsive
*"Don't be **repulsive**," my sister said. "It's rude to pick your nose."*

revolting
*The corned beef hash that Dad made when we were camping tasted **revolting**.*

unpleasant
*Clearing drains is one of life's more **unpleasant** experiences.*

foul (2) ADJECTIVE

Foul language is very unpleasant.

coarse
*Mrs Giles did not approve of old Mr Giles's **coarse** vocabulary.*

obscene
*The player was sent off for making an **obscene** gesture at the crowd.*

rude
*If you use **rude** language at school you will get into trouble.*

vulgar
*"Don't be so **vulgar**!" Mum said, after I had been rude to my sister.*

fragile ADJECTIVE

Something that is **fragile** is easily broken or damaged.

breakable
*The poisonous chemicals had been stored carelessly in **breakable** flasks.*

brittle
*As we grow older, our bones become more **brittle** and can break easily.*

delicate
*Flora was a **delicate** child who regularly had to go into hospital.*

flimsy
*The box was **flimsy**, and the groceries crashed to the ground.*

free (1) ADJECTIVE

If something is **free**, you can have it without paying for it.

complimentary
*Through Mum's work, we received **complimentary** tickets to the exhibition.*

free of charge
*My little brother, being under five, was allowed into the match **free of charge**.*

on the house
*"Drinks are **on the house**!" called the bar owner, having heard of his lottery win.*

free (2) ADJECTIVE

Someone who is **free** is no longer a prisoner.

at large
*The escaped prisoner was still **at large** after three days.*

liberated
*The dictator fled and the country was **liberated**.*

A B C D E F G H I J K L M N O P Q R S T U V W X Y Z

released
*The **released** hostages were taken to hospital.*

free (3) VERB

If you **free** someone or something that is trapped, you release them.

liberate
*In 1944, the Allies **liberated** France from enemy occupation.*

release
*"**Release** those number balls!" the lottery announcer cried excitedly.*

set free
*The hostages were **set free** in a daring rescue.*

turn loose
*Spring had come, and the cattle were **turned loose** in the fields.*

freezing ADJECTIVE

If someone or something is **freezing**, they are very cold indeed.

arctic
*The wind was almost **arctic**, and our breath froze in the air.*

biting
*A **biting** chill gnawed at Cratchit's bones as he worked in the gloom.*

bitter
***Bitter** February was followed by windy March.*

chilled to the bone
*After two hours in the carnival parade, Coco the clown was **chilled to the bone**.*

frozen
*The reporters were **frozen**, having waited for the star for three hours.*

icy
*On an **icy** bend, the car skidded off the road.*

perishing
*Despite it being summer, the weather on our holiday was **perishing**.*

ANTONYM: hot

fresh ADJECTIVE

If something feels **fresh**, it is clean, cool and refreshing.

bracing
*After lunch we needed a walk in the **bracing** sea air.*

clean
*Back home after camping, the best thing was to sleep in **clean** sheets.*

clear
*They breathed in the **clear** early morning air outside the cottage.*

pure
*We drank deeply of the **pure** water that bubbled up from the spring.*

friend NOUN

A **friend** is someone you know well and like, but who is not related to you.

buddy
*Padma and I have been **buddies** since we were at nursery school.*

mate
*Dominic and Hyram are best **mates**.*

pal
*My sister Sadie is a real **pal**.*

LANGUAGE TIP
An **acquaintance** is someone you know but who is not a full friend.

friendly ADJECTIVE

A **friendly** person is kind and pleasant to others.

amiable
*The woman gave me an **amiable** smile.*

amicable
*Dad came to an **amicable** agreement with our neighbour about sharing a lawn mower.*

good-natured
*Although Grandad is basically a **good-natured** soul, he gets angry about politics.*

kind
*Everyone was very **kind** to Marie on her first day at school.*

welcoming
*When the carol singers called on her, Mrs Moss was very **welcoming**.*

ANTONYM: unfriendly

fright NOUN

Fright is a sudden feeling of fear.

alarm
*The air-raid siren's eerie wailing filled householders with **alarm**.*

dismay
*To Sissy's utter **dismay**, the train pulled out of the station without her.*

horror
*The pilot was filled with **horror** when his plane began to judder and jolt.*

panic
__Panic__ set in, and people fled in all directions.

terror
You could see the __terror__ in the eyes of the people watching the scary movie.

frighten VERB

If something or someone **frightens** you, they make you afraid.

alarm
The barking dog __alarmed__ the kitten.

petrify
To say I was __petrified__ of the dark was an understatement.

scare
"You can't __scare__ me!" I called into the darkness, my knees knocking with fear.

terrify
Some people are simply __terrified__ of spiders.

terrorise
Until they were jailed, the three brothers had __terrorised__ their neighbourhood.

> **Try these lively words and phrases:**
>
> **make your blood run cold**
> *He could hear a sudden roaring and it __made his blood run cold__.*
>
> **make your flesh creep**
> *It __makes my flesh creep__ to think about spiders.*

frightened ADJECTIVE

Someone who is **frightened** thinks that something nasty might happen.

afraid
Who's __afraid__ of the big bad wolf?

alarmed
Ben was __alarmed__ when he heard something tapping at the window.

scared
Miss Muffet was __scared__ when a spider sat down beside her.

startled
The pony was __startled__ when a paper bag blew across its path.

terrified
One of the new ducklings is __terrified__ of water.

> **Try these lively words and phrases:**
>
> **numb with fear**
> *I was __numb with fear__ as we sped towards the traffic lights.*
>
> **scared to death**
> *Mum is __scared to death__ of heights.*

frightening ADJECTIVE

If something or someone is **frightening**, they make you afraid.

fearsome
The __fearsome__ monster roared ferociously.

hair-raising
That new theme-park ride is an absolutely __hair-raising__ experience.

menacing
The music stopped as the __menacing__ stranger thrust open the doors of the saloon.

terrifying
The car crash was a __terrifying__ ordeal.

front NOUN

The **front** is the part of something that is furthest forward.

head
Davina went straight to the __head__ of the queue.

lead
In the __lead__ was a runner from East Africa.

ANTONYM: rear

LANGUAGE TIP
The front end of a ship or boat is the **bow**. The front end of an ancient ship (e.g. a Viking longboat) is the **prow**.

full (1) ADJECTIVE

Something that is **full** contains as much as it is possible to hold.

brimming
I had left the tap on and the bath was __brimming__ when I got back.

chock-a-block
When we reached the cinema, the foyer was __chock-a-block__ with people.

crammed
The underground train was __crammed__ with people, like a tin of sardines.

loaded
__Loaded__ with presents, the sleigh absolutely refused to budge.

A B C D E F G H I J K L M N O P Q R S T U V W X Y Z

packed
*Our class newspaper was **packed** with useful information.*

ANTONYM: empty

full (2) ADJECTIVE

The **full** amount of something is the complete or whole amount.

complete
*In a three-CD package, the author read the **complete** novel, unabridged.*

comprehensive
*To view the **comprehensive** range of our products, go to our website.*

entire
*Mr Fox had spent his **entire** life living in the same cottage.*

whole
*Mandy told me the **whole** story.*

fun NOUN

Fun is a pleasant, enjoyable and light-hearted activity.

amusement
*I got stuck in the mud, which caused the others some **amusement**.*

enjoyment
*We all had terrific **enjoyment** out of our battered old-style surfboards.*

entertainment
*Listening to my uncle crack jokes was torture, not **entertainment**!*

pleasure
*It was with great **pleasure** that the soldier received his bravery award.*

make fun of PHRASE

If you **make fun of** someone or something, you tease them or make jokes about them.

mock
*At school, we secretly **mock** Mrs Caywood, imitating her warbly voice.*

poke fun at
*Bullies enjoy **poking fun at** weaker people.*

ridicule
*Jamal's sisters **ridiculed** him because of his new haircut.*

tease
*If you ignore people who **tease** you, they soon give up.*

funny (1) ADJECTIVE

Funny people or things cause amusement or laughter.

amusing
*Grandma read out an **amusing** article.*

comical
*Mr Mahler thought he was **comical**; we thought otherwise.*

hilarious
*For once my brother told a **hilarious** story.*

humorous
*Grandpa used to write **humorous** poems.*

witty
*Everyone laughed at my **witty** reply to Mrs Skinner's question – except Mrs Skinner.*

funny (2) ADJECTIVE

Funny people or things are strange or puzzling.

curious
*Holmes found it **curious** that the window was open when we arrived.*

mysterious
*We shadowed the **mysterious** stranger around the town.*

odd
*"That's **odd**," Will thought. "Lyra was here just a second ago."*

peculiar
*Mr Agnelli has a **peculiar** sense of humour.*

puzzling
*How **puzzling** to find a ship abandoned, with the crew's table set for a meal.*

weird
*It's **weird** to think how much change Gran must have seen in her lifetime.*

furious ADJECTIVE

Someone who is **furious** is extremely angry.

beside yourself
*The colonel was **beside himself** at the prospect of a ban on hunting.*

enraged
*The bull, **enraged**, charged across the field towards him.*

infuriated
*My big sister was **infuriated** that her boyfriend had forgotten her birthday.*

livid
*You could tell the shopkeeper was **livid** by the way her voice shook.*

up in arms
*The whole town was **up in arms** about the planned new superstore.*

fuss NOUN

A **fuss** is unnecessarily anxious or excited behaviour.

agitation
*The new rule caused **agitation** among the parents at the school gate.*

bother
*"What's all the **bother** about?" demanded Mrs Edwards sternly.*

commotion
*The escaped circus elephant caused something of a **commotion** in town.*

fussy ADJECTIVE

If you are **fussy**, you worry too much about unnecessary details.

choosy
*James is so **choosy**, he refuses to eat anything that has lumps in it.*

hard to please
*In the store, the loud tourist was proving **hard to please**.*

particular
*My sister is very **particular** about her food.*

future ADJECTIVE

Future things relate to or occur at a time after the present.

eventual
*The **eventual** outcome of global warming is still unknown.*

forthcoming
*There is a great spy film among the **forthcoming** cinema releases.*

impending
*My sister was rather worried about her **impending** operation.*

subsequent
*Stan scored three goals on his debut, but his **subsequent** appearances were disappointing.*

ANTONYMS: past, previous

Gg

gain (1) VERB

If you **gain** something, you get more of it, or get something you didn't have before.

achieve
*"Just what did you **achieve** by doing that?" Mum asked.*

acquire
*Amisha **acquired** an old velvet coat for her fancy-dress box.*

increase
*My bike **increased** in speed alarmingly down the steep hill.*

ANTONYM: lose

gain (2) NOUN

A **gain** is an increase or improvement in something.

growth
*There has been a **growth** in pupil numbers at our school.*

increase
*When a car accelerates, there's an **increase** in its speed.*

rise
*I'm hoping for a **rise** in my pocket money this year.*

ANTONYM: loss

gamble (1) VERB

If you **gamble**, you risk losing something in the hope of gaining an advantage.

bet
*The man foolishly **bet** all his money on a useless horse.*

risk
*Toby **risked** his life to save his sister.*

stick your neck out (*informal*)
*You may have to **stick your neck out** if you want to succeed.*

A B C D E F G H I J K L M N O P Q R S T U V W X Y Z

take a chance
*Dad **took a chance** when he started his own business.*

gamble (2) NOUN

A **gamble** is a risk.

chance
*The firefighter took a **chance** when he entered the burning house.*

risk
*That's a **risk** only a fool would take!*

game (1) NOUN

A **game** is an activity with a set of rules that is played by individuals or teams against each other.

competition
*A swimming **competition** was held for all children in the school.*

contest
*They had a **contest** to see who could run home the fastest.*

match
*I love playing in cricket **matches**.*

game (2) NOUN

A **game** is an activity that involves playing.

amusement
*Snowball fights are our main **amusement** in winter.*

pastime
*Jenny's favourite **pastime** was playing chess.*

sport
*Football is the most popular **sport** in many countries.*

gang NOUN

A **gang** is a group of people who join together for some purpose.

band
*A **band** of robbers attacked the stagecoach.*

crowd
*Wayne went round with a **crowd** that I didn't like much.*

group
*The pop star was mobbed by a **group** of screaming fans.*

gap NOUN

A **gap** is a space between two things or a hole in something solid.

break
*The sun shone through a **break** in the clouds.*

chink
*There was a tiny **chink** of light coming through the cell door.*

opening
*The miners saw an **opening** in the wall of the tunnel ahead of them.*

space
*Dad managed to find a **space** in which to park the car.*

gasp VERB

When you **gasp**, you take a short quick breath through your mouth.

breathe heavily
*When they reached the top of the hill, they were **breathing heavily**.*

choke
*The firefighters found a woman **choking** in the dense smoke.*

pant
*"Quick!" she **panted**. "I must have a drink of water."*

puff
*They **puffed** and groaned as they finished the race.*

wheeze
*Paul was **wheezing** and coughing because of his very bad cold.*

gate NOUN

A **gate** is a barrier which is used at the entrance to a garden or field.

barrier
*A **barrier** prevented cars from driving into the park.*

entrance
*Soldiers guarded the **entrance** to the palace.*

gateway
*The bride and groom paused at the **gateway** to the churchyard.*

gather (1) VERB

To **gather** is to bring things together in one place.

accumulate
*As it rolled down the hill, the snowball **accumulated** more and more snow.*

amass
*Over the years, Gran had **amassed** a huge pottery collection.*

collect
*The waiter went round **collecting** up the dirty dishes.*

hoard
*The miser **hoarded** gold coins.*

gather (2) VERB

When people **gather**, they come together in a group.

assemble
*When the fire alarm sounds, **assemble** in the playground.*

collect
*Protesters **collected** in the park before starting their march.*

come together
*Every Monday, the whole school **came together** for assembly.*

congregate
*We **congregated** in the hall, waiting for instructions.*

ANTONYM: disperse

general (1) ADJECTIVE

Something that is **general** is true in most cases, or applies to most people or things.

broad
*This is a film with **broad** appeal to people of all ages.*

common
*Putting apostrophes into plurals is a **common** mistake which people make.*

universal
*There are **universal** rules for soccer.*

widespread
*Famine is a **widespread** problem in that country.*

general (2) ADJECTIVE

Something that is **general** includes or involves a range of different things.

broad
*The winner of the quiz had a **broad** general knowledge.*

comprehensive
*Shannon's guidebook to the city was **comprehensive**.*

generous ADJECTIVE

Someone who is **generous** gives or shares what they have, especially time or money.

benevolent
*The millionaire author was **benevolent** to many charities.*

big-hearted
*The **big-hearted** star was always ready to help new musicians.*

charitable
*Mrs Sood is always **charitable** when I ask her for sponsorship.*

unselfish
*An **unselfish** boy gave up his seat for the pregnant woman.*

ANTONYM: selfish

gentle ADJECTIVE

Someone or something that is **gentle** is mild and calm.

calm
*My mum's voice always remained **calm**, no matter how flustered other people were.*

mild
*The doctor's **mild** manner relaxed her nervous patients.*

peace-loving
*Being a **peace-loving** man, Dad hated fights.*

tender
*Emma gave John a **tender** kiss.*

genuine ADJECTIVE

Something that is **genuine** is real and exactly what it appears to be.

authentic
*Is this autograph of Elvis Presley **authentic**?*

original
*This is an **original** painting by Van Gogh, not a print.*

sincere
*You could tell by Allana's face that her apology was **sincere**.*

true
*Is this a **true** likeness of the man you saw?*

ANTONYM: fake

get (1) VERB

Get can mean to change from one thing to another.

become
*The sky **became** darker as the moon crossed in front of the sun.*

grow
*Each day the weather **grew** warmer as spring finally arrived.*

turn
*The nights were starting to **turn** cold.*

A B C D E F G H I J K L M N O P Q R S T U V W X Y Z

get (2) VERB

If you **get** something, you fetch it or receive it.

collect
*We spent hours **collecting** different shells for our sand castle.*

fetch
*I asked Simeon to **fetch** some paper for me.*

retrieve
*Spot **retrieved** the stick from the river.*

get (3) VERB

If you **get** a joke or the point of something, you understand it.

comprehend
*It was hard to **comprehend** the instructions the first time Maria explained them.*

follow
*"Did you **follow** what I said?" asked the science professor.*

grasp
*Everyone laughed when they **grasped** the joke.*

understand
*The French lady **understood** what I meant, when I spoke slowly.*

get off VERB

To **get off** can mean to leave a certain kind of transport.

alight
*We **alighted** from the school bus at the stop close to our house.*

disembark
*Because the plane had a fault, we were forced to **disembark.***

dismount
*The mountain-bike rider **dismounted** and trudged off miserably.*

get on (1) VERB

If you **get on** with a task, you start or continue doing it.

continue
*Abdul **continued** with his piano practice even though he was tired.*

keep on
*Although I had a sore knee, I **kept on** with the sponsored walk.*

persevere
*Even when it started raining, the rock band **persevered** with the concert.*

get on (2) VERB

If you are **getting on** well, you are making good progress.

cope
*I **coped** well in the test, even though I felt quite nervous.*

fare
*"How did you **fare** in your exam?" asked Dad.*

manage
*"Can you **manage** all right carrying those heavy bags?" the man asked Gran.*

get on (3) VERB

To **get on** can mean to board a particular kind of transport.

board
*We **boarded** the bus for the campsite.*

embark
*The passengers **embarked** on the cruise liner.*

mount
*The highwayman **mounted** his horse and was gone in seconds.*

get out of VERB

If you **get out of** something, you avoid doing it.

avoid
*The lazy students **avoided** PE by pretending to be ill.*

dodge (*informal*)
*Keith tried to **dodge** doing the washing-up by creeping upstairs.*

escape
*Gertrude made a weak excuse to try and **escape** her piano practice.*

ghost NOUN

A **ghost** is the spirit of a dead person that appears to someone who is still alive.

phantom
*The **phantom** of the opera walked the stage at the dead of night.*

spectre
*Scrooge quaked before the **spectre** of his former friend.*

spirit
*The old inn was haunted by some form of evil **spirit** who made noises in the night.*

giant (1) NOUN

A **giant** is a huge person in a myth or legend.

colossus
*In Greek mythology, Atlas was a **colossus** of the ancient gods.*

monster
*A **monster** was guarding the entrance to the cave where the treasure was kept.*

ogre
*The **ogre** took another thunderous step towards the beanstalk.*

giant (2) ADJECTIVE

Something **giant** is much larger than other similar things.

colossal
*The sequel was a **colossal** success – even better than the original film.*

enormous
*The dinosaur's body was **enormous** compared with its brain.*

gigantic
*A **gigantic** wave swept towards the shore.*

huge
*The **huge** castle loomed out of the darkness in front of the elves.*

massive
*The **massive** bulldozer dwarfed everything around it.*

ANTONYM: tiny

gift NOUN

A **gift** is a present.

contribution
*Our teacher was collecting **contributions** for children in hospital.*

donation
*A **donation** from the parents helped the school buy more books.*

offering
*The roses were only a small **offering** but Mum was really pleased.*

present
*Everyone brought a **present** when they came to the party.*

give (1) VERB

If you **give** something to someone, you hand it to them, or provide it for them.

hand
*Nassir **handed** me the hammer.*

pass
*"**Pass** me the salt, please," I requested.*

present
*Our teacher **presented** the trophy to Keisha.*

supply
*A network of spies **supplied** secrets to the enemy government.*

give (2) VERB

If you **give** something, you grant, present or donate it.

award
*The girl was **awarded** a medal for her bravery during the flood.*

contribute
*Mum **contributed** money to Mrs Jones's farewell present.*

donate
*Tara's father **donated** one of his kidneys to save her life.*

present
*He **presented** a cheque to the charity.*

LANGUAGE TIP
A person who gives blood is a **blood donor**.

give in VERB

If you **give in**, you admit that you are defeated.

concede
*Chess players have to **concede** when their king is in checkmate.*

submit
*The intense pain in his back forced the wrestler to **submit.***

surrender
*The troops **surrendered** after they were surrounded by the enemy.*

give out VERB

If you **give** things **out**, you hand out or distribute them to people.

distribute
*The aid workers **distributed** food to the starving people.*

issue
*"Please **issue** these uniforms to the sailors," said the captain.*

supply
*The organisers **supplied** vests to all the marathon runners.*

A B C D E F G H I J K L M N O P Q R S T U V W X Y Z

give up VERB

If you **give up**, you stop doing something.

abandon
*Another fire forced the crew to **abandon** their efforts to save the ship.*

quit
*The DJ threatened to **quit** the show if he didn't get his way.*

resign from
*She had to **resign from** her work because of a serious illness.*

surrender
*The marines **surrendered** after their ship was attacked.*

glad ADJECTIVE

If someone is **glad**, they are happy or pleased.

contented
*Gran led a **contented** life in her little bungalow.*

delighted
*Seamus was **delighted** when he heard that he had won a prize.*

happy
*Mum was **happy** to have my cousin to stay.*

pleased
*Dad was **pleased** that we had offered to help.*

ANTONYM: displeased

glitter VERB

If something **glitters**, it shines in a sparkling way.

glint
*The farmer spotted something **glinting** in the soil – a gold coin!*

glisten
*Snowy treetops **glistened** in the sunshine.*

shimmer
*The lake **shimmered** in the golden light of the setting sun.*

gloomy (1) ADJECTIVE

If a place is **gloomy**, it is dark and dull.

dark
*The room was **dark**, with cobwebs hanging down everywhere.*

dismal
*It was a **dismal** landscape with hardly any trees or bushes.*

dreary
*She lived in a **dreary** town full of dirty grey buildings.*

gloomy (2) ADJECTIVE

If people are **gloomy**, they are unhappy and not at all hopeful.

dejected
*She felt **dejected** when she didn't win.*

glum
*Angela felt **glum** when the time came to leave her new friend.*

sad
*After his gerbil died, John felt **sad**.*

glow VERB

If something **glows**, it shines with a steady dull light.

gleam
*The polished brass knocker **gleamed** in the torchlight.*

glimmer
*It was getting dark when they saw a light **glimmering** in a cottage window.*

shine
*The paintwork on Jen's new car **shone** in the sunlight.*

smoulder
*The remains of the bonfire were still **smouldering** the next day.*

glue NOUN

Glue is a thick sticky liquid used for joining things together.

adhesive
*By the time they finished, their fingers were sticky with **adhesive**.*

cement
*I need some **cement** for my model aircraft.*

gum
*Nicola spread **gum** carefully on the back of her drawing.*

paste
*"We'll use this **paste** to make our collages," said the art teacher.*

go (1) VERB

If you **go** somewhere, you walk, move or travel there.

advance
*Troops **advanced** over the enemy lines.*

depart
*No sooner had we **departed** than Dad realised he'd forgotten his wallet.*

journey
*Marco Polo **journeyed** to eastern lands.*

set off
*Some of the group **set off** in the wrong direction.*

travel
*The car was **travelling** far too fast.*

go (2) VERB

If something **goes** somewhere, it leads or passes through there.

lead to
*This street **leads to** the Roman city walls.*

pass through
*We need to **pass through** that town in order to get home.*

reach
*The rocky road **reaches** out onto the peninsula, beside the lighthouse.*

go (3) VERB

Go can mean to become.

become
*At the sight of the pop star, Millie **became** weak at the knees.*

turn
*Mike **turns** green whenever the plane hits any turbulence.*

go (4) VERB

If something **goes**, it works properly.

function
*The old car refused to **function**.*

operate
*Water sprinklers **operate** when the smoke alarm starts ringing.*

work
*The stereo wouldn't **work** after I spilt my drink on it.*

go (5) NOUN

A **go** is an attempt or a turn at doing something.

attempt
*It was the weightlifter's second **attempt** at 100 kilograms.*

shot
*I didn't win any prizes with my first **shot** at the hoop game.*

stab
*Luckily, Jacob's first **stab** at guessing the answer was correct!*

try
*Lucinda had a **try** at horse riding, but unfortunately fell off.*

go back VERB

If you **go back**, you return to a place you have been before.

retrace your steps
*Lost in the jungle, our only hope was to **retrace our steps.***

retreat
*Faced with foul weather, we **retreated** to the cosy café.*

return
*As he began his descent, the climber promised he would **return** to his injured friend.*

gobble VERB

To **gobble** can mean to eat food or drink very quickly.

bolt
*Harvey **bolted** his meal and rushed off to play rugby.*

devour
*The hungry leopard **devoured** the remains of the antelope.*

gulp
*Charlene **gulped** down her tea and ran upstairs to phone her friends.*

guzzle (*informal*)
*I **guzzled** down a bottle of water when I finished the race.*

wolf
*Holly **wolfed down** her sandwich.*

good

→ Look at the **Word Power** page!

goodbye INTERJECTION

You say **goodbye** when you are leaving someone or ending a telephone conversation.

cheerio (*informal*)
*I shouted **cheerio** before I went out of the front door.*

farewell (*old-fashioned*)
*The captain said **farewell** to his crew and disembarked for the last time.*

so long
*"**So long**, partner!" cried the sheriff as he rode away from the ranch.*

LANGUAGE TIP
So long is used in America.

A B C D E F G H I J K L M N O P Q R S T U V W X Y Z

good

(1) ADJECTIVE Something that is **good** is pleasant or enjoyable.

delightful
*"What a **delightful** visit it's been!" said the president in his speech.*

enjoyable
*We had an **enjoyable** time at the zoo.*

pleasant
*The weather was **pleasant** for our walk.*

(2) ADJECTIVE If you are **good**, you are kind and thoughtful.

considerate
*I thought it was very **considerate** of him to do it just for me.*

decent
*They were a **decent** family who would never do anything dishonest.*

generous
*It was so **generous** of you to spend so much time helping me.*

kind
*To get close to your friends, think of **kind** things to do for them.*

merciful
*The **merciful** king spared the life of the peasant.*

thoughtful
*It was **thoughtful** of them to send flowers.*

(3) ADJECTIVE Something **good** is of high quality.

excellent
*"This is **excellent** writing," Mrs Watts said.*

splendid
*Mr Kaye said we had made a **splendid** effort.*

thorough
*I gave my room a **thorough** clean.*

useful
*Our guidebook proved very **useful** on holiday.*

good

(4) ADJECTIVE If you are **good** at something, you are competent or talented at it.

capable
*Elliot was a **capable** writer but he was poor at history.*

competent
*I am a **competent** enough speller, but my writing is poor.*

expert
*Chris was an **expert** mechanic when it came to mending vintage cars.*

skilful
*Aseem proved to be a **skilful** tennis player.*

talented
*He realised that she was a naturally **talented** singer.*

Try these other lively words and phrases!

amazing	*We had an **amazing** time at the concert.*
awesome	*The book I've just read was absolutely **awesome**.*
excellent	*The weather was **excellent** on Saturday when we went camping.*
fabulous	*What a **fabulous** idea!*
fantastic	*Her dad is a **fantastic** cook.*
magnificent	*You get a **magnificent** view from the top of the tower.*
out of this world (*informal*)	*The cake she made was **out of this world**.*
tremendous	*It will be a **tremendous** achievement to complete the challenge.*
wonderful	*I hope you had a **wonderful** holiday in France.*

→ Also have a look at the **Word Power** page for **bad**!

A B C D E F G H I J K L M N O P Q R S T U V W X Y Z

go off VERB

If something such as a bomb **goes off**, it explodes.

detonate
The beach was cleared quickly, before the bomb could ***detonate****.*

explode
Land mines are dangerous because they ***explode*** *when you step on them.*

go on VERB

If something is **going on**, it is happening.

happen
What ***happened*** *while we were away?*

occur
The incident ***occurred*** *at the swimming pool on a hot summer day.*

take place
Sanjay's party will ***take place*** *in the village hall at three o'clock.*

go round (1) VERB

Something that **goes round** moves in a circular motion.

circle
The plane ***circled*** *the airport several times before landing.*

revolve
The hotel porter told me that ***revolving*** *doors prevent draughts.*

rotate
When the pilot turned on the helicopter engine, the huge blade started to ***rotate****.*

go round (2) VERB

If you **go round** something, you avoid it by moving around it.

avoid
My mum, riding her bike, ***avoided*** *the dog but hit the lamppost.*

dodge
We ***dodged*** *the crowds by walking through backstreets.*

go through VERB

If something **goes through** another thing, it pierces it.

penetrate
No bullet could ***penetrate*** *the robot's thick body armour.*

pierce
The nail ***pierced*** *the skin of my foot when I trod on it.*

puncture
Broken glass in the road ***punctured*** *the tyre on my new bike.*

grab VERB

If you **grab** something, you take or pick it up roughly.

pluck
In the nick of time, the helicopter winchman ***plucked*** *the girl from the raging river.*

seize
The weightlifter ***seized*** *the bar and thrust it above his head.*

snatch
Muggers ***snatched*** *the bag and ran off with it.*

graceful ADJECTIVE

Someone or something that is **graceful** moves in a smooth, pleasant way.

effortless
She turned towards them with an ***effortless*** *swing of her body.*

elegant
The famous actress crossed the stage with ***elegant*** *movements.*

flowing
His pencil quickly covered the page with ***flowing*** *lines.*

smooth
They stood watching the ***smooth*** *glide of a swan on the river.*

supple
Dancers moved around each other with ***supple*** *ease.*

gradually ADVERB

Gradually means happening slowly over a long period of time.

little by little
Little by little*, the climber inched his way up the rock face.*

slowly
The classroom alterations are being done far too ***slowly*** *for my liking.*

step by step
I'm learning to play the piano ***step by step.***

ANTONYM: suddenly

grateful ADJECTIVE

If you are **grateful** for something, you feel thankful for it.

appreciative
*The old lady was very **appreciative** of my help in crossing the road.*

thankful
*After hours in the blizzard, we were **thankful** for a warm fire.*

ANTONYM: ungrateful

grave ADJECTIVE

Something that is **grave** is important, serious and worrying.

gloomy
*We knew the news was bad as soon as we saw his **gloomy** expression.*

serious
*"I'm afraid her condition is **serious**," said the doctor.*

solemn
*The head teacher made the announcement in **solemn** tones.*

sombre
*I noticed the postman looked unusually **sombre** today.*

worrying
*There was a **worrying** lack of medical supplies in the war zone.*

graveyard NOUN

A **graveyard** is a place where dead people are buried.

burial ground
*The **burial ground** overlooked the beach where the sailors had perished.*

cemetery
*My gran was buried in the town **cemetery**.*

great (1) ADJECTIVE

Something that is **great** is very large in size.

colossal
*The tidal wave was **colossal.***

enormous
*Until you actually see them, you don't realise just how **enormous** space rockets are.*

gigantic
*A **gigantic** boom echoed round the hillsides.*

vast
*The Sahara desert covers a **vast** area of land.*

ANTONYM: small

great (2) ADJECTIVE

Something that is **great** is very good.

excellent
*"That was an **excellent** meal, thank you," said my cousin.*

superb
*The gymnast gave a **superb** display of floor exercises.*

wonderful
*"It's **wonderful** to see you," she gushed as she hugged her friend.*

great (3) ADJECTIVE

A **great** person is very important and highly respected.

eminent
*The **eminent** scientist has won the Nobel Prize two years in a row.*

important
*Picasso had made an **important** contribution to art.*

outstanding
*Muhammad Ali was the **outstanding** boxer of his generation.*

ANTONYMS: unknown, insignificant

great (4) ADJECTIVE

A **great** event is very important.

grand
*The coronation was a **grand** occasion.*

magnificent
*The invention of the steam engine was a **magnificent** achievement.*

spectacular
*The millionaire's party ended in a **spectacular** firework display.*

great (5) ADJECTIVE

Something that is **great** is very large in amount or degree.

considerable
*It takes **considerable** skill to walk a tightrope.*

extreme
*The passer-by showed **extreme** courage in rescuing the children from the water.*

LANGUAGE TIP
Don't confuse **great** with the word **grate**.

A B C D E F G H I J K L M N O P Q R S T U V W X Y Z

greedy ADJECTIVE
Someone who is **greedy** wants more of something than is necessary or fair.

gluttonous
*Augustus was a **gluttonous** child who never seemed to stop eating.*

selfish
*The **selfish** lottery winner kept all his winnings for himself.*

voracious
*Charlie had a **voracious** appetite, especially for chocolate.*

green ADJECTIVE
If something is **green**, it has the colour of grass or leaves.

Shades of green:		
emerald	lime	olive
sea green	turquoise	

grief NOUN
Someone who feels **grief** is very sad, often because a person or animal they love has died.

distress
*When they examined the baby, it was showing signs of **distress**.*

heartache
*He wasn't prepared for the **heartache** that followed the death of his hamster.*

misery
*We couldn't find any way of helping Daniel get over his **misery**.*

sadness
*It was the **sadness** in her eyes that told us what had happened.*

sorrow
*It was a time of great **sorrow** for the whole family.*

grim ADJECTIVE
If someone looks **grim**, they seem worried or angry about something.

bad-tempered
*Mr Jones had a **bad-tempered** expression when he handed back our ball.*

grave
*The head teacher looked **grave** when he told us about the accident.*

serious
*Tim knew something was wrong when he saw her **serious** face.*

severe
*His mouth was set in a **severe** line. "What have you been up to?" he asked.*

unfriendly
*I try not to go in that shop because the man always looks so **unfriendly**.*

groan VERB
If you **groan**, you make a long, low sound of pain, unhappiness or disappointment.

cry out
*He **cried out** as his head struck the rock.*

moan
*Tom **moaned** in his sleep, and turned over.*

sigh
*When he heard my corny joke, Jim **sighed** and walked away.*

ground (1) NOUN
Ground is the surface of the land.

earth
*The meteorite made a vast crater in the **earth** when it landed.*

land
*Mr Palfrey farms the **land** next to our house.*

soil
*The **soil** in our garden is good for growing vegetables.*

ground (2) NOUN
Ground is an area of land, especially land that is used for a particular purpose.

pitch
*That baseball **pitch** gets very muddy in winter.*

stadium
*You could see the lights of the sports **stadium** from miles around.*

group NOUN
A **group** is a number of things or people that are linked in some way.

category
*There were five nominations in the "Best Actor" **category**.*

class
*Lucy won a rosette in her **class** at the show.*

set
*To her surprise, Mum won a matching **set** of screwdrivers in the raffle.*

→ Have a look at the **Illustration** page!

grow (1) VERB
When someone or something **grows**, it gets bigger.

GROUPS OF ANIMALS

murder of crows

school of whales

kindle of kittens

pack of wolves

flock of birds

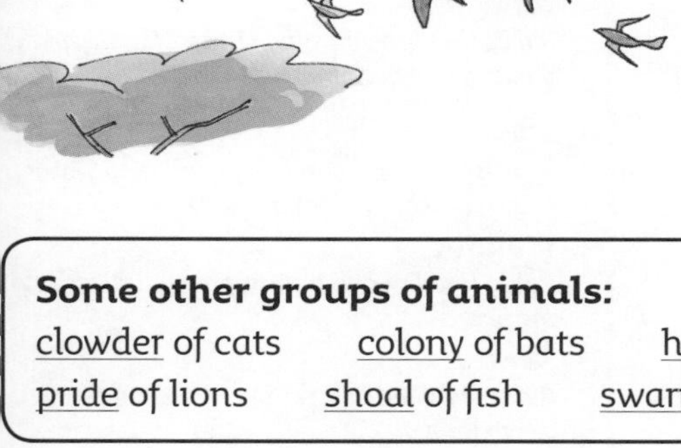

gaggle of geese

Some other groups of animals:

<u>clowder</u> of cats   <u>colony</u> of bats   <u>herd</u> of cows   <u>litter</u> of puppies

<u>pride</u> of lions   <u>shoal</u> of fish   <u>swarm</u> of bees   <u>troop</u> of monkeys

develop
*In their teenage years, children **develop** into adults.*

expand
*That city has **expanded** into the countryside.*

spread
*The bush's branches **spread** all over the place.*

swell
*Each bud **swells** until it bursts open as a leaf.*

ANTONYM: shrink

grow (2) VERB

When plants **grow**, they increase in size or develop.

flourish
*While we were on holiday, weeds had **flourished** everywhere.*

germinate
*The flower seeds **germinated** in the warmth of the greenhouse.*

sprout
*The magic tree suddenly **sprouted** legs, and ran off, chuckling.*

grown-up ADJECTIVE

Someone who is **grown-up** is adult in age or behaviour.

adult
*His **adult** behaviour made him seem older than he was.*

fully-grown
*At 4 hands high, the horse was considered **fully-grown.***

mature
*Mr Jessop said he expected us to behave in a **mature** way.*

grow up VERB

Grow up can mean to become an adult.

develop
*Calves soon **develop** into cows.*

mature
*Nadia has **matured** into a kind and sensitive person.*

grumble VERB

If you **grumble**, you complain in a bad-tempered way.

moan
*Grant is always **moaning** about having no money.*

whine
*After he lost his sweets, my little brother wouldn't stop **whining.***

whinge
*"It's no good **whingeing**," said Dad. "You said you wanted piano lessons."*

grumpy ADJECTIVE

Someone who is **grumpy** is bad-tempered and fed up.

bad-tempered
*"Just because your team lost, there's no need to be **bad-tempered**," said Victoria.*

cross
*I was **cross** when my mum wouldn't let me play outside.*

crotchety
*Babies often get **crotchety** when they are teething.*

irritable
*I tend to get **irritable** when I'm hungry, but I soon cheer up once I've eaten.*

sulky
*My big sister gets very **sulky** if her boyfriend doesn't phone her.*

→ *See* **angry**

guard (1) VERB

When you **guard** someone or something, you watch them carefully to protect them.

keep watch
*While the other bandits slept, the Ringo Kid **kept watch** by the campfire.*

protect
*Twenty soldiers **protected** the queen's palace.*

shield
*The police **shielded** the prisoner from the protesters.*

tend
*It was the shepherd's job to **tend** the sheep and goats in the rocky mountains.*

guard (2) NOUN

A **guard** is a person whose job is to watch over a person, object or place.

lookout
*Robin Hood posted **lookouts** on all roads into the forest.*

sentry
***Sentries** stood to attention as the royal car swept through the palace gates.*

warden
*The jail was staffed by 200 **wardens** who worked in shifts.*

guess (1) VERB

If you **guess** something, you form an opinion about it without knowing all the relevant facts.

estimate
*At the fête, we had to **estimate** how many sweets were in the jar.*

reckon
*I **reckon** the Blues are a certainty to win the league this year.*

suppose
*"With all this rain, I **suppose** the race will be cancelled," pondered Faraji.*

suspect
*Roberto **suspected** that someone was following him home.*

guess (2) NOUN

A **guess** is an opinion formed without knowing all the facts.

estimate
*Harry's **estimate** was that the spell would last for half an hour.*

hunch
*Nancy's **hunch** was that her friend was in danger.*

guide VERB

If you **guide** someone somewhere, you lead or show them the way there.

conduct
*The historian **conducted** the party round the ancient manor house.*

direct
*"Can you **direct** me to the city centre, please?" asked Berta.*

lead
*The delicious smell of bread **led** us straight to the bakery.*

steer
*With my hands on his shoulders, I **steered** the blindfolded boy towards his target.*

guilty (1) ADJECTIVE

If you are **guilty** of doing something wrong, you did it.

at fault
*After the collision, the lorry driver admitted he was **at fault.***

responsible
*When we saw the mess after the party, everyone felt **responsible**.*

to blame
*We couldn't tell which of the puppies was **to blame** for the chewed furniture.*

ANTONYM: innocent

guilty (2) ADJECTIVE

If you feel **guilty**, you are unhappy because you think you have done something wrong.

ashamed
*I felt **ashamed** that I had eaten all of Ashley's sweets.*

repentant
*The **repentant** thief resolved to return what he had stolen.*

sorry
*Mai-Lin felt **sorry** about the lies she had told.*

gullible ADJECTIVE

If someone is **gullible**, they are easily tricked.

innocent
*The **innocent** children thought that all the magician's tricks were real.*

naive
*Only a very **naive** person would believe the statements made by the fraudster.*

trusting
*My aunt has an open, **trusting** nature, so she falls for all my jokes.*

unsuspecting
*The class played a joke on their **unsuspecting** teacher.*

ANTONYM: suspicious

gun NOUN

A **gun** is a weapon that fires bullets or shells.

The name for...
lighter guns is **firearms**.
heavy guns is **artillery**.
a group of heavy guns is a **battery**.

a b c d e f g h i j k l m n o p q r s t u v w x y z

Hh

habit NOUN

A **habit** is something that you do often or regularly.

custom
*There's an old Greek **custom** of smashing plates for good luck.*

routine
*It was Wallis's **routine** to brush his teeth twice a day, morning and evening.*

hair NOUN

Hair is the fine threads that grow on the heads and bodies of people and animals.

LANGUAGE TIP
Hair on animals can be called their **fur** or **coat**. The long hair on the necks of horses and lions is called their **mane**.

Some types of hairstyle:

Afro	bob	braids
bun	bunches	cornrows
crew cut	dreadlocks	pigtail
plaits	ponytail	ringlets

hairy ADJECTIVE

Something or someone **hairy** is covered in hair.

bristly
*Dad rubbed his **bristly** chin thoughtfully. "I think I can manage that," he said.*

furry
*A hamster is a small **furry** rodent that sleeps during the day.*

shaggy
*Our dog has got a long **shaggy** coat.*

woolly
*I had a nice **woolly** jacket for my birthday.*

handle (1) VERB

If you **handle** something, you touch or feel it with your hands.

feel
*She liked to **feel** the cool sand as she built sandcastles on the beach.*

finger
*Don't **finger** that pear unless you're going to eat it.*

hold
*She liked picking up spiders, but they were difficult to **hold**.*

stroke
*Lily liked to **stroke** the kitten to hear it purr.*

touch
*The teacher said we could **touch** the baby hamsters very gently.*

handle (2) VERB

If you **handle** something, you deal with it.

cope with
*Can you **cope with** the plates while I make the tea?*

look after
*Mrs Smith said she would **look after** the flower arrangements.*

manage
*Will you be able to **manage** the rest if I leave now?*

supervise
*I need to **supervise** the face painting.*

handsome ADJECTIVE

A **handsome** person is very attractive in appearance.

attractive
*Melanie has a very **attractive** smile.*

good-looking
*The film star is **good-looking** and skilful.*

ANTONYM: ugly

handy (1) ADJECTIVE

If something is **handy**, it is conveniently near.

accessible
*The hotel is **accessible** by rail and road.*

convenient
*Our school's location is quite **convenient** – we can walk there in ten minutes.*

nearby
*We also have a post office **nearby**, which is behind the supermarket.*

ANTONYM: inconvenient

handy (2) ADJECTIVE

If something is **handy**, it is useful.

convenient
*Credit cards are a **convenient** way of paying for things over the phone.*

helpful
*The instructions that came with the game are very **helpful**.*

practical
*Dad had given me very **practical** advice on mending a puncture.*

user-friendly
*The instruction book was **user-friendly** – short, very clear and with helpful diagrams.*

hang VERB

If something **hangs** from a hook, nail or line, it is attached so that it does not touch the ground.

be suspended
*The sides of beef **were suspended** from hooks in the cold room.*

dangle
*The climber fell off the rock face and **dangled** on her rope.*

droop
*The flag **drooped** on the pole in the still air.*

swing
*The inn sign **swung** creakily in the wind.*

hang about; also hang around VERB

(informal)

If you **hang about** or **hang around** somewhere, you stay or wait there.

dawdle
*"Will you stop **dawdling** and get a move on?" Mum shouted.*

linger
*Moira **lingered** by the bakery window. Those cakes looked so tempting!*

loiter
*The spy **loitered** in the shadows, hoping that no one would see her.*

remain
*We **remained** in our seats for some time after the match was over.*

happen VERB

When something **happens**, it occurs or takes place.

arise
*The secret to being organised is to deal with problems as they **arise**.*

crop up
*"A meeting has **cropped up**, so I'll have to see you next week instead," apologised Daniel.*

occur
*When I was three, a strange event **occurred** in our family.*

take place
*The concert will **take place** next Tuesday.*

LANGUAGE TIP

Something that happens before something else **precedes** it. Something that happens after something else **follows** it. Something that happens again **recurs** or **reoccurs**.

happiness NOUN

Happiness is a feeling of great contentment or pleasure.

cheerfulness
*Her **cheerfulness** despite her problems was a lesson to us all.*

contentment
*The couple lived a life of great **contentment**.*

delight
*Zara opened her presents with great **delight**.*

ecstasy
*Luke was in **ecstasy** – at last he'd got the puppy he'd always wanted.*

joy
*The missing sailor's parents were filled with **joy** when they knew he was safe.*

jubilation
*There were scenes of **jubilation** in the winning team's changing room.*

pleasure
*"It gives me great **pleasure** to open this library," announced the chairwoman.*

satisfaction
*Gran got **satisfaction** from the blankets she made for charity.*

ANTONYM: sadness

happy

→ Look at the **Word Power** page!

harbour NOUN

A **harbour** is a protected area of deep water where boats can be moored.

jetty
*There was a barge moored alongside the **jetty**.*

pier
*Several small, open boats were tied up to the **pier**.*

Places where ships can dock or shelter:

dock	marina
quay	wharf

hard (1) ADJECTIVE

An object that is **hard** is not easy to bend or break.

firm
*The snow had been packed **firm** by dozens of sledges sliding over it.*

rigid
*We left the washing hanging out overnight and the frost had turned it **rigid**.*

solid
*There is no land at the North Pole – just metres of thick, **solid** ice.*

stiff
*His waterproof trousers were brand new and **stiff**.*

tough
*Castles needed walls **tough** enough to survive an attack.*

ANTONYM: soft

hard (2) ADJECTIVE

If something is **hard** to do, it requires a lot of effort.

arduous
*Women and children did **arduous** work in Victorian mills.*

backbreaking
*Shifting the rocks was a **backbreaking** task.*

exhausting
*The walk up the hill was **exhausting**.*

strenuous
*The more **strenuous** the exercise, the more calories you burn up.*

tiring
*Garden work can be **tiring**, especially if the weather is hot.*

tough
*It was a **tough** job keeping the lawn clear of fallen leaves.*

ANTONYM: easy

hard (3) ADJECTIVE

Something that is **hard** is difficult to understand.

complicated
*The problem was far too **complicated** for me to understand.*

difficult
*"Work's **difficult** enough without phone calls interrupting me," Dad said tetchily.*

perplexing
*It was a **perplexing** decision: one tunnel led to freedom, the other to a trap, but which was which?*

puzzling
*I found my maths homework quite **puzzling**. I should have listened harder in the lesson.*

ANTONYMS: easy, simple

hard (4) ADVERB

If you do something **hard**, you do it with a lot of force.

sharply
*The magician pulled the cloth **sharply** and the plates stayed on the table!*

vigorously
*Grandad shook my hand so **vigorously** I thought it would come off.*

with all your might
*"Now, make a wish **with all your might**," the fairy godmother said.*

ANTONYM: gently

hard (5) ADVERB

If you work **hard**, you give a lot of time and effort to the work.

doggedly
*Aksana didn't find it easy, but studied **doggedly** and passed the test.*

industriously
*For days, the divers worked **industriously** to salvage the treasure.*

happy

ADJECTIVE If you are **happy**, you feel full of contentment and joy.

Very happy:

delighted
*Mum and Dad were **delighted** with the book I bought them.*

ecstatic
*My big sister was **ecstatic** that she had got tickets for the concert.*

joyful
*The wedding was a day of **joyful** celebration.*

jubilant
*We were **jubilant** that the team's hard training had paid off.*

Try these lively words and phrases!

on cloud nine (*informal*)	*Seeing my gran after so long put me **on cloud nine**.*
over the moon (*informal*)	*Her mum was **over the moon** with her exam results.*
walking on air	*I felt like I was **walking on air** after such a fantastic evening.*

Quite happy:

cheerful
*The popular boy greeted everyone with a **cheerful** smile.*

cheery
*He had a **cheery** word for everyone.*

content
*I could have scored more, but in the end I was **content** with having scored two goals.*

glad
*"I'll be **glad** when the holidays are over," said Mum with a big sigh.*

jolly
*Reginald was a **jolly** old man who always had a smile on his face.*

merry
*The whole family had a **merry** time thanks to the generosity of their neighbours.*

pleased
*Victoria was **pleased** that people noticed her new hairstyle.*

satisfied
*Whatever the result, I was **satisfied** that I had tried my hardest.*

➔ Also have a look at the **Word Power** page for sad!

harden VERB

If something **hardens**, it sets or stops being soft.

set
*"Wait for that concrete to **set** before you walk on it," Dad ordered.*

solidify
*The paint had **solidified** in the tin.*

stiffen
*The fluffy egg whites **stiffened** into meringues as they were cooked.*

ANTONYM: soften

hardly ADVERB

If you can **hardly** do something, you can only just do it.

barely
*The fog was so thick, I could **barely** see the tree in the back yard.*

only just
*Because of the heavy traffic, we **only just** caught the train.*

scarcely
*A Roman coin in our garden! Dad could **scarcely** believe his luck.*

hard-working ADJECTIVE

A **hard-working** person works hard.

conscientious
*Craig was very **conscientious**, feeding the hamsters every day without fail.*

diligent
*Mr Hassan said I was a **diligent** worker.*

industrious
*Mum and I had been very **industrious**, with lots of jam to prove it.*

ANTONYM: lazy

harm VERB

To **harm** means to injure someone or damage something.

damage
*The use of too many chemicals can **damage** the environment.*

hurt
*It won't **hurt** her to do a bit of work for a change.*

ill-treat
*The children were taught never to **ill-treat** an animal.*

injure
*He beat down the brambles so that they would not **injure** anybody.*

ruin
*"Careless washing could **ruin** this delicate material," said Amanda.*

wound
*It was obvious the arrow was meant to **wound** him.*

harmful ADJECTIVE

Something **harmful** has a bad effect on something.

damaging
*Chemicals are **damaging** to the ozone layer.*

dangerous
*"That quarry is **dangerous**. Stay away," warned my uncle.*

destructive
*Locusts are hugely **destructive** to crops, eating everything in minutes.*

detrimental
*Late nights had a **detrimental** effect on Keisha's school work.*

ANTONYM: harmless

harsh ADJECTIVE

Harsh conditions are severe, difficult and unpleasant.

cruel
*Rain and a **cruel** wind cut through his clothes and froze him to the bone.*

hard
*Dickens's stories tell how **hard** life was in Victorian London.*

merciless
*Few people survive the **merciless** conditions of this desert.*

severe
*A **severe** winter made things difficult for the farmers.*

hat NOUN

A **hat** is a covering for the head.

→ Have a look at the **Illustration** page!

hate VERB

If you **hate** someone or something, you dislike them very much.

abhor
*Pauline **abhors** cheese.*

HATS

baseball cap

fez

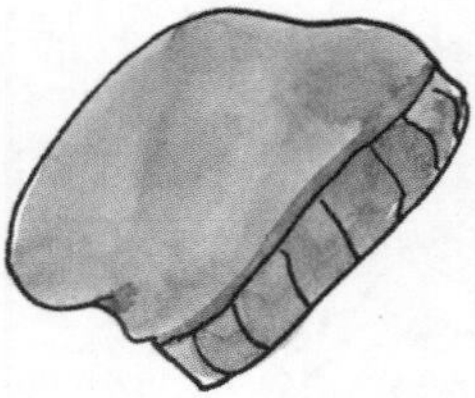

beanie

cork hat

boater

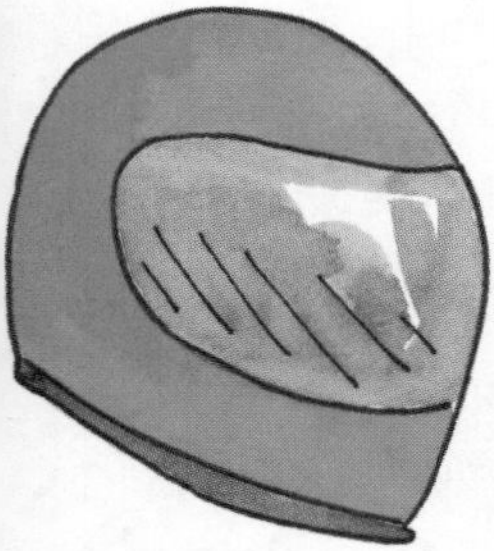

crash helmet

beret

top hat

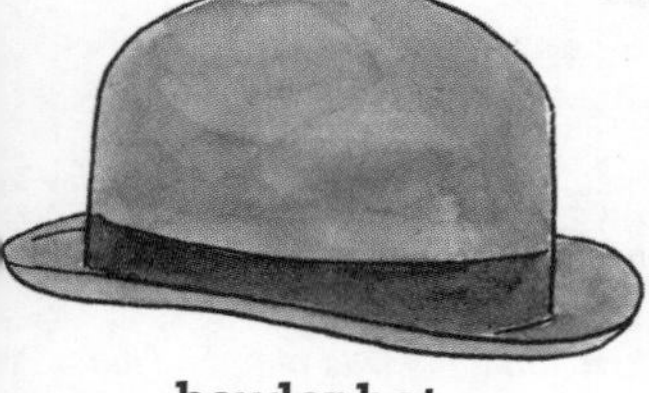

bowler hat

sombrero

Some other types of hat:

bonnet	cowboy hat	hard hat	helmet	Stetson®
sun hat	trilby	turban	woollen hat	yarmulke

A B C D E F G H I J K L M N O P Q R S T U V W X Y Z

despise
*If there's one thing I **despise**, it's people who tell lies.*

detest
*My brother **detests** me tweaking his ears.*

loathe
*My dad **loathes** getting up early on Saturday mornings.*

ANTONYM: love

have (1) VERB

If you **have** something, it belongs to you or you possess it.

own
*The millionaire **owned** far more houses and cars than he needed.*

possess
*My report read, "Abby **possesses** a good sense of humour".*

have (2) VERB

If you **have** something such as a cold or an accident, you feel or experience it.

endure
*The climbers **endured** three days of blizzards.*

experience
*Going on holiday, we **experienced** a few delays, but nothing too dreadful.*

undergo
*The footballer **underwent** an operation on his injured knee.*

have to VERB

If you **have to do** something, you must do it.

be compelled to
*When Grandad was in the army, the soldiers **were compelled to** have cold showers.*

be forced to
*Because her injury proved too painful, the runner **was forced to** drop out of the race.*

must
*We **must** drink plenty of water each day in order to stay healthy.*

should
*"You really **should** see that film. It's terrific!" Kelly told me.*

healthy (1) ADJECTIVE

Someone who is **healthy** is fit and well, and is not suffering from any illness.

in good condition
*The dog is **in good condition**, considering her age.*

in good shape
*The champion felt **in good shape** for his bout with Basher Muggs.*

physically fit
*For their job, soldiers, sailors and air crew need to be **physically fit**.*

ANTONYM: sick

healthy (2) ADJECTIVE

Something that is **healthy** is good for you.

beneficial
*A glass of orange juice a day can be **beneficial** to your immune system.*

nutritious
***Nutritious** food is full of vitamins.*

wholesome
*A **wholesome** diet does not include junk food.*

ANTONYM: unhealthy

heap NOUN

A **heap** is an untidy pile of things.

mound
*Mum despaired at the **mound** of washing that greeted her.*

mountain
*A **mountain** of comics is hidden in my bedroom cupboard.*

pile
*A **pile** of unopened letters lay on the doormat.*

stack
*Unfortunately, in the kitchen there was a **stack** of dirty dishes.*

hear (1) VERB

When you **hear** sounds, you are aware of them because they reach your ears.

catch
*"I didn't quite **catch** what you said, dear," Gran confided.*

overhear
*I **overheard** Mum and Dad planning a day at the seaside for the family.*

→ *See* **listen**

LANGUAGE TIP
To hear someone else's conversation by accident is to **overhear**. To listen to someone else's conversation deliberately is to **eavesdrop**.

hear (2) VERB
If you **hear** about something, you get to know about it.

discover
Myles ***discovered*** *that his friend had been telling lies.*

learn
My mum ***learnt*** *by phone last night that Grandpa was seriously ill.*

receive the news
The king ***received the news*** *of his army's defeat in dignified silence.*

heavy (1) ADJECTIVE
Something that is **heavy** weighs a lot.

bulky
A delivery man brought us a ***bulky*** *parcel.*

hefty
Mum said the sofa was too ***hefty*** *for my dad to try lifting on his own.*

weighty
With PE kit and books in it, my school bag was fairly ***weighty****.*

ANTONYM: light

heavy (2) ADJECTIVE
Heavy rain falls hard and in great quantities.

pouring
The ***pouring*** *rain ruined our day at the beach.*

torrential
The downpour was ***torrential****, flooding roads.*

ANTONYM: light

help (1) VERB
If you **help** someone, you make something easier or better for them.

aid
I think that it is a rich country's duty to ***aid*** *poorer countries.*

assist
The off-duty nurse rushed to ***assist*** *the man lying at the roadside.*

cooperate with
The companies ***cooperated with*** *one another to develop the new medicine.*

lend a hand
Most people are happy to ***lend a hand*** *to their neighbours.*

→ *See* **support (2)**

help (2) NOUN
If you get **help** from someone, they give you assistance.

a helping hand
Most mums appreciate ***a helping hand*** *every now and then.*

aid
When I sprained my ankle, I needed my friend's ***aid*** *to walk.*

assistance
Dad offered his pal our ***assistance*** *in moving house.*

cooperation
The police thanked the public for their ***cooperation*** *with the investigation.*

helpful (1) ADJECTIVE
If you are **helpful**, you cooperate with others and support them.

cooperative
It's important to be ***cooperative*** *with others if you're part of a team.*

obliging
The shop assistant was very ***obliging****, taking Gran's shopping to her car.*

supportive
When Grandad died, Gran's friends were very ***supportive****.*

helpful (2) ADJECTIVE
If something is **helpful**, it helps you in some way.

beneficial
That bit of extra homework was ***beneficial*** *to Khalid's maths.*

useful
My old tracksuit is ***useful*** *when I have to help in the garden.*

ANTONYMS: useless, of no help

helpless ADJECTIVE
If you are **helpless**, you are unable to protect yourself or do anything useful.

defenceless
The refugees were ***defenceless*** *as the fighters swooped in.*

powerless
The Australian family were ***powerless*** *as the bush fire roared towards their home.*

unprotected
The abandoned dog wandered the streets, ***unprotected*** *in the blizzard.*

a b c d e f g h i j k l m n o p q r s t u v w x y z

vulnerable
The enemy realised that the castle was ***vulnerable*** *to attack from the air.*

weak
When they were born, the puppies were small and ***weak****, but they soon grew strong.*

hesitate VERB

If you **hesitate**, you pause or show uncertainty.

dither
"Stop ***dithering*** *and make a decision," he begged.*

falter
The little plane's engine ***faltered****, died, then roared into life again.*

pause
The group ***paused*** *at the monument to think of the brave people who had died in the war.*

hidden ADJECTIVE

If something is **hidden**, you cannot see it.

buried
The painting lay ***buried*** *beneath old furniture in the loft.*

concealed
My big sister's spot was ***concealed*** *beneath a ton of make-up.*

out of sight
Mum found the empty biscuit tin, but my brother and I were safely ***out of sight****.*

secreted
The money was ***secreted*** *in a box beneath the floorboards.*

ANTONYM: visible

hide (1) VERB

If you **hide**, you go somewhere where you cannot be seen or found easily.

go into hiding
The pop star ***went into hiding*** *when news of her wedding got out.*

lie low
The train robbers hoped to ***lie low*** *at the farm for a while.*

stow away
The refugee ***stowed away*** *in the ship's hold.*

take cover
*"****Take cover*** *everyone!" the sheriff ordered as the Clancy Gang rode into town.*

hide (2) VERB

If you **hide** something, you put it where it cannot be seen, or prevent it from being discovered.

conceal
The singer managed to ***conceal*** *her grief, but burst into tears when the show was over.*

mask
Skilful use of make-up ***masked*** *the scars Adhira had from the accident.*

secrete
She ***secreted*** *the box of chocolates in the kitchen cabinet.*

ANTONYM: reveal

high (1) ADJECTIVE

If something is **high**, it reaches a long way above the ground.

lofty
From the ***lofty*** *ceiling of the castle's main hall hung a beautiful chandelier.*

soaring
The ***soaring*** *columns of the temple filled me with wonder.*

tall
In the top of a ***tall*** *fir tree, the vulture awaited its chance.*

towering
We were surrounded by ***towering*** *volcanic peaks.*

ANTONYM: low

high (2) ADJECTIVE

Something that is **high** is great in degree, quantity or intensity.

exceptional
The head teacher did not often give such ***exceptional*** *praise.*

excessive
She wrapped up the delicate ornaments with ***excessive*** *care.*

extreme
Electronic work requires an ***extreme*** *degree of concentration.*

ANTONYM: low

high (3) ADJECTIVE

A **high** voice is pitched high in tone.

high-pitched
I was immediately aware of the toddler's ***high-pitched*** *cries.*

piercing
*A **piercing** scream cut through the tranquillity of the wood.*

piping
*The **piping** voices of children at play drifted over the village roof tops.*

shrill
*With a **shrill** whistle, the steam locomotive began to depart.*

ANTONYM: deep

hinder VERB

If you **hinder** someone or something, you get in their way and make it difficult for them to do what they want to do.

hamper
*Returning down the mountain, Celine was **hampered** by her twisted ankle.*

hold back
*"Don't let us **hold** you **back**," Mum said. "You go on ahead."*

obstruct
*The major did all he could to **obstruct** the building work.*

prevent
*The protests delayed the new bypass, but could not **prevent** it.*

hit VERB

If you **hit** someone or something, you strike or knock them with force.

bash (informal)
*"Sir, Syd **bashed** me on the nose," he whined.*

batter
*Police **battered** on the door, but no one answered.*

clout (informal)
*Grandad told me that when he was a boy he would often be **clouted** for being late.*

pound
*I watched the TV chef **pound** the steak to make it tender before he cooked it.*

punch
*The two heavyweights **punched** each other to a standstill.*

slap
*I saw my big sister **slap** her boyfriend's face!*

smack
*At school we had a debate about whether parents should **smack** children.*

thump
*The ball **thumped** me in the stomach and I doubled up.*

wallop (informal)
*Dennis the Menace is often getting **walloped** with his dad's slipper.*

whack
*I **whacked** the ball with the bat.*

hoarse ADJECTIVE

A **hoarse** voice sounds rough and unclear.

croaky
*With her sore throat, all Karen could manage was a **croaky** hello.*

husky
*The singer's deep, **husky** voice is her trademark.*

rasping
*Mr Quelch's **rasping** voice gave Bunter the creeps.*

throaty
*The large motorbike gave a **throaty** roar as it surged away.*

hold (1) VERB

When you **hold** something, you keep it in your hands or arms.

clasp
*The eagle **clasped** its prey with its strong, crooked claws.*

cling to
*As the Titanic sank, people **clung to** wreckage in the icy water.*

clutch
*The panic-stricken driver **clutched** the wheel in terror.*

get hold of
*To remove the wheel, undo the nuts, **get hold of** the tyre and pull hard.*

grip
*Lisa **gripped** her sister's hand in fear.*

hold (2) VERB

If something **holds** a certain amount of something, it can contain or carry that amount.

bear
*The old bridge will not **bear** too much weight.*

contain
*Mrs Abernathy asked, "How much liquid does this cup **contain**?"*

support
*A pyramid of gymnasts **supported** the triumphant girl.*

LANGUAGE TIP
The number of people a theatre stadium holds is the number of people it **seats**.

hold out VERB

If you **hold out** something to someone, you offer it to them.

extend
*The captain **extended** his hand, expecting his opponent to shake it.*

offer
*With a slight bow, the waiter **offered** us black pepper for our pizza.*

hold up VERB

If something **holds** you **up**, it delays you.

delay
*The unfortunate accident **delayed** the procession by half an hour.*

detain
*"You mustn't let me **detain** you," the injured explorer begged his colleagues.*

hinder
*Rebellious workers did their best to **hinder** the introduction of the new system.*

hole NOUN

A **hole** is an opening or hollow space in something.

gap
*Through a **gap** in the curtains, Mrs White saw her neighbours drive away.*

opening
*In an instant, the Pied Piper had created an **opening** in the rock before him.*

a small hole:

cavity
*"Hmm! Plenty of **cavities** there," said the dentist disapprovingly.*

perforation
*The tiny **perforations** in tea bags allow the water to get to the tea leaves.*

puncture
*Mum's tyre had a **puncture** and went flat.*

split
*The **split** in the acorn widened. An oak tree was beginning to grow.*

tear
*The x-ray showed I had a **tear** in a leg muscle.*

a hole in the ground:

crater
*The meteorite left a massive **crater** in the desert landscape.*

excavation
*The archaeologists dug a huge **excavation**.*

hollow
*The squirrel stared at Vicky from a **hollow** at the foot of the tree.*

pothole
*There were too many **potholes** in the road for a bicycle to travel safely.*

a deep hole in the ground:

abyss
*Beneath them, a yawning **abyss** descended to infinite depths.*

chasm
*Smoke signals could be seen from the far side of the enormous **chasm**.*

shaft
*The lift cage full of miners descended the **shaft** to the coalface.*

home NOUN

Your **home** is the building or place in which you live.

dwelling
*"Welcome to my humble **dwelling**," said Rat.*

residence
*The ambassador's **residence** was an impressive villa among palm trees.*

→ *See* **house**

The home made by...
ants is called a **hill**.
a badger is called a **sett** or **set** or **earth**.
a bear is called a **den** or **lair**.
bees is called a **hive**.
a bird is called a **nest**.
a fox is called an **earth** or a **lair**.
a hare is called a **form**.
a mole is called a **fortress**.
an otter is called a **holt**.
a rabbit is called a **burrow** or **warren**.
a snake is called a **nest**.
a squirrel is called a **drey**.

honest ADJECTIVE

If you are **honest**, you can be trusted to tell the truth.

frank
*"Now," Bhoomi's dad asked, "I want you to be **frank** with me. Is anything the matter?"*

sincere
*Mrs Fletcher felt that Susan had made a **sincere** effort to behave well.*

trustworthy
*My gran often said, "If you're not **trustworthy**, you're nothing!"*

truthful
*As the girl was normally **truthful**, her version of events was accepted.*

ANTONYM: dishonest

hooligan NOUN

A **hooligan** is a destructive and violent young person.

delinquent
*Mum said she would like to get hold of the **delinquents** who wrecked the scout hut.*

lout
*"You looking for trouble?" the **lout** said, his face two centimetres from mine.*

vandal
***Vandals** had broken the windows.*

yob (*informal*)
*Some **yobs** came into the youth club, but Mr Trainer sent them packing.*

hope (1) VERB

If you **hope** that something will happen, you want or expect it to happen.

anticipate
*Krishnan **anticipated** that his mum would bake him a cake on his birthday.*

count on
*"You mustn't **count on** me," my friend Wendy warned. "I might not be there."*

dream
*Vicky **dreamt** that one day she would be on that stage.*

look forward to
*Mrs Phillips was **looking forward to** going to the cinema when her car broke down.*

trust
*"I **trust** you all had a good holiday," said the head teacher at first assembly.*

hope (2) NOUN

A **hope** is the wish or expectation that things will go well in the future.

ambition
*It was Jasmine's **ambition** to be a professional ice skater one day.*

anticipation
*The sailor's proud parents put up decorations in **anticipation** of his homecoming.*

dream
*Napoleon's **dream** was to conquer Europe.*

ANTONYMS: desperation, hopelessness

hopeful (1) ADJECTIVE

If you are **hopeful** about something, you hope it will turn out well.

confident
*Our team were **confident** that we could win the trophy.*

optimistic
*My **optimistic** uncle is always looking on the bright side.*

ANTONYM: doubtful

hopeful (2) ADJECTIVE

If a situation is **hopeful**, it looks as if it will turn out well.

encouraging
*"An **encouraging** report" was all that the head teacher had written.*

promising
*The conductor told my mum that I was a **promising** violinist.*

ANTONYM: hopeless

hopeless (1) ADJECTIVE

You say something is **hopeless** when it is very bad and you do not feel it can get any better.

futile
*The dog made **futile** attempts to run away, but it was firmly tied to the railings.*

pointless
*"It's **pointless** asking me," my sister protested. "I don't know anything."*

vain
*The commuter puffed up the platform in a **vain** attempt to catch the train.*

ANTONYM: promising

→ *See* **impossible**

A B C D E F G H I J K L M N O P Q R S T U V W X Y Z

hopeless (2) ADJECTIVE

Someone who is **hopeless** is unable to do something well.

incompetent
*Yet again, the **incompetent** stuntman hobbled to the waiting ambulance.*

pathetic (*informal*)
*"I've never seen such a **pathetic** effort," Miss Marsden ranted.*

useless
*David was a **useless** salesman. Even his mother wouldn't buy from him.*

ANTONYMS: able, competent

horrible ADJECTIVE

Someone or something that is **horrible** is disagreeable and unpleasant.

abominable
*"That was an **abominable** thing to do," said the police officer.*

appalling
*There was an **appalling** smell coming from the drains.*

awful
*My new haircut is **awful**.*

dreadful
*My grandma made me a **dreadful** sweater for Christmas, but I had to pretend I liked it.*

hideous
*Into view came a beast so **hideous** that none could behold it.*

horrid
*Having one's property stolen is a **horrid** thing to happen.*

nasty
*"Investigating murders must be a **nasty** business," Dad remarked.*

terrible
*The lion uttered a **terrible** roar.*

horror NOUN

Horror is a strong feeling of alarm caused by something very unpleasant.

alarm
*Filled with **alarm**, the mother rushed to stop her baby falling in the pool.*

disgust
*Katrina's **disgust** at such a mean trick showed in her face.*

dismay
*To the shy man's **dismay**, the spotlight suddenly turned onto him.*

dread
*My mum has a **dread** of heights.*

fear
*There was a look of **fear** on Miss Muffet's face when she saw the spider.*

terror
***Terror** turned to anger when Latisha found ou I had put a worm in her lunchbox.*

→ *See* **fright** and **panic (2)**

hot

→ Look at the **Word Power** page!

house NOUN

A **house** is a building where people live.

dwelling
*Badger's **dwelling** lay deep in the heart of the Wild Wood.*

home
*House martins made their **home** under the eaves of the cottage.*

property
*The house agent said that the **property** had been empty for some time.*

residence
*Immaculate lawns ran from the ambassador's **residence** down to the river.*

Some types of houses:

bungalow	cabin
castle	chalet
cottage	detached house
farmhouse	flat
maisonette	manor
mansion	palace
ranch house	semidetached house
terraced house	tower block
villa	

hug VERB

If you **hug** someone, you put your arms round them and hold them close to you, usually to comfort them or to show affection.

cuddle
*A nurse **cuddled** the poorly child in her arms to comfort him.*

embrace
*The man and his elderly father **embraced** each other after years apart.*

squeeze
*I thought Auntie Flo was going to **squeeze** me to death. Ugh!*

hot

ADJECTIVE Something that is **hot** has a high temperature.

Very hot:

baking
*It was a **baking** July day.*

blistering
*Her birthday, for once, was a **blistering** summer day.*

boiling (hot)
*When everyone else is **boiling hot**, I'm freezing!*

burning
*People will cross **burning** deserts to get there.*

scorching (hot)
*The marathon took place in **scorching** weather.*

sultry
*It began one **sultry** August evening.*

sweltering
*The roads were remarkably quiet despite the **sweltering** weather.*

tropical
*The temperature soared to a **tropical** heat.*

Quite hot:

lukewarm
*The coffee was only **lukewarm**.*

tepid
*She put her mouth to the tap and drank the **tepid** water.*

warm
*It was **warm** in the house and David only wore shorts.*

Hot-flavoured food:

fiery
*He said it was 'a **fiery** combination of chicken, chillies and rice'.*

peppery
*She served it with **peppery** radishes.*

piquant
*The mustard gives a **piquant** edge to the dressing.*

spicy
*He made a **spicy** tomato sauce.*

Hot liquid:

piping hot
*There's nothing better than curling up with a bowl of **piping hot** soup.*

scalding
*I tried to sip the tea but it was **scalding**.*

steaming
*She carried two **steaming** mugs of coffee to the door and handed him one.*

➧ Also have a look at the **Word Power** page for **cold**!

A B C D E F G H I J K L M N O P Q R S T U V W X Y Z

huge ADJECTIVE

Something that is **huge** is extremely large in amount, size or degree.

colossal
Unexpectedly, the school show turned out to be a ***colossal*** *success.*

enormous
Towed behind six horses came a truly ***enormous*** *carriage.*

gigantic
There was a ***gigantic*** *cake at the film star's birthday party.*

immense
It was an ***immense*** *favour to ask, but what else could I do?*

massive
When the filling fell out, the crater in my tooth was ***massive****.*

vast
The Sahara desert covers a ***vast*** *area of land in North Africa.*

ANTONYM: tiny

hunch NOUN

If you have a **hunch** about something, you have a feeling or suspicion about it that is not based on facts or evidence.

idea
"I've an ***idea*** *that you may be just the girl for the job!" the manager said.*

inkling
Mrs Lindsey had an ***inkling*** *the class was planning a surprise for her.*

hungry ADJECTIVE

If you are **hungry**, you need or want food.

empty
"Please hurry up with that food, Mum, I'm ***empty****!" Lisa called from upstairs.*

famished
Our rations had run out, and we sat in the rain, soaked and ***famished****.*

ravenous
After helping with the harvest all day, Hugh was ***ravenous****.*

starving
While we waste food, millions of children in the developing world are ***starving****.*

hunt (1) VERB

When people **hunt**, they chase and kill wild animals for food or sport.

pursue
The hunters ***pursued*** *the elephants.*

stalk
The gamekeeper silently ***stalked*** *the red deer as it grazed.*

hunt (2) VERB

If you **hunt** for something, you search for it.

ferret about (*informal*)
For some reason, my sister was ***ferreting about*** *in the loft above my room.*

look high and low
"There it is!" Mum said. "I've ***looked high and low*** *for that remote control."*

scour
The neighbours helped us ***scour*** *the area for our missing cat.*

search
Although Ron ***searched*** *for the book, there was no trace of it.*

hurry (1) VERB

If you **hurry** somewhere, you go there quickly.

dash
Dad had to ***dash*** *down to the shop to buy a lottery ticket before it was too late.*

hasten
She ***hastened*** *to the headteacher's study for fear of being punished for lateness.*

rush
Anxious to see the end of the golf match, the crowd ***rushed*** *towards the final green.*

scurry
When Whiskers appeared, mice ***scurried*** *to al[l] parts of the garden.*

step on it (*informal*)
*"****Step on it****, old bean, we're late," Wooster said to his chauffeur.*

hurry (2) NOUN

If you are in a **hurry** to do something, you want to do it quickly.

haste
In her ***haste****, Mrs Pepperpot left her umbrella behind.*

rush
"What's the ***rush****?" Dad asked. "We'll get ther[e] two hours early."*

hurt (1) VERB

If you **hurt** yourself or someone else, you injure or cause physical pain to yourself or someone else.

bruise
*The hockey ball **bruised** Jamie's leg when Craig cracked it towards goal.*

harm
*I managed to get the butterfly out of the window without **harming** it.*

injure
*Dozens of people were **injured** in the pile-up.*

wound
*The ricocheting bullet **wounded** the old sheriff in the arm.*

hurt (2) VERB

If you **hurt** someone, or hurt their feelings, you upset them by being unkind towards them.

distress
*It **distressed** my dad to think that Sean wasn't very happy at school.*

upset
*We could tell that Miss Kielty was **upset** by the news she had received.*

wound
*Devesh was **wounded** to think that a friend would believe such lies about him.*

hurt (3) ADJECTIVE

If you are **hurt**, you are injured.

harmed
*Although the ceiling collapsed, no one was **harmed**.*

injured
*A nurse bandaged my **injured** wrist.*

wounded
***Wounded** troops were evacuated from the beach by the landing craft.*

hurt (4) ADJECTIVE

If you feel **hurt**, you are upset because of someone's unkindness towards you.

offended
*Scarlet felt **offended** that her friend had not invited her.*

upset
*My mum was visibly **upset** when she saw how poorly Gramps looked, but the nurse assured her he was on the road to recovery.*

hut NOUN

A **hut** is a small house or shelter.

cabin
*The old Canadian trapper lived in a log **cabin** in the woods.*

shack
*A few tumbledown **shacks** was all that remained of the gold miners' village.*

shed
*On Grandad's allotment is a **shed** where he keeps his tools.*

Ii

icy ADJECTIVE
Something that is **icy** has ice on it, or is very cold.

arctic
*Without a fire, conditions in our front room were nearly **arctic**.*

bitter
*A **bitter** wind was blowing off the sea as we walked along the promenade.*

freezing
*When we arrived in Canada for our holiday, it was the middle of winter and the weather was **freezing**.*

frozen
*With the sub-zero temperatures, all the lakes were **frozen** to some depth.*

raw
*A **raw** wind penetrated Shackleton's inadequate clothing.*

idea (1) NOUN
An **idea** is a plan or possible course of action.

brainwave
*Someone had the **brainwave** to use old tyres in making road surfaces.*

proposal
*The **proposal** to build an electric dishwasher was made as early as 1912.*

suggestion
*"That's a spiffing **suggestion**, Jeeves," replied Bertie Wooster.*

idea (2) NOUN
If you have an **idea** of something, you have a general but not a detailed knowledge of it.

inkling
*We had an **inkling** that something odd was going on.*

notion
*He was the one who first had the **notion** of humans flying.*

suspicion
*I had a strong **suspicion** that Letitia was lying to me.*

have an idea PHRASE
If you **have an idea**, you think something up.

conceive
*Sir Frank Whittle first **conceived** the jet engine in 1930.*

devise
*People are trying to **devise** new television game shows all the time.*

dream up
*"Who on earth could have **dreamt up** that strange-looking car?" Dad remarked.*

suggest
*Darren **suggested** we should go bowling and then for a pizza.*

idiot NOUN
An **idiot** is someone who is stupid or foolish.

fool
*"Don't touch those wires, you **fool**!" the electrician shouted.*

imbecile
*"Get out of my sight, you clumsy **imbecile**!" bellowed Clouseau's boss.*

nincompoop (*informal*)
*What a **nincompoop** I was to get up for school on Saturday!*

twit
*What a **twit** my little sister is – she believed me when I told her that I could fly.*

idiotic ADJECTIVE
Someone or something that is **idiotic** is very stupid.

crazy (*informal*)
*I must have been **crazy** to let my friend talk me into bungee jumping.*

foolish
*It was **foolish** to think that I could carry all those plates at once.*

hare-brained
*"Whoever thought of this **hare-brained** new scheme?" moaned the head teacher.*

senseless
*The way we damage the atmosphere by burning fuels is **senseless**.*

ANTONYM: sensible

ll ADJECTIVE

Someone who is **ill** is unhealthy or sick.

ailing
*The old man was **ailing**, but then he recovered and lived for many more years.*

laid up (*informal*)
*I went upstairs to see Dad, who was **laid up** with flu.*

poorly
*The nurse saw at once that the lady was very **poorly** and needed an ambulance.*

sick
*Moira was off **sick** last week, but she's back at school this week.*

unwell
*The visitor complained of feeling **unwell**, and asked to sit down.*

ANTONYM: healthy

llness NOUN

An **illness** is a particular disease.

ailment
*The explorer came back from the tropics with a mystery **ailment**.*

complaint
*Mum took me to the doctor's because I had a stomach **complaint**.*

disease
*Tuberculosis was once a common **disease**.*

sickness
*Many children suffer from travel **sickness**.*

naginary ADJECTIVE

Something that is **imaginary** exists only in your mind, not in real life.

fictitious
*My favourite **fictitious** characters are The Twits, from Roald Dahl's book of that name.*

mythological
*The Minotaur was a **mythological** creature, said to have lived in the catacombs of Crete.*

unreal
*The incredible beauty of the Himalayan mountains seemed almost **unreal**.*

ANTONYMS: real, actual

nagine VERB

If you **imagine** something or someone, you create a picture of them in your mind.

dream
*Rebecca **dreamed** she was back at the home where she had once lived.*

envisage
*Dillon **envisaged** what his bedroom in their new house would be like.*

fantasise
*As I trudged through the snow I **fantasised** about being at home in front of the fire.*

picture
*"Before you write, just **picture** yourself in a boat on a river," Mr Lennon said.*

visualise
*I tried to **visualise** what would happen if all cars grew legs.*

imitate VERB

If you **imitate** someone or something, you copy them.

do an impression of
*Sally made me laugh by **doing an impression of** our teacher.*

impersonate
*My brother is very good at **impersonating** my dad in a bad mood.*

mimic
*The clown walked behind the circus master, **mimicking** him perfectly.*

immediate ADJECTIVE

If something is **immediate**, it happens or is done without delay.

instant
*To make **instant** coffee, just add boiling water to the granules.*

instantaneous
*The huge flash of lightning was followed by an **instantaneous** peal of thunder.*

prompt
*Kamal's **prompt** action in phoning an ambulance saved the girl's life.*

urgent
*The message needed an **urgent** answer.*

immediately ADVERB

If something happens **immediately**, it happens at once.

directly
*The phrase: "Go **directly** to jail. Do not pass 'Go'." can be found on a Monopoly board.*

instantly
*Michaela recognised the film star **instantly** when she saw him in the street.*

A B C D E F G H I J K L M N O P Q R S T U V W X Y Z

promptly
*My annoying brother borrowed my watch and **promptly** broke it.*

right away
*I told Auntie Maureen I would run the errand **right away**.*

straight away
***Straight away**, Marie resolved to find out what the fuss was all about.*

important (1) ADJECTIVE

Something that is **important** is very valuable, necessary or significant.

crucial
*It was absolutely **crucial** that supplies reached the famine zone soon.*

serious
*"The school is in a **serious** position," the head teacher said. "We need more staff."*

urgent
*The matter was **urgent**, and needed a quick response.*

vital
*"If you want to do well as an adult, it's **vital** that you work hard now," my father advised.*

ANTONYM: unimportant

important (2) ADJECTIVE

An **important** person has a lot of influence or power.

distinguished
*Many **distinguished** guests attended the banquet.*

eminent
*My Uncle Armand is an **eminent** scientist.*

influential
*When it comes to government policy, Sir Brian is an extremely **influential** man.*

powerful
*The Canadian was a **powerful** man, owning a global business empire.*

ANTONYM: unimportant

impossible ADJECTIVE

Something that is **impossible** cannot happen or cannot be done.

hopeless
*The situation seemed **hopeless**, but the rescuers found another survivor.*

out of the question
*"A holiday abroad is not **out of the question**," Mum said. "We'll have to wait and see."*

unworkable
*The government's plan proved **unworkable**, and schools reverted to the old system.*

ANTONYM: possible

LANGUAGE TIP

If a place is impossible to reach, it is **inaccessible**. If someone's story is impossible to believe, it is **incredible**.

impressive ADJECTIVE

If something is **impressive**, people admir[e] it, usually because it is large or important.

awe-inspiring
*Edmund gazed up at the mountain. It was **awe-inspiring**.*

grand
*They came upon a huge house with a **grand** garden.*

great
*I stared at the **great** stone statue in the hotel courtyard.*

magnificent
*The trees were **magnificent**. They were the tallest he'd ever seen.*

improve VERB

If something **improves**, or if you **improve** it, it gets better.

advance
*Medical technology has **advanced** a great deal since my grandparents were children.*

develop
*Thomas's batting has **developed** this year.*

make progress
*My report said that I was **making progress** in most subjects.*

upgrade
*"Why should I **upgrade** my computer, when this one works perfectly?" John protested.*

include VERB

If one thing **includes** another, the second thing is part of the first thing.

comprise
*Mathematics **comprises** three main parts: arithmetic, geometry and algebra.*

contain
*A lot of food today **contains** chemicals.*

incorporate
*The package holiday **incorporates** excursio[ns] and a flight over the Grand Canyon.*

involve
"Will Mum's new job ***involve*** *a lot of time away?" I asked.*

ANTONYM: exclude

ncrease (1) VERB

If something **increases**, or if you **increase** it, it becomes larger in number, level or amount.

add to
Hywell ***added to*** *his reputation by scoring three goals.*

build up
"I want you to ***build up*** *your exercise slowly," the doctor advised after I sprained my ankle.*

enhance
My brother hoped a smart suit would ***enhance*** *his chances of getting the job.*

enlarge
The photograph was ***enlarged****, and is now pinned on my wall.*

extend
To reach the gutters, Dad had to ***extend*** *his ladder by two metres.*

ANTONYM: decrease

ncrease (2) NOUN

An **increase** is a rise in the number, level or amount of something.

boost
The ***boost*** *in the number of goals meant that the team would be in the semifinals.*

development
There has been a ***development*** *in organic farming over the past few years.*

growth
Rapid population ***growth*** *is a problem that affects many countries.*

rise
There has been a ***rise*** *in pupil numbers.*

ANTONYM: decrease

ncredible ADJECTIVE

Something that is **incredible** is totally amazing or impossible to believe.

astonishing
The Roman coins were an ***astonishing*** *discovery.*

astounding
To put a man on the moon was an ***astounding*** *achievement.*

beyond belief
It is ***beyond belief*** *to think that someone could row across the Atlantic on their own.*

extraordinary
"How ***extraordinary****! That's the third time I've seen Mrs Grimes today," Mum observed.*

marvellous
The choirboy had a ***marvellous*** *voice for one so young.*

sensational
A ***sensational*** *performance by the captain helped the team to victory.*

unbelievable
We had ***unbelievable*** *luck in catching the ferry after so many delays.*

infect VERB

To **infect** is to cause disease in someone or something.

affect
Our school was closed for two days to stop more people being ***affected*** *by the virus.*

contaminate
Most food is ***contaminated*** *with pesticides, preservatives and other chemicals.*

infection NOUN

An **infection** is an illness caused by germs.

bug (*informal*)
The sick people were put in quarantine to prevent the ***bug*** *spreading.*

disease
Measles is a highly contagious ***disease*** *that causes red spots on the skin.*

virus
Amanda missed three weeks of school because she had a throat ***virus****.*

informal ADJECTIVE

Informal means relaxed and casual.

casual
My dad wears ***casual*** *clothes to work on a Friday.*

easy
Our doctor has a very ***easy*** *manner.*

friendly
It was just a ***friendly*** *match.*

natural
He wasn't at all pompous and just chatted in a ***natural*** *way.*

relaxed
It was a very ***relaxed*** *interview.*

A B C D E F G H I J K L M N O P Q R S T U V W X Y Z

information NOUN

If someone gives you **information** about something, they tell you about it.

facts
The police said they had several leads in the case, but needed more ***facts****.*

material
You'll find plenty of ***material*** *on this subject in the library.*

news
The soldier's friends and family were anxiously awaiting ***news****.*

notice
We'll get plenty of ***notice*** *nearer the time.*

word
The head teacher said he'd received ***word*** *that a famous author was coming.*

inhabitant (1) NOUN

If you are an **inhabitant** of a place, you live there.

citizen
Although born in Great Britain, Steve became a ***citizen*** *of New Zealand.*

native
A ***native*** *of New York, Christina moved with her family to California at the age of 10.*

resident
My aunt and uncle are ***residents*** *of Denton, a suburb close to where we live.*

LANGUAGE TIP
The general name for all the inhabitants of a town or area is its **population**.

inhabitant (2) NOUN

If you are an **inhabitant** of a building, you live there.

occupier
We weren't sure who was the ***occupier*** *of the flat on the top floor.*

resident
Mrs O'Connell is a ***resident*** *of the old people's home near us.*

tenant
The landlord rented out several flats, and had all kinds of ***tenants****.*

injure VERB

If something **injures** someone, it hurts or harms them in some way.

damage
The accident ***damaged*** *Iain's shoulder.*

harm
Electricity has great power to ***harm*** *people, if used carelessly.*

wound
My great grandad was ***wounded*** *by shrapnel in the Second World War.*

innocent ADJECTIVE

Someone who is **innocent** is not guilty of a crime or of doing something wrong.

blameless
The Roman governor thought the prisoner was ***blameless****, and wanted to release him.*

not guilty
The jury found that the accused was ***not guilty*** *of the robbery charge.*

ANTONYM: guilty

inside (1) ADJECTIVE

Inside refers to the inner part of something.

inner
The monastery's ***inner*** *courtyard was where monks worked and taught.*

interior
A car's ***interior*** *lights come on when you open the door.*

internal
The stomach, liver, kidneys and lungs are all ***internal*** *organs of the body.*

ANTONYMS: external, outside

LANGUAGE TIP
Inside out means with the inside part facing outwards.

inside (2) ADVERB

Inside can mean in something.

indoors
It was raining heavily, so we had to play ***indoors****.*

within (*old-fashioned*)
"Who dwells ***within*** *this castle?" the knight enquired of the guard.*

ANTONYM: outside

instant ADJECTIVE

Something **instant** happens immediately and without delay.

fast
Fast *food tends to be quickly available, but lacking in nutrition.*

immediate
*New Whizzo cleaner gets **immediate** results on stubborn stains!*

on-the-spot
*With scratchcards, if you're lucky, you get an **on-the-spot** win.*

prompt
*The café impressed us by the **prompt** service we received on arrival.*

nstead ADVERB

If you choose one thing **instead** of another, you choose it as an alternative to the other.

alternatively
*I thought to myself, "Shall I have a cup of tea or, **alternatively**, a soft drink?"*

in place
***In place** of a forward, the coach brought on another defender.*

nsult VERB

If you **insult** someone, you upset them by being rude to them.

offend
*I didn't mean to **offend** you when I said you were grumpy.*

slight
*She felt **slighted** when she was not invited to the party.*

upset
*It will **upset** her if you criticise her hairstyle.*

terest (1) NOUN

If you have an **interest** in something, you want to know more about it.

concern
*Mitchell had always had an avid **concern** for wildlife.*

curiosity
*Nell's **curiosity** took her towards an ancient antique shop.*

involvement
*For some years, my parents have had an **involvement** with our local tennis club.*

terest (2) NOUN

An **interest** is something you enjoy doing.

activity
*My baby sister's favourite **activity** is shaking her rattle.*

hobby
*The **hobby** Nimesh most fancied was dinghy sailing.*

pastime
*Jigsaws are a very popular **pastime** with all ages.*

pursuit
*Angling is one of the most common leisure **pursuits** in the world.*

interest (3) VERB

If something **interests** you, you want to know more about it.

attract
*Supposedly, anything shiny **attracts** jackdaws.*

fascinate
*The birds which perched on the tree's branches **fascinated** the young girl.*

intrigue
*It **intrigued** Will to find out how you were able to pick up a new language so easily.*

interesting ADJECTIVE

If something is **interesting**, you enjoy it or want to know more about it.

absorbing
*Mum and Dad had a very **absorbing** conversation over dinner.*

appealing
*"I think the patterned dress is more **appealing** than the plain one," I said to Lisa.*

captivating
*The audience found the show **captivating**.*

enthralling
*"I found the model dinosaurs **enthralling**," Jodie told her dad excitedly.*

fascinating
*Bob thought the magic show was **fascinating**.*

gripping
*The story that Dad read to us was so **gripping** that I couldn't stop thinking about it.*

riveting
*We followed the **riveting** news story of the missing actor with interest.*

spellbinding
*It was quite **spellbinding** to watch the glass maker blowing and spinning the glass.*

ANTONYM: uninteresting

a b c d e f g h i j k l m n o p q r s t u v w x y z

A B C D E F G H I J K L M N O P Q R S T U V W X Y Z

interfere VERB

If you **interfere** in a situation, you try to influence it, although it does not concern you.

meddle
*My aunt's problem was that she would always **meddle** in other people's business.*

poke your nose in (*informal*)
*"Don't you **poke your nose in** what doesn't concern you," Gran said.*

pry
*"I hope I'm not **prying**, but I'd love to know your cake recipe," Mum said to the baker.*

tamper
*The accident was caused because someone had **tampered** with my bike wheel.*

international ADJECTIVE

Something that is **international** involves different countries.

global
*These days, **global** communications are achieved via satellites.*

intercontinental
***Intercontinental** flights leave from Terminal 3, domestic flights from Terminal 4.*

universal
*Many Hollywood actors and actresses have become **universal** superstars.*

worldwide
*The singer was hoping for **worldwide** success with his latest release.*

interrupt (1) VERB

If you **interrupt** someone, you start talking while they are talking.

barge in
*Mum and I were chatting when my brother **barged in**, asking for sweets.*

butt in
*Dad **butted in** to say that my uncle had left his car lights on.*

chip in
*Mrs Ellis was pleased that Priya had **chipped in** with her comments.*

intrude
*"I don't want to **intrude**," the man panted, "but I've an urgent message for you."*

interrupt (2) VERB

If you **interrupt** a process or activity, you stop it for a time.

disrupt
*The match was **disrupted** by some people invading the pitch.*

halt
*Rain **halted** play at Wimbledon for a second day yesterday.*

hold up
*Our journey was **held up** by a few minutes, when some cows got loose ahead.*

invade VERB

If an army **invades** a country, it enters it by force.

attack
*Boadicea's wild hordes **attacked** the Roman township.*

occupy
*Soldiers **occupied** the town within a few minutes.*

seize
*In a daring raid, the outlaws **seized** the Sheriff's castle.*

invasion NOUN

An **invasion** is the entering or attacking of a place.

assault
*Air strikes paved the way for an **assault** on the beaches.*

attack
*The **attack** was timed for 06:30 hours.*

offensive
*A huge enemy **offensive** was planned, involving 12 armoured divisions.*

raid
*In a lightning **raid**, Drake's crews captured several enemy ships.*

ANTONYM: withdrawal

invent VERB

If you **invent** something, you are the first person to think of it or make it.

come up with
*My friend's dad **came up with** a gadget to relieve hay fever.*

conceive
*Laszlo Biro **conceived** the idea of a pen with small ball at its tip.*

create
*It takes many people to **create** a film.*

design
*A light vacuum cleaner was **designed** by Mr Spangler, but marketed by Mr Hoover.*

devise
Sir Isaac Newton built the first telescope, using an idea ***devised*** *by Galileo.*

dream up
People ***dream up*** *all sorts of ideas about what life in the future will be like.*

invention NOUN

An **invention** is something that is a completely new idea.

brainchild
The bicycle was the ***brainchild*** *of a Scottish blacksmith, Kirkpatrick Macmillan.*

creation
The first practical telephone was the ***creation*** *of Alexander Graham Bell.*

inventor NOUN

An **inventor** is a person who invents something.

creator
He was the ***creator*** *of many popular children's television programmes.*

designer
A man called Levi Strauss was the ***designer*** *of the first jeans, around 1850.*

founder
The businesswoman is the ***founder*** *of several websites.*

originator
The ***originator*** *of the printing press was a 15th-century German called Gutenberg.*

pioneer
The Wright brothers of the USA were ***pioneers*** *of aeroplane flight.*

investigate VERB

If someone **investigates** something, they try to find out all the facts about it.

explore
Mum gave us permission to ***explore*** *the cave in the cliff.*

make enquiries
After the burglary, police ***made enquiries*** *at all the houses on the estate.*

probe
The lander's mission was to ***probe*** *the surface of Mars for evidence of life.*

research
Scientists are constantly ***researching*** *the causes of cancer.*

snoop (*informal*)
"What are you doing ***snooping*** *round here?" the doorman asked the private investigator.*

→ *See* **examine**

invisible ADJECTIVE

If something is **invisible**, you cannot see it.

hidden
The hill-top monument was ***hidden*** *in the clouds.*

out of sight
As soon as Mrs Frost was ***out of sight****, some of us started a pillow fight.*

unseen
Guided by an ***unseen*** *hand, the candle moved upwards towards the ceiling.*

ANTONYM: visible

involve VERB

If a situation or activity **involves** something, that thing is a necessary part of it.

entail
This mission will ***entail*** *long hours and great bravery.*

mean
Taking on a business ***meant*** *a lot of hard work for my parents.*

necessitate
The making of concrete ***necessitates*** *mixing cement, sand, gravel and water.*

require
Driving a car ***requires*** *concentration, skill and common sense.*

J j

jagged ADJECTIVE

Something **jagged** has an uneven edge with sharp points on it.

broken
*The wall was topped with **broken** glass.*

rough
*Steven tore his sleeve on the **rough** edge of a rock.*

uneven
*She trimmed the photo rapidly with careless, **uneven** cuts.*

jail (1) NOUN

A **jail** is a building where criminals are locked up.

nick (*slang*)
*He spent seven years in the **nick**.*

penitentiary
*"The state **penitentiary** is where the bad guys go," the American guide told us.*

prison
*Despite attempts to improve them, most old **prisons** are grim-looking places.*

LANGUAGE TIP

The **nick** is slang used in Britain, Australia and New Zealand. **Penitentiary** is a word used in America.

---

jail (2) VERB

To **jail** someone can mean to lock them up in a jail.

detain
*Police **detained** the suspect until he was due in court.*

imprison
*For her outburst in court, the woman was **imprisoned** for a further three months.*

jam (1) NOUN

A **jam** is a situation where there are so many people or things that it is difficult to move.

bottleneck
*Those traffic lights are a notorious **bottleneck**, with queues every day.*

hold-up
*Minor roadworks caused a major **hold-up**.*

queue
*"Expect long **queues** at Junction 5," my radio warned.*

tailback
*Fortunately, Dad saw the long **tailback** ahead, and managed to turn off.*

jam (2) NOUN (*informal*)

If you are in a **jam**, you are in a difficult situation.

dilemma
*The family faced a **dilemma** in the floods: to stand on the roof or to swim.*

quandary
*I was in a **quandary** when I lost my purse.*

tight spot
*When the other plane opened fire from behind, Officer Kite knew he was in a **tight spot**.*

jam (3) VERB

If you **jam** something into a place, you squeeze it in.

cram
*At rush hour in the city, people **cram** themselves into trains and buses.*

force
*Guards **forced** the gates shut as the enemy battered the other side.*

pack
*The school hall was **packed** for our end-of-term concert.*

ram
*Mum always **rams** salad into her help-yourself tub until it's overflowing.*

stuff
*Milos **stuffed** his PE kit into his bag and ran for the bus.*

wedge
*My brother **wedged** a book under the leg of his desk to stop it rocking.*

jam (4) VERB

If something **jams**, it becomes stuck or is unable to work properly.

block
*The ball **blocked** the drain and water flooded the back yard.*

clog
*Never put candle holders in a dishwasher, because the wax will **clog** the pipes when it sets.*

ealous ADJECTIVE

If you feel **jealous**, you feel envious of others, wanting to have what they have or wanting to be like them.

envious
*Clark was **envious** of his brother's new bike.*

green with envy
***Green with envy**, the wicked witch plotted revenge on her beautiful sister.*

resentful
*It is not worth being **resentful**, as there will always be people richer than you.*

et NOUN

A **jet** is a stream of liquid or gas forced out under pressure.

fountain
*The firework exploded in a **fountain** of coloured lights.*

gush
*They had to leap back to avoid the sudden **gush** from the tap.*

spray
*The horse kicked up a **spray** of water as it cantered through the river.*

spurt
*There was a small **spurt** of blood when Debbie cut her finger.*

squirt
*A **squirt** of ink from the fountain pen went across his homework.*

ewel NOUN

A **jewel** is a precious stone, such as a diamond or a ruby, used to make things like rings and necklaces.

gem
*Her ring had a single **gem** set in silver.*

gemstone
*The duchess wore a tiara sparkling with rare **gemstones**.*

ornament
*King Ralph wore several valuable **ornaments** around his neck.*

precious stone
*The treasure chest was overflowing with **precious stones**.*

rock
*The singer wore **rocks** the size of marbles on his fingers.*

stone
*"What a beautiful **stone**," gushed Sandra. "Was it expensive?"*

job (1) NOUN

A **job** is the work that someone does to earn money.

career
*Fiona decided she was going to make a **career** in industry.*

occupation
*Being a teacher is not an easy **occupation**.*

profession
*My brother is studying to go into the nursing **profession**.*

trade
*Dad's **trade** is plumbing and heating.*

job (2) NOUN

A **job** is a particular task that has to be done.

assignment
*Ethan's **assignment** was to get the stolen painting back.*

chore
*On Saturdays, all of us have to help with the household **chores**.*

errand
*Mum asked me to do an **errand** for our next-door neighbour.*

mission
*The astronauts' **mission** was to repair the satellite telescope.*

task
*Moving the whole vegetable patch was a huge **task** for the gardener.*

job (3) NOUN

A **job** is a duty or responsibility.

duty
*A doorman's **duty** is to check that no one unsuitable comes in.*

function
*The generator's **function** was as a back-up if the electricity failed.*

responsibility
*"Felicity, it's your **responsibility** to put out the games equipment," Mrs Beerbohm said.*

role
*A head teacher's **role** is to manage the school effectively.*

join (1) VERB

To **join** can mean to fasten or connect things.

attach
*The dry-cleaners **attached** the label to the garment with a safety pin.*

connect
*"Once the pipes are **connected**, the sink will be finished," the plumber announced.*

couple
*The man in overalls jumped down to **couple** the carriages together.*

link
*For the TV programme, they built tree houses in the jungle **linked** by rope bridges.*

join (2) VERB

When two things **join**, or when one thing **joins** another, they come together.

combine
*Our school **combined** with St Mary's for the Christmas carol service.*

merge
*The two companies **merged** to form a giant corporation.*

unite
*The countries have **united** to form one team.*

ANTONYM: separate

join (3) VERB

If you **join** a club or organisation, you become a member of it.

enlist
*She **enlisted** in the army at seventeen.*

enrol
*My sister has **enrolled** in an acting class at our local college.*

sign up for
*Several children **signed up for** the after-school gym club.*

joke (1) NOUN

A **joke** is something that you say to make people laugh.

gag (*informal*)
*The comedian's **gags** were too rude for Mum.*

pun
*My favourite **pun** is: It was a sad wedding. Even the cake was in tiers!*

wisecrack (*informal*)
*Uncle Ted can never be serious; he's always coming out with **wisecracks**.*

joke (2) VERB

If you are **joking**, you are teasing someone.

jest
*Callum said he was **jesting**, but Morag was in tears nevertheless.*

kid (*informal*)
*Dad tried to **kid** me that he had sold my bike, but I knew he wouldn't be that mean.*

tease
*I knew Jazlyn was **teasing**, but my mate took her seriously.*

journey NOUN

A **journey** is the act of travelling from one place to another.

drive
*My parents made the long **drive** from Paris to the south of France.*

expedition
*Mr Malone told us we were going on an **expedition** through the mountains.*

trek
*The long **trek** ended at a youth hostel.*

voyage
*Columbus's four **voyages** took him to North and Central America.*

judge VERB

If you **judge** someone or something, you decide what they are like.

assess
*It was the inspector's job to **assess** how clean the kitchen was.*

determine
*He had a job **determining** whether the fish was fully cooked.*

estimate
*The tour guide **estimated** we would arrive in an hour's time.*

evaluate
*At the end of the debate, Mrs Fitch **evaluates** how we have done.*

weigh up
*Paula **weighed up** whether to take the jumps slowly or to go full tilt.*

A B C D E F G H I J K L M N O P Q R S T U V W X Y Z

juice NOUN

Juice is the liquid that comes from fruit such as oranges when you squeeze them.

fluid
*He opened the container and **fluid** ran onto the table.*

liquid
*As she squeezed the fruit, drops of **liquid** fell into the cake mixture.*

jumble (1) NOUN

A **jumble** is an untidy muddle of things.

chaos
*My sister's room was a scene of utter **chaos**.*

clutter
*You could have filled ten sacks with the **clutter** in the attic.*

muddle
*The wind reduced Mrs Jackson's papers to a complete **muddle**.*

jumble (2) VERB

If you **jumble** things, you mix them up untidily.

muddle
*Mum is always **muddling** her papers then losing them.*

shuffle
*With an expert flourish, the gambler **shuffled** the cards and dealt.*

tangle
*The angler **tangled** his lines up and consequently lost the fish.*

jump VERB

When you **jump**, you spring off the ground using the muscles in your legs.

bound
*The greyhound **bounded** up to the terrier, who let out a huge growl.*

hurdle
*All the runners managed to **hurdle** the fence, except Kyle, who fell on his face.*

leap
*Chased by the guards, the escaped prisoner tried to **leap** across the ditch.*

pounce
*Our cat waits near the shed to **pounce** on unsuspecting mice.*

spring
*When she heard the word "chocolate", my sister **sprang** out of bed.*

vault
*In the cross-country race, we had to **vault** a gate.*

junk NOUN

Junk is old, unwanted or worthless things that are sold cheaply or thrown away.

clutter
*"Some day I will clear that **clutter** from our loft," Dad promised.*

jumble
*We bagged up the **jumble** and took it to the charity shop.*

scrap
*The millionaire had made his fortune as a **scrap** metal merchant.*

→ *See* **rubbish (1)**

Kk

keen ADJECTIVE

If you are **keen** to do something, or for something to happen, you want very much to do it or for it to happen.

eager
Nazirah was ***eager*** *to help set up the school sports day.*

enthusiastic
My report said, "John is an ***enthusiastic*** *worker."*

willing
Our neighbour was very ***willing*** *for us to borrow his lawn mower.*

keep (1) VERB

If you **keep** something somewhere, you store it there.

collect
My brother ***collected*** *swap cards in a secret tin.*

deposit
We ***deposited*** *our money in the hotel safe.*

hold
"Our stock is ***held*** *in the warehouse," explained the manager.*

retain
At the theatre, the ushers tear off half your ticket, and you ***retain*** *the other half.*

stock
"I'm sorry, madam, we don't ***stock*** *that brand," the shopkeeper said.*

store
You can ***store*** *apples for several months if you do it properly.*

keep (2) VERB

If you **keep** doing something, you do it again and again.

carry on
Despite being told to stop, they ***carried on*** *throwing things at each other.*

continue
Despite the pouring rain, we ***continued*** *kicking our ball around.*

persist
"If you ***persist*** *in talking," Miss Hassan said, "there's going to be big trouble."*

keep (3) VERB

If you **keep** a promise, you do what you say you will do.

carry out
The council ***carried out*** *its promise to restore the crumbling church.*

fulfil
The knight ***fulfilled*** *his oath to the princess and slew the dragon.*

honour
Dad ***honoured*** *his promise to take us all bowling.*

kidnap VERB

If someone **kidnaps** someone else, they take them away by force and demand something in exchange for returning them.

abduct
While travelling, the millionaire's son was ***abducted*** *by bandits.*

hold to ransom
The pirates ***held*** *the boy* ***to ransom*** *for a million dollars.*

seize
Having ***seized*** *the hostage, the guerrillas didn't know what to do with her.*

snatch (*informal*)
The message came through to HQ: "The boss's wife has been ***snatched****!"*

LANGUAGE TIP
Money that is demanded to free someone who has been kidnapped is a **ransom**.

---

kill VERB

If someone **kills** a person, animal or plant, they make them die.

assassinate
The police uncovered a plot to ***assassinate*** *the President.*

bump off (*informal*)
"Send Legs to ***bump off*** *Fat Antonio," drawled Luigi, the Mafia boss.*

do away with
The evil duke planned to ***do away with*** *all his enemies.*

murder
*Roberts went on trial for **murdering** a man and was imprisoned for life.*

slay (*old-fashioned*)
*The book of legends contains a picture of St George **slaying** the dragon.*

take someone's life
*At the command of the king, the four knights **took the archbishop's life**.*

kill as a punishment:

execute
*King Henry VIII had two of his wives **executed**.*

put to death
*Ann Boleyn was **put to death** at the Tower of London.*

kill many people or animals:

annihilate
*The terrible disease caused whole herds of cattle to be **annihilated**.*

exterminate
*The council sent someone to **exterminate** the cockroaches that had invaded our flat.*

massacre
*The army was **massacred** by rebel forces.*

kill people or animals brutally:

butcher
*Anyone who disagreed with the leader was **butchered** by his henchmen.*

slaughter
*Hundreds of people were **slaughtered** during the conflict.*

kill animals humanely:

cull
*Because of foot-and-mouth disease, many cattle had to be **culled**.*

put down
*Our rabbit had to be **put down** yesterday.*

slaughter
*Many animals are **slaughtered** for human consumption.*

LANGUAGE TIP
If someone kills themselves, they **commit suicide** or **take their own life**. To kill someone famous or important is to **assassinate** them.

kind (1) NOUN

A **kind** of thing is a particular thing of the same type as other things.

brand
*The interviewer asked Mum which **brand** of soap she used.*

breed
*Our favourite **breed** of dog is the Staffordshire bull terrier.*

class
*Dad admitted that his friend played a better **class** of tennis altogether.*

species
*The finch is the **species** of bird that helped Darwin form his theory of evolution.*

type
*A baguette is my favourite **type** of sandwich.*

variety
*It is amazing how many **varieties** of rose there are.*

kind (2) ADJECTIVE

Someone who is **kind** behaves in a caring and helpful way towards other people.

caring
*Mum was very **caring** when it came to looking after Gran in her old age.*

humane
*Our cat was old and ill; it was only **humane** to have her put down.*

kindly
*"What a **kindly** gesture," my aunt said, when I gave her the flowers.*

sympathetic
*I wish my sister had been more **sympathetic** when I fell off my bike.*

thoughtful
*It was **thoughtful** of Dad to take Mum out on Mother's Day.*

understanding
*Nurses have to be **understanding** when dealing with distressed patients.*

warm-hearted
*Mrs Thomas will be remembered as a **warm-hearted**, generous lady.*

ANTONYMS: unkind, cruel

kindness NOUN

Kindness is the act of being kind.

goodness
*The monk's **goodness** showed in his gentle manners and understanding nature.*

humanity
*Despite his fame and success, the rock star showed **humanity** and concern for all he met.*

sympathy
*Many townsfolk offered their **sympathy** to the man whose wife had died.*

understanding
*It takes **understanding** to deal with people who are ill.*

king NOUN

A **king** is a man who is the head of state in a country, and who inherited his position from his parents.

emperor
*The **Emperor** of Japan sat serenely on his gilded throne.*

monarch
*After almost 40 years as **monarch**, the king handed over to his son, the crown prince.*

sovereign
*In mythology, Neptune was the **sovereign** of the seas.*

LANGUAGE TIP
The wife of a king is a **queen**. The son of a king and queen is a **prince** and their daughter is a **princess**.

---

kit NOUN

A **kit** is a collection of equipment and clothing that you use for a sport or other activity.

gear
*We were told to put our **gear** into waterproof bags.*

tools
*Nicholas was under strict instructions not to touch the **tools** in the shed.*

knock VERB

If you **knock** on something, you hit it hard with your hand to make a noise.

pound
*In rage, the angry diner **pounded** on the table.*

rap
*The messenger **rapped** smartly on the door.*

tap
*A sound awoke Karl. It was someone **tapping** gently on the window.*

know (1) VERB

If you **know** something, you have it in your mind and you do not need to learn it.

be aware of
*Sunil **was aware of** the rules of the competition.*

understand
***Understanding** how dangerous some crooks can be, the detective reached for the revolver.*

know (2) VERB

If you **know** a person, place or thing, you are familiar with them.

be acquainted with
*"Are you **acquainted with** the school rules?" Mr Holdsworthy asked, sarcastically.*

be familiar with
*"I wonder if you **are familiar with** the rule about eating in class?" he enquired.*

knowledge NOUN

Knowledge is all the facts and information that you know.

education
*He was a man with little **education** but a kind heart.*

learning
*After a lifetime of quiet study, the old man was full of wisdom and **learning**.*

scholarship
*My grandma enjoyed a lifetime of **scholarship**, completing her third degree when she was 70.*

understanding
*At last Jacintha felt she had an **understanding** of algebra.*

wisdom
*The old man was a source of great **wisdom**.*

ANTONYM: ignorance

Ll

lag VERB

If a person or a thing **lags** behind, they make slower progress than other people or other things and do not keep up.

dawdle
*"Stop **dawdling** at the back," Miss Finch called out, as we walked to the playing field.*

linger
*Two fans **lingered** outside the grounds after the rest of the crowd had left.*

straggle
*The sheepdog dashed off to round up the sheep that were **straggling** at the back.*

trail
*Marcie and Grace **trailed** behind the rest of the class on the walk up the steep hill.*

lame ADJECTIVE

Someone who is **lame** has an injured leg and cannot walk easily.

crippled
*They stretchered the **crippled** athlete off the field with a thigh injury.*

disabled
*The ex-soldier was now **disabled** as the result of a bullet wound to the leg.*

hobbling
*The **hobbling** player signalled that he needed to come off the pitch.*

limping
*The sheriff had a **limping** deputy.*

land (1) NOUN

Land is the parts of the earth's surface that are not covered by water.

dry land
*When the boat reached **dry land**, the pirates leapt out silently.*

earth
*A plough slices downwards and beneath the surface, turning the **earth** over.*

ground
*A supermarket is being built on waste **ground** behind our house.*

land (2) NOUN

Land is an area of ground.

estate
*The millionaire's **estate** was surrounded by an electric fence.*

grounds
*"Guests are welcome to wander around the **grounds**," the hotel brochure told us.*

property
*I had no idea that I was trespassing on someone's **property**.*

land (3) NOUN

A **land** is a country.

country
*Switzerland had borders with four other **countries**.*

nation
*Churchill told the **nation** that the war would be a long, hard struggle.*

land (4) VERB

When you **land** somewhere on a plane or a ship, you arrive there.

berth
*Coming in on the high tide, the cruise liner **berthed** at Southampton.*

dock
*"What time will we **dock**, skipper?" the deckhand asked.*

touch down
*Despite the aeroplane's burst tyre, the pilot managed to **touch down** safely.*

language (1) NOUN

A **language** is a system of words used by a particular group of people to communicate with each other.

dialect
*Some people find Shona's Scottish **dialect** difficult to understand.*

jargon
*The report was full of scientific **jargon** that I couldn't understand.*

tongue
*French was his mother **tongue**, but Cyril spoke three other languages fluently.*

A B C D E F G H I J K L M N O P Q R S T U V W X Y Z

language (2) NOUN

Language is the style in which you speak or write.

phrasing
*The meaning was clear, even if the **phrasing** of the email was rather basic.*

style
*"Sandra's **style** of speaking is very grown-up," commented Mum.*

wording
*Mrs Cahill suggested changing the **wording** to add punch to the sentence.*

large ADJECTIVE

Someone or something **large** is bigger than usual.

big
*Joe wasn't a **big** man, but he could certainly hit a ball hard!*

colossal
*Our uncle in New York says that the Empire State Building is a **colossal** structure.*

enormous
*At over two metres tall, the man looked **enormous** in the model village.*

giant
*King Kong picked up the helpless Miss Darrow in one **giant** paw.*

gigantic
*My favourite football team has got a **gigantic** new stadium.*

great
*A **great** swathe of golden corn covered the rolling hillside.*

huge
*There is a **huge** medieval cathedral in the city's main square.*

immense
*Our town's sports centre has an **immense** swimming pool.*

massive
*The Colossus at Rhodes was a **massive** statue straddling the harbour entrance.*

vast
*The majority of Mongolia is a **vast** desert.*

ANTONYM: small

last (1) ADJECTIVE

The **last** part of something happens after all the others.

closing
*The head teacher's **closing** remarks were aimed at the parents.*

concluding
*In the **concluding** chapter, Lyra and Will are parted.*

final
*"As a **final** word, I want to thank all of you for coming," the mayor said.*

ANTONYM: opening

at last PHRASE

At last can mean after a long time.

eventually
***Eventually**, the lost hikers saw the lights of a distant farmhouse.*

finally
*After ten hours, the train **finally** reached the capital.*

last (2) ADJECTIVE

The **last** thing or event is the most recent one.

latest
*"Have you heard the **latest** news?" my sister asked excitedly.*

most recent
*The **most recent** report from the hospital says that Gran is doing well.*

last (3) VERB

If something **lasts**, it continues to exist or happen.

continue
*"We hope," said the mayor, "that the friendship between our towns **continues** for years."*

endure
*Gran's marriage to Gramps had **endured** through all life's ups and downs.*

hold out
*"Let's hope that wing **holds out** till we land," muttered the pilot.*

remain
*On its hill top, the monument **remained** as a memorial to the great general.*

survive
*The Oxford–Cambridge boat race **survives** today after over 170 years.*

late ADJECTIVE

If you are **late** arriving somewhere, you get there after the time that was arranged or expected.

delayed
*The plane was **delayed** because of fog.*

last-minute
*The delay in our departure meant we had a **last-minute** dash to catch the train.*

overdue
*As we were **overdue**, Mum began to worry.*

ANTONYM: punctual

laugh

→ Look at the **Word Power** page!

laughter NOUN

Laughter is the action of laughing or the sound of people laughing.

amusement
*"I cannot see any cause for **amusement**," Mr Jones said stonily.*

hilarity
*During the pantomime there was much **hilarity** in the audience.*

law NOUN

A **law** is a rule that is made by the government.

code
*Drivers are expected to follow strict **codes** of behaviour on the road.*

regulation
*There are **regulations** to control the hours pilots spend flying.*

rule
*An important **rule** is that children go to school regularly.*

lay VERB

If you **lay** something somewhere, you put it there carefully.

place
*They collected the papers and **placed** them on her desk.*

put
*"Just **put** it down anywhere on the table," she said.*

set down
*He **set down** the book in front of her.*

spread
*Dad **spread** a rug on the damp grass.*

layer NOUN

A **layer** is a single thickness of something that lies underneath or above something else.

blanket
*A **blanket** of snow lay on the ground.*

coating
*The pond was covered in a **coating** of ice.*

film
*A **film** of wax protected the new car.*

seam
*The miners found a **seam** of gold in the rock.*

sheet
*The car skidded on a **sheet** of black ice.*

lazy ADJECTIVE

If you are **lazy**, you are idle and are unwilling to work.

idle
*"You have no chance of success, if you're **idle**," Mrs Krishnan warned.*

slack
*Mum warned me that I would be in trouble if I was **slack** about my homework.*

ANTONYM: hard-working

lead (1) VERB

If you **lead** someone somewhere, you go in front of them to show them the way.

conduct
*A talkative guide **conducted** us round the mansion.*

escort
*The prisoner was **escorted** to the van by two armed guards.*

guide
*We were **guided** to our seats by a member of the cabin crew.*

steer
*Mum **steered** the little boy through the crowd to where his mother was looking for him.*

PRONUNCIATION TIP
When it is a verb, **lead** is pronounced **leed**.

lead (2) VERB

Someone who **leads** a group of people is in charge of them.

command
*The colonel **commanded** a regiment in Cyprus.*

A
B
C
D
E
F
G
H
I
J
K
L
M
N
O
P
Q
R
S
T
U
V
W
X
Y
Z

laugh

(1) VERB When you **laugh**, you make a noise that shows you are amused or happy.

chortle
*He **chortled** quietly to himself.*

chuckle
*Jojo **chuckled** at the thought of her brother covered in mud.*

crease up (*informal*)
*Mum **creased up** when she first saw Dad in his long shorts.*

giggle
*As usual, the twins were **giggling** at the back of the class.*

guffaw
*The colonel **guffawed** loudly at the regiment's annual show.*

snigger
*I **sniggered** when my brother fell.*

titter
*She **tittered** weakly at the joke.*

(2) NOUN A **laugh** is the sound you make when you laugh.

chuckle
*We could hardly suppress our **chuckles**.*

giggle
*My sister has an infectious **giggle**.*

guffaw
*The professor let out a **guffaw** at the student's remark.*

roar of laughter
*You could hear the **roar of laughter** from outside the theatre.*

shriek of laughter
*As soon as he came in, there was a **shriek of laughter** from the kids.*

snigger
*Karim was having a quiet **snigger** at the back of the class.*

titter
*The girl gave a **titter** of embarrassment when she saw me.*

Try these lively words and phrases!

be in stitches (*informal*) — *The audience **was in stitches** when the clown came on.*

laugh your head off (*informal*) — *We were all **laughing our heads off** at his dancing.*

to laugh...

heartily — *The audience **laughed heartily** at every joke.*

hysterically — *Omar continued to **laugh hysterically**.*

uproariously — *She was **laughing uproariously** at everything.*

→ Also have a look at the **Word Power** page for cry!

govern
*The king **governed** the country firmly but fairly for many years.*

head
*Professor Saharawi **headed** a team of research scientists.*

manage
*Ron Knee **manages** our local soccer team.*

rule
*Republics are **ruled** by presidents, monarchies by kings and queens.*

supervise
*My mum **supervises** a team of sales people.*

PRONUNCIATION TIP
When it is a verb, **lead** is pronounced **leed**.

leader NOUN

If you are the **leader** of a group, you are in charge of it.

boss
*A good **boss** cares for his or her workforce.*

captain
*Camilla is the **captain** of our netball team.*

chief
*Native American **chiefs** once wore elaborate headdresses of feathers.*

commander
*During the assault, the **commander** of the troops was severely wounded.*

director
*"Meet the **director** of studies, Mr Rivett," our young guide said.*

head
*Auntie Diane is **head** of the history department at a secondary school.*

ringleader
*"This damage is serious, and I want to know who the **ringleader** is!" snapped Mr Matheson.*

LANGUAGE TIP
The leader of a country is the **ruler**, **president** or **prime minister**.

leak NOUN

A **leak** is a hole that lets gas or liquid escape.

chink
*Gas was escaping through a small **chink** in the pipe.*

crack
*The roots of a tree had caused a **crack** in the waste pipe.*

hole
*Water seeped through several small **holes** in the swimming pool.*

puncture
*She watched the tyre go flat as air hissed from the **puncture**.*

learn (1) VERB

When you **learn** something, you gain knowledge or a skill by practice or by being taught.

acquire the ability
*After many hours of practice, Amy **acquired the ability** to juggle.*

grasp
*Equations were hard to **grasp**, but Alex eventually did so.*

master
*Matilda **mastered** the art of coaxing more pocket money from her parents.*

pick up
*As her mother was Spanish, little Anna soon **picked up** the language.*

learn (2) VERB

When you **learn** something, you get to know it off by heart.

commit to memory
*For the school play, Tariq had to **commit** many lines **to memory**.*

memorise
*"It is important to **memorise** your tables," said Miss Graham, our maths teacher.*

learn (3) VERB

If you **learn** of something, you get to know about it.

discover
*Selima was shocked to **discover** what her friend had done.*

find out
*I hoped Mum wouldn't **find out** that I'd broken her favourite mug before I replaced it.*

gather
*"I **gather** from the expression on your face that you haven't done your homework," Mr Jason said.*

hear about
*"I was sorry to **hear about** your illness," said Miss Copperfield.*

A B C D E F G H I J K L M N O P Q R S T U V W X Y Z

understand
"I ***understand*** *that you're moving away," our neighbour said to Mum.*

least ADJECTIVE

The **least** of something is the smallest possible amount of it.

lowest
The winning golfer is the one who takes the ***lowest*** *number of strokes.*

minimum
The ***minimum*** *requirement for the job is a degree in French.*

ANTONYM: most

LANGUAGE TIP
Least and **fewest** are often confused. **Least** applies to singular nouns (e.g. least butter, least money), while **fewest** applies to plurals (e.g. fewest errors, fewest marks).

leave (1) VERB

When you **leave** a place, you go away from it.

depart
The train ***departed*** *on time, leaving my dad behind because he was late.*

exit
When I mentioned what she owed me, Aislinn ***exited*** *hurriedly.*

withdraw
Unable to hold the city, King Charles ***withdrew*** *with his forces to a nearby hilltop.*

ANTONYM: arrive

→ *See* **disappear**

leave (2) VERB

When you **leave** a person, you go away from them, often when they do not want you to go.

abandon
The explorers were forced to ***abandon*** *their injured colleague at base camp.*

desert
My brother ***deserted*** *me just as our parents were coming in to find the mess we'd made.*

leave (3) VERB

If you **leave** something somewhere, you let it stay there or put it there before you go away.

deposit
We ***deposited*** *our bags in a left-luggage locker and went off to explore the city.*

place
The technician ***placed*** *the test tube in the rack.*

ANTONYM: take

leave (4) VERB

If you **leave** a job or a school, you stop being a part of it.

give up
Matthew ***gave up*** *his job to go travelling round the world for a year.*

quit
My big brother ***quit*** *school as soon as he finished his exams.*

LANGUAGE TIP
The noun **leave** is a period of holiday or absence from a job.

leave (5) VERB

If someone **leaves** money or property to you, you will receive it after they die.

bequeath
My grandad ***bequeathed*** *me the telescope from his naval days.*

LANGUAGE TIP
A **will** is a legal document in which you say what you want to happen to your money and property when you die.

length (1) NOUN

The **length** of something is the distance from one end to the other.

distance
The carpet fitters had to measure the ***distance*** *from one end of the corridor to the other.*

extent
Even the full ***extent*** *of the wire wouldn't reach the plug.*

span
The ***span*** *of suspension bridges is amazing, considering that they don't have any support beneath them.*

LANGUAGE TIP
The **length** of something from one side to the other is its width.

length (2) NOUN

The **length** of an event or activity is the amount of time it continues.

duration
*The three-hour **duration** of the film made me fidgety.*

term
*The judges suggested a short **term** of imprisonment followed by community service.*

let VERB

If you **let** someone do something, you allow them to do it.

allow
*"Will you **allow** Sumehra to come as well?" I implored.*

authorise
*The government **authorised** James Bond to take any action necessary.*

give permission
*I asked Gran to **give permission** for my friends to sleep over.*

permit
*"I cannot **permit** you to enter this area," said the police officer.*

let down VERB

If you **let** someone **down**, you don't do what they expected you to do for them.

disappoint
*Arkan **disappointed** me when he didn't back up what I said.*

fail
*"You fools have **failed** me," roared Dr Evil. "You will be punished!"*

leave in the lurch
*Marie **left** me **in the lurch**, just when I needed her help.*

let off (1) VERB

If someone **lets** you **off**, they do not punish you for something you have done wrong.

forgive
*As I apologised, Dad **forgave** me for breaking the spade.*

pardon
*Lord Asriel **pardoned** the intruders.*

reprieve
*After a year expecting to be beheaded, Sir Walter Raleigh was **reprieved**.*

let off (2) VERB

If you **let off** a firework, you make it explode.

detonate
*After making sure everyone was at a safe distance, Mum **detonated** the firework.*

ignite
*Fireworks are **ignited** by lighting the touchpaper.*

let out VERB

If you **let** someone **out** of somewhere, you release them.

free
*Lucy and Peter **freed** a bird that had flown into the house.*

liberate
*I sometimes wish I could **liberate** all the poor chickens kept in sheds.*

release
*The lions were **released** into the wild.*

LANGUAGE TIP

If you **let the cat out of the bag**, you tell someone something that is a secret.

---

level (1) ADJECTIVE

A surface that is **level** is flat and even.

even
*Pool tables must have an **even** surface to be played on properly.*

horizontal
*Builders always have to check that rows of bricks and blocks are **horizontal**.*

smooth
*For once, the sea was **smooth** and the sky was clear.*

ANTONYMS: rough, uneven

level (2) NOUN

A **level** is a standard or grade of achievement.

grade
*Hanan achieved a good **grade** in her piano exam.*

standard
*Even Mrs Jennings was forced to admit that the **standard** of our work was high.*

lie (1) VERB

If someone or something **lies** somewhere, they rest there in a flat position.

lounge
*My big sister spends most of the weekend **lounging** around.*

recline
*My grandad likes to **recline** in front of the fire in the evening.*

sprawl
*When Dad sleeps in a chair, he **sprawls** with his arms and legs out.*

lie (2) VERB

If you **lie**, you say something that you know is not true.

bluff
*Caught leaving the store, the shoplifter tried to **bluff** her way out of the situation.*

fib (*informal*)
*To avoid hurting Eddie's feelings, I **fibbed** that I liked his haircut.*

ANTONYM: tell the truth

lie (3) NOUN

A **lie** is something you say that you know is not true.

deceit
*My mate tried to say he was from America, but the lady saw through the **deceit**.*

falsehood
*When the police looked at the man's statement, it was full of **falsehoods**.*

fib (*informal*)
*"Now, no **fibs**," said my mum. "Where did that chocolate come from?"*

whopper (*informal*)
*I don't know how Dennis tells such **whoppers** to his parents and gets away with it.*

life (1) NOUN

Your **life** is the way you live.

existence
*Melanie lived an ideal **existence**, full of happiness and wealth.*

lifestyle
*The **lifestyle** of people in developing countries is hugely different from our own.*

way of life
*Tired of the commuter **way of life**, they decided to move to the country.*

life (2) NOUN

If you say someone is full of **life**, you mean they are lively and enthusiastic.

energy
*Despite his age, Grandad has loads of **energy**.*

get-up-and-go (*informal*)
*Arthur came down to breakfast full of **get-up-and-go**.*

spirit
*The team showed real **spirit** in coming back from three goals down.*

vitality
*All our class like Miss Sherwood. She's so full of **vitality** and jokes.*

lift VERB

If you **lift** something, you move it to a higher position.

elevate
*Over the altar, the priest ceremonially **elevated** the golden dish.*

hoist
*Medieval builders used a human treadwheel to **hoist** stones to the roof of buildings.*

raise
***Raising** his glass, my uncle proposed a toast to the bride and groom.*

ANTONYM: lower

light (1) NOUN

Light is the brightness from the sun, moon, fire or lamps, that lets you see things.

brightness
*For a second, the driver was dazzled by the **brightness** of the headlights.*

brilliance
*The **brilliance** of the moon as it rose over the horizon took our breath away.*

glow
*At night, the **glow** of the forest fires could be seen many miles away.*

radiance
*The sun rose majestically, spreading its **radiance** over the sea.*

ANTONYMS: darkness, dark

Some types of natural light:

daylight	moonlight
starlight	sunlight

Some types of artificial light:

candle	fairy light
flare	floodlight
fluorescent tube	lamplight
lantern	light bulb
neon light	searchlight
spotlight	torch

light (2) VERB

If you **light** a fire, you make it start burning.

ignite
*The burning paper **ignited** the sticks above.*

kindle
*There's no doubt that firelighters help **kindle** a barbecue fire.*

set light to
*Dad used matches to **set light to** the camp fire.*

ANTONYM: extinguish

light (3) VERB

If the sun, moon, a fire or lamps **light** a room, they make it brighter.

brighten
*The rising sun **brightened** Bonnie's normally dingy room.*

illuminate
*Neon gas is used to **illuminate** city advertisements.*

ANTONYM: darken

like (1) VERB

If you **like** someone or something, you find them pleasing.

admire
*Vega **admired** the way her mum coped after her dad died.*

appreciate
*Gran really **appreciated** the flowers I picked for her.*

be fond of
*Chocolate is one of the things I **am** most **fond of**.*

be keen on
*My big brother **is keen on** a girl in his class.*

be partial to
*"I **am partial to** a slice of cake now and again," Dad admitted.*

enjoy
*All our family **enjoys** holidays by the seaside.*

love
*My family **loves** going for walks at the weekend.*

ANTONYM: dislike

like (2) ADJECTIVE

If one thing is **like** another, it is similar to it.

alike
*The twins were so **alike**, only their family could tell them apart.*

comparable with
*The Dutch language is in many ways **comparable with** Afrikaans.*

identical to
*The singer turned purple when she realised the dress was **identical to** hers.*

similar to
*Your new car is **similar to** ours.*

ANTONYM: unlike

→ *See* **same (1)**

LANGUAGE TIP
If one thing is like another, you can say that it **resembles** it.

likely ADJECTIVE

If something is **likely**, it will probably happen or is probably true.

expected
*It was **expected** that the old man would recover before long.*

liable
*"Be careful," warned the farmer. "This road is **liable** to flood without much warning."*

probable
*It was **probable** that the students would reach their destination safely.*

ANTONYM: unlikely

limp VERB

If you **limp**, you walk in an uneven way because you have hurt your leg or foot.

hobble
*After twisting her ankle, the tennis player **hobbled** off the court.*

hop
*When I trod on a drawing pin I had to **hop** over to a chair to sit down.*

shuffle
*For a month after her stroke, Gran could only **shuffle** along.*

A B C D E F G H I J K L M N O P Q R S T U V W X Y Z

line (1) NOUN

A **line** of people or things is a number of them in a row.

chain
Firefighters formed a ***chain*** *to pass buckets of water along.*

column
A huge ***column*** *of people waited to pay their respects to the dead president.*

file
We walked silently in single ***file*** *to the playing fields.*

queue
When we arrived at the cinema, the ***queue*** *stretched round the block.*

rank
Ranks *of police stood in full riot gear, waiting for the brawl to erupt.*

row
The ***row*** *of old shops was demolished.*

line (2) NOUN

A **line** is a long, thin mark.

dash
Sometimes people use a ***dash*** *to separate parts of a sentence.*

groove
He used a sharp knife to cut a ***groove*** *in the stick.*

rule
Keep your writing on top of the ***rules*** *on the paper.*

score
A vandal had left ***scores*** *in the side of the car.*

stripe
She wore a long skirt with blue and white ***stripes****.*

stroke
She added a ***stroke*** *of colour to the painting.*

LANGUAGE TIP
A line on your skin is a **crease** or **wrinkle**.

link (1) VERB

If someone or something **links** people, places or things, they join them together.

attach
Amber ***attached*** *the competition slip to her drawing with a paperclip.*

connect
The switchboard operator ***connected*** *me immediately.*

couple
Dad ***coupled*** *the car and the caravan together.*

fasten
Safety pins are useful for ***fastening*** *babies' nappies.*

join
On a vehicle, the axle ***joins*** *a pair of wheels together.*

link (2) NOUN

The **link** between two things is the relationship or connection between them.

association
The two families had a close ***association****.*

connection
There's a strong ***connection*** *between a mother and her child.*

relationship
One ***relationship*** *between five and ten is that five is half of ten.*

liquid NOUN

A **liquid** is a substance such as water, which is neither a solid nor a gas, and which can be poured.

fluid
Blood and water are the two main ***fluids*** *in the body.*

solution
Dr Jekyll drank the ***solution*** *in one gulp, and turned into Mr Hyde.*

list (1) NOUN

A **list** is a set of words or items written one after another.

catalogue
I picked up a ***catalogue*** *of toys to choose one I would like.*

register
Schools are obliged by law to keep a ***register*** *of pupils.*

series
I sat down to memorise a ***series*** *of spellings before the test.*

list (2) VERB

If you **list** a number of things, you write them or say them one after another.

catalogue
My mum's job was to ***catalogue*** *all the paintings in the gallery.*

itemise
*Dad says it's a good job the phone company **itemises** every call on our phone bill so that he can keep track of them.*

record
*The names of the dead were **recorded** in stone on the war memorial.*

listen VERB

If you **listen** to something, you pay attention to its sound.

be all ears
*Ben **was all ears** when he heard his name mentioned.*

eavesdrop
*Sneakily, Emily decided to **eavesdrop** on her friend's phone call.*

→ *See* **hear (1)**

litter NOUN

Litter is rubbish in the street and other public places.

debris
*After the bomb attack, it took months to clear the **debris**.*

refuse
*The county aims to recycle as much **refuse** as it can.*

rubbish
*"Why can't people put their **rubbish** in the bin, instead of littering the streets?" I wondered.*

waste
*Not too long ago, **waste** was just dumped into the sea.*

little (1) ADJECTIVE

Little can mean small in size or amount.

compact
*"This **compact** music centre can be yours for next to nothing!" the advertisement read.*

diminutive
*Chihuahuas are **diminutive** dogs.*

mini
*A **mini** hurricane struck the island, but fortunately it didn't do too much damage.*

miniature
*My Auntie Joan brought me a **miniature** Eiffel Tower back from her holiday in Paris.*

minute
*Carly's writing is so **minute** that I can hardly read it.*

tiny
*My sister is quite **tiny**, and would pass for someone much younger.*

ANTONYMS: big, large

little (2) ADJECTIVE

Little can mean young in age.

infant
***Infant** children often go to nursery school.*

young
*The trouble with my **young** sister is that she always wants me to play silly games with her.*

ANTONYMS: grown-up, mature

little (3) NOUN

A **little** of something is a small amount or degree of it.

A little of something is:
- a **bit** of attention
- a **bite** of lunch
- a **dab** of paint
- a **dash** of romance
- a **drop** of milk
- a **hint** of garlic
- a **pinch** of salt
- a **sip** of tea
- a **spot** of gardening
- a **taste** of soup
- a **touch** of frost

live (1) VERB

If someone or something **lives**, they are alive.

exist
*Dinosaurs **existed** long before humans lived on the earth.*

survive
*Fortunately, all the passengers in the bus **survived** the crash.*

ANTONYM: die

PRONUNCIATION TIP
When it is a verb, **live** rhymes with "give".

a b c d e f g h i j k l m n o p q r s t u v w x y z

A B C D E F G H I J K L M N O P Q R S T U V W X Y Z

live (2) VERB

If you **live** in a place, that is where your home is.

inhabit
*Stig, once a cave dweller, now **inhabited** a rubbish dump.*

occupy
*Last summer, several swallows **occupied** our garage.*

reside
*The old duchess expressed a wish to **reside** in a house by the sea.*

PRONUNCIATION TIP
When it is a verb, **live** rhymes with "give".

lively (1) ADJECTIVE

Someone who is **lively** is full of energy and enthusiasm.

active
*Despite her age, my aunt is very **active**.*

energetic
*"I don't know how you can be so **energetic**," Mum said from the depths of her armchair.*

fit
*It pays to stay **fit**. Good health is important.*

sprightly
*Grandad is a **sprightly** old gent of 76, who enjoys going for walks.*

vigorous
*After a **vigorous** game of squash, Dad looked shattered.*

ANTONYM: listless

lively (2) ADJECTIVE

If someone has a **lively** personality, they are enthusiastic and full of energy.

bubbly
*The checkout lady with the **bubbly** personality always said a cheery "hello".*

high-spirited
***High-spirited** lambs were jumping about the field together.*

ANTONYM: dull

lively (3) ADJECTIVE

If you say a place is **lively**, it is busy, noisy and full of people.

bustling
*The city centre is always a **bustling** place on a Saturday afternoon.*

buzzing
*As the rocket launch approached, the control room was **buzzing** with activity.*

ANTONYM: quiet

living ADJECTIVE

If someone or something is **living**, they are alive.

alive
*Sniffer dogs found someone **alive** under the rubble of the earthquake.*

existing
*The **existing** species on earth are very different from the animals they evolved from.*

surviving
*Kiara's only **surviving** great grandparent lives in Australia.*

ANTONYMS: dead, extinct

load (1) NOUN

A **load** is something large or heavy that is being carried.

burden
*The elderly peasant was stooped from a lifetime of carrying heavy **burdens**.*

weight
*To lift a heavy **weight** safely, bend your knees and keep your back straight.*

load (2) NOUN

A **load** is a large quantity of goods that is being transported.

cargo
*Customs officers inspected the ship's **cargo**.*

consignment
*In this container is a **consignment** of televisions from Japan.*

lock VERB

If you **lock** something, you fasten it with a key.

bolt
*I heard Mum **bolt** the door and come upstairs to bed.*

fasten
*"Please would you **fasten** the gate, Grant?" I asked.*

latch
*Gran said to **latch** the door when we came in from the garden.*

padlock
*The yard was securely **padlocked** to keep the Alsatian dogs in and thieves out.*

secure
*Police recommend **securing** all doors and windows before going out.*

ANTONYM: unlock

lonely (1) ADJECTIVE

If you are **lonely**, you are unhappy because you are alone.

forlorn
*The tiny terrier looked **forlorn** on its own in the show ring.*

friendless
*The wealthy widow died in a seaside hotel, **friendless** and alone.*

solitary
*Old Wes was a **solitary** person, but quite happy with his own company.*

lonely (2) ADJECTIVE

A **lonely** place is one which very few people visit.

isolated
*The house was **isolated** in a field, quite apart from the rest of the village.*

remote
*A huge sea bird population colonised the **remote** Scottish island.*

secluded
*In a **secluded** corner of the beach, Summer sat and had her picnic.*

Try these lively words and phrases:

off the beaten track
*My aunt likes visiting villages that are **off the beaten track**.*

out-of-the-way
*It can be difficult to travel to **out-of-the-way** places.*

long (1) ADJECTIVE

Something that is **long** is great in length or distance.

extended
*To avoid roadworks, we had an **extended** journey to reach Glasgow.*

extensive
*The newly built country mansion had an **extensive** drive.*

lengthy
*We had to drive down a **lengthy** track before we reached the farm.*

ANTONYM: short

long (2) ADJECTIVE

Something that is **long** continues for a great amount of time.

drawn-out
*Dad looked shattered after his **drawn-out** meeting.*

interminable
*Our wait at the dentist's seemed **interminable**.*

lengthy
*We had a **lengthy** wait before the level crossing gates lifted.*

prolonged
*We had a **prolonged** discussion about where to go on our class outing.*

ANTONYM: brief

look

→ Look at the **Word Power** page!

look after VERB

If you **look after** someone or something, you take care of them.

care for
*Bradley **cared for** the bird with the broken wing until it could fly again.*

protect
*It is everyone's responsibility to help to **protect** wildlife.*

tend
*My grandad **tends** his garden with loving care so that it always looks pretty.*

→ *See* **guard (1)**

loose (1) ADJECTIVE

Something that is **loose** is not firmly held or fixed in place.

slack
*The dog's collar was **slack**, and he slipped out of it to chase the cat.*

unsecured
*The load of hay was **unsecured**, and had tumbled off the trailer.*

A B C D E F G H I J K L M N O P Q R S T U V W X Y Z

Look

(1) VERB If you **look** at something, you turn your eyes towards it so that you can see it.

look briefly:

glance
*The driver **glanced** right, then turned into the main road.*

glimpse
*They **glimpsed** smoke on the horizon.*

peep
*Then he realised that someone was **peeping** through the keyhole.*

look carefully:

examine
*"**Examine** this," said Mr Parnevik, pointing to the microscope.*

observe
*The police officers **observed** the house from their unmarked car.*

scrutinise
*Independent experts **scrutinised** the process to ensure it was fair.*

study
*Javier spent some time **studying** the game's instruction booklet.*

look hard:

stare
*"It's rude to **stare**," I whispered.*

peer
*Without his specs, Harry was forced to **peer** at the notice.*

look for something:

hunt
*Liam **hunted** high and low for the missing ticket.*

search
*Although we **searched** for several hours, we couldn't find the keys.*

seek
*"The treasure ye **seek** be found up the creek," the ancient parchment read.*

look for a long time:

feast your eyes on
*I **feasted my eyes on** the vast array of cakes.*

gaze
*Rupert **gazed** lovingly at his new bike.*

view
*For some time, the prince **viewed** the paintings in the gallery.*

look rudely:

gawp
*"Stop **gawping** at me!" hissed Beth.*

gawk
*The youth continued to **gawk** at her and did not answer.*

Look

look in surprise:

gape
*Mum said she **gaped** when she saw the size of the Grand Canyon.*

goggle
*I **goggled** at the huge present before me. I could hardly believe my eyes.*

look around:

scan
*"Every ten seconds that radar dish **scans** the horizon," explained the guide.*

survey
*The farmer smiled as he **surveyed** his fields of swaying corn.*

2) NOUN If you have a **look** at something, you look at it.

gaze
*Nothing could deflect her steady **gaze**.*

glance
*"Can I have a **glance** at the TV guide?" my brother asked.*

glimpse
*We caught a **glimpse** of the sparkling blue sea through the gap in the hedge.*

peek
*"You can come and have a very quick **peek** at the puppies," the farmer told us.*

3) NOUN The **look** on your face is the expression on it.

air
*My brother wore an **air** of innocence when Mum asked who had spilt their juice on the floor.*

appearance
*I tried to give the **appearance** of being confident, but really I was rather nervous.*

expression
*Gran's **expression** of delight when she saw the cake we'd baked made the effort worthwhile.*

A B C D E F G H I J K L M N O P Q R S T U V W X Y Z

wobbly
*Angelica's tooth was **wobbly**, and she knew it would soon fall out.*

ANTONYM: firm

loose (2) ADJECTIVE

If clothing is **loose**, it does not fit tightly.

baggy
***Baggy** trousers are comfortable clothes for travelling in.*

sloppy
*Jo loves wearing **sloppy** jumpers.*

ANTONYM: tight

LANGUAGE TIP
The adjective and adverb **loose** is spelt with two *os*. Do not confuse it with the verb **lose**.

lose (1) VERB

If you **lose** something, you cannot find it, or you no longer have it because it has been taken away from you.

mislay
*"Can you see my purse? I've **mislaid** it," Fiona said desperately.*

misplace
*Scott had **misplaced** the ticket and now it was time to leave for the show!*

ANTONYM: find

lose (2) VERB

If you **lose** an argument or a game, you are beaten.

be beaten
*"I'll admit it. We **were beaten** by a better team," said Gamal.*

be defeated
*In a debate today, the government **was defeated** by a small majority.*

suffer defeat
*United **suffered defeat** in three matches in succession.*

ANTONYM: win

lost ADJECTIVE

If something is **lost**, you cannot find it.

mislaid
*We were late because Dad's keys were **mislaid** yet again!*

misplaced
*Faizah finally found her **misplaced** glasses in the laundry basket!*

missing
*Mrs Howe was delighted that her **missing** cat had been found.*

ANTONYM: found

lot NOUN

A **lot** of something is a large amount of it.

a great deal
***A great deal** of time and effort has gone into this thesaurus.*

a large quantity
*For our patio, Dad required **a large quantity** of paving slabs.*

a vast number
*From the helicopter we could see **a vast number** of antelope.*

heaps (*informal*)
*"I've had **heaps** of replies to my party invitations," Daisy said excitedly.*

masses (*informal*)
*Pop stars receive **masses** of fan mail.*

stacks (*informal*)
*"You should see Lucy's CD collection. She's got **stacks** of them!" Atifa exclaimed.*

loud ADJECTIVE

A **loud** noise produces a lot of sound.

booming
*The **booming** bass note of the foghorn echoed along the misty decks.*

deafening
*At the air show, we sat patiently through the **deafening** fly-past.*

noisy
*Mum's samba band are really **noisy** when they get going.*

piercing
*Suddenly, a **piercing** scream cut through the peaceful night.*

rowdy
*My parents have complained about the **rowdy** neighbours.*

Try these lively words and phrases:

ear-piercing
*The device triggers an **ear-piercing** alarm.*

ear-splitting
*According to our neighbour, my sister's music was an **ear-splitting** racket.*

ANTONYM: quiet

love (1) VERB

If you **love** someone or something, you have strong feelings of affection for them.

adore
*My baby sister **adores** her teddy bear, Scruff.*

dote on
*I **dote on** my Grandma and Grandpa.*

idolise
*Mum and Dad **idolise** one or two of the old heavy metal rock groups.*

Try these lively words and phrases:

be crazy about
*My sister **is crazy about** one band, then another.*

be mad about
*I **am mad about** sports.*

ANTONYM: hate

love (2) VERB

If you **love** doing something, you like doing it very much.

delight in
*I'm told that my great grandmother **delighted in** skating on frozen canals.*

enjoy
*"**Enjoy** your honeymoon!" everyone shouted, as the newlyweds drove off.*

relish
*The Roman emperor **relished** watching the gladiators in the ring.*

ANTONYMS: hate, loathe

love (3) NOUN

Love is a strong feeling of affection for someone or something.

adoration
*The pop star basked in the **adoration** of his devoted fans.*

fondness
*My uncle was ruined by having too great a **fondness** for gambling.*

ANTONYM: hatred

lovely ADJECTIVE

Someone or something **lovely** is very beautiful, attractive or pleasant.

adorable
*"Isn't that baby just **adorable**?" the lady in the pink hat cooed.*

attractive
*Simone has an **attractive** personality and is always smiling.*

beautiful
*Even I had to admit my sister looked **beautiful** in her new dress.*

delightful
*A **delightful** scene met our eyes as we came round the bend in the road: a river, willow trees and swans.*

enchanting
*The desert sky at night was **enchanting**, with stars everywhere.*

gorgeous
*"Wow, he's **gorgeous**!" my big sister said as the pop star came on television.*

pleasant
*All in all, we had a very **pleasant** afternoon on the lake.*

pretty
*Both bridesmaids looked **pretty** in their matching outfits.*

ANTONYMS: unattractive, unpleasant

low ADJECTIVE

A **low** noise is low in tone and not always easy to hear.

muffled
***Muffled** voices could be heard coming from within the hut.*

muted
*The **muted** sound of music travelled across the bay.*

quiet
*The **quiet** lapping of the waves against the shore was very soothing.*

A B C D E F G H I J K L M N O P Q R S T U V W X Y Z

soft
*Lyra spoke in a **soft** whisper.*

subdued
*From behind the heavy door came the **subdued** sounds of conversation.*

ANTONYM: high

luck NOUN

Luck can mean something that happens by chance.

chance
*It was only **chance** that brought Mum and Dad together.*

destiny
*Some people think that **destiny** brings people together who will be friends.*

fate
*By a simple twist of **fate** we both went to the same school.*

fortune
*By amazing **fortune**, the hostel was empty when the fire started.*

good luck PHRASE

Good luck is anything good that happens to you which is not a result of your own efforts.

blessing
*It was a **blessing** when the rain started after the long drought.*

godsend
*"Auntie's money was a real **godsend** when we were so hard-up," my mum said.*

good fortune
*At the air show, I had the **good fortune** to see a very rare Second World War plane.*

lucky break (*informal*)
*The young tenor's **lucky break** came when another singer fell ill.*

a stroke of luck
*"Finding that Roman coin was a **stroke of luck**!" Travis said.*

ANTONYM: bad luck

bad luck PHRASE

Bad luck is anything bad that happens to you which is not a result of your own efforts.

hard luck
*The sudden storm was **hard luck** on the organisers of the barbecue.*

misfortune
*Was the Titanic's sinking a case of **misfortune** or mismanagement?*

stroke of bad luck
*It was a **stroke of bad luck** for Dad when he broke his leg playing basketball.*

ANTONYM: good luck

lucky ADJECTIVE

Something that is **lucky** has good effects or consequences.

fortuitous
*It was **fortuitous** that someone handed in my money when I lost it.*

fortunate
*It was **fortunate** that just after Mum's car had broken down, Dad happened to be driving past.*

ANTONYM: unlucky

luggage NOUN

Your **luggage** is the bags and suitcases that you take with you when you travel.

baggage
*Our **baggage** arrived two days after us!*

belongings
*"We'll look after your **belongings** while you shop," said the shop assistant at the airport.*

lump (1) NOUN

A **lump** is a solid piece of something.

cake
*Neil stamped his feet and **cakes** of snow fell off the soles of his boots.*

chunk
*The explosion sent **chunks** of metal flying everywhere.*

clod
*The clumsy golfer sliced a great **clod** of earth from the fairway.*

hunk
*All I wanted was a **hunk** of cheese and a few chunky slices of bread.*

nugget
*At the sight of the gold **nugget**, the prospector began to dance with glee.*

slab
*Great **slabs** of rock slid down the hillside during the earthquake.*

lump (2) NOUN

A **lump** is a small, hard piece of flesh on someone's body.

bump
*After her fall, Sîan developed a large **bump** on the head.*

hump
*In the story, the man who lived in Notre Dame cathedral had a **hump** on his back.*

swelling
*The dog had a **swelling** on her right leg.*

luxury (1) NOUN

Luxury is a great comfort, especially among expensive and beautiful surroundings.

comfort
*The five-star hotel oozed **comfort** from every plush corner.*

richness
*Scores of people queued to view the famous **richness** of the palace decorations.*

splendour
*The **splendour** of the water gardens really impressed us.*

luxury (2) NOUN

A **luxury** is something that you would like to have but do not need, and is usually expensive.

extra
*Because I have a Saturday job, I can afford a few **extras**.*

indulgence
*The expensive chocolates were sheer **indulgence**, but we loved them!*

treat
*For a special **treat**, Dad took us all to the cinema and then bowling.*

ANTONYM: necessity

Mm

machine NOUN

A **machine** is a piece of equipment designed to do a particular job. It is usually powered by an engine or electricity.

apparatus
*Firefighters use breathing **apparatus** to enter smoke-filled buildings.*

appliance
*For some reason, most kitchen **appliances** seem to be white.*

contraption (*informal*)
*"What on earth's that **contraption**?" Dad asked when he saw my DIY go-kart.*

mad (1) ADJECTIVE

Someone who is **mad** has a mental illness that causes them to behave in strange ways.

crazy (*informal*)
*The princess was driven **crazy** by love for the prince she could not marry.*

insane
*Neighbours claimed they were being driven **insane** by the loud music.*

out of your mind
*"I think I'm going **out of my mind**," said Mum. "I've lost my keys again!"*

ANTONYM: sane

mad (2) ADJECTIVE

Someone who is **mad** is angry.

berserk
*They went **berserk** when they heard the news.*

crazy (*informal*)
*My brother went **crazy** when he found out I'd broken his guitar.*

furious
*What started as a reasonable discussion developed into a **furious** argument.*

A B C D E F G H I J K L M N O P Q R S T U V W X Y Z

incensed
Gran became ***incensed*** *when she realised the burglar had stolen her wedding ring.*

irate
Mum was really ***irate*** *when I dismantled the cuckoo clock.*

livid
Mrs Vine was ***livid*** *when she heard about the bad behaviour on the school trip.*

→ *See* **angry**

mad (3) ADJECTIVE

If you describe an idea as **mad**, you mean that it very foolish or silly.

absurd
It is ***absurd*** *to believe the earth is flat, but that is what people used to think.*

crazy (*informal*)
It was ***crazy*** *to think we'd win the lottery, but we couldn't help hoping.*

daft
Jade had the ***daft*** *idea of riding on my bicycle handlebars.*

ludicrous
"That's a ***ludicrous*** *suggestion," said Dad. "Of course you can't stay out until midnight!"*

preposterous
It was ***preposterous*** *to bring a snake to school, but that's what Carly did for "show and tell"!*

ridiculous
"A mongrel? Don't be ***ridiculous****. It's a pedigree poodle!" the lady said snootily.*

mad (4) ADJECTIVE

If you are **mad** about someone or something, you like them very much.

enthusiastic
People in some countries are very ***enthusiastic*** *about playing cricket.*

fanatical
Many Americans are ***fanatical*** *about baseball.*

passionate
Uncle Tim is ***passionate*** *about travel, and tries to get abroad at least three times a year.*

magic (1) NOUN

In fairy stories, **magic** is a special power that can make impossible things happen.

sorcery
Merlin was famed for his spells and ***sorcery****.*

witchcraft
Dorothy was thwarted by ***witchcraft*** *on her journey to the Emerald City.*

wizardry
People from the past would think modern technology is some form of ***wizardry****.*

LANGUAGE TIP
A magician in fairy stories is a **sorcerer**, **witch** or **wizard**.

magic (2) NOUN

Magic is the art of performing tricks to entertain people.

conjuring
The magician's ***conjuring*** *tricks went down well at the party.*

LANGUAGE TIP
A magician who entertains people is a **conjuror**.

magical ADJECTIVE

Something that is **magical** is wonderful and exciting.

fascinating
The magician wore a cloak covered in ***fascinating*** *designs.*

marvellous
We had a ***marvellous*** *tree completely covered in decorations.*

spellbinding
The lights in the city were ***spellbinding****.*

magnificent ADJECTIVE

Something that is **magnificent** is extremely beautiful or impressive.

glorious
The packed stadium in the sunshine made a ***glorious*** *setting for the final.*

grand
Venice has many ***grand*** *buildings and the Grand Canal.*

impressive
There are few sights more ***impressive*** *than the pyramids of Egypt.*

splendid
King Charles was rowed down the Thames in a ***splendid*** *barge.*

ANTONYM: unimpressive

main ADJECTIVE

If something is the **main** thing, it is the most important or largest.

chief
*The boss's **chief** reason for holding the meeting was to announce his retirement.*

foremost
*Italy is the **foremost** producer of pasta in the world.*

major
*Language skills form a **major** part of primary education.*

principal
*Brasilia is the capital of Brazil, but Rio is the **principal** city.*

ANTONYM: least important

mainly ADVERB

Mainly can mean mostly, chiefly or usually.

chiefly
*"This morning," said Mrs Lucas, "we'll **chiefly** be doing maths."*

generally
*Mum said that **generally** she was pleased with how well the project was managed.*

largely
*The Congo is **largely** covered by rainforest.*

mostly
*Although he was tired, Will's weakness was **mostly** due to his illness.*

on the whole
***On the whole**, I think our city is a great place to live.*

usually
*We **usually** go to Cornwall for our holidays, but this year we are going to Spain.*

make (1) VERB

If you **make** something, you create or produce it.

assemble
*It was very funny watching Dad trying to **assemble** the wardrobe.*

build
*"I'm hoping to **build** my own den in that oak tree," Morgan told Ron.*

construct
*Mrs Jones asked us to **construct** different shapes with the same area.*

create
*As well as inventions, Leonardo da Vinci **created** the Mona Lisa and other paintings.*

manufacture
*At my mum's work, they **manufacture** brakes for cars.*

produce
*My brother and his friend **produced** their own film. It was awful!*

make (2) VERB

If you **make** someone do something, you force them to do it.

compel
*An injury **compelled** the athlete to retire.*

force
*The gale-force wind **forced** them to drop the anchor.*

oblige
*All of the pupils at our school are **obliged** to wear school uniform.*

order
*The colonel **ordered** the troops to surrender.*

make (3) VERB

If you **make** something happen, you cause it.

bring about
*The revolution **brought about** many changes in the country.*

cause
*James **caused** a fire by letting the frying pan overheat.*

provoke
*My sister is always **provoking** arguments, especially with me.*

make (4) VERB

Two amounts added together **make** a sum.

add up to
*Six and six **add up to** twelve.*

amount to
*My pocket money and yours **amount to** enough for a game of tennis.*

total
*Our school's fundraising **totalled** the amount needed to build the new sports hall.*

make (5) NOUN

A **make** is the name of a product of a particular manufacturer.

brand
*"Which **brand** of washing-up liquid do you use?" asked the man conducting the survey.*

a b c d e f g h i j k l m n o p q r s t u v w x y z

model
*Our neighbour always has to have the latest **model** of car.*

variety
*"This **variety** of jewellery is well known for its quality," said the sales assistant.*

make up VERB

If you **make** something **up**, you invent it.

concoct
*To explain his absence, my friend **concocted** an amazing story about being kidnapped.*

create
*Mum is great at **creating** tasty meals out of very few ingredients.*

devise
*Over the years, the production team had **devised** many game shows.*

dream up
*"What plans have you **dreamt up** for your future?" my uncle asked.*

invent
*My grandad once **invented** a new type of rollerskate.*

man (1) NOUN

A **man** is an adult, male human being.

bloke (*informal*)
*"A **bloke** in the street tried to sell me a watch," Dad said.*

chap (*informal*)
*My uncle was a nice **chap**, always willing to help.*

fellow
*The **fellow** being interviewed looked more like a farmer than a professor.*

gentleman
*"Ladies and **gentlemen**, a toast to the bride and groom!" said the best man.*

guy (*informal*)
*"You're a great **guy**," the tourist said. "Thanks for your help."*

ANTONYM: woman

A man...
who is unmarried is a **bachelor**.
who is engaged is someone's **fiancé**.
on his wedding day is a **bridegroom**.
who is married is a **husband**.
whose spouse has died is a **widower**.
who has children is a **father**.

man (2) NOUN

Human beings, both male and female, are sometimes referred to as **man**.

mankind
***Mankind** has existed for only a tiny fraction of the life of the earth.*

the human race
***The human race** has evolved over thousand of years.*

manage (1) VERB

If someone **manages** an organisation or business, they are responsible for controlling it.

be in charge of
*Joseph **was in charge of** preparing for the great famine.*

control
*The Australian **controlled** a vast television and publishing empire.*

direct
*My mum **directed** a play for the local drama group.*

run
*Granny and Grandad **run** a car parts busines*

manage (2) VERB

If you **manage** to do something, you succeed in doing it even if it is difficult.

be successful in
*Dad **was successful in** getting the job he ha applied for.*

bring off
*Despite the awful weather, the helicopter crew **brought off** the rescue.*

succeed in
*The crew of the rescue boat **succeeded in** winching aboard five shipwrecked fishermen.*

manage (3) VERB

If you **manage** in difficult circumstances, you carry on successfully.

cope
*After the airline lost our cases, we had to **cop** for three days without our things.*

get by
*When the car broke down, the family **got by** using the bus.*

manners PLURAL NOUN

Your **manners** are the way you behave.

behaviour
*Mr O'Leary complimented us on our **behaviour** at camp.*

conduct
*The coach driver complained about the **conduct** of Class 3B on the school outing.*

etiquette
*The duchess considered **etiquette** to be very important in a young woman.*

many ADJECTIVE

If there are **many** people or things, there are a large number of them.

abundant
*Thanks to irrigation, **abundant** crops grow in some parts of the desert.*

countless
*There are parts of the world where **countless** people do not have enough food.*

numerous
*Dad showed me **numerous** ways to do the same sum.*

several
*We have **several** newts in our garden pond.*

umpteen (*informal*)
*"I've asked you **umpteen** times to make your bed," my mother said.*

ANTONYM: few

mark (1) NOUN

A **mark** is a small stain or damaged area on a surface.

blotch
*Siobhan's Biro made **blotches** on every word she wrote.*

smudge
*A massive **smudge** of ink had somehow made its way on to my exercise book.*

spot
*Luckily, it was difficult to see the **spot** of grease on her shirt.*

mark (2) VERB

If something **marks** a surface, it stains or damages it in some way.

smear
*Greasy thumbprints were **smeared** all over the new window.*

smudge
*My little sister's face was **smudged** with dirt when she came in from the garden.*

mark (3) VERB

When a teacher **marks** a student's work, they decide how good it is and give it a mark.

assess
*Teachers from another school had to **assess** my brother's coursework.*

correct
*We hand in our maths for Mrs Abiola to **correct**.*

marvellous ADJECTIVE

Something that is **marvellous** is wonderful or excellent.

amazing
*The Niagara Falls are an **amazing** sight to behold.*

incredible
*From the cliff top there was an **incredible** view over the bay below.*

miraculous
*The dog made a **miraculous** recovery after being run over.*

phenomenal
*In my opinion, anyone who runs a marathon has **phenomenal** strength and stamina.*

terrific
*"Thanks very much. We've had a **terrific** day out," I said to Della's mum.*

massive ADJECTIVE

Someone or something that is **massive** is extremely large in size and weight.

colossal
*Some of the skyscrapers in New York are **colossal** buildings.*

enormous
*Some cranes can extend to an **enormous** height.*

gargantuan
*Many dinosaurs were **gargantuan** compared to today's creatures.*

great
*The **great** stone rolled back to reveal a hidden passageway beneath the mountain.*

huge
*Putting his head through the cloud at the top of the beanstalk, Jack spied a **huge** man.*

immense
*We gasped as we saw the **immense** banquet in front of us.*

vast
*I was very excited to see the **vast** array of flavours the ice-cream parlour had.*

A B C D E F G H I J K L M N O P Q R S T U V W X Y Z

whopping (*informal*)
*"Buy a ticket and you could win a **whopping** prize!" read the sign.*

ANTONYM: tiny

match (1) NOUN

A **match** is an organised game of football, cricket or some other sport.

bout
*It was an evenly fought **bout** between the two wrestlers.*

competition
*Our chess **competition** was a great success.*

contest
*Lucy and I held a chocolate-eating **contest**.*

head-to-head
*A tennis singles final is a **head-to-head** between the two unbeaten players.*

match (2) VERB

If one thing **matches** another, it is similar to it.

correspond
*What we see in a mirror **corresponds** with what we are really like.*

go with
*Charlotte's shoes **went with** her dress.*

ANTONYM: clash

mathematics NOUN

Mathematics is the study of numbers, quantities and shapes.

maths (*informal*)
*Many adults are scared of **maths**, but it's straightforward really.*

numeracy
*We have a **numeracy** lesson most mornings.*

LANGUAGE TIP
The main branches of mathematics in schools are **arithmetic**, **geometry** and **algebra**. A person who studies mathematics is a **mathematician**.

matter (1) NOUN

A **matter** is a task or situation that you have to attend to.

affair
*They have sent one of their best men to investigate the whole **affair**.*

business
*The **business** of moving house upset Gran.*

issue
*Mum and Dad couldn't agree on the **issue** of where to go for the day.*

situation
*The **situation** in the Middle East causes a lot of discussion.*

subject
*Mr Carew asked us to talk on any **subject** we were keen on.*

topic
*In the playground, the only **topic** of conversation was the school trip.*

matter (2) VERB

If something **matters**, it is important.

be significant
*Sherlock Holmes realised that the man's red hair **was significant** in the case.*

count
*Small details can **count** just as much as big issues when it comes to making decisions.*

make a difference
*Every penny you can give to charity **makes a difference**.*

maybe ADVERB

If you think there is a possibility that something will happen, but you are not sure, you use **maybe**.

perhaps
***Perhaps** you'll catch a fish; perhaps not.*

possibly
***Possibly** Mrs Jenkins, our science teacher, will take us to the power station.*

meal NOUN

A **meal** is an occasion when people eat, and the food people eat at meal times.

Some types of meal:

breakfast	brunch	dinner
elevenses	lunch	supper
tea		

A meal that is...

small is a **bite** or **snack**.

large is a **feast**.

large and formal is a **banquet**.

eaten outdoors is a **barbecue** or **picnic**.

self-service is a **buffet**.

ready-cooked and hot is a **takeaway**.

mean (1) ADJECTIVE

Someone who is **mean** is unwilling to share with others.

miserly
*The **miserly** old woman turned the carol singers away.*

penny-pinching
***Penny-pinching** people are reluctant to part with their money.*

stingy
*My **stingy** sister wouldn't give me a bite of her ice cream.*

tightfisted
*"Don't be so **tightfisted**," I exclaimed when my brother wouldn't share his sweets.*

ANTONYM: generous

mean (2) ADJECTIVE

Someone who is **mean** is unkind.

horrible
*I can't believe how **horrible** my sister sometimes is to me.*

malicious
*The neighbour delighted in spreading **malicious** gossip.*

nasty
*The **nasty** witch gave a cruel laugh.*

spiteful
*Because he was **spiteful**, Malfoy looked for any chance of revenge.*

ANTONYM: nice

mean (3) VERB

If you ask someone what something **means**, you want them to explain it to you.

denote
*The squiggle at the bottom of the letter **denoted** that Gran had signed the card.*

indicate
*Polly's red face **indicated** that she was embarrassed.*

signify
*"What does this red dot **signify**?" I asked, pointing at the diagram.*

mean (4) VERB

If you **mean** to do something, you intend to do it.

aim
*"We **aim** to raise plenty of money for charity from the fête," announced Mrs Partridge.*

intend
*I hadn't **intended** to be home late, but I lost track of time.*

plan
*"What do you **plan** to do over the summer?" Malika asked.*

meaning NOUN

The **meaning** of a word, expression or gesture is what it refers to or expresses.

definition
*Dictionaries contain the **definitions** of words.*

explanation
*The **explanation** for Paul's late arrival was that he had got lost.*

gist
*Although I couldn't understand everything, I got the **gist** of the French conversation.*

sense
*There are several different **senses** to the word "bright".*

significance
*At last, Luke understood the **significance** of the note.*

measure VERB

If you **measure** something, you find out the size or amount of it.

assess
*The firefighters tried to **assess** how far the fire had spread.*

calculate
*In maths, we had to **calculate** the area of a triangle.*

gauge
*The skipper found the wind direction difficult to **gauge**.*

survey
*Map makers need to **survey** an area in order to map it.*

measurement NOUN

A **measurement** is the result you obtain when you measure something.

dimensions
*"We need to measure the **dimensions** of the cupboard before we buy it," said Dad.*

extent
*It was difficult to assess the **extent** of the forest fires from the ground.*

size
*Scientists were amazed at the **size** of the crater left by the meteorite.*

> **The measurement of...**
> the space in a flat (two-dimensional) surface is **area**.
> the space within a three-dimensional shape is **volume**.
> how much a container will hold is its **capacity**.

meet VERB

If you **meet** someone, you happen to be in the same place as them.

bump into (*informal*)
*"Guess who I **bumped into** today?" said Mum when she got home.*

come across
*At the show, we **came across** our next door neighbour.*

encounter
*The troops **encountered** more troublemakers than they expected.*

meeting (1) NOUN

A **meeting** is an occasion when you meet someone by arrangement.

appointment
*I groaned when Dad told me I had an **appointment** with the dentist.*

rendezvous
*Daniel arranged a secret **rendezvous** to discuss what could be done.*

meeting (2) NOUN

A **meeting** is an event at which people discuss things or make decisions.

assembly
*At an **assembly**, we showed the school the work we had done.*

conference
*Mrs Guptah said she was off to a teachers' **conference**.*

get-together (*informal*)
*Mum has a **get-together** with the book club every fortnight.*

melt VERB

When something **melts**, or when you **melt** it, it changes from a solid to a liquid because it has been heated.

defrost
*The ice cream had to be slightly **defrosted** before we could scoop it out of the tub.*

thaw
*As the snow and ice **thawed**, the witch's power over Narnia waned.*

ANTONYM: freeze

mend VERB

If you **mend** something that is broken, you repair or fix it.

fix
*"Can you **fix** the fridge, or do we need a new one?" Mum asked the repair man.*

patch
*My brother was in the garden helping Dad **patch** the broken fence.*

renovate
*Our sofa has been completely **renovated** and is now as good as new.*

repair
*The mechanic lay under the van trying to **repair** the exhaust.*

> **LANGUAGE TIP**
> If you mend a sock with a hole in, you **darn** it.

mention VERB

If you **mention** something, you speak or write briefly about it.

bring up
*"I'm glad you **brought** that **up**," the mayor said. "I wanted to thank you."*

comment on
*Grandma **commented on** how lovely the weather was.*

point out
*Mum **pointed out** that I had forgotten my school bag.*

refer to
*In her speech, the head teacher **referred to** the parents' support.*

mess (1) NOUN

A **mess** is something dirty or untidy.

chaos
*After the explosion, the whole area was in complete **chaos**.*

clutter
*Max decided to get rid of a lot of the **clutter** in his room.*

pigsty (*informal*)
*The twins' bedroom was an absolute **pigsty** until they were made to tidy it.*

shambles
When my parents took it over, the hotel was a total ***shambles****.*

mess (2) NOUN

A **mess** is a situation full of problems.

dilemma
My parents were in a ***dilemma****: should they sell the business and move to Spain?*

predicament
I was in a ***predicament*** *about which party to go to, as they were both on the same day.*

mess (3) VERB

If you **mess** with something, you play around with it.

meddle
"Don't ***meddle*** *with that box. It's your father's," Mum warned.*

tamper
Someone had been ***tampering*** *with the padlock.*

tinker
I've always enjoyed ***tinkering*** *with car engines.*

mess about; also mess around VERB

If you **mess about** or **mess around**, you spend time doing silly or casual things.

fool around
Amy and I were ***fooling around*** *when she fell and hurt herself.*

muck about (*informal*)
It's great to ***muck about*** *in the snow with sledges.*

play around
Playing around *on the railway is a very foolish thing to do.*

message NOUN

A **message** is a piece of information or a request from one person to another.

Some types of message:		
call	communication	email
fax	letter	memo
note	text message	

mess up (1) VERB

If you **mess up** something, you make it untidy.

dirty
The wretched dog had ***dirtied*** *the floor with his muddy paws.*

jumble
By accident, we had totally ***jumbled*** *all Dad's papers.*

muddle
"You have to be careful not to ***muddle*** *the wires," Dad explained as he changed the plug.*

spoil
Jess ***spoilt*** *her work by doodling around the edges.*

mess up (2) VERB

If you **mess up** something, you do it badly.

botch
The cowboy builders had really ***botched*** *the roof repair.*

bungle
We had ***bungled*** *the arrangements, and now confusion reigned.*

make a hash of
Carrie can ***make a hash of*** *any situation.*

muck up (*informal*)
By turning up late, Izzy ***mucked up*** *her chance to be in the first team.*

ANTONYMS: fix, sort out

messy ADJECTIVE

Something **messy** is dirty, untidy or confused.

chaotic
Carter's bedroom was ***chaotic****, with clothes and shoes everywhere.*

mucky
There were lots of ***mucky*** *pots and pans to clear up when we had finished baking.*

muddled
Miss Harrison told me off for producing a ***muddled*** *piece of writing.*

untidy
Untidy *work is something Mr Hill won't tolerate.*

ANTONYM: neat

method NOUN

A **method** is a particular way of doing something.

approach
Iorek's ***approach*** *to battle was simple: hit them, and hit them hard.*

procedure
"As part of the ***procedure****, you have to fill out this form," the clerk said.*

technique
In sport, try to learn ***techniques*** *that will help you perform better.*

way
My sister has a special ***way*** *of revising for her exams.*

middle (1) NOUN

The **middle** of something is the part furthest from the edges, ends or surface.

centre
In the ***centre*** *of the field was a crop circle.*

core
At the ***core*** *of the earth, temperatures are extremely high.*

heart
At night, you may find foxes even in the ***heart*** *of the city.*

hub
The control room was the ***hub*** *of all the emergency services.*

ANTONYMS: edge, end, surface

middle (2) ADJECTIVE

The **middle** thing in a series is the one with an equal number of things on each side.

central
Only the ***central*** *bowling pin remained standing.*

inner
The castle had a protected ***inner*** *courtyard.*

ANTONYM: outer

mild ADJECTIVE

Someone or something **mild** is gentle and does no harm.

gentle
The male gorilla had a very ***gentle*** *nature.*

kind
My knee hurt but the nurse was very ***kind****.*

meek
In a ***meek*** *voice, she explained what had happened.*

placid
My great-grandfather has the same ***placid*** *reaction to almost everything.*

pleasant
She made a ***pleasant*** *comment as she let them through.*

mind (1) VERB

If you **mind** when something happens to you, you are annoyed or bothered by it.

be bothered
"I ***am bothered*** *that so many of you have turned in your homework late," Mr Juffar said.*

be offended
I ***was*** *quite* ***offended*** *when I wasn't invited to the party.*

disapprove
Granny ***disapproves*** *if we arrive late.*

object
Mum really ***objects*** *when people smoke in the kitchen.*

resent
We ***resented*** *being woken up by our neighbour's noisy guests.*

mind (2) VERB

If you **mind** something for someone, you look after it for a while.

keep an eye on
At the airport, a lady asked us to ***keep an eye on*** *her luggage.*

look after
"Please ***look after*** *this bear," read Paddington Bear's label.*

take care of
Megan and I ***took care of*** *little Bethany while her mum bathed the baby.*

minimum ADJECTIVE

The **minimum** amount of something is the smallest amount that is possible, allowed or needed.

least
Trust me to get the ***least*** *amount of roast potatoes at lunch!*

lowest
The ***lowest*** *mark we needed to pass the test was 50 per cent.*

smallest
Ten euros was the ***smallest*** *amount with which you could open a bank account.*

ANTONYM: maximum

minute ADJECTIVE

Something that is **minute** is extremely small.

microscopic
It was ***microscopic*** *bacteria, not weapons, that brought the alien invaders to their knees.*

minuscule
*You should have seen the **minuscule** amount of food they gave us at camp!*

tiny
*A **tiny** glitch can cause a computer to crash.*

ANTONYMS: gigantic, huge, massive

niserable ADJECTIVE

If you are **miserable**, you are very unhappy.

brokenhearted
***Brokenhearted**, the knight said a farewell to his faithful horse.*

dejected
*After being turned down for college, my sister was **dejected** for days.*

depressed
*We were all quite **depressed** when the holiday was cancelled.*

melancholy
*I couldn't understand why Suzannah looked so **melancholy**.*

wretched
*I felt **wretched** after I'd been mean to George, my little brother.*

ANTONYM: cheerful

nisery NOUN

Misery is great unhappiness.

despair
*Mr Jones was full of **despair** when he lost his job.*

grief
*The swan showed signs of **grief** when its mate died.*

sadness
*We tried to discover the reason for the little boy's **sadness**.*

sorrow
*It was a time of great **sorrow** for the whole family.*

unhappiness
*Luckily, her **unhappiness** did not last for more than a day.*

ANTONYM: joy

niss (1) VERB

If you **miss** something that nearly hits you, it does not hit you.

avoid
*Dad just managed to **avoid** a cyclist who had no lights on her bike.*

dodge
*When he was a soldier, Grandad once **dodged** a bullet from an enemy rifle.*

evade
*The pop stars **evaded** the waiting fans by escaping in a meat van.*

ANTONYM: hit

miss (2) VERB

If you **miss** someone or something, you feel sad because they are no longer with you.

grieve for
*All our family **grieved for** our cat, Barnaby, when he died.*

mourn for
*For many years, Queen Victoria **mourned for** her late husband, Albert.*

pine for
*Daniel **pined for** his children, and decided then and there to see them next weekend at all costs.*

mistake NOUN

If you make a **mistake**, you do something wrong without intending to.

blunder
*It was a bit of a **blunder** to let the dog loose in a field full of sheep.*

error
*A simple **error** led to the loss of all the computer data.*

slip
*One **slip** of the pen meant writing the whole page again.*

misty ADJECTIVE

If it is **misty**, there are lots of tiny drops of water in the air, and you cannot see very far.

blurred
*His eyes were full of tears and everything looked **blurred**.*

dim
*In the early morning, they watched the **dim** outline of trees becoming clearer.*

faint
*A **faint** glimmer shone through the clouds.*

hazy
*The **hazy** sunshine promised a hot day.*

A B C D E F G H I J K L M N O P Q R S T U V W X Y Z

indistinct
*The figures behind the fountain were **indistinct**, but even through the spray they seemed familiar.*

mix VERB

If you **mix** things, you combine them.

blend
*Instant coffee is **blended** from several types of coffee bean.*

combine
*This dish **combines** the flavour of beef with the tang of horseradish.*

mingle
*Security guards **mingled** with the crowd, watching like hawks.*

ANTONYM: separate

mixed ADJECTIVE

If a quantity of something is **mixed**, it combines two or more different types.

assorted
*I bought a box of **assorted** Christmas cards.*

miscellaneous
*Miss Mason brought in **miscellaneous** stamps from her collection.*

various
*It was great when we went out for tea – we could choose from **various** types of cake.*

mixture NOUN

A **mixture** is two or more things mixed together.

assortment
*Grandma brought us a big box of chocolates containing an **assortment** of flavours.*

blend
*We used a **blend** of paints to get the colour we wanted for the bathroom.*

combination
*A **combination** of drugs helped bring Grandad's pain under control.*

compound
*The scientist used a **compound** of several chemicals to perfect his formula.*

fusion
*The meal was a **fusion** of Caribbean- and British-style cooking.*

jumble
*Mrs Harris gave us a **jumble** of word cards that we had to sort into verbs and nouns.*

mix up VERB

If you **mix up** things, you get confused.

confuse
*Grandad **confused** his washing with ours.*

muddle
*In maths, my sister still **muddles** multiplication and division.*

moan (1) VERB

If you **moan**, you make a low, miserable sound because you are in pain or unhappy

groan
*I couldn't help **groaning** when Elijah accidentally trod on my sore toe.*

sigh
*Mr Gupta **sighed** when he saw what a mess my tray was in.*

moan (2) VERB

If you **moan** about something, you complain about it.

complain
*My sister is always **complaining** about one thing or another.*

grumble
*Our upstairs neighbour **grumbled** about the state of the building.*

whine
*Jerry wouldn't stop **whining** about the fact that I'd forgotten his birthday, even though I'd got him a present eventually.*

whinge
*"Stop **whingeing**!" Dad said. "You're not having an ice cream."*

model NOUN

A **model** is a copy of something that show what it looks like or how it works in real life

dummy
*Shop window **dummies** don't usually look at all like real people.*

imitation
*Although the jewels were **imitations**, they looked real to me.*

replica
*My aunt has a business marketing **replicas** of Roman coins.*

modern ADJECTIVE

Something **modern** is new and involves the latest ideas or equipment.

advanced
***Advanced** technology means that you can plan your journey by satellite navigation.*

newfangled
*Grandad doesn't want to get involved with **newfangled** things like computers.*

state-of-the-art
*Dad spends a fortune on all the **state-of-the-art** camera equipment.*

the latest
*"Our health suite contains all **the latest** exercise equipment," read the gym notice.*

up-to-date
*It's an expensive business having **up-to-date** computers at school.*

ANTONYM: old-fashioned

➔ *See* **recent**

moment NOUN

A **moment** is a very short period of time.

instant
*The **instant** Mum arrived, I hid her present in the cupboard.*

second
*"Just wait. I won't be a **second**," Dad said as I headed out of the door.*

split second
*I was a **split second** too late. The bus was already leaving.*

in a moment PHRASE

If something happens **in a moment**, it happens very quickly.

in a flash
***In a flash**, the greyhounds had left the traps.*

in a jiffy (*informal*)
*"Don't worry, I'll have your car fixed **in a jiffy**," the cheery mechanic announced.*

in a trice
***In a trice**, the kettle was on and Badger was getting cups ready.*

in an instant
*The thief was out of the door **in an instant**.*

in no time at all
*We were very late, but **in no time at all**, Mrs Abrahams had made us a meal.*

money NOUN

Money is the coins and banknotes that you use to buy things.

cash
*When I asked for my pocket money, Dad pretended he was short of **cash**.*

currency
*After the holiday, we had some foreign **currency** left over.*

dosh (*informal*)
*"Do you have any **dosh** I could borrow?" my brother asked.*

dough (*informal*)
*"I've made loads of **dough** washing cars," Gupta told us.*

monkey NOUN

A **monkey** is an agile animal that has a long tail and climbs trees.

➔ Have a look at the **Illustration** page!

monster NOUN

A **monster** is a large, imaginary creature that looks very frightening.

beast
*The **beast** had cruel eyes and sharp teeth.*

brute
*With an upward thrust of his sword, St George felt the **brute** stiffen and then go limp.*

fiend
*What foul **fiend** could have inflicted such terrible havoc?*

giant
*Lumbering across the cloud, the **giant** stared at the top of the beanstalk.*

ogre
*Jack could hear the **ogre** crashing moodily about in his castle.*

mood NOUN

Your **mood** is the way you are feeling at a particular time.

frame of mind
*To win at games, you have to be in a positive **frame of mind**.*

temper
*It pays to try to keep an even **temper**.*

moody (1) ADJECTIVE

Moody people change their mood often and very quickly, seemingly for no reason.

changeable
*I find **changeable** people difficult to handle.*

temperamental
*The **temperamental** tennis player banged his racket on the ground.*

unpredictable
*Fiery and **unpredictable**, the artist was always sacking her assistants.*

a b c d e f g h i j k l m n o p q r s t u v w x y z

MONKEYS

capuchin

proboscis

gibbon

orangutan

baboon

chimpanzee

gorilla

mandrill

Some other types of monkey:

howler monkey Japanese macaque marmoset noisy night monkey Rhesus monkey spider monkey squirrel monkey tamarin

moody (2) ADJECTIVE
If you are **moody**, you feel miserable and bad-tempered.

down in the mouth (*informal*)
*"You're looking **down in the mouth**. What's the matter?" Phillipa asked.*

in a huff
*Just because I had borrowed her brush, my sister went **in a huff**.*

irritable
*Trouble at work was making Dad **irritable** in the evenings.*

sulky
*I hate it when my best friend is **sulky**.*

sullen
*Sharon gave her mum a **sullen** look.*

more ADJECTIVE
More of something is an additional thing or amount of something.

added
***Added** salt can make many snacks very bad for you.*

additional
*The club needed **additional** money to finish the project.*

extra
*Wesley asked for **extra** ice cream, as there was some spare.*

further
*"One **further** thing," she asked, "where is my umbrella?"*

ANTONYM: less

most ADJECTIVE
Most of a group of things or people means nearly all of them.

almost all
***Almost all** my friends are around the same age as I am.*

the majority of
***The majority of** the class walked to school.*

mountain NOUN
A **mountain** is a very high piece of land with steep sides.

Mount
***Mount** Olympus is where the flame starts its journey to the Games.*

peak
*A **peak** overlooks the wonderful sight of Hong Kong harbour.*

Some words to do with mountains:

The top of a mountain is its **peak** or **summit**.

A long stretch of mountains is a **range**.

A narrow, high stretch of a mountain is a **ridge**.

A high valley between two mountains is a **pass**.

move (1) VERB
If you **move** something, or when it **moves**, its position changes.

budge (*informal*)
*We couldn't **budge** the tree trunk that was blocking the path.*

shift
*It was clear from the crack that the earth beneath the house had **shifted**.*

move slightly or slowly:

crawl
*Traffic **crawled** down the busy high street in the rush hour.*

creep
*Every day, the stark frame of the skyscraper **crept** upwards.*

edge
*Hardly daring to breathe, we **edged** past the unexploded bomb.*

inch
*The giant crane **inched** its way into position.*

nose
*With its bow doors opening, the ferry **nosed** towards the docking ramp.*

stir
*The house was dark and silent. Nothing **stirred** within.*

move fast:

hurtle
*I stood in amazement as the lorry **hurtled** past me, down the hill.*

race
*Monica **raced** into the room, grabbed a comic and **raced** out again.*

shoot
*As soon as it saw us, the red squirrel **shot** up the tree.*

speed
*Soon the fire engine was **speeding** towards the scene of the accident.*

zoom
*My brother **zoomed** past me on his way out of the house.*

move forward or closer to:

advance
The invading army had ***advanced*** *several miles inland.*

approach
Approaching *the house, we could see a shadow moving in the front room.*

near
As the plane ***neared*** *its destination, we had to fasten our seat belts.*

proceed
Proceeding *towards the summit, the climbers turned on their oxygen.*

progress
Building had ***progressed*** *swiftly since Dad had last been to check.*

move backwards:

back
Some drivers have awful difficulty ***backing*** *into parking spaces properly.*

retreat
As the rain began to teem down, the golfers ***retreated*** *to a hut.*

reverse
Reversing *a canal boat is always a tricky operation.*

withdraw
The colonel decided to ***withdraw*** *rather than risk his troops being wiped out.*

move upwards:

ascend
With a deafening racket, the hovercraft ***ascended*** *on its cushion of air.*

climb
The desert temperature ***climbed*** *as the lost explorers staggered onward.*

soar
High above, a golden eagle swooped and ***soared*** *in the sunlight.*

move downwards:

descend
Holmes cautiously ***descended*** *the stairs, aware that the intruder might still be below.*

dive
Looking for somewhere to hide, they ***dived*** *under the table.*

fall
When they were ripe, the apples ***fell*** *to the ground beneath the tree.*

swoop
The hawk hovered above the roadside, ready to ***swoop*** *at any second.*

move smoothly:

float
In a total dream, Carly ***floated*** *past wearing a long dress.*

glide
Modern trains ***glide*** *along with remarkably little noise.*

skate
Totally out of control, the car ***skated*** *across the icy surface.*

move clumsily:

lumber
The bulky lorry ***lumbered*** *up the steep mountain pass.*

trundle
Bouncing and clattering, the cart ***trundled*** *along the bumpy road.*

move suddenly:

dart
A kingfisher ***darted*** *from the bank and flashed away down the canal.*

lunge
The Sheriff ***lunged*** *for the dagger, but Robin Hood was too quick for him.*

lurch
Dev ***lurched*** *forward when he tripped on the uneven paving stones.*

move quietly:

prowl
Cats ***prowl*** *at night, looking for small mammals to kill.*

slink
The spy ***slunk*** *through the bushes, dressed in black to blend with the night.*

steal
The attack party ***stole*** *past the sleeping guards at the gate.*

move (2) VERB

If you **move** things, you take them from one place to another.

convey
Containers are used for ***conveying*** *goods by ship.*

transfer
I was upset when my favourite player ***transferred*** *to another club.*

transport
Fragile items are more difficult to ***transport*** *than robust ones.*

→ *See* **carry**

move (3) VERB

If you **move**, you go to live in a different place.

move house
*People who serve in the armed forces tend to **move house** quite often.*

relocate
*Rob's parents were keen to **relocate** to the country.*

LANGUAGE TIP
When you move from one country to another, you **emigrate**. When animals move in a particular season, usually to breed or find food, they **migrate**.

mud NOUN

Mud is wet, sticky earth.

muck
*I came in covered head to toe in **muck**.*

slime
*After the rain, **slime** oozed from the pig pens.*

sludge
*"Put your wellies on," Mum shouted. "The rain has turned the path to **sludge**."*

muddle (1) NOUN

If there is a **muddle**, things get confused.

confusion
*There was a **confusion** over dates, and only three people turned up.*

misunderstanding
*The firm apologised for the **misunderstanding**, and offered Mum a free holiday.*

mix-up
*What a **mix-up**! Dad was in Australia and his luggage was in Singapore.*

muddle (2) NOUN

A **muddle** is a state of disorder or untidiness.

jumble
*Our loft is a **jumble** of unwanted items that we can't bring ourselves to throw out.*

mess
*The **mess** in my sister's bedroom looked like the aftermath of a riot.*

tangle
*Amid the **tangle** of wires, I managed to find the plug I was looking for.*

muddle (3) VERB

If things **muddle** you, they confuse you.

bewilder
*Computers may be clever things, but they **bewilder** some people.*

perplex
*We stood at the crossroads, unable to find it on the map and totally **perplexed** about which way to go.*

muddle (4) VERB

If you **muddle** things, you mix them up.

jumble
*My friend Adhira managed to **jumble** the cards she had to deliver.*

mess up
*Over the years, Grandad's papers had become totally **messed up**.*

murder (1) VERB

To **murder** someone means to kill them deliberately.

assassinate
*Police uncovered a plot to **assassinate** the king and queen.*

bump off (*informal*)
*The gangster **bumped off** those people who annoyed him.*

slaughter
*In the First World War, machine guns **slaughtered** men in their thousands.*

slay (*old-fashioned*)
*Legend has it that St George **slew** a dragon with his mighty sword.*

LANGUAGE TIP
Someone who kills another person is a **killer** or **murderer**.

murder (2) NOUN

Murder is the deliberate killing of a person.

assassination
*The **assassination** of President Kennedy took place in 1963.*

homicide
*We often hear the term **homicide** in American films and television programmes.*

killing
*No one knew how many **killings** the dictator had ordered.*

slaughter
Chicago gangsters of the 1920s used to go in for wholesale ***slaughter*** *of rivals.*

LANGUAGE TIP
Homicide is a word used in America. The killing of someone without intending to do so is **manslaughter**.

mutiny NOUN
A **mutiny** is a rebellion against someone in authority.

rebellion
The ***rebellion*** *began because the regiment was being underfed.*

revolt
Deck hands staged a ***revolt*** *at the unfair treatment of one of their shipmates.*

revolution
Many people were killed in the French ***Revolution****.*

uprising
An ***uprising*** *in the North was brutally put down by the king's men.*

mutter VERB
If you **mutter**, or if you mutter something, you speak very quietly so that it is difficult for people to hear you.

mumble
As Farmer Gabriel ***mumbled****, we often had to ask him to repeat things.*

murmur
In the wood many creatures were ***murmuring*** *and singing.*

mysterious ADJECTIVE
Something **mysterious** is strange and puzzling.

baffling
Even more ***baffling****: why was the light on in the attic?*

curious
"This Baskerville case is a ***curious*** *business," Holmes said.*

eerie
Eerie *howlings had been heard, coming from the moor.*

inexplicable
It was ***inexplicable****. Why should anyone wish to go out on a stormy night?*

mystifying
What was behind the ***mystifying*** *message written on the wall?*

mystery NOUN
A **mystery** is something that is not understood or known about.

conundrum
Mr Powers had to figure out Dr Evil's little ***conundrum****, or die.*

puzzle
It was a real ***puzzle****: how on earth could she have escaped?*

riddle
The meaning of the ancient signs was a ***riddle*** *that took years to solve.*

Nn

nag VERB

If you **nag** someone, you keep complaining to them or pestering them about something.

badger
*My little brother kept **badgering** me to take him to the park.*

hassle (*informal*)
*If you're famous, you can expect to be **hassled** by all sorts of people.*

pester
*"Stop **pestering** me!" Jasmine said. "I'll tidy my room very soon."*

name (1) NOUN

A **name** is a word that you use to identify a person, animal, place or thing.

term
*The **term** for a doing word is a verb, for example "run" and "say".*

title
*On forms, when it asks for your **title**, you have to write Mr, Mrs, Miss, Ms, Lord or Lady.*

> **Some words for different names:**
>
> Your first names can be called **forenames** or **Christian names**.
>
> In most European languages, your last name is your **family name** (also called a **surname** in English).
>
> In languages such as Chinese and Urdu, your first name is your family name.
>
> A false name for someone trying to hide or escape is an **alias**.
>
> A writer's false name is a **pen name** or **pseudonym**.
>
> An actor or musician's false name is their **stage name**.

name (2) VERB

If you **name** someone or something, you give them a name.

baptise
*My friend's little brother is going to be **baptised** on Sunday as George.*

call
*We **called** our new kitten Paws, as she has a black body and white paws.*

christen
*My mum was **christened** Patricia, but everyone calls her Pat.*

narrow ADJECTIVE

Something that is **narrow** measures a small distance from one side to the other.

slender
*The tall, **slender** poplar tree swayed gently in the breeze.*

slim
*Cinderella's **slim** foot fitted perfectly into the glass slipper.*

thin
*The black cat slipped easily through the **thin** gap in the fence.*

ANTONYM: wide

nasty (1) ADJECTIVE

Nasty behaviour is very unpleasant.

disgusting
*"Don't speak with your mouth full. It's **disgusting**!" complained my sister.*

foul
*When the joiner hit his thumb, he came out with some **foul** language.*

horrible
*"Mya, that was a **horrible** thing to say!" protested Alex.*

offensive
*The behaviour of the football hooligans was most **offensive**.*

rude
*"It's **rude** to interrupt," said Grandma when I tried to get a word in edgeways.*

sickening
*It was **sickening** to see the way the journalist tried to flatter the pop star.*

unpleasant
*My brother is sometimes **unpleasant** to me, but we always make up.*

vile
*Blackmail is a **vile** crime.*

A B C D E F G H I J K L M N O P Q R S T U V W X Y Z

nasty (2) ADJECTIVE

Nasty comments are very unpleasant.

cruel
*I don't like it when the other children say **cruel** things to new children.*

malicious
*In the **malicious** letter, the writer threatened to kidnap the businessman's son.*

mean
*My brother made some **mean** remarks about my haircut, but his isn't so smart!*

spiteful
*Her **spiteful** comments lost Jocelyn her best friend.*

unkind
*"You mustn't say **unkind** things like that," Mum warned me.*

natural (1) ADJECTIVE

Something **natural** is normal and to be expected.

common
*It was a **common** occurrence for us to pass the pop star on his daily jog.*

normal
*The doctor reassured Givon that his spots were **normal**, and would go.*

ordinary
*To the world, the spy seemed just an **ordinary**, everyday sort of person.*

➔ *See* **regular** and **usual**

natural (2) ADJECTIVE

Something **natural** exists or happens in nature, rather than being caused or made by people.

organic
*Our local shop sells **organic** food that is free from pesticides and has grown naturally.*

plain
*I loved the **plain** wood finish of the panels in the old manor.*

wholesome
*Mum's meals were always made of good, **wholesome** ingredients.*

ANTONYM: artificial

natural (3) ADJECTIVE

If you have a **natural** ability, you are born with it.

inherent
*Gymnasts need an **inherent** sense of balance to succeed.*

innate
*Henry had an **innate** ability to get on well with people.*

instinctive
*It was only the racing driver's **instinctive** reaction that saved his life.*

ANTONYM: unnatural

naughty ADJECTIVE

A child who is **naughty** behaves badly.

badly-behaved
*The twins were suspended from school for being persistently **badly-behaved**.*

disobedient
*My brother isn't usually **disobedient**, but does what he's told.*

mischievous
*While his mother was on the phone, the **mischievous** toddler pulled everything out of the cupboard.*

troublesome
*Mum says I was quite **troublesome** when I was little, but I'm much better behaved now.*

ANTONYMS: well-behaved, obedient

near (1) PREPOSITION

If something is **near** a particular place, it is a short distance from it.

adjacent
***Adjacent** to the old pigsty was a room for storing horse harnesses.*

close
*When we go swimming we can walk to the pool, as it is so **close** to home.*

nearby
*Mrs Irons told us to wait while she asked the way in a **nearby** shop.*

neighbouring
*Bilal and I built a den beneath a tree in **neighbouring** woods.*

within easy reach
*Our house is **within easy reach** of the station.*

near (2) ADJECTIVE

If an event is **near**, it will happen soon.

approaching
*Anish was excited at the thought of the **approaching** concert.*

close at hand
*The midnight hour was **close at hand**, as the coffin lids creaked open.*

forthcoming
*The local newspaper has details of **forthcoming** events.*

imminent
*We knew from the countdown that the rocket launch was **imminent**.*

nigh (*old-fashioned*)
*"As night is **nigh**, prithee stay with us, kind sir," said the innkeeper.*

nearly ADVERB

Something which is **nearly** done is not completely finished, but almost.

almost
*I'd **almost** finished my homework when Alan called round.*

practically
*Our supplies were **practically** exhausted, and water was short too.*

virtually
*Building was **virtually** completed when fire destroyed the house.*

→ *See* **roughly**

neat (1) ADJECTIVE

Something that is **neat** is tidy and smart.

orderly
*Mr Khan told us to form an **orderly** queue as we waited to get on the bus.*

shipshape
*Gramps praised me for leaving my room **shipshape**.*

smart
*Mum likes me to look **smart** when we visit my aunt and uncle.*

spick-and-span
*The holiday apartment was **spick-and-span** when we arrived.*

tidy
*Skylar was always **tidy** in her school work.*

ANTONYM: messy

neat (2) ADJECTIVE

If someone makes a **neat** move, they do it skilfully.

clever
*The way that my mum worded the birthday card was really **clever**.*

nifty (*informal*)
*With a **nifty** sidestep, the forward was through to the goal.*

skilful
*Alastair admired the **skilful** way the magician handled the cards.*

necessary ADJECTIVE

Something that is **necessary** is needed or must be done.

essential
*Napoleon insisted that good food was **essential** for his troops.*

imperative
*"It is **imperative** that this message gets through," the sergeant urged the rider.*

required
*To become a teacher, a good education is **required**.*

vital
*At the end of an exam, it's **vital** to check what you've written.*

ANTONYM: unnecessary

need VERB

If you **need** something, you cannot achieve what you want without having it or doing it.

demand
*Being a good nurse **demands** stamina, intelligence and a caring attitude.*

require
*The advert read, "**Required**: honest boy or girl for newspaper deliveries."*

neighbourhood NOUN

Your **neighbourhood** is the area where you live.

area
*There are many tower blocks in our **area**.*

community
*Each Wednesday, there's a luncheon club for old people in the **community**.*

district
*Our school is the best in the **district**.*

locality
*Our **locality** does not have very many facilities for young people.*

vicinity
*"Police warn that a thief is operating in the **vicinity**," announced the newsreader.*

a b c d e f g h i j k l m n o p q r s t u v w x y z

A B C D E F G H I J K L M N O P Q R S T U V W X Y Z

nervous ADJECTIVE

If someone is **nervous**, they are easily worried and agitated.

anxious
*Ben seemed **anxious** so Laura asked him what was wrong.*

apprehensive
*I always feel a little **apprehensive** before I go to the dentist.*

edgy
*As the day of his test approached, Karl became increasingly **edgy**.*

jittery (*informal*)
*Many actors and actresses get **jittery** before they go on stage.*

jumpy (*informal*)
*The man was so **jumpy** that I knew he was up to no good.*

worried
*When Mum was in hospital, we could tell Dad was **worried**.*

ANTONYM: calm

never ADVERB

Something that has **never** happened, has happened at no time in the past, and will not happen at any time in the present or future.

at no time
*"**At no time** did I leave the room, sir," the witness insisted.*

on no account
*They were warned **on no account** to ever touch the wires.*

under no circumstances
*Mr Osman said that **under no circumstances** would he let us off our homework.*

new (1) ADJECTIVE

Something **new** is recently made.

fresh
*I love the smell of **fresh** bread.*

unused
*The car was advertised as being in **unused** condition.*

LANGUAGE TIP

A new, unused coin or stamp is in **mint condition**.

---

new (2) ADJECTIVE

Something **new** is recently created or discovered.

current
*"You can bet that **current** trends will be tomorrow's old news," said the reporter.*

latest
*"For my birthday I got the **latest** version of my favourite computer game," said Gamal.*

modern
*Our school is a **modern** building near the town centre.*

recent
*My mum's car is the most **recent** model.*

up-to-date
*My brother insists on buying all the **up-to date** computer gadgets.*

ANTONYM: old

next (1) ADJECTIVE

The **next** thing, person or event is the one that comes immediately after the present one.

following
*We went to the seaside one day, and the **following** day to the hills.*

subsequent
*On Tuesday I planned my story, and wrote it the **subsequent** day.*

ANTONYM: previous

next (2) ADJECTIVE

The **next** place or person is the one nearest to the person in question.

adjacent
*My friends Ivan and Isabella live in the flat **adjacent** to ours.*

neighbouring
*The ball hit the headpin, which then knocked all the **neighbouring** pins down.*

next (3) ADVERB

You use **next** to refer to an action that follows immediately after the present one.

afterwards
*Shane and I had a swim and **afterwards** sat by the pool.*

subsequently
*The man was injured in the accident but **subsequently** made a full recovery.*

ANTONYM: previously

nice

➔ Look at the **Word Power** page!

nice

(1) ADJECTIVE A **nice** person is pleasant and kind.

charming
Scoresby, the balloonist, turned out to be a ***charming*** *fellow.*

delightful
A ***delightful*** *old lady offered us a cup of tea.*

kind
It was ***kind*** *of Alexia to invite me.*

likeable
Crystal was a ***likeable*** *character who had lots of friends.*

pleasant
The interviewer was ***pleasant****, with a kind smile and a nice voice.*

(2) ADJECTIVE A **nice** event is pleasant and enjoyable.

delightful
"What a ***delightful*** *evening," said Pete.*

enjoyable
We spent an ***enjoyable*** *hour chatting on the phone.*

pleasant
The sun shone and the whole barbecue was a ***pleasant*** *event.*

(3) ADJECTIVE A **nice** view is pleasant to look at.

pleasing
The hotel balcony had a ***pleasing*** *outlook over the estuary.*

scenic
The mountains are very ***scenic****.*

stunning
We had a ***stunning*** *view of the lake.*

(4) ADJECTIVE A **nice** meal is tasty.

appetizing
An ***appetizing*** *smell wafted in.*

delicious
Strawberry jam, cream and scones make a ***delicious*** *combination.*

scrumptious (*informal*)
"That was a ***scrumptious*** *supper," Omar said to my mum.*

tasty
"Thanks for the dinner," said Fred. "It was really ***tasty****."*

(5) ADJECTIVE **Nice** weather is warm and pleasant.

fine
The day we left was ***fine*** *and warm.*

pleasant
It was ***pleasant*** *weather for a picnic.*

lovely
Saturday was a ***lovely*** *crisp autumn day.*

(6) ADJECTIVE **Nice** clothes are stylish and smart.

beautiful
The dress in the window was ***beautiful*** *but very expensive.*

elegant
I thought Mum and Dad looked ***elegant*** *in their evening clothes.*

smart
He wore a ***smart*** *new suit.*

A
B
C
D
E
F
G
H
I
J
K
L
M
N
O
P
Q
R
S
T
U
V
W
X
Y
Z

nip VERB

If you **nip** somewhere, you go there quickly.

dart
*The squirrel **darted** across the garden.*

dash
*As the rain bucketed down, we **dashed** from the car to the doorway.*

hurry
***Hurrying** past, our next-door neighbour didn't notice me.*

rush
*Jade banged the door, threw her bag on the chair and **rushed** upstairs.*

no INTERJECTION

You say **no** when you do not want something or do not agree.

LANGUAGE TIP
To say no to someone's request is to **deny** it, **refuse** it or **turn** it **down**. To say no when asked if you have done something is to **deny** it.

noise (1) NOUN

A **noise** can be a loud or unpleasant sound.

cacophony
*There was a **cacophony** from the orchestra as the musicians warmed up.*

commotion
*There was a **commotion** at the back, and someone burst forward, shouting.*

din
*In the **din** of the cotton mill, it was impossible to hear yourself speak.*

hubbub
*Gran doesn't like the **hubbub** of the city.*

hullabaloo (*informal*)
*"What's all this **hullabaloo** about?" the sergeant enquired.*

racket
*My brother's music makes quite a **racket**.*

row
*Mum asked us not to make too much of a **row** out in the garden.*

uproar
*When the pop star finally came on stage there was **uproar** in the crowd.*

noise (2) NOUN

The **noise** of people talking is what they sound like as they speak.

babble
*The head teacher raised a hand, and the **babble** of voices subsided.*

chatter
*A ceaseless **chatter** comes from my sister's room when her friend Hope comes round.*

hubbub
*There is usually quite a **hubbub** in the school dining hall at dinner time.*

noisy (1) ADJECTIVE

When something is **noisy**, it makes a lot of noise.

deafening
*The sound of the waterfall was **deafening**.*

ear-splitting
*With an **ear-splitting** crash, the building was demolished.*

loud
*From windows throughout the neighbourhood, **loud** music boomed into the summer streets.*

piercing
*The **piercing** screech of the parrot echoed through the house.*

thunderous
*The **thunderous** boom of artillery fire can be heard many miles away.*

ANTONYM: quiet

noisy (2) ADJECTIVE

When someone is **noisy**, they make a lot of noise.

boisterous
*The **boisterous** children were obviously enjoying the party.*

rowdy
*The crowds in the street were **rowdy** but friendly.*

ANTONYM: quiet

nonsense NOUN

Nonsense is foolish or meaningless words or behaviour.

drivel
*My dad reckons that modern radio DJs mostly talk **drivel**.*

rot
*"Bunter, you do talk **rot**!" the fourth-former snapped.*

rubbish
*"I think a lot of television programmes are utter **rubbish**," I told my best friend, Keisha.*

twaddle (*informal*)
*What she was saying was **twaddle**, and everyone there knew it.*

normal (1) ADJECTIVE
If people or things are **normal**, they are usual and ordinary.

average
*The **average** person doesn't go to the opera very often.*

common
*Mrs Parham was very special – certainly not the **common** type of teacher.*

conventional
*Vanya never likes to wear **conventional** clothes – always something a bit different.*

typical
*The weather was **typical** for this time of year.*

ANTONYM: different

normal (2) ADJECTIVE
If someone's behaviour is **normal**, it is usual for them to behave this way.

habitual
*Gran's **habitual** routine is to sit down with a cup of coffee at eleven o'clock each morning.*

regular
*They looked like a **regular** pair of shoes, but they actually had magic powers.*

usual
*Mum said she'd pick me up from school at the **usual** time.*

nosy; also **nosey** ADJECTIVE
Nosy people always want to know about other people's business, and like to interfere where they are not wanted.

curious
***Curious** to discover more, we followed the sound of the voices.*

inquisitive
*Mum's quite **inquisitive** and loves to hear all the gossip from the neighbours.*

meddlesome
*"Go away, you **meddlesome** children!" shouted the caretaker.*

nothing NOUN
Nothing means not a single thing, or not a single part of something.

none
*When I asked my brother to pass the roast potatoes, there were **none** left.*

nought
*I was quite ashamed when I got **nought** out of ten in the test.*

zero
*My sister checked her bank balance and was horrified to see that it was **zero**.*

LANGUAGE TIP
In tennis, no points is called **love**. In sports such as rugby or soccer, no points is called **nil**.

notice (1) VERB
If you **notice** something, you become aware of it.

detect
*The sniffer dog **detected** the stolen jewels in the woman's luggage.*

observe
*I **observed** that, unusually, no trains had passed for an hour.*

perceive
*"I **perceive** more in you than you realise," Gandalf the wizard told the hobbit.*

spot
*Mum **spotted** a mark on my shirt.*

notice (2) NOUN
A **notice** is a written announcement.

advertisement
*Dad placed an **advertisement** for the bike in the local paper.*

poster
*For our garage sale, we put **posters** all round the neighbourhood.*

now (1) ADVERB
If someone asks you to do something **now**, they want it done straight away.

at once
*She flung open the door and shouted, "Stop this racket **at once**!"*

immediately
*"Do it **immediately**, or there'll be trouble," Mum ordered.*

straight away
*"We need an ambulance, **straight away**, please," the caller said.*

A B C D E F G H I J K L M N O P Q R S T U V W X Y Z

now (2) ADVERB

Now can mean at the present time or moment.

at the moment
Because of the fog, no planes are taking off ***at the moment****.*

nowadays
Nowadays*, we can travel abroad much more easily than in the past.*

these days
*"****These days****, I can't run around like I did," my grandad said.*

nuisance NOUN

A **nuisance** is someone or something that is annoying or causing problems.

annoyance
Our neighbour found my brother's loud music a great ***annoyance****.*

bother
"Let me help you with those bags. It's no ***bother****," I said as I took my gran's shopping into the house.*

hassle *(informal)*
"If you come shopping, I want no ***hassle****," warned my mother.*

inconvenience
The company apologised for the ***inconvenience*** *caused by their roadworks.*

→ *See* **problem**

number (1) NOUN

A **number** is a word or symbol used for counting or calculating.

digit
The number one million (1 000 000) has seven ***digits*** *in it.*

figure
"Think of a number with three ***figures****," the magician commanded.*

numeral
The ***numerals*** *we use come from the Arab countries of the Middle East.*

number (2) NOUN

A **number** of things or people is several of them.

collection
For the TV series, a ***collection*** *of old vehicles was needed.*

crowd
A large ***crowd*** *of supporters gathered to cheer the team as they left.*

host *(old-fashioned)*
Seeing a ***host*** *of golden daffodils beside the lake, the poet sat down to write.*

quantity
"What ***quantity*** *of bricks do you need?" the builder's merchant enquired*

nut NOUN

A **nut** is a dry fruit with a hard shell.

→ Have a look at the **Illustration** page!

NUTS

almond

brazil nut

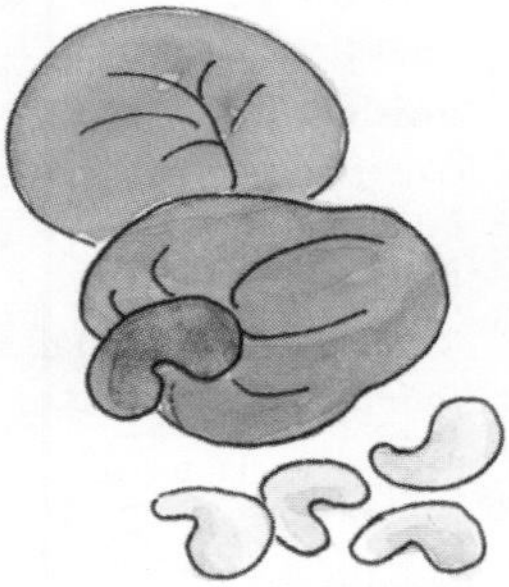

cashew

walnut

peanut/monkey nut

hazelnut

pecan

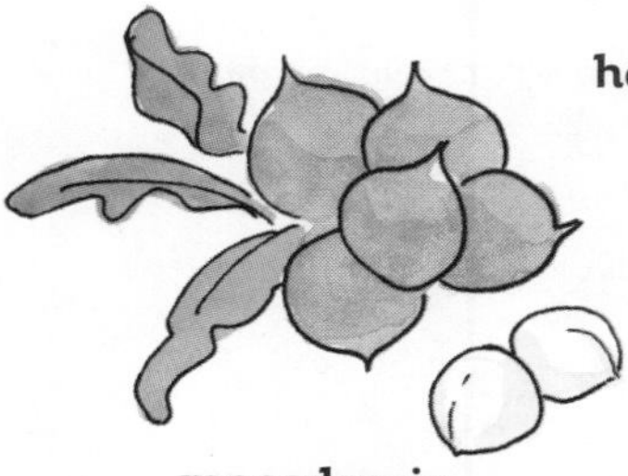

macadamia

Some other types of nut:

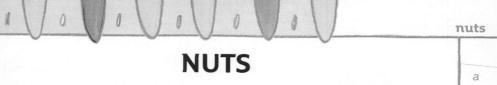

chestnut coconut pilinut pine nut pistachio

A B C D E F G H I J K L M N O P Q R S T U V W X Y Z

Oo

obey VERB

If you **obey** a person or an order, you do what you are told to do.

abide by
*Games are much more fun when people **abide by** the rules.*

follow
*Building models from kits is easier if you **follow** the instructions.*

ANTONYM: disobey

object VERB

If you **object** to something, you dislike it, disagree with it or disapprove of it.

disagree
*Shania **disagreed** with Wayne's choice of DVD, but she watched it anyway.*

disapprove
*Gran **disapproves** of us playing our music too loudly.*

oppose
*Many local people **opposed** the new road.*

protest
*Thousands of people turned out to **protest** against the missiles.*

ANTONYMS: approve, support

→ *See* **argue (1)**

observant ADJECTIVE

An **observant** person notices things that are not usually noticed.

alert
*Fortunately Dad was **alert** enough to avoid the deer that ran out in front of the car.*

eagle-eyed
*Thanks to the **eagle-eyed** lookout, the tanker avoided the sailing dinghy.*

perceptive
*Mrs Bower said how **perceptive** Jack was to notice her new shoes.*

ANTONYM: unobservant

obvious ADJECTIVE

Something that is **obvious** is easy to see or understand.

apparent
*As soon as she spoke, it was **apparent** that Lyndsay came from the USA.*

blatant
*Tripping the player up was a **blatant** foul by the opposition's team captain.*

clear
*It was **clear** that the climber was totally stuck and would need some help.*

evident
*"It's **evident**, Yoshi," said Mr Leonard, "that you have learned nothing."*

plain
*From her wonderful performance, it was **plain** that Alana had been practising hard.*

ANTONYM: unclear

occasionally ADVERB

If something happens **occasionally**, it happens sometimes, but not often.

from time to time
***From time to time**, Granny and Grandad come to visit us.*

now and then
*Mum takes us to the seaside **now and then**.*

once in a while
***Once in a while**, my computer will do strange things.*

periodically
*My father has to go abroad **periodically**, but not very often.*

ANTONYMS: often, regularly

odd (1) ADJECTIVE

If something is **odd**, it is strange or unusual.

curious
*It was **curious** how tame the baby birds were.*

peculiar
*How **peculiar**! There's a dog on the roof of that house!*

queer
*The king noticed there was something **queer** about the woods beyond the castle.*

odd (2) ADJECTIVE
If someone is **odd**, they do not behave in a normal way.

eccentric
*My Aunty Rose is rather **eccentric**.*

unconventional
*Deena has always been **unconventional**. Now she rides a unicycle to school.*

zany
*I love the old silent films, especially ones with that **zany** chap with his eyes crossed.*

ANTONYM: conventional

off ADJECTIVE
If an event is **off**, it is cancelled or postponed.

cancelled
*Because of cattle disease, the agricultural show was **cancelled**.*

postponed
*United's game with City was **postponed** owing to the fog.*

ANTONYM: on

offend VERB
If you **offend** someone, you upset them by saying or doing something rude.

annoy
*Claire said she was sorry she had **annoyed** her grandmother.*

displease
*They found it was a mistake to **displease** their teacher.*

insult
*"Don't **insult** your brother," said Mum. "It's not funny."*

upset
*It will **upset** her if you criticise her hairstyle.*

often ADVERB
Something that happens **often**, happens many times or a lot of the time.

frequently
*My father **frequently** takes us to the beach in the summer.*

regularly
***Regularly** in July, old Mr Lowry went to stay at the seaside.*

repeatedly
*He warned her **repeatedly** that he was unlikely to change his mind.*

time after time
*"You forget your kit **time after time**," Mrs Quincy sighed.*

ANTONYM: occasionally

okay (1); also **OK** ADJECTIVE (*informal*)
If you say something is **okay**, it is all right.

acceptable
*Miss Chowdri said it was **acceptable** for me to miss PE, as I'd hurt my ankle.*

in order
*"Is it **in order** for me to have Tuesday off?" the clerk asked.*

satisfactory
*It was a fairly **satisfactory** solution to the problem.*

okay (2); also **OK** ADJECTIVE (*informal*)
If something is **okay**, it is moderately good.

adequate
*The expedition's supplies were **adequate** for their needs.*

fair
*According to the head teacher, my report was **fair**, but nothing more.*

passable
*"This lasagne is **passable**, but not as good as I usually make," remarked Dad.*

satisfactory
*Mrs Freeman said my work was **satisfactory**.*

old (1) ADJECTIVE
If a person is **old**, they have lived for a long time.

aged
*The **aged** actor received a "Lifetime Achievement" award.*

elderly
*Each week, my gran meets three other **elderly** ladies for lunch.*

getting on (*informal*)
*Grandad is **getting on**, and finds climbing stairs a problem.*

past their prime
*The tennis players were **past their prime**, but they were still entertaining to watch.*

ANTONYMS: young, youthful

A B C D E F G H I J K L M N O P Q R S T U V W X Y Z

old (2) ADJECTIVE

If something is **old**, it has existed for a long time.

ancient
*Europe has many **ancient** cathedrals and my dad intends to visit them all.*

antique
*The **antique** chairs were worth a great deal of money.*

archaic
*"Shakespeare uses some **archaic** language," explained Mrs Tordoff.*

original
*Our cottage still has some of its **original** features from the 19th century.*

primitive
*The **primitive** way of moving heavy stones was to roll them along on logs.*

veteran
*Some **veteran** radio broadcasters keep going until they are 80 or more.*

vintage
*Our neighbour has a lovely **vintage** car.*

LANGUAGE TIP
Something **prehistoric** is from the time before written records were kept.

old (3) ADJECTIVE

An **old** tradition has existed for a long time.

long-established
*The school has the **long-established** tradition of a feast in April.*

long-standing
*"Our firm has a **long-standing** reputation for fine meat," the butcher said proudly.*

traditional
*The harbour town has a **traditional** street parade in May.*

ANTONYM: new

old (4) ADJECTIVE

You use **old** to talk about something that is no longer used or has been replaced by something else.

ex-
*We still get Christmas cards from my sister's **ex-**boyfriend.*

former
*Because she was a **former** ballerina, Mrs Fountain still looked very slim and fit.*

one-time
*The **one-time** player is now a coach.*

previous
*My mum's **previous** car was a real old banger.*

ANTONYM: current

old-fashioned ADJECTIVE

Something **old-fashioned** is out of date and no longer fashionable.

antiquated
*My dad's shed is rather **antiquated**, but he likes working there.*

dated
*With their black-and-white pictures, some of our school textbooks look very **dated**.*

obsolete
*The school is changing some of its **obsolete** computers for more up-to-date ones.*

outdated
*The factory manager aimed to get rid of the **outdated** machinery.*

traditional
*Lumley's **traditional** oatcakes have been made here since 1758.*

unfashionable
*These clothes were once very trendy, but are now **unfashionable**.*

ANTONYMS: up-to-date, modern

once ADVERB

If something was **once** true, it was true in the past, but is no longer true.

at one time
***At one time**, Mrs Schwarz used to read us a story every day.*

formerly
*Geraldine was **formerly** at a different high school.*

in the past
***In the past**, Dad used to be able to carry me upstairs to bed.*

at once (1) PHRASE

If several things happen **at once**, they all happen at the same time.

at the same time
*"If you all talk **at the same time**, no one can hear what anyone's actually saying," said Miss Bell.*

simultaneously
*On the night of the golden jubilee, celebratory bonfires were lit **simultaneously** all over the country.*

at once (2) PHRASE
If you do something **at once**, you do it immediately.

immediately
*The bell rang for break time, and **immediately** children streamed out of their classrooms.*

instantly
*A clever vet **instantly** knew what was wrong with our hamster.*

right away
*I promised to do the errand **right away**.*

this minute
*"If you don't come down here **this minute**, your supper will get cold!" Mum yelled.*

without hesitation
***Without hesitation**, the firefighter raced into the burning house to save the woman.*

only (1) ADVERB
You use **only** to emphasise that something is unimportant or small.

barely
*We had **barely** a teaspoonful of sugar left in the bowl.*

just
*"It's **just** a simple operation," the doctor said.*

merely
*"Julie is **merely** the office junior, but she tries to act like the boss," complained my cousin.*

simply
*It was **simply** a matter of snipping one of the wires to prevent the bomb from exploding.*

only (2) ADJECTIVE
If you talk about **only** one thing or person, you mean that there are no others.

single
*Mrs Cameron was the **single** person Lydia felt she could talk to.*

sole
*Robinson Crusoe thought he was the **sole** inhabitant of his island.*

solitary
*The prisoner was the **solitary** occupant of a whole row of cells.*

LANGUAGE TIP
If you are an **only child**, you have no brothers or sisters.

open (1) ADJECTIVE
Something that is **open** is not closed or fastened, allowing things to pass through.

ajar
*As the door was **ajar**, Hadiya peeped in.*

gaping
*The explosion left a **gaping** hole in the wall.*

unlocked
*"I've left the door **unlocked**," Mum shouted, as she went out.*

yawning
*In front of the two hobbits lay a **yawning** chasm. How were they to cross it?*

open (2) VERB
When you **open** something, or when it **opens**, it is moved so that it is no longer closed.

unfasten
*Fiona **unfastened** the gate and the chickens rushed to meet her.*

unlock
*"**Unlock** this door and let me out!" the prison warder bawled.*

unwrap
*I went through to Mum and Dad's room to **unwrap** my presents.*

ANTONYM: close

open (3) VERB
If something **opens**, or is opened, it starts or begins.

begin
*Each day business **begins** at the shop at nine o'clock.*

commence
*The chairman **commenced** the meeting by introducing his new assistant.*

get going
*My birthday party really **got going** when Mum brought the cake out.*

ANTONYM: finish

open (4) ADJECTIVE
Someone who is **open** is honest and not secretive.

candid
*"Please be **candid** in your replies," the judge asked the witness.*

frank
*"To be **frank**," Mum told Dad, "I'd rather go to the cinema than the theatre."*

A B C D E F G H I J K L M N O P Q R S T U V W X Y Z

honest
Mrs Ghandi told us that it is always best to be ***honest****.*

opening NOUN

An **opening** is a hole or space that things or people can go through.

break
The sun shone briefly through a ***break*** *in the clouds.*

chink
A ***chink*** *between the curtains allowed a strip of light to escape.*

crack
Smoke was rising through a ***crack*** *between the floorboards.*

hole
The boys peered into the garden through a ***hole*** *in the fence.*

slot
The car keys fell down through a ***slot*** *in the grating.*

space
There was just a ***space*** *where the door should have been.*

opinion NOUN

An **opinion** is a belief or view.

belief
It's my ***belief*** *that he is a very talented young artist.*

view
You should make your ***views*** *known to the head teacher.*

opposite (1) ADJECTIVE

If things are **opposite**, they are completely different.

conflicting
The journalists were receiving ***conflicting*** *reports about how the talks were going.*

contrary
Contrary *to what people thought, the old man was very generous to charity.*

contrasting
Contrasting *with last year's disaster, the school play was a great success this year.*

opposing
We were friends even though we had ***opposing*** *points of view.*

ANTONYM: alike

opposite (2) NOUN

If people or things are **opposites**, they are completely different from each other.

contrary
Aditi thought that she had done badly in the test, but she had, on the ***contrary****, done well.*

converse
Three times two is six, and the ***converse*** *is also true.*

reverse
If ever I ask my brother to do something, he always does the ***reverse****.*

LANGUAGE TIP
If you say the opposite of what someone has said, you **contradict** them.

order (1) VERB

If you **order** someone to do something, you tell them firmly to do it.

command
When he got to the roundabout he ***commanded*** *his driver to stop.*

direct
The coach ***directed*** *all the players to say nothing to the newspapers.*

instruct
Mrs Caruso ***instructed*** *us to walk along the cliff path in single file.*

order (2) VERB

When you **order** something, you ask for it to be brought or sent to you.

apply for
My older brother has ***applied for*** *his provisional driving licence.*

book
Dad ***booked*** *our train tickets in advance.*

request
Mr Kwami ***requested*** *some new equipment for the sports hall.*

order (3) NOUN

An **order** is a command given by someone in authority.

command
For disobeying the ***command*** *of his officer, the airman was dismissed.*

instruction
The boss's ***instructions*** *were to finish the job whatever the cost.*

ordinary ADJECTIVE

Something that is **ordinary** is not special or different in any way.

conventional
*Gran likes a **conventional** hairstyle.*

normal
*It is quite **normal** for people to have sleepless nights now and then.*

routine
*"Don't worry, madam," the police officer said. "It's just a **routine** enquiry."*

standard
*"At the cinema, even a **standard** size of popcorn would feed a regiment," laughed Dad.*

usual
*It seemed like a **usual** Saturday, but then something unexpected happened.*

Try these lively words and phrases:

common-or-garden
*This isn't just a **common-or-garden** phone!*

run-of-the-mill
*I am just an average **run-of-the-mill** person.*

ANTONYMS: unusual, rare

organise (1) VERB

If you **organise** something, you plan and arrange it.

arrange
*Mum **arranged** a surprise party for Dad's 40th birthday.*

coordinate
*Our class was asked to **coordinate** the preparation of the hall for speech day.*

direct
*Dad **directs** plays for the local drama group.*

manage
***Managing** a sports team is never an easy job.*

plan
*My sister and her fiancé **planned** their wedding reception in great detail.*

organise (2) VERB

If you **organise** a group of things, you arrange them in a sensible order.

arrange
*Dawn enjoyed **arranging** the pottery sheep in a different order.*

catalogue
*It took ages to **catalogue** all the books in the school library.*

classify
*Mrs Zubin asked us to **classify** the flowers according to colour.*

sort
*Before mail is delivered, it is **sorted** into areas, then towns, then streets.*

ANTONYM: jumble

other ADJECTIVE

Other people or things are different from those already mentioned.

additional
*The general called for **additional** troops to reinforce the lines.*

alternative
*"Is there an **alternative** date we could travel on?" Mum asked.*

further
*Mrs Given asked us if we had any **further** suggestions.*

outfit NOUN

An **outfit** is a set of clothes.

clothes
*Brad didn't really bother about what sort of **clothes** he wore.*

costume
*You should have seen my sister's fancy-dress **costume**!*

gear
*"If you're going sailing, don't forget your wet-weather **gear**,"Mum called.*

kit
*I left my sports **kit** in the changing room.*

outing NOUN

An **outing** is a trip made for pleasure.

excursion
*The coach company runs **excursions** to all sorts of places.*

jaunt
*Dad fancied a **jaunt**, so off we all went to the seaside.*

trip
*Before we went on our class **trip**, we had lots of work to prepare for it.*

A B C D E F G H I J K L M N O P Q R S T U V W X Y Z

outside (1) NOUN

The **outside** of something is the part that surrounds or encloses the rest of it.

exterior
*The tatty **exterior** of the old hotel gave the wrong impression.*

face
*On the **face** of it, the problem looked simple.*

surface
*The outer **surface** of the rocket is designed to withstand terrific heat.*

ANTONYM: inside

outside (2) ADJECTIVE

Something that is **outside** is not inside.

exterior
*My brother was up a ladder finishing the **exterior** paintwork.*

external
***External** doors have to be thicker and sturdier than internal ones.*

outdoor
*We had a scrumptious picnic before the **outdoor** concert.*

outer
*The castle's **outer** wall had slits, through which arrows were fired.*

ANTONYMS: inner, inside

over (1) ADJECTIVE

Something that is **over** is completely finished.

at an end
*The term was **at an end**, and the holidays stretched before us.*

complete
*The work of restoring the old farmhouse is now **complete**.*

concluded
*With business **concluded**, the two women were pleased to head home.*

finished
*With his career **finished** because of ill health, the politician retired to the country.*

over (2) PREPOSITION

Something that is **over**, is more than what is required.

above
*The driver was stopped for travelling **above** the speed limit.*

higher than
*I was very pleased when I got a mark **higher than** I had expected in the test.*

in excess of
*The lottery winner received a sum **in excess of** 10 million pounds.*

ANTONYM: under

own ADJECTIVE

If something is your **own**, it belongs to you or is associated with you.

personal
*My **personal** opinion is that the film was dull.*

private
*Behind the locked door was the duke's **private** suite of rooms.*

Pp

pad NOUN

A **pad** is a set of sheets of paper glued together at one end.

jotter
*I couldn't understand the notes I'd scribbled in my **jotter**.*

notebook
*Writing in his **notebook**, the police officer took down details from the witness.*

writing pad
*My **writing pad** has holes punched in it, so that pages can be filed.*

pain NOUN

Pain is a feeling of discomfort and hurt in your body, caused by an illness or injury.

ache
*The **ache** in Gran's leg improved overnight.*

discomfort
*Sitting in the same seat for hours often causes **discomfort**.*

soreness
*Marina had a lot of **soreness** in her legs when she finished the marathon.*

twinge
*A sudden **twinge** made me stop and hold my arm for a moment.*

LANGUAGE TIP
Words for severe pain include **agony**, **distress** and **suffering**.

---

painful (1) ADJECTIVE

Something that is **painful** causes physical pain.

aching
*I had an **aching** side from laughing so hard.*

agonising
*Marlon said that when he fractured his knee the pain was **agonising**.*

excruciating
*You could tell from Mum's face that the pain was **excruciating**.*

sore
*With a **sore** throat, Almira was in no condition to sing in the choir.*

tender
*My thumb was **tender** for days after I slammed it in the door.*

throbbing
*The pop star's ears were **throbbing** with the screams of the crowd.*

ANTONYMS: painless, pain-free

painful (2) ADJECTIVE

Something that is **painful** causes emotional pain.

agonising
*Dad had an **agonising** wait to know if he'd got the job.*

distressing
*It must be **distressing** for the police to have to break bad news to people.*

upsetting
*The girl's spiteful remarks were deeply **upsetting** to her friends.*

paint VERB

If you **paint** a picture of someone or something, you make a picture of them using paint.

depict
*In The Fighting Temeraire, Turner **depicts** a heroic old ship being towed to the shipyard.*

portray
*I tried to **portray** Khalil's face, but his skin ended up tomato-coloured.*

pair NOUN

A **pair** is two things of the same type, often meant to be used together.

couple
*In the race, a **couple** of horses threw their riders.*

duo
*Comic-book characters Batman and Robin were known as "The Dynamic **Duo**".*

twosome
*I call my big sister and her friend "the gruesome **twosome**".*

A B C D E F G H I J K L M N O P Q R S T U V W X Y Z

pale ADJECTIVE

If someone or something is **pale**, they are not strong or bright in colour.

ashen
*I could tell something was terribly wrong by my mum's **ashen** face.*

colourless
*The sun had bleached the curtains until they were fairly **colourless**.*

faded
***Faded** from being sat on by a million people, the cinema seats were past their best.*

light
*The shirt was a **light** shade of blue.*

wan
*By the end of winter I always look a bit **wan**.*

panic (1) VERB

If you **panic**, you become so afraid or anxious that you cannot act sensibly.

become hysterical
*My aunt almost **became hysterical** when she lost her purse.*

go to pieces
*My cousin never **goes to pieces** in a crisis.*

lose your nerve
*The parachute jumper **lost his nerve** and stayed on board the plane.*

panic (2) NOUN

Panic is a sudden strong feeling of fear or anxiety.

alarm
*Filled with **alarm**, Keifer realised that he only had one way of escape..*

dismay
*With **dismay** Amitava saw the child run out into the road.*

fright
*When the lion sprang forward, the antelope scattered in **fright**.*

hysteria
***Hysteria** spread through the crowd and people started screaming and crying.*

terror
*The mountaineers were struck with **terror** as they saw the avalanche heading towards them.*

pant VERB

If you **pant**, you take short, quick breaths through your mouth.

gasp
*I was **gasping** by the end of the race.*

puff
*The large lady **puffed** up the hill, only to see the bus disappearing.*

wheeze
*With her asthma, Lydia used her inhaler to sto herself **wheezing**.*

parcel NOUN

A **parcel** is something wrapped up in pape

package
*A white van delivered a mystery **package** addressed to my dad.*

packet
*At my party Mum brought out a huge **packet** for pass-the-parcel.*

part (1) NOUN

A **part** of something is a piece of it, and nc all of it.

component
*There were several different **components** to the board game.*

element
*A big **element** of success in any sport is the will to win.*

fraction
*Kym won the egg and spoon race by a **fraction** of a second.*

fragment
*We kept finding **fragments** of glass for days after I'd dropped the bottle.*

portion
*"Just a small **portion** of pie for me, please," Kristin said.*

segment
*Oranges divide easily into **segments**.*

ANTONYM: whole

A part of...

a book is called a **chapter**, **passage** or **extract**.

a journey is called a **stage**.

a meal is called a **course**.

a play is called a **scene** or **act**.

a poem is called a **line** or **verse**.

a song is called a **verse** or **chorus**.

part (2) NOUN

Part of a business or organisation is a section of it.

branch
*My mum works in the local **branch** of a bank*

department
*In any big store, my sister always heads for the toy **department**.*

division
*Dad's company is just one **division** of a huge corporation.*

section
*The **section** where Dad works deals with the staff wages.*

part (3) NOUN

A **part** of a place is an area or section of it.

area
*One **area** of the lawn was brown where Ian had sprinkled weedkiller.*

district
*Cities are divided up into many **districts**.*

region
*Brittany is a large **region** of western France.*

zone
*At an airport, there are clearly marked **zones** where planes park.*

part (4) NOUN

A **part** is one of the roles in a play or film.

character
*The main **character** in Shakespeare's play Hamlet is the Prince.*

role
*We thought that the actress was excellent in the **role** of the Princess.*

take part in PHRASE

If you **take part in** an activity, you do it together with other people.

be involved in
*My mum **is involved in** some charity work.*

join in
*It took some time for the shy boy to **join in** with the game.*

participate in
*Mrs Nemeth wants the school to **participate in** an area quiz.*

play a part in
*Through his alertness, Ricky **played a part in** saving the yachtsman's life.*

partly ADVERB

Partly can mean to some extent, but not completely.

partially
*From our seats, the view of the stage was **partially** blocked by a pillar.*

somewhat
*We were **somewhat** surprised to find a stray dog on our doorstep.*

to some extent
*Although I didn't start it, **to some extent** the argument was my fault.*

up to a point
*"I agree with you **up to a point**," said Mr Blake," but it's not as simple as that."*

ANTONYM: completely

party (1) NOUN

A **party** is a social occasion when people meet to enjoy themselves, often in order to celebrate something.

celebration
*The evening was a **celebration** of Gran and Grandad's silver wedding anniversary.*

get-together
*That night, Mum was going to a **get-together** with her office friends.*

reception
*It was a brilliant wedding **reception**, with mountains of tasty food.*

party (2) NOUN

A **party** is a group of people who are doing something together.

crew
*In a theatre, it is the stage **crew**'s job to move the scenery.*

gang
*Most of the original canals were hand-dug by **gangs** of workmen.*

squad
*Major Benjamin sent an explosives **squad** to blow up the bridge.*

team
*Working as a **team**, we soon solved the problem.*

pass (1) VERB

If you **pass** someone or something, you go past them without stopping or you exceed them.

exceed
*The driver was fined for **exceeding** the speed limit.*

go beyond
*The train **went beyond** the platform before it stopped, and had to reverse.*

overtake
*Did you see that car **overtake** on a bend?*

surpass
*The quality of our work **surpassed** Mrs Mistry's expectations.*

pass (2) VERB

If you **pass** an examination, you are successful in it.

qualify
*After taking her final exams, my aunt **qualified** as a doctor.*

succeed
*After three attempts at the driving test, my brother **succeeded**.*

ANTONYM: fail

pass (3) VERB

If you **pass** something to someone, you give it to them.

convey
*Mr Djemba asked me to **convey** his thanks to my parents.*

give
*I paid the shopkeeper and she **gave** the bag of shopping to me.*

send
*The ice hockey goalkeeper **sent** the puck across to the winger.*

transfer
*Picking up the ball, the fielder **transferred** it to her right hand.*

transmit
*A spy was caught **transmitting** messages to the enemy.*

past (1) NOUN

The **past** is the period of time before the present.

days gone by
*In **days gone by**, cars had to have a man walking in front of them with a flag.*

former times
*Leslie's family were wealthy cotton manufacturers in **former times**.*

long ago
*The old men told stories of **long ago**.*

olden days (*old-fashioned*)
*In **olden days**, travel was either by horse or on foot.*

the old days
*Gran often tells me about **the old days**, when rock'n'roll first started.*

yesteryear (*old-fashioned*)
*Some people look back fondly on **yesteryear***

ANTONYM: future

past (2) ADJECTIVE

If you say someone is a **past** pupil, athlete and so on, you mean that they were once that.

ex-
*The soccer coach was an **ex-**miner.*

former
*As a **former** pupil of the school, my mum still remembers some of the teachers.*

previous
*Apparently, the **previous** head teacher, Mrs Kirkland, was a curious character.*

ANTONYMS: current, present

pattern NOUN

A **pattern** is a design of shapes repeated a regular intervals.

decoration
*Round my story I drew a **decoration** in a border.*

design
*Wedgwood pottery has a distinctive blue and white **design**.*

motif
*My bedroom curtains have a rose **motif**.*

pause NOUN

A **pause** is a short period when something stops.

break
*There was a **break** in the conversation when a stranger walked in.*

delay
*The clown announced a **delay** in his act while he hunted for his shoes.*

gap
*Sometimes TV programmes have **gaps** for advertisements.*

halt
*The games teacher signalled a **halt** in the race; two children were running in the wrong direction.*

intermission
*The show started with advertisements, then there was an **intermission** before the animal film began.*

interruption
*Fire practice created an **interruption** in the lesson.*

interval
*Spencer went to get an ice cream in the **interval** between the acts.*

rest
*Mel demanded a **rest** before pressing on with the hike.*

pay (1) VERB

If you **pay**, you give someone money in exchange for something.

cough up (*informal*)
*"Come on, **cough up**!" my brother told me after I lost the bet.*

reimburse
*Dad **reimbursed** Mr Ghosh for the window I had broken with my ball.*

settle
*Working overtime for some weeks, my cousin was able to **settle** his debts.*

pay (2) VERB

If it **pays** to do something, it is to your advantage to do it.

be worthwhile
*The effort you put into school now will **be worthwhile** in the future.*

benefit
*The tennis coaching really **benefited** Simon.*

pay (3) NOUN

Someone's **pay** is the money they receive for working.

earnings
*I've no idea what my parents' **earnings** are.*

income
*Mr Micawber wisely thought that one's **income** should be more than one's spending.*

salary
*A person's **salary** is paid monthly into their bank account.*

wages
***Wages** are often paid weekly, and perhaps in cash.*

peace NOUN

Peace is a state of undisturbed calm and quiet.

calm
*When the last pupil departed, Mr Kiely felt an inner **calm** descend.*

quiet
*"While you're reading we'll have absolute **quiet**," Mrs Enckleman insisted.*

silence
*At the dead of night, there was **silence**.*

stillness
*City people either love or hate the **stillness** of the countryside.*

tranquillity
*The **tranquillity** of the hills was shattered by the roar of a jet fighter.*

LANGUAGE TIP
If a country is at **peace**, it is not at war. Another word that sounds like peace is **piece**.

peaceful ADJECTIVE

Someone or something that is **peaceful** is quiet and calm.

placid
*My sweet little sister is a very **placid** child.*

restful
*The ballet music from Swan Lake is very **restful**.*

serene
*The baby looked very **serene**, asleep in his cot.*

tranquil
*With no wind, the lake was **tranquil**, reflecting the hills beyond.*

undisturbed
*My mum works night shifts and likes to be **undisturbed** during the day.*

peculiar ADJECTIVE

Something **peculiar** is strange and unusual.

bizarre
*The fire-eater on the unicycle made a **bizarre** spectacle.*

extraordinary
*It's **extraordinary** that some people don't realise how wonderful books are.*

odd
*"That's **odd**," Ted remarked. "There's someone in the derelict cottage."*

weird
*"It is **weird** to think that, two days from now, we will be on holiday," my best friend said.*

A
B
C
D
E
F
G
H
I
J
K
L
M
N
O
P
Q
R
S
T
U
V
W
X
Y
Z

peep VERB

If you **peep** at something, you have a quick, secretive look at it, or you look at it through a small opening.

catch a glimpse
*We managed to **catch a glimpse** of the film star through the crowd.*

peek
*"This is my wedding dress, so no **peeking**!" my big sister said.*

sneak a look
*Carmel **sneaked a look** through the window to see her birthday cake.*

pen (1) NOUN

A **pen** is an instrument with a pointed end used for writing with ink.

LANGUAGE TIP
A **pen friend** is someone living in a different place or country whom you write to regularly, although you may never have met each other.

pen (2) NOUN

A **pen** is a small, fenced area where farm animals are kept.

A pen for...
cattle is called a **cattle pen**, **cowshed** or **byre**.
hens is called a **coop**.
horses is called a **loose box** or **stable**.
pigs is called a **sty**.
sheep is called a **fold**.

people (1) PLURAL NOUN

People are human beings – men, women and children.

humans
***Humans**, unlike other creatures, walk upright on two legs.*

mankind
***Mankind** is made up of many races.*

people (2) NOUN

The **people** of a particular country or race are all the men, women and children of that country or race.

citizens
*In 1789, the **citizens** of Paris rose up against the king.*

inhabitants
*The **inhabitants** of Manchester are known as Mancunians.*

population
*By 2025, three-quarters of the world's **population** will live in cities.*

public
*This path is for the **public** to walk on.*

perfect ADJECTIVE

Something that is **perfect** is as good as it possibly can be.

faultless
*The ballerina gave a **faultless** dancing display.*

flawless
*I never know how solo musicians manage to give **flawless** performances.*

immaculate
*Dad looked **immaculate** as he prepared for my sister's wedding.*

impeccable
*The old duke had **impeccable** manners.*

ANTONYMS: faulty, imperfect

perhaps ADVERB

You use **perhaps** when you are not sure if something is true or possible.

maybe
*"Hmmm, **maybe** I'll go," Mitchi said, "but **maybe** I won't."*

possibly
*It was **possibly** the best drink I had ever tasted.*

permission NOUN

If you have **permission** to do something, you are allowed to do it.

approval
*We asked for the head teacher's **approval** to have a class charity sale.*

authorisation
*"No entry without **authorisation**", the sign read.*

consent
*Mum and Dad gave their **consent** for me to go on the school trip.*

person NOUN

A **person** is a man, woman or child.

human
*Before 1969, no **human** had stood on the moon.*

human being
*A **human being** is an amazingly complex and wonderful piece of machinery.*

individual
*"Which wretched **individual** did this?" Mr Wright thundered.*

soul
*Not a **soul** was on the beach.*

personal ADJECTIVE

Something **personal** belongs or relates to a particular person.

individual
*On the plane we were all given **individual** meals on trays.*

private
*Bhavin and I didn't dare go in the office marked "**Private**".*

persuade VERB

If you **persuade** someone to do something, or **persuade** them that something is true, you get them to do or believe it by giving them good reasons.

cajole
*My mother **cajoled** me into going shopping.*

coax
*The donkey took a lot of **coaxing** before it would shift.*

convince
*I was glad that Marjani **convinced** me to go to the cinema with her, as I enjoyed the film.*

talk someone into
*Chris **talked me into** playing cards.*

pester VERB

If you **pester** someone, you keep bothering them.

annoy
*The big wasp was **annoying** Marcus with its buzzing.*

badger
*Amy's little brother **badgered** her until she agreed to play with him.*

bother
*Don't **bother** Grandma now. She's trying to sleep.*

nag
*Sam kept **nagging** his dad to get him a new bike.*

plague
*They took a picnic to the river but were soon **plagued** by mosquitoes.*

phoney; also phony ADJECTIVE

Something that is **phoney** is false, not genuine and meant to trick.

bogus
*The police warned people in the area to beware of **bogus** callers.*

counterfeit
*You could tell it was **counterfeit** money, as the ink rubbed off.*

fake
*I thought the whole programme was **fake**. No one would behave like that!*

false
*Great Grandma puts her **false** teeth in a glass by her bed.*

forged
*The spy travelled the world with various **forged** passports.*

imitation
*The house was clad in **imitation** stone – it looked awful.*

ANTONYMS: authentic, real, genuine

pick (1) VERB

If you **pick** someone or something, you choose them.

choose
*I **chose** a creamy chocolate with a swirly top.*

decide on
*Dad and Mum couldn't **decide on** where to go for our holidays.*

nominate
*Our class **nominated** Kemal as team captain.*

opt for
*My brother **opted for** History and French at secondary school.*

select
*When buying melons, it's important to **select** ripe ones.*

vote for
*Taylor was upset because only one or two of us **voted for** her.*

pick (2) VERB

If you **pick** a flower or a fruit, you break it off from where it is growing.

gather
*We **gathered** a lovely bunch of daffodils for our mother.*

harvest
*Before wheat can be **harvested**, it has to be a golden colour.*

a b c d e f g h i j k l m n o p q r s t u v w x y z

pluck
*Marylyn **plucked** an apple from the tree.*

pick on VERB

If you **pick on** someone, you treat them unkindly and unfairly.

bully
*Cattle in a herd will often **bully** a cow that is in some way weaker.*

tease
*When he annoys me, I **tease** my big brother about his messy hair.*

torment
*My brother gets his own back by **tormenting** me because I'm little.*

picture NOUN

A **picture** is a drawing, painting, photograph or television image of someone or something.

illustration
*Roald Dahl's books have lively **illustrations**.*

image
*Will had a mental **image** of his father as an Arctic explorer.*

sketch
*Some painters make a **sketch** before they start to paint.*

piece NOUN

A **piece** of something is a portion or part of it.

bit
*"Anybody got a **bit** of paper?" Martin asked from behind me.*

chunk
*The hungry traveller ripped a **chunk** of bread from the loaf.*

fragment
When I dropped the mug, fragments of china were scattered across the floor.

morsel
*"Not a **morsel** of food will I give you, boy!" boomed the workhouse supervisor.*

share
*Everyone in the family had a **share** of Mum's lottery win.*

→ *See* **part (1)**

LANGUAGE TIP
Another word that sounds like piece is **peace**.

pierce VERB

If a sharp object **pierces** something, it goe through it, making a hole.

bore
*The drill **bored** smoothly through the wall an into the water pipe.*

penetrate
*As soon as the drill **penetrated** the pipe, wate gushed everywhere.*

prick
*When nurses test your blood, they **prick** your thumb.*

puncture
*The piece of protruding metal **punctured** the tyre.*

stab
*The upturned drawing pin **stabbed** the sole o my foot when I trod on it.*

pile (1) NOUN

A **pile** is a quantity of things lying on top o one another.

heap
*All round the garden lay **heaps** of leaves that we'd raked up.*

mass
*In the angler's tin was a **mass** of wriggling maggots.*

mound
*In order to create the slide in the playground, a bulldozer piled up a **mound** of earth.*

mountain
*Within the shed was a huge **mountain** of turnips.*

stack
*The **stack** of baked-bean cans toppled noisily to the shop floor.*

pile (2) VERB

If you **pile** things somewhere, you put them on top of one another.

heap
*Gran would always insist on **heaping** scrambled egg on to my plate.*

stack
*After Dad had **stacked** the hay bales, we played commandoes on top of them.*

pill NOUN

A **pill** is a small, round tablet of medicine that you swallow.

capsule
*I don't mind taking **capsules**, because they slip down easily.*

tablet
*"Take one **tablet** twice a day," the nurse said.*

pinch (1) VERB

If you **pinch** something, you squeeze it between your thumb and first finger.

nip
*Jana has the annoying habit of **nipping** me to get my attention.*

squeeze
*My brother is always **squeezing** his spots.*

tweak
*When my dad's asleep, I **tweak** his beard.*

pinch (2) VERB (*informal*)

If someone **pinches** something, they steal it.

pilfer
***Pilfering** is a problem in some supermarkets.*

snatch
*Thieves **snatched** the lady's bag and ran off with it.*

steal
*He accused me of **stealing** his bicycle.*

swipe (*informal*)
*"Okay, who has **swiped** my pencil?" I asked.*

walk off with
*By accident, Leila had **walked off with** my pen.*

pitch NOUN

A **pitch** is an area of ground marked out for playing a game such as football or cricket.

ground
*When we arrived at the **ground**, the rain was teeming down.*

playing field
*The team ran onto the **playing field**.*

sports field
*Recently, the **sports field** has been extended.*

LANGUAGE TIP
Sports such as tennis and badminton are played on a **court**.

pity (1) NOUN

Pity is a feeling of sadness and concern for someone.

compassion
*The duke couldn't help feeling **compassion** for the penniless widow.*

concern
*The father's **concern** for his sick child showed in his face.*

sympathy
*Anyone who teaches my big sister has my utmost **sympathy**!*

pity (2) VERB

If you **pity** someone, you feel sorry for them.

feel sorry for
*Mum **felt sorry for** the poorly old gentleman and took him round some soup.*

sympathise with
*Grace **sympathised with** anyone who was out in the storm.*

place (1) NOUN

A **place** is a particular point, position, building or area.

location
*"Please give me your exact **location**," the radio operator said.*

position
*From our **position** in the circle, we had a great view of the stage.*

site
*"This field," the guide said, "was the **site** of a battle 600 years ago."*

spot
*We found a lovely **spot** by the river for our picnic.*

place (2) VERB

If you **place** something somewhere, you put it there.

deposit
*I **deposited** my book on Mrs Jalali's desk and went out to play.*

lay
*"I'll now call upon the mayoress to **lay** the first brick," the chairman said.*

position
*We **positioned** ourselves so that we could see the finish of the race.*

stand
*The painter **stood** his ladder against the wall and got into his overalls.*

A B C D E F G H I J K L M N O P Q R S T U V W X Y Z

station
*Guards were **stationed** every 10 metres along the route of the procession.*

→ *See* **leave (3)**

LANGUAGE TIP
Lay and **lie** are often confused. Remember that you **lie** down and hens **lay** eggs.

take place PHRASE
When something **takes place**, it happens.

come about
*"It all **came about** when I was in the air force," Gramps began.*

happen
*"At what time did the accident **happen**?" asked the nurse.*

occur
*Curiously, Shakespeare's death **occurred** on the same date as his birth.*

plain (1) ADJECTIVE
Something that is **plain** is very simple in style, with no pattern or decoration.

bare
*The room had **bare** wooden floors, but still felt cosy.*

basic
*Cadets wear a **basic** uniform with few badges.*

simple
*Monks and nuns wear very **simple** clothes, known as habits.*

ANTONYMS: fancy, ornate

plain (2) ADJECTIVE
Something that is **plain**, is obvious or easy to understand.

apparent
*It was **apparent** that something was wrong with the plane's engine.*

clear
*The instructions on the box were very **clear**.*

distinct
*A **distinct** sound of voices travelled across the quiet lake.*

evident
*Looking at the time, it was **evident** that we were going to miss the bus.*

obvious
*The relief on the passengers' faces when the plane landed was **obvious** to see.*

unmistakable
*There was the **unmistakable** smell of baking in the air.*

ANTONYM: unclear

plan (1) NOUN
A **plan** is a method of achieving something that has been worked out beforehand.

plot
*The originators of the Gunpowder **Plot** planned to blow up Parliament.*

scheme
*Fortunately, the baddies' dastardly **scheme** failed.*

strategy
*The footballers' **strategy** had taken months to perfect.*

plan (2) VERB
If you **plan** something, you decide in detail what you are going to do.

arrange
*I helped Mum **arrange** my little brother's birthday party.*

devise
*The duke **devised** a cunning plan to escape from the castle dungeons.*

draft
*Mrs Schwarz always makes us **draft** our stories before we actually write them.*

prepare
*Because of the weather forecast, no one had **prepared** for rain.*

think up
*Dylan and I **thought up** an idea for a den.*

plan (3) VERB
If you **plan** to do something, you intend to do it.

aim
*My sister **aims** to join the navy.*

intend
*Meredith's brother **intends** to train as a nurse.*

mean
*Dad keeps asking me what I **mean** to do with my life.*

propose
*"So, how do you **propose** to pay for this new computer game you want?" asked Mum.*

play (1) VERB
When people **play**, they take part in games or use toys for fun.

amuse yourself
*Babies often **amuse themselves** with rattles and other noisy things.*

enjoy yourself
*Dad was quietly **enjoying himself** with my train set.*

entertain yourself
*We were told to **entertain ourselves** outside for a while.*

frolic (*old-fashioned*)
*The young children **frolicked** in the meadow.*

romp
*Gran said that in her young days, they used to **romp** around in the hay field.*

play (2) VERB

If you **play** someone at a game or sport, you compete against them.

challenge
*Our neighbouring school **challenged** us to a game of netball.*

compete against
*Our school will **compete against** Gorton in the quiz final.*

take on
*My brother and I **took on** Dad and Uncle Mansur at pool.*

play (3) VERB

If an actor **plays** a character in a play or film, they perform that role.

act the part of
*It was great! When we read it aloud, Euan had to **act the part of** Mrs Twit.*

play the role of
*The director was not sure who would **play the role of** the King.*

portray
*My sister **portrayed** Sleeping Beauty well.*

play (4) NOUN

A **play** is a story acted out in the theatre, on the radio or on television.

drama
*Most **dramas** from ancient Greece have a chorus of women in them.*

performance
*In all, the theatre company put on three **performances**, plus a dress rehearsal.*

show
*The end-of-term **show** was a great success.*

player NOUN

A **player** is someone who plays a game or sport.

competitor
*It is important to be a keen **competitor** if you want to win at sports.*

contestant
*"Bring the next **contestants** in, please!" called the game-show host.*

participant
*Grandad was no longer a **participant** in cricket, but enjoyed watching it.*

playful ADJECTIVE

A person or animal who is **playful** is friendly and light-hearted.

frisky
*Our cat was very **frisky** when we first had her.*

lively
*Mr Hislop is a **lively** teacher, and we've always learnt a lot by the end of his lessons.*

mischievous
*My **mischievous** sister is always playing tricks on me.*

ANTONYM: serious

pleasant (1) ADJECTIVE

If a person is **pleasant**, they are nice and their company is enjoyable.

amiable
*Fortunately, Mum thinks most of my friends are very **amiable**.*

charming
*The landlord was **charming** – always well-mannered and very humorous.*

cheerful
*You could guarantee that the lady in the corner shop would be **cheerful**.*

friendly
*"A **friendly** smile goes a long way," my granny says.*

likeable
*I find Mrs Walker more **likeable** than our previous teacher.*

pleasant (2) ADJECTIVE

If an event is **pleasant**, it is enjoyable.

delightful
*"It is **delightful** to meet you," Mum said as our new neighbours walked in.*

enjoyable
Bhupendra and I had an ***enjoyable*** *time skimming stones over the water.*

lovely
The weather was ***lovely****: plenty of sun and a gentle breeze.*

ANTONYM: unpleasant

please VERB

If something **pleases** you, it makes you feel happy and satisfied.

amuse
"Something obviously ***amuses*** *you," said Mr Murray, somewhat sneeringly.*

delight
The firework display ***delighted*** *the crowds.*

entertain
The puppet show ***entertained*** *dozens of children for an hour.*

give pleasure to
Concerts ***give pleasure to*** *many people.*

satisfy
The inspector was ***satisfied*** *by what she saw in our school.*

ANTONYMS: displease, annoy, upset

pleased ADJECTIVE

If you are **pleased** with something, it makes you feel happy and satisfied.

contented
Even though it was a few years old, John was very ***contented*** *with his car.*

delighted
Dad wrote to say how ***delighted*** *he was with the new conservatory.*

glad
We were very ***glad*** *to get home after our long journey.*

over the moon (*informal*)
"I'm ***over the moon*** *with our win," the coach purred.*

satisfied
My brother is never ***satisfied****, whatever he is given for his birthday.*

thrilled
The millionaire summoned the chef to say how ***thrilled*** *he was with the meal.*

ANTONYM: dissatisfied

pleasure NOUN

Pleasure is a feeling of happiness, satisfaction or enjoyment.

amusement
TV provides ***amusement****, but it's no substitute for getting out and doing things yourself.*

delight
To her ***delight****, Nimah passed the piano exam.*

enjoyment
It's amazing what ***enjoyment*** *you can get from just throwing a ball about.*

happiness
Many people find ***happiness*** *in helping others.*

satisfaction
Mum gained great ***satisfaction*** *from the quilt she made.*

plenty NOUN

If you have **plenty** of something, you have more than enough for your needs.

a great deal
Mrs Suleiman needs ***a great deal*** *of patience to teach our class!*

an abundance
Deserts have ***an abundance*** *of sand but a shortage of water.*

masses (*informal*)
It was a brilliant tea, with ***masses*** *of cakes.*

plot (1) NOUN

A **plot** is a secret plan made by a group of people.

conspiracy
Several plotters joined the ***conspiracy*** *to overthrow the king.*

plan
The ***plan*** *was to pretend we were going out, then sneak back for the surprise party.*

scheme
The traitors' ***scheme*** *failed and they all had to flee the country.*

plot (2) NOUN

The **plot** of a film, novel or play is the story.

narrative
The ***narrative*** *of the book was rather complicated but very exciting.*

story line
For a soap opera, one team decides the ***story line****, while another team writes the script.*

A B C D E F G H I J K L M N O P Q R S T U V W X Y Z

plot (3) VERB

If people **plot** to do something, they plan it secretly.

conspire
*Three of us **conspired** to have a midnight feast, but it would take a lot of planning if we were to pull it off.*

plan
*Sauron **planned** to take possession of the all-important ring.*

scheme
*Flashman was always **scheming** to make life hard for others.*

plug VERB

If you **plug** a hole, you block it with something.

block
*Fallen leaves **blocked** the drain cover and prevented the rain from draining away.*

seal
*Mum used some white gooey stuff to **seal** the gap round the bath.*

stop up
*Beavers **stop up** whole rivers by building dams made of trees.*

poem NOUN

A **poem** is a piece of writing, usually arranged in short rhythmic lines, with words chosen for their sound or impact.

Some types of poem:

acrostic	ballad	blank verse
calligram	cinquain	concrete poem
couplet	elegy	epic
free verse	haiku	jingle
limerick	narrative poem	nursery rhyme
ode	rap	shape poem
sonnet	tanka	

poetry NOUN

Poetry is writing in which the lines have a rhythm and sometimes rhyme.

poems
*They were asked to write **poems** about something that interested them.*

rhymes
*Jessie was good at thinking up funny **rhymes** to entertain her friends.*

verse
*The author handed out books of **verse** for the children to look at.*

point (1) NOUN

A **point** is the thin, sharp end of something such as a needle or knife.

prong
*I accidentally jabbed myself with the **prong** of my fork.*

spike
*As bills are paid, the restaurant manager puts them on a **spike**.*

tip
*The **tip** of the cardinal's sword grazed the musketeer's cheek.*

point (2) NOUN

A **point** is the purpose or the most important part of something.

aim
*The **aim** of the lesson was to improve our handwriting.*

goal
*The **goal** of the jumble sale was to raise money for charity.*

object
*I couldn't quite see the **object** of the game until I had read the instructions.*

purpose
*"What's the **purpose** of that twiddly bit?" I enquired of the salesperson.*

point (3) NOUN

A **point** is a particular time.

instant
*At that **instant**, Ron disappeared behind a large tree.*

moment
*We had reached the **moment** when the winner would be announced.*

point (4) VERB

If you **point** at or to something, you hold out your finger towards it to show where it is.

draw attention to
*Grandpa **drew attention to** a hawk hovering nearby.*

indicate
*The sign **indicated** to the right for the city centre and left for other attractions.*

poisonous ADJECTIVE

A **poisonous** substance will harm or kill you if you swallow it or absorb it.

toxic
*The sign warned that the tanker's cargo was highly **toxic**.*

venomous
*The cobra is a particularly **venomous** snake.*

ANTONYMS: harmless, nontoxic

poke VERB

If you **poke** someone or something, you give them a push with your finger or a sharp object.

dig
*I had to **dig** Zaid gently in the ribs to keep him awake through the film.*

elbow
*Kylie **elbowed** me, so I elbowed her back.*

jab
*"If you **jab** me with that pencil again ...," I warned Dean.*

nudge
*I **nudged** my pal to warn him that Mrs Hussein was watching.*

prod
*As I tried to sleep, my kid sister kept **prodding** me.*

polite ADJECTIVE

Someone who is **polite** has good manners and is not rude to other people.

courteous
*The hotel manager welcomed the guests in a **courteous** manner.*

respectful
*It's important to be **respectful** to older people.*

well-behaved
*All the children were **well-behaved** when they met the queen.*

well-mannered
***Well-mannered** people remember to say "please" and "thank you".*

ANTONYMS: impolite, rude

pollute VERB

If something **pollutes** water, air or land, it makes it dirty and dangerous to use or live in.

contaminate
*Farm fertilisers and pesticides sometimes **contaminate** streams.*

foul
*The school had a problem with dogs **fouling** the sports field.*

poison
*Industrial smoke from factories and power plants **poisons** the atmosphere.*

poor (1) ADJECTIVE

Someone who is **poor** has very little money.

badly off
*My parents were quite **badly off** when they were first married.*

broke
*"I'm **broke**," the gambler confessed.*

penniless
*The **penniless** orphan wandered the streets of the city.*

poverty-stricken
*In Victorian times, a lot of families were **poverty-stricken**.*

ANTONYMS: rich, wealthy

LANGUAGE TIP
If someone owes a lot of money they are **in debt**. If someone cannot pay their debts they are **bankrupt**.

poor (2) ADJECTIVE

Something that is **poor** is of a low quality or standard.

inferior
*Built of **inferior** materials, the flats eventually started to crumble.*

mediocre
*"This is a **mediocre** effort," Mrs Cole warned.*

shoddy
*The factory manager warned that he would not tolerate **shoddy** workmanship.*

unsatisfactory
*The head teacher wrote that my school report was **unsatisfactory**.*

poor (3) ADJECTIVE

A **poor** person is deserving of pity or unlucky.

miserable
*Thoroughly **miserable**, Ellie and Nadine sat on the steps and wept.*

pathetic
*The small group of onlookers on the corner presented a **pathetic** sight.*

unfortunate
*The **unfortunate** child had lost both his parents in an accident.*

wretched
*They have raised a lot of money to help some of the **wretched** children caught up in the conflict.*

poorly ADJECTIVE

If you are **poorly**, you feel ill.

off colour
*"I'm feeling a little **off colour**," Mum confided.*

out of sorts (*informal*)
*Linda felt **out of sorts**, and asked if she could stay at home.*

under the weather (*informal*)
*By the end of the day, Miss Taylor really looked **under the weather**.*

➔ *See* **ill**

popular ADJECTIVE

Someone or something that is **popular** is liked or approved of by a lot of people.

fashionable
*The south of France is very **fashionable** for holidays.*

favourite
*The Caribbean is a **favourite** part of the world for ship cruises.*

in demand
*My brother's band was **in demand** for dances and parties.*

trendy
*They turned the local bank into a **trendy** wine bar.*

well-liked
*Bhoomi's report said she was **well-liked** by others in the class.*

ANTONYM: unpopular

port NOUN

A **port** is a town or area that has a harbour or docks.

docks
*All along the **docks** were huge cranes for shifting containers.*

harbour
*Round the **harbour**, fishermen in oilskins were unloading small boats.*

➔ *See* **harbour**

position (1) NOUN

A **position** is the place where someone or something is.

location
*Using the map's grid, you can plot the exact **location** of almost anything.*

site
*"This is the exact **site** of the ancient burial chamber," explained the tour guide.*

whereabouts
*It was quite tricky for the divers to find the **whereabouts** of the old shipwreck.*

position (2) NOUN

When someone or something is in a particular **position**, they are sitting or lying in that way.

posture
*Working at a computer, it's important to have the right **posture**.*

stance
*Maurice has a good batting **stance**.*

position (3) NOUN

The **position** that you are in is the situation that you are in.

circumstances
*Having won the lottery, our neighbour's **circumstances** changed for the better.*

situation
*The soldier was in a serious **situation**.*

possible (1) ADJECTIVE

If something is **possible**, it can be done.

feasible
*"Is it **feasible** to put a window here?" Mum asked the architect.*

practicable
*"It wouldn't be **practicable** to cross the Channel in this weather," the ferry captain announced.*

ANTONYM: impossible

possible (2) ADJECTIVE

If something is **possible**, it can happen.

conceivable
*"It's **conceivable** that the town could flood," the mayor said.*

imaginable
*"For me, the best place **imaginable** to go on holiday is Skegness," Gran told us.*

ANTONYM: impossible

a b c d e f g h i j k l m n o p q r s t u v w x y z

A B C D E F G H I J K L M N O P Q R S T U V W X Y Z

pour (1) VERB

If something **pours** somewhere, it flows there quickly and in large quantities.

cascade
*During the downpour, water **cascaded** from overflowing gutters.*

flow
*The dam is designed so that surplus water **flows** over the top.*

gush
*Water from the broken pipe **gushed** upwards into the street.*

stream
*People **streamed** through the gates and out into the street.*

pour (2) VERB

If it is **pouring** with rain, it is raining very heavily.

bucket down (*informal*)
*"Don't go out yet, it's **bucketing down**," my gran warned.*

pelt
*Rain was **pelting** down, so I sheltered in a doorway.*

raining cats and dogs (*informal*)
*We were going to go to the park, but then it started **raining cats and dogs**.*

power (1) NOUN

Power is control over people and events.

authority
*In our school, the head teacher has the most **authority**.*

command
*During the revolution, the army generals seized **command**.*

control
*Dictators are people who have absolute **control** over their country.*

domination
*Goldfinger was intent on world **domination**.*

influence
*The judge was a woman of great **influence**, which she used wisely.*

rule
*In 1645, the **rule** of the English king was broken by Parliament.*

power (2) NOUN

Power is a physical strength.

energy
*Mr Chakrabarty seems to have boundless **energy**.*

force
*Using all her **force**, the woman pushed the broken-down car off the road.*

might
*The wizard's army attacked the fortress with all their **might**.*

strength
*Wrestlers need great **strength** to hurl each other around.*

power (3) NOUN

Your **power** to do something is your ability to do it.

ability
*Mrs Finch reckoned Daksha had the **ability** to be a writer.*

capability
*The submarines had the **capability** to launch missiles.*

potential
*You could see that the young actress had the **potential** to be a star.*

powerful (1) ADJECTIVE

Someone or something that is **powerful** has a lot of strength.

mighty
*The weightlifter flexed his **mighty** muscles.*

robust
*Fortunately, the castle gate was **robust** enough to withstand the ram.*

strong
*The boxer was as **strong** as an ox.*

sturdy
*The camera was mounted on a **sturdy** tripod.*

ANTONYMS: puny, weak

powerful (2) ADJECTIVE

Someone or something **powerful** has control or influence over others.

commanding
*Our team was in a **commanding** position at half-time.*

dominant
*The lead singer was the **dominant** member of the pop group.*

influential
*My uncle is an **influential** businessman.*

ANTONYM: powerless

practice NOUN

Practice is regular training or exercise that you do to improve your skill at something.

drill
*Every term the whole school goes through the fire **drill**.*

exercise
*The army **exercise** involved tanks, helicopters and landing craft.*

preparation
*My sister had to do a lot of **preparation** for her part in the play.*

rehearsal
*Doing lots of **rehearsal** can be tough, but the result is worthwhile.*

training
*When they join up, soldiers have to undergo rifle **training**.*

LANGUAGE TIP
The noun **practice** ends in *ice*.

practise VERB

If you **practise** something, you do it regularly in order to do it better.

go over
*Mrs Murray made us **go over** what we would do if a fire broke out.*

go through
*We **went through** how to line up and file out into the yard in case of fire.*

rehearse
*After **rehearsing** for two hours, we felt more confident.*

train
*The team **trains** hard all week, but rests before a match.*

LANGUAGE TIP
The verb **practise** ends in *ise*.

praise (1) VERB

If you **praise** someone, you say good things about them, or tell them they have done well.

applaud
*The press **applauded** the passer-by who had dived into the river to save the child.*

compliment
*It was nice of Grandad to **compliment** me on my table manners.*

congratulate
*Mr Silvester **congratulated** Rio on his painting.*

pay tribute to
*At the funeral, a friend **paid tribute to** Grandma's kindness.*

praise (2) NOUN

Praise is what you say or write when you praise someone or something.

compliment
*The head teacher paid me a **compliment** about my work.*

congratulations
*Ratty offered **congratulations** to Toad on his new car.*

tribute
*The number of people at her leaving party was a **tribute** to how much Mrs Ahmed was liked.*

precious (1) ADJECTIVE

Something that is **precious** is important to you and should be looked after or used carefully.

cherished
*"Be careful. That clock is a **cherished** item!" Mum warned.*

treasured
*For many years, the desk had been a **treasured** possession in our family.*

precious (2) ADJECTIVE

Something **precious** is valuable.

priceless
*The jewels were **priceless**, so the duchess only wore them on special occasions.*

valuable
*"Any painting by that artist is now very **valuable**," said the gallery owner.*

→ *See* **expensive**

predict VERB

If you **predict** something, you say what you think will happen in the future.

forecast
*The weather person on the TV **forecasts** a showery day.*

foresee
*Before I'd even lifted the tray, Mum **foresaw** what would happen.*

a b c d e f g h i j k l m n o p q r s t u v w x y z

A B C D E F G H I J K L M N O P Q R S T U V W X Y Z

foretell
"I'm convinced that some gifted people can ***foretell*** *the future," said Auntie Clare.*

prophesy
The wizard ***prophesied*** *that a new king would come to the throne.*

prefer VERB

If you **prefer** one thing to another, you like it better than the other thing.

favour
I ***favour*** *going on holiday to Spain, but Dad wants to go to the Lake District.*

go for
"Will you ***go for*** *a cola or a lemonade?" Dad asked.*

incline towards
I would ***incline towards*** *going for a bike ride rather than watching TV.*

prepare VERB

If you **prepare** something, or **prepare** for something, you get it ready or get ready for it.

arrange
My auntie had ***arranged*** *the party for Saturday afternoon.*

make arrangements
"Can I rely on you to ***make arrangements*** *for the music?" Sophie asked me.*

organise
Mum ***organised*** *everything for choir practice in the evening.*

pave the way
The generals hoped the air strikes would ***pave the way*** *for the land attack.*

present (1) NOUN

A **present** is something that you give to someone for them to keep.

donation
The school received a generous ***donation*** *from a former pupil.*

gift
As a special ***gift****, Mum bought Dad a mountain bike.*

offering
At the temple altar, the Inca priest raised an ***offering*** *to the gods.*

PRONUNCIATION TIP
When it is a noun, **present** is pronounced **prez**-ent.

present (2) ADJECTIVE

If someone is **present** at a place or an event, they are there.

at hand
Fortunately, a doctor was ***at hand*** *when the lady collapsed.*

in attendance
Queen Victoria's doctors were ***in attendance*** *at her deathbed.*

on hand
First-aiders were ***on hand*** *at the festival in case of emergency.*

ANTONYM: absent

PRONUNCIATION TIP
When it is an adjective, **present** is pronounced **prez**-ent.

present (3) VERB

If you **present** someone with something, or if you present it to them, you formally give it to them.

bestow
The king ***bestowed*** *a great honour on the town.*

donate
It was good of the group to ***donate*** *their fee to the charity.*

grant
Smiling secretly, the genie offered to ***grant*** *Aladdin three wishes.*

PRONUNCIATION TIP
When it is a verb, **present** is pronounced pri-**zent**.

present (4) VERB

If someone **presents** a show, they put it on.

perform
Our class ***performed*** *a play for the parents.*

put on
The orchestra ***puts on*** *an outdoor concert here each summer.*

stage
It is always exciting to find out which city will ***stage*** *the Commonwealth Games.*

PRONUNCIATION TIP
When it is a verb, **present** is pronounced pri-**zent**.

press VERB

If you **press** something, you push or hold it firmly against something else.

compress
Recycled cardboard is shredded, soaked and ***compressed****.*

crush
Grapes are ***crushed*** *to make grape juice and wine.*

squash
"If I were an ant, I'd always be afraid of getting ***squashed****," said my funny little sister.*

squeeze
Auntie Betty ***squeezed*** *me so hard I thought I would burst!*

pretend VERB

If you **pretend** that something is the case, you try to make people believe that it is true when it is not.

act as if
When the ball sailed through the window, I ***acted as if*** *nothing had happened.*

feign
Graham ***feigned*** *not to have seen the sign: "Do not eat in corridors".*

make believe
When I was small, I used to ***make believe*** *my bed was a flying carpet.*

LANGUAGE TIP
To pretend that you are someone else is to **impersonate** them. To pretend that you are doing an action is to **simulate** it.

pretty (1) ADJECTIVE

If someone or something is **pretty**, they are attractive and pleasant to look at.

attractive
My sister thinks the boy next door is really ***attractive****.*

beautiful
The ballerina looked ***beautiful*** *in her tutu.*

bonny
My little cousin may be a ***bonny*** *baby, but she certainly makes a noise!*

good-looking
"If my sister is ***good-looking****, I'm a teapot!" said my horrid brother.*

lovely
The view from the balcony was ***lovely****.*

ANTONYM: ugly

pretty (2) ADVERB *(informal)*

Pretty can mean quite or rather.

fairly
Mr Bissu said it was a ***fairly*** *good effort, but that I could improve.*

moderately
Lisa was ***moderately*** *happy with her work.*

rather
I was ***rather*** *disappointed with my mark in the spelling test.*

reasonably
Mum said the hotel bed was ***reasonably*** *comfortable.*

somewhat
Jenny was ***somewhat*** *surprised to see her cousin at her school.*

prevent VERB

If you **prevent** something, you stop it happening.

avert
The Railway Children ***averted*** *a disaster by stopping the train.*

block
The government ***blocked*** *the proposal to raise taxes.*

foil
"Thanks to a tip-off, police today ***foiled*** *an armed robbery," said the newsreader.*

hinder
My baby brother does his best to ***hinder*** *me when I'm working.*

impede
Fallen rocks are ***impeding*** *the progress of the rescue workers.*

thwart
The plotters were ***thwarted*** *in their attempt to blow up Parliament.*

ANTONYM: encourage

previous ADJECTIVE

A **previous** time or thing is one that occurred before the present one.

earlier
The artist's ***earlier*** *work includes some impressive still-life paintings.*

former
The car had two ***former*** *owners, but seemed to be in good condition.*

past
The school invited all its ***past*** *teachers to the opening ceremony.*

A B C D E F G H I J K L M N O P Q R S T U V W X Y Z

preceding
*Our family had been away the **preceding** summer.*

ANTONYMS: following, subsequent

price NOUN

A **price** is the amount of money that you pay to buy something.

charge
*"That's the standard **charge** for a car service, sir," the garage man said.*

cost
*"There is a small **cost** for entry to the castle grounds," the tour guide said.*

expense
*Dad felt that the trip to Disneyland was worth the **expense**.*

rate
*The **rate** for a haircut has gone up recently.*

The price you pay...

for a journey on a bus, taxi, train or plane is the **fare**.

to send a letter or parcel is the **postage**.

to use a private road or bridge is a **toll**.

to join a club or organisation is the membership **fee**.

prick VERB

If you **prick** something, you stick a sharp object into it.

jab
*I **jabbed** my thumb on a pair of compasses.*

pierce
*When the needle **pierced** my skin, very little blood came out.*

puncture
*A sharp rock **punctured** my bicycle tyre.*

stab
*Mum **stabbed** her finger on a thorn when she was pruning the rose bush.*

prickly ADJECTIVE

Something that is **prickly** has many sharp, fine points.

sharp
*Roses are noted for their lovely smell and their **sharp** thorns.*

spiky
*Horse chestnuts hide conkers inside **spiky** casings.*

spiny
*Porcupines are **spiny** creatures with huge pointed quills.*

thorny
*Inevitably, the ball rolled into the heart of the **thorny** bush.*

prison NOUN

A **prison** is a building where people who have broken the law are locked up as a punishment.

detention centre
*The accused woman was sent to a **detention centre** before her trial.*

dungeons (*old-fashioned*)
*"My **dungeons** await you," said the wicked baron to his enemy.*

jail
*My mum teaches pottery to the inmates of a local **jail**.*

penitentiary
*Kimble was a fugitive from the state **penitentiary**.*

LANGUAGE TIP
Penitentiary is a word used in America.

prisoner NOUN

A **prisoner** is someone who is kept in prison or held in captivity.

captive
*In a daring raid, the platoon of brave soldiers released all the **captives**.*

convict
***Convicts** are usually required to do some sort of work in jail.*

hostage
*"Bank robbers snatched three **hostages** in an armed raid today," read the newspaper article.*

LANGUAGE TIP
Someone who is captured by an enemy in a time of war is a **prisoner of war**.

private (1) ADJECTIVE

Something that is **private** is for the use of only one person or group of people, rather than for the general public.

exclusive
*"On this liner, the Royal Suite has its own **exclusive** sun deck," Mum read from the brochure.*

personal
*A letter marked "**personal**" should only be opened by the person to whom it is addressed.*

ANTONYM: public

private (2) ADJECTIVE

Something that is **private** is meant to be kept secret.

confidential
*As it was **confidential** that Mum was expecting a baby, I told no one.*

secret
*Moneypenny told Bond that the information was **secret**, for his ears only.*

ANTONYM: in public

prize NOUN

A **prize** is a reward given to the winner of a competition or game.

award
*Dad's firm received an **award** for the quality of its cheese.*

honour
*"I'm very proud to accept this **honour**," the moist-eyed actress said as she was handed the statuette.*

trophy
*The champion had tears in his eyes as he held the **trophy** aloft.*

LANGUAGE TIP
The top-money prize in a lottery is known as the **jackpot**. The money prize that someone wins can be called their **winnings**.

probable ADJECTIVE

Something that is **probable** is likely to happen or likely to be true.

expected
*As trouble was **expected**, there were more police than usual on duty.*

likely
*"It's **likely** we'll have showers today," the weatherman said.*

on the cards (*informal*)
*Gamblers always kid themselves that a big win is **on the cards**.*

ANTONYM: improbable

LANGUAGE TIP
When something is so likely it is almost certain, it is **inevitable**.

probably ADVERB

If something will **probably** happen, it is likely but not certain to happen.

almost certainly
*Mrs Macumba told the driver we would **almost certainly** need a brief stop.*

doubtless
*"**Doubtless** you've heard today's big news," Mum said.*

in all probability
*United will win the league, **in all probability**.*

presumably
*"You would **presumably** like the box wrapped?" the saleswoman enquired.*

problem (1) NOUN

A **problem** is an unsatisfactory situation that causes difficulties.

complication
*In theory, the operation was simple, but there were **complications**.*

dilemma
*It was a real **dilemma**: to catch the train or wait for my friends.*

headache
*The non-arrival of the new desks was just one of Mrs Carragher's **headaches**.*

snag
*Building work was going well, until the plumbers hit a **snag**.*

problem (2) NOUN

A **problem** is a puzzle or question that you solve using logical thought or mathematics.

brain-teaser
*Mrs Southgate enjoyed setting us **brain-teasers** on Friday afternoons.*

puzzle
*Which way out of the maze, that was the **puzzle**!*

question
There was the serious ***question*** *of whether the school could raise enough money.*

ANTONYMS: answer, solution

produce (1) VERB

If someone or something **produces** something, they make it.

construct
The factory ***constructs*** *aeroplanes.*

create
TV writers have ***created*** *a new series about a cook who loves gardening.*

manufacture
Mum's firm ***manufactures*** *garden furniture.*

produce (2) VERB

If someone or something **produces** something, they cause it to happen.

bring about
This is the only way to ***bring about*** *any kind of change.*

cause
Our new car ***caused*** *much excitement in my family.*

give rise to
High summer temperatures ***give rise to*** *many bush fires.*

result in
The hot weather ***resulted in*** *a huge demand for soft drinks.*

programme NOUN

A **programme** is something that is broadcast on television or radio.

broadcast
The ***broadcast*** *went out three days after it was recorded.*

production
The ***production*** *was directed by Hamish Haddock.*

show
Kayleigh's favourite television programmes are quiz ***shows****.*

progress (1) NOUN

Progress is the process of gradually improving or getting near to achieving something.

development
"There has been considerable ***development*** *in Ben's writing," said Mr Flannagan.*

improvement
My report said I had shown steady ***improvement*** *during the year.*

LANGUAGE TIP
Sudden, significant progress is a **breakthrough**.

PRONUNCIATION TIP
When it is a noun, **progress** is pronounced **proh**-gress.

progress (2) VERB

If you **progress**, you become more advanced or skilful at something.

advance
Techniques in medicine have ***advanced*** *greatly in the last 20 years.*

improve
My gran's condition was ***improving****, the nurse said.*

make headway
After weeks of rehearsal, our show was ***making headway****.*

PRONUNCIATION TIP
When it is a verb, **progress** is pronounced pro-**gress**.

prohibit VERB

If someone **prohibits** something, they forbid it or make it illegal.

ban
Smoking is ***banned*** *in most public buildings.*

forbid
Running in corridors is ***forbidden*** *at school.*

make illegal
Using mobile phones while driving has been ***made illegal****.*

outlaw
Cigarette advertising is gradually being ***outlawed****.*

ANTONYM: allow

LANGUAGE TIP
You prohibit a person *from* doing something.

project NOUN

A **project** is a carefully planned task that requires a lot of time or effort.

assignment
*Qadira handed her **assignment** in just before the deadline.*

scheme
*China has completed a **scheme** to build a massive reservoir.*

task
*"Ladies and gentlemen, the **task** before us is a hard one," the chairman said.*

promise (1) VERB

If you **promise** to do something, you say that you will definitely do it.

assure
*Ethan **assured** his boss that he would carry out the mission successfully.*

guarantee
*"Do you **guarantee** that this bridge is safe to cross?" asked the tank driver.*

pledge
*The businessman **pledged** to give his staff a pay rise.*

swear
*The clerk asked the witness to **swear** that her evidence would be the truth.*

vow
*Sir Lancelot **vowed** that he would serve King Arthur faithfully.*

Try these lively words and phrases:

cross your heart
*I **cross my heart**, I won't tell anyone.*

give your word
*"I **give my word** that I will return," the explorer exclaimed.*

promise (2) NOUN

A **promise** is a statement made by someone that they will definitely do something.

assurance
*I gave Dad my **assurance** that I would be home on time.*

guarantee
*"I give you my **guarantee** that I'll do better next time," I told Mum.*

pledge
*The gambler signed a **pledge** that he would never bet again.*

vow
*Rebecca made a **vow** that, one day, she would live in that very house.*

proper ADJECTIVE

If you do something in the **proper** way, you do it correctly.

appropriate
*Quiet speaking is **appropriate** in libraries.*

correct
*Giving an elderly person your seat is the **correct** thing to do.*

fitting
*After the meal, at a **fitting** moment, Mum made her speech.*

suitable
*Carina hoped that her dress was **suitable** for the occasion.*

ANTONYMS: improper, unsuitable

property NOUN

A person's **property** is something, or all the things, that belong to them.

belongings
*The guard reminded us to take all our **belongings** when we got off the train.*

possessions
*All Oliver's **possessions** in the world could be tied up in a handkerchief.*

protect VERB

If you **protect** someone or something, you prevent them from being harmed.

defend
*It is a bodyguard's job to **defend** their client.*

guard
*In banks, a glass screen is there to **guard** against robberies.*

safeguard
*The miser **safeguarded** his money by putting it under his bed.*

shelter
*The old log cabin **sheltered** us from the downpour.*

shield
*A line of police **shielded** the politician from the protesters.*

A B C D E F G H I J K L M N O P Q R S T U V W X Y Z

protection NOUN

Protection is something that protects you from being harmed.

armour
Police in dangerous situations have to wear body ***armour****.*

defence
Ordinary glass is no ***defence*** *against bullets.*

safeguard
Fitting a decent alarm is one ***safeguard*** *against burglary.*

security
The old people's home offered comfort and ***security****.*

shield
Knights of old went into battle with a sword and ***shield****.*

protest (1) VERB

If you **protest**, you say or do something to show that you strongly disapprove of something.

argue
The unions were ***arguing*** *for better pay.*

complain
Jivin's mother ***complained*** *that he had been bullied.*

demonstrate
A huge crowd ***demonstrated*** *in the streets against the new tax.*

disagree
Dad ***disagrees*** *with lots of government policies.*

object
When the chairlady wanted to end the meeting, my Mum stood up and ***objected****.*

oppose
About half the people in town ***opposed*** *the new bypass.*

PRONUNCIATION TIP

When it is a verb, **protest** is pronounced pro-**test**.

---

protest (2) NOUN

A **protest** is a demonstration or statement to show that you strongly disapprove of something.

complaint
There were several ***complaints*** *about what the mayor had said.*

demonstration
The ***demonstration*** *was large but the crowd remained peaceful.*

outcry
A public ***outcry*** *resulted when plans for the new road were published.*

PRONUNCIATION TIP

When it is a noun, **protest** is pronounced **pro**-test.

---

proud ADJECTIVE

If you are **proud** of something, you feel satisfaction and pleasure because of something you own or have achieved.

gratified
The actor was ***gratified*** *by the applause.*

honoured
"I feel ***honoured*** *to work with such a respected scientist," said the assistant.*

pleased
My big sister was ***pleased*** *with the results she had achieved.*

ANTONYM: ashamed

prove VERB

If you **prove** that something is true, you show by means of argument or evidence that it is definitely true.

confirm
Police ***confirmed*** *that the stolen goods had been recovered.*

demonstrate
This experiment ***demonstrates*** *that flames need oxygen to burn.*

establish
Eventually, Mrs Bridge ***established*** *that there was no missing purse.*

show
Jonathan ***showed*** *that he wasn't afraid of heights by diving off the high board.*

verify
In court, the witness was asked to ***verify*** *the statement he had made earlier.*

provide VERB

If you **provide** someone with something, you give it to them or make it available to them.

contribute
Governments agreed to ***contribute*** *food and equipment to the earthquake victims.*

equip
*The millionaire **equipped** himself with all the latest gadgets.*

supply
*That firm **supplied** all the expedition's tents and ropes.*

pull VERB

If you **pull** something, you get hold of it and move it towards you with force.

drag
*The fisherman **dragged** his boat into the water.*

haul
*The two red-faced tug-of-war teams dug in with their heels and **hauled** on the rope.*

heave
***Heaving** for all they were worth, the sailors raised the anchor.*

tug
*When the diver **tugged** on her line, the surface crew brought her up.*

pull delicately:

pick
*I hate having to **pick** cat hairs off my coat.*

pluck
*You can strum a guitar or **pluck** strings individually.*

pull out:

extract
*Using tweezers, Mum **extracted** the splinter from my thumb.*

remove
*Very delicately, the vet **removed** the marble that our cat had swallowed.*

withdraw
*The nurse **withdrew** the needle so gently after my injection that I didn't even feel it.*

pull suddenly:

jerk
*When you tow a car, the rope often **jerks**, which can snap it.*

wrench
*Desperate to escape, the trapped man **wrenched** the door off its hinges.*

yank
*Gaman **yanked** the door handle, which then dropped off.*

pull out VERB

If you **pull out** of an arrangement, you decide not to do it.

quit
*When she was caught cheating, the woman had to **quit** the game show.*

withdraw from
*Owing to sickness, our team **withdrew from** the league.*

punch VERB

If you **punch** someone or something, you hit them hard with your fist.

jab
*My brother **jabbed** me playfully in the arm to get my attention.*

pummel
*The boxer **pummelled** the punchbag nonstop for five minutes.*

strike
*The angry man **struck** the table in frustration.*

thump
*The little bully who **thumped** my brother landed himself in detention for the rest of the week.*

punish VERB

To **punish** someone means to make them suffer for doing wrong.

discipline
*The coach resolved to **discipline** anyone who was late for practice.*

penalise
*Our fullback was **penalised** for bringing down an attacker.*

sentence
*The young offender was **sentenced** to one year's community service.*

punishment NOUN

Punishment is the action taken to make someone suffer for doing wrong.

penalty
*The **penalty** for walking on the grass is a £20 fine.*

sentence
*There are different **sentences** given for different crimes.*

pupil NOUN

The **pupils** at a school are the children who attend it.

schoolboy
*Shakespeare wrote about the **schoolboy** going reluctantly to school.*

a b c d e f g h i j k l m n o p q r s t u v w x y z

A B C D E F G H I J K L M N O P Q R S T U V W X Y Z

schoolgirl
*When Mum was a **schoolgirl**, she used to carry her satchel on her back.*

student
*My big brother is a **student** at the local further education college.*

pure (1) ADJECTIVE

Something that is **pure** is not mixed with anything else.

natural
*"Our cereal contains only **natural** ingredients," the packet boasted.*

wholesome
*Eating **wholesome** food is the first step to being healthy.*

ANTONYM: impure

pure (2) ADJECTIVE

Something that is **pure** is clean and free from harmful substances.

germ-free
*Hospitals try to keep their wards as **germ-free** as possible.*

unpolluted
*Country air is **unpolluted** compared with city air.*

ANTONYM: impure

pure (3) ADJECTIVE

Something that is **pure** is complete and total.

absolute
*Mum said her stay at the health farm was **absolute** bliss.*

complete
*They said my story was **complete** fiction, but it actually happened!*

total
*From start to finish, for me the film was **total** enjoyment.*

utter
*"You're talking **utter** nonsense," my brother laughed.*

purpose (1) NOUN

The **purpose** of something is the reason for it.

function
*The **function** of the decimal point is to separate whole numbers from fractions.*

object
*"The **object** of this lesson is to learn more about the environment," Miss O'Sullivan told the class.*

point
*I don't really get the **point** of horse riding. All I do is fall off.*

reason
*"What's the **reason** for that dial?" I asked my grandad.*

purpose (2) NOUN

Your **purpose** is the thing that you want to achieve.

aim
*My **aim** is to collect stamps from every country in Europe.*

intention
*My **intention** is to hold a world record by the age of 25.*

object
*"The **object** of the game is to make the most money," explained Deepak.*

point
*"What was the **point** of saying that?" I asked Mandy.*

on purpose PHRASE

If you do something **on purpose**, you do it deliberately.

deliberately
*"You did that **deliberately**!" my brother shouted.*

intentionally
*I didn't **intentionally** trip him – it really was an accident.*

ANTONYM: unintentionally

push (1) VERB

If you **push** someone or something, you use force to move them away from you.

drive
*The farmer **drove** the fence posts into the ground with a huge mallet.*

force
*The attackers tried to **force** the gate inward.*

ram
*Once more the huge tree trunk **rammed** the wooden entrance.*

shove
*They **shoved** her so hard that she fell over backwards.*

thrust
*The cowboy **thrust** open the saloon doors and strode in.*

ANTONYM: pull

push (2) VERB

If you **push** someone, you use force to move them out of the way.

elbow
*The bully tried to **elbow** me out of the way.*

jostle
*The people in the crowd were all **jostling** to move forward.*

put VERB

If you **put** something somewhere, you move it into that position.

deposit
*"Please **deposit** your keys on the desk when you leave the hotel," said the receptionist.*

lay
*"**Lay** your gun down, and come out with your hands up!" the sheriff shouted.*

place
*Mum **placed** the box carefully on the table. What on earth was in it?*

rest
*I lay back and **rested** my legs on the stool.*

stand
*"Make sure you **stand** that ladder firmly in place," Grandad advised.*

put off (1) VERB

If something **puts** you **off**, it stops you from concentrating on what you are doing.

distract
*I find that the radio **distracts** me from writing.*

faze
*However hard I try to sidetrack her, nothing **fazes** my sister when she's concentrating.*

throw
*The tennis champion wasn't **thrown** by booing from some spectators.*

unsettle
***Unsettled** by problems at home, the actress gave a poor performance.*

put off (2) VERB

If you **put off** doing something, you delay it.

defer
*"I propose," said the mayor, "that we **defer** our decision until next week."*

delay
*We had to **delay** our holiday because of strikes at the airport.*

postpone
*The match was **postponed** due to bad weather.*

put off (3) VERB

If something **puts** you **off** something else, it causes you to stop being interested in or enjoying it.

deter
*A few falls didn't **deter** Kate from wanting to ride a horse.*

discourage
*I was **discouraged** by my poor mark in the maths test.*

put out VERB

If you **put out** a fire or flame, you stop it from burning.

extinguish
*Instead of **extinguishing** the flames, the wind fanned them to a new fury.*

snuff out
*With a pinch of her wetted fingers, Gran **snuffed out** the candle.*

put up (1) VERB

If you **put up** something, you build or erect it.

assemble
*The model I tried to **assemble** turned out a gluey monstrosity.*

construct
*The neighbour **constructed** a swing for us in the yard.*

erect
*Builders need permission to **erect** scaffolding near a road.*

pitch
*The flood made us regret **pitching** our tent near the stream.*

ANTONYMS: dismantle, pull down

put up (2) VERB

If someone **puts up** prices, they raise them.

increase
*The government intends to **increase** taxes.*

raise
*As from next month, train fares will be **raised** by three per cent.*

ANTONYM: reduce

put up with VERB

If you **put up with** something, you let it happen without complaining.

bear
*Even the tough explorer found the bitter cold hard to **bear**.*

endure
*The shipwrecked sailors **endured** weeks in an open boat.*

stand
*"I can't **stand** that din any more," Dad shouted upstairs.*

tolerate
*Mrs O'Shea refused to **tolerate** bad behaviour of any kind.*

puzzle VERB

If something **puzzles** you, it confuses you and you do not understand it.

baffle
*Completely **baffled** by the maze, I was forced to look at the plan in my pocket.*

bewilder
*Gary was **bewildered** by the complicated instructions for putting up the shelves.*

confuse
*"Don't let maths **confuse** you," said Mr Najeev. "It's simple really."*

mystify
*Having seen the whole film, I was still **mystified** at the end.*

perplex
*The explorers were **perplexed**. Surely they had been at this spot before!*

Qq

quality NOUN

The **quality** of something is how good or bad it is, compared with other things of the same kind.

excellence
*It was a chance to show the **excellence** of their work.*

grade
*King Henry's tailor always used cloth of the finest **grade**.*

standard
*"I expect your writing to be of a high **standard**," said the teacher.*

value
*Things from that greengrocer are always good **value**.*

quantity NOUN

A **quantity** is an amount that you can measure or count.

amount
*The recipe said to add a small **amount** of salt – just a pinch.*

number
*A sizeable **number** of people wanted to go on the trip.*

A quantity of...

drink is a **measure**.
food is a **portion**.
land is an **expanse**.
money is a **sum**.
timber is a **length**.
water is a **volume**.

quarrel (1) NOUN

A **quarrel** is an angry argument.

argument
*My brother and I had an **argument** over who would use the computer.*

difference of opinion
*Mrs Hardy and Miss Mellberg had a **difference of opinion** about homework.*

disagreement
*There was a **disagreement** between Mum and Dad about our holiday destination.*

dispute
*The workers had a **dispute** with management about the length of tea breaks.*

feud
*The Campbells and the MacDonalds had a long-running **feud**.*

fight
*Kiesha and I made up after we'd had a **fight**.*

row
*Heidi had a **row** with her parents about the state of her room.*

quarrel (2) VERB

If people **quarrel**, they have an angry argument.

argue
*I didn't like to **argue**, but I'm sure what Mr Barry said was wrong.*

bicker
*My sister and brother spent the whole journey **bickering**.*

disagree
*Ratty and Badger **disagreed** about how to deal with Mr Toad.*

fall out
*Jamal and I **fell out** over who won the game.*

fight
*I hardly ever **fight** with my brothers and sisters, and when I do we soon make up.*

squabble
*"Stop **squabbling**, you two!" Dad shouted up the stairs.*

question (1) NOUN

A **question** is a sentence that asks for information.

enquiry
*Dad went to the school office with an **enquiry** about holiday dates.*

query
*"Before you start the test, have you any **queries**?" Mrs Unsworth asked.*

ANTONYM: answer

question (2) VERB

If you **question** someone, you ask them questions.

cross-examine
*The counsel for the prosecution **cross-examined** the defence witness.*

interrogate
*The spy was taken away to be **interrogated** by secret agents.*

query
*Mrs Kenna **queried** my use of the word "nice" when other words would have been better.*

quiz
*Mum **quizzed** my big sister to find out why she was so late back.*

quick (1) ADJECTIVE

If you are **quick**, you move or do things with great speed.

brisk
*Dad and I went for a **brisk** walk.*

fast
*My grandad was a very **fast** runner.*

hasty
*Katie had a habit of being too **hasty** to judge other people.*

hurried
*After a **hurried** sandwich, Mr Henshaw dashed off to an afternoon meeting.*

rapid
*A **rapid** tyre change meant that the driver was still in the lead when he left the pits.*

speedy
*Emails are a **speedy** way of sending messages.*

swift
*The actor had a **swift** costume change at the end of the first scene.*

ANTONYM: slow

quick (2) ADJECTIVE

Someone who is **quick** is intelligent and able to understand things easily.

alert
*The company was looking for an **alert**, lively office junior.*

bright
*A **bright** officer on the beat spotted the burglars behaving suspiciously.*

intelligent
*Khaled's report said that he was an **intelligent** boy who worked hard.*

quick-witted
*The **quick-witted** girl grabbed the dog and pulled it to safety.*

a b c d e f g h i j k l m n o p q r s t u v w x y z

A B C D E F G H I J K L M N O P Q R S T U V W X Y Z

sharp
*Some **sharp** work by the wicketkeeper dismissed the batsman.*

smart
*"It was **smart** of you to come up with an idea like that," Mum said.*

ANTONYM: slow

quickly ADVERB

Something that happens **quickly** happens with great speed.

fast
*My Uncle Ted drives very **fast**.*

hastily
*As her dad walked in, Nadine **hastily** switched the video game off and turned to her homework.*

hurriedly
***Hurriedly** throwing a few things in an overnight bag, Dad rushed Mum to hospital because the baby was coming.*

rapidly
*The courier dashed **rapidly** through the door with a message from HQ.*

speedily
*"I want this article written **speedily**," the editor told the reporter.*

swiftly
*After his mistakes, the tennis umpire was **swiftly** replaced by someone else.*

ANTONYM: slowly

quiet (1) ADJECTIVE

If someone or something is **quiet**, they are not making much noise, or they are not making any noise at all.

hushed
*Speaking in a **hushed** voice, the guide told us about the cathedral.*

silent
*When the director called "Action", everyone except the actors had to be **silent**.*

soundless
*With a **soundless** movement, Bond sprang from behind the door.*

ANTONYMS: loud, noisy

quiet (2) ADJECTIVE

A **quiet** place, time or situation is calm and peaceful.

calm
*The **calm** evening with the light sea breeze was a great change from the storm of the night before.*

peaceful
*Scotland's highland scenery is **peaceful** as well as beautiful.*

serene
*She relaxed in the beautiful, **serene** park.*

tranquil
*The shore of the lake was a **tranquil** setting for the wedding.*

quiet (3) ADJECTIVE

A **quiet** person is shy and does not usually say much.

reserved
*The artist was a **reserved** man who kept himself to himself.*

retiring
*Being a **retiring** sort of person, Miss McCall wanted no fuss on her birthday.*

shy
*From being very **shy**, my brother has suddenly become noisy and confident.*

ANTONYMS: loud, outgoing

quiet (4) NOUN

Quiet can mean silence or lack of noise.

peace
*Mum says she loves the **peace** and quiet after we've gone to bed.*

silence
*As the last child departed, **silence** fell on the school corridors.*

stillness
*The **stillness** of the summer night was soothing.*

tranquillity
*The memorial garden was a haven of **tranquillity** in a busy city.*

quit VERB

If you **quit** something, you leave it or stop doing it.

leave
*Barry finally **left** the army after 25 years' service.*

resign
*Dad **resigned** from the police force to become a private detective.*

step down
After a string of poor results, the coach decided to ***step down****.*

quite (1) ADVERB

Quite can mean fairly but not very.

fairly
I was ***fairly*** *happy with my test results, but aimed to do better next time.*

moderately
"Tomorrow will be ***moderately*** *warm," the weatherman said confidently.*

rather
Mum was ***rather*** *disappointed not to be elected as a councillor.*

somewhat
Johnathan was ***somewhat*** *pleased that the parachute jump was postponed.*

quite (2) ADVERB

Quite can mean completely.

absolutely
Dad was ***absolutely*** *adamant that we needed to turn left.*

entirely
I was ***entirely*** *taken aback by my sister's decision to join the navy.*

fully
"I am ***fully*** *confident that my decision is correct," my friend said pompously.*

perfectly
"I am ***perfectly*** *sure you'll manage while I'm away," said Mum's boss.*

totally
Bhoomi had not ***totally*** *recovered from her cold when she came back to school.*

wholly
Frodo decided he had been ***wholly*** *mistaken in undertaking such a perilous journey.*

Rr

race (1) NOUN

A **race** is a competition to see who is fastest at something.

competition
Brandon and I had a ***competition*** *to see who could be first in the playground.*

contest
Our town holds a famous pie-eating ***contest*** *each year.*

dash
Grandad used to run in the 100-yard ***dash*** *when he was a boy.*

race (2) VERB

If you **race** somewhere, you go there as quickly as possible.

dash
Paul ***dashed*** *out of the room laughing.*

fly
"I must ***fly****," said Kit, "or I'll miss my train."*

hurry
"We'll have to ***hurry*** *Dad, or the shops will be shut!" Jenny said.*

run
Alison started to ***run*** *as she saw the bus coming round the corner.*

speed
The car came ***speeding*** *round the corner with a police car behind it.*

tear
The door flew open and Wendy ***tore*** *into the house and up the stairs.*

rage NOUN

A **rage** is a strong, uncontrollable anger.

anger
Consumed with ***anger****, the evil wizard sent thunderbolts from the heights of his tower.*

fit of temper
In a ***fit of temper****, my sister threw my socks out of the window.*

A B C D E F G H I J K L M N O P Q R S T U V W X Y Z

fury
Jason stomped off in a ***fury*** *when I told him I'd lost his phone.*

tantrum
Mum say that when I was two I used to have ***tantrums*** *all the time.*

ragged ADJECTIVE

If fabric is **ragged**, it is torn or frayed, with rough edges.

frayed
My baby brother drags his blanket everywhere, so now it's all ***frayed*** *around the edges.*

shabby
We got a new sofa as our old one was starting to look ***shabby****.*

tattered
My teddy is very ***tattered*** *these days, because I used to take it everywhere.*

threadbare
Despite his wealth, a ***threadbare*** *suit was all he ever wore.*

worn-out
The long-distance walker abandoned yet another ***worn-out*** *pair of shoes.*

raid (1) NOUN

A **raid** is a sudden, surprise attack.

attack
The ***attack*** *on the US battleships was sudden and unexpected.*

break-in
Police thought the ***break-in*** *had occurred between one o'clock and two o'clock in the morning.*

invasion
The D-Day ***invasion*** *of 1941 was the world's biggest-ever amphibious landing.*

raid (2) VERB

When people **raid** a place, they enter it by force in order to attack it or to look for something or someone.

attack
Howling with rage, Boadicea's fierce army ***attacked*** *the Roman citadel.*

invade
In 1066, the Normans ***invaded*** *the shores of Britain.*

plunder
Having ***plundered*** *the town, the Vikings returned to their longboats.*

rain (1) NOUN

Rain is water falling from the clouds in small drops.

cloudburst
We were in the lead, but a ***cloudburst*** *put an end to the match.*

deluge
The ***deluge*** *left the field several centimetres deep in water.*

downpour
After the ***downpour****, the sky cleared and the sun came out.*

rainfall
Mountainous areas attract the highest level of ***rainfall****.*

LANGUAGE TIP
Steady, fine rain is **drizzle**. Rain that frequently starts and stops is **showers**.

rain (2) VERB

When it **rains**, small drops of water fall from clouds in the sky.

rain heavily:

bucket down
It ***bucketed down****, and rain poured from overflowing gutters.*

pelt
Typical! I hadn't brought a coat so it ***pelted*** *with rain.*

pour
For the entire day of our outing, it ***poured*** *down.*

rain cats and dogs (*informal*)
We had to stay in at playtime because it was ***raining cats and dogs****.*

teem
In tropical climates, it ***teems*** *with rain on many days during the rainy season.*

rain lightly:

drizzle
As we left the house it started to ***drizzle****.*

spit
As it was only ***spitting****, I decided to go out bu[t] took an umbrella with me.*

range NOUN

A **range** is a selection or choice of differen[t] things of the same kind.

assortment
On the sweet trolley was an ***assortment*** *of delicious desserts.*

selection
*For her prize, Mum could choose from a **selection** of perfumes.*

variety
*You can buy an amazing **variety** of trainers.*

apid ADJECTIVE
Something that is **rapid** is happening or moving very quickly.

brisk
*Mr Goma set off at a **brisk** trot.*

hasty
*After using the phoney credit card, the fraudsters made a **hasty** exit.*

hurried
*Because of an early bedtime, my homework was rather **hurried**.*

speedy
*In our card, we wished Mrs Keown a **speedy** recovery from the flu.*

swift
*The alert girl's **swift** action saved the day.*

ANTONYM: slow

are ADJECTIVE
Something that is **rare** is not common or does not often happen.

scarce
*"Oak carving like this is **scarce** these days," said the expert.*

uncommon
*The young Wolfgang Mozart had an **uncommon** gift for music.*

unique
*"This style of painting is quite **unique**," said the curator of the art gallery.*

unusual
*It was **unusual** to hear a cuckoo so early in the year.*

ANTONYM: common

LANGUAGE TIP
Note that **unique** can only be used to describe something if there is only one of its kind.

ather (1) ADVERB
Rather can mean fairly or to a certain extent.

fairly
*Our car is **fairly** old, but it still goes well.*

moderately
*Mrs Bernard said she was **moderately** pleased with our test results.*

quite
*"I'm **quite** surprised to see you here," Auntie Madge said.*

relatively
*It was **relatively** early when we got home, so we had time to play before tea.*

somewhat
*I was excited, but **somewhat** scared, to be doing a bungee jump.*

slightly
*We were **slightly** late, but hoped we wouldn't be in too much trouble.*

to a certain extent
***To a certain extent**, I was pleased to be going back to school.*

rather (2) ADVERB
If you would **rather** do one thing than another, you would prefer to do it.

preferably
*Mum said she would **preferably** have had a Chinese meal.*

sooner
*"Personally, I would **sooner** eat Greek food," said my sister.*

raw (1) ADJECTIVE
Raw food is uncooked.

fresh
*Sushi is a small piece of **fresh** fish within a rice surround.*

uncooked
***Uncooked** or partly cooked meat can cause stomach upsets.*

ANTONYM: cooked

raw (2) ADJECTIVE
A **raw** substance is in its natural state, before being processed.

basic
*In aluminium manufacture, the **basic** material used is bauxite.*

natural
*Our central heating and hot water are heated by **natural** gas.*

A B C D E F G H I J K L M N O P Q R S T U V W X Y Z

unprocessed
__Unprocessed__ wool is greasy and needs to be cleaned.

ray NOUN
A **ray** is a beam of light.

beam
Every few seconds, the __beam__ from the lighthouse swept round the bay.

shaft
Deep within the cave, Frodo saw a __shaft__ of sunlight ahead.

stream
A __stream__ of light shone down between the clouds.

reach (1) VERB
When you **reach** a place, you arrive there.

arrive at
__Arriving at__ America in 1620, the Pilgrim Fathers set up their own colony.

get to
The mountaineers planted their flag in the snow when they __got to__ the summit.

make
The first transatlantic flight only just __made__ the coast of Ireland.

reach (2) VERB
When something **reaches** somewhere, it extends as far as that place or point.

climb to
The road __climbed to__ the top of the hill and then snaked down the other side.

extend
By 1870 the railway __extended__ as far as the USA's west coast.

stretch to
The desert __stretched to__ the horizon.

touch
The suburbs of the city now __touched__ the foot of the mountain.

reach (3) VERB
When you **reach** your goal, you achieve it.

achieve
The rower was the first to __achieve__ five gold medals in different years.

attain
My brother __attained__ the highest maths mark in the school's history.

read (1) VERB
When you **read** something that is written, you look at it and understand or say aloud the words that are there.

dip into
Bonnie liked to browse through the library, __dipping into__ several books.

pore over
Engineers __pored over__ the plans, trying to find where the fault might lie.

scan
Dad __scanned__ the job adverts in the newspaper.

skim through
With reference books, you often have to __skim through__ an entry to make sure it's useful.

study
I sat at my desk __studying__ my school report in cheerful disbelief.

read (2) VERB
If you can **read** someone's mind or moods, you can judge what they are feeling or thinking.

comprehend
Her expression was difficult to __comprehend__.

decipher
Kim could not __decipher__ from Mr Abdul's expression whether she had done well in the test.

interpret
I __interpreted__ Mum's cross look to mean that I was late.

ready (1) ADJECTIVE
If something or someone is **ready**, they are prepared for doing something.

all set
The family was __all set__ to go on holiday when Mum had her accident.

geared up (*informal*)
We were all __geared up__ for the school trip.

prepared
Having our waterproofs with us, we were __prepared__ for rain.

ANTONYM: unprepared

ready (2) ADJECTIVE
If someone is **ready**, they are willing to do something.

eager
The young soldiers were __eager__ to go on exercise, the older ones less so.

glad
*"If you need assistance, I'll be **glad** to help," our neighbour said.*

keen
***Keen** to do well, the student studied day and night for the exam.*

willing
*My sisters were **willing** to do any job that needed doing.*

eal (1) ADJECTIVE
Something that is **real** is genuine and not artificial.

authentic
*Most of the autographs were **authentic**, but one or two were fake.*

genuine
*"That chair is a **genuine** Chippendale," the expert exclaimed.*

ANTONYMS: artificial, fake

eal (2) ADJECTIVE
Something that is **real** is actually true and not imagined.

actual
*"This is the **actual** throne on which King Arthur sat," said the guide.*

genuine
*The millionaire's wish to help save the rainforests was **genuine**.*

true
*"Is this a **true** record of what you said?" the magistrate asked the first witness.*

ANTONYMS: imagined, insincere

ealise VERB
If you **realise** something, you become aware of it or understand it.

appreciate
*The twins did not **appreciate** the danger they were in.*

become aware
*Dad slowly **became aware** that the crocodile was looking at him.*

grasp
*At first I didn't **grasp** what was happening.*

recognise
*It is important to **recognise** the importance of regular exercise.*

understand
*"You must **understand** how important maths is," the head teacher said.*

really (1) ADVERB
You use **really** when you are talking of the true facts about something.

actually
*"To think we are **actually** flying to Australia!" I marvelled.*

honestly
*"I **honestly** don't know what to say," Mrs Neill sighed.*

in fact
*Grandad looked well enough, but **in fact** he was quite poorly.*

truly
*We had a **truly** wonderful day on the island.*

really (2) ADVERB
You use **really** to emphasise a point.

absolutely
*My teacher is **absolutely** terrified of spiders.*

extremely
*"I'm **extremely** sorry, but we have sold out," the shopkeeper said.*

reason NOUN
A **reason** is the fact that explains why something happens.

cause
*Months after the disaster, scientists were no nearer to finding the **cause**.*

excuse
*Miss Gresko pointed out that there was no **excuse** for disobedience.*

explanation
*"Is there an **explanation** for this?" the sergeant asked, picking up the dirty boots.*

justification
*The worker could see no **justification** for his sacking.*

motive
*Holmes was puzzled about the suspect's **motive** for committing the crime.*

reasonable (1) ADJECTIVE
Someone or something that is **reasonable** is fair and sensible.

fair
*Mrs Rufus is always **fair** when she marks our homework and tests.*

sensible
*A meeting seemed the only **sensible** way to deal with the issue.*

ANTONYM: unreasonable

reasonable (2) ADJECTIVE

A **reasonable** price is fair and not too high.

fair
*They both thought that the dealer was asking a **fair** price for the old car.*

inexpensive
*Charity shops are an **inexpensive** source of clothes and books.*

moderate
*The developer bought the house at a **moderate** price, and sold it for a fortune.*

ANTONYM: expensive

receive (1) VERB

When you **receive** something, you get it after someone has given or sent it to you.

accept
*The show's producer **accepted** the award on behalf of all the cast.*

collect
*Mum **collected** a free gift with her first order from the catalogue.*

obtain
*It takes three weeks to **obtain** a new passport.*

receive (2) VERB

To **receive** something can mean to have it happen to you.

suffer
*Gran began to **suffer** unpleasant headaches.*

sustain
*In the accident, my sister **sustained** a fractured arm.*

undergo
*The ex-soccer star had to **undergo** a liver transplant.*

recent ADJECTIVE

A **recent** event is something that happened a short time ago.

current
***Current** affairs are the events which are happening in today's world.*

fresh
*The reporter had just received **fresh** information about the kidnap.*

latest
*Where my dad works, they have all the **latest** computer gadgets.*

new
*The head teacher sent a letter to parents explaining some **new** school rules.*

up-to-date
*The internet can be a good source of **up-to-date** information.*

ANTONYM: old

record (1) NOUN

A **record** is a written account of something.

diary
*I started my **diary** on New Year's Day, but gave up after the 4th of January.*

file
*In the past, **files** were kept in cabinets. Now more and more are stored on computers.*

log
*The captain kept a **log** of his voyage to the outer galaxies.*

minutes
*"Who'll take the **minutes** of our meeting?" the chairperson asked.*

register
*Names of pupils and details of attendance are kept in a **register**.*

PRONUNCIATION TIP
When it is a noun, **record** is pronounced **rek**-ord.

record (2) VERB

If you **record** information, you write it down so that it can be referred to later.

document
*The events were **documented** in the local newspapers.*

log
*Captain Picard **logged** the explosion of a distant planet.*

note
*"**Note** the main points of the story in your exercise books," Mr Bailey said.*

register
*When you arrive at a hotel, you have to **register** your name.*

PRONUNCIATION TIP
When it is a verb, **record** is pronounced ri-**kord**.

cover VERB
When you **recover**, you get better after being ill.

convalesce
Grandma is still ***convalescing*** *in hospital after her operation.*

get better
It took me a couple of weeks to ***get better*** *after having my tonsils out.*

get well
When Mrs Buckle was ill, we sent her a card saying ***"Get well*** *soon!"*

improve
According to the nurse, Grandad was ***improving*** *slowly.*

pull through
In spite of his grave injuries, the motorcyclist ***pulled through****.*

recuperate
After operations, patients go back to the ward to ***recuperate****.*

revive
Reviving *after her faint, the old lady sat and sipped water.*

cycle VERB
When you **recycle** something, you use it again for a different purpose.

reclaim
Materials such as paper, card and metal can be ***reclaimed*** *for reuse.*

reprocess
Nuclear waste is ***reprocessed*** *to extract usable substances.*

reuse
"Not enough of what we throw away is ***reused*** *in other forms," said Mum.*

salvage
Many things that we take to dumps are ***salvaged*** *and resold.*

ed ADJECTIVE
If something is **red**, it has the colour of blood or a tomato.

Shades of red:

auburn	burgundy	claret
crimson	maroon	russet
scarlet	vermilion	

reduce VERB
If you **reduce** something, you make it smaller in size or amount.

cut
The politician promised that his party would ***cut*** *taxes if they won the election.*

decrease
In built-up areas, a driver's speed should ***decrease*** *considerably.*

lessen
A healthy diet ***lessens*** *the risks of disease.*

lower
Air conditioning ***lowers*** *the temperature in hot interiors.*

ANTONYM: increase

refuse VERB
If you **refuse** something, you say no to it, or decide firmly that you will not do it or do not accept it.

decline
My dad ***declined*** *the offer of a job in the USA.*

reject
Haughtily, the princess ***rejected*** *Sir Mordred's proposal of marriage.*

turn down
The player ***turned down*** *the chance of a move to Italy.*

ANTONYM: accept

regular (1) ADJECTIVE
Regular events happen at equal or frequent intervals.

constant
The ***constant*** *throb of the ship's engines lulled me to sleep.*

even
When doctors take your pulse, they hope to hear an ***even*** *beat.*

rhythmic
The wind kept up a ***rhythmic*** *flapping of the flags.*

steady
In any band, the drummer's job is to maintain a ***steady*** *rhythm.*

regular (2) ADJECTIVE
Something that is **regular** is usual or normal.

a b c d e f g h i j k l m n o p q r s t u v w x y z

customary
Our neighbour was going out for his ***customary*** *evening walk.*

everyday
Helicopters were an ***everyday*** *sight over our valley.*

habitual
"You are a ***habitual*** *thief and liar," the judge told the defendant.*

normal
It was ***normal*** *for us to visit Aunt Emma each spring.*

usual
It is ***usual*** *for my sister and brother to argue at least once a day.*

ANTONYMS: abnormal, irregular

relation NOUN

Your **relations** are the people who are related to you, such as aunts, uncles and grandparents.

kin
"Most of our ***kin*** *come originally from Ireland," said the American visitor.*

kinsman or **kinswoman**
The wicked prince killed his ***kinsmen*** *in order to become king.*

relative
Amrit had many ***relatives*** *in India.*

relax VERB

When you **relax**, you become calm and less worried or tense.

laze
We spent the holiday ***lazing*** *on the beach.*

rest
The doctor advised Faizah to ***rest*** *as much as possible after the operation.*

take it easy
"Now just ***take it easy****," the police officer advised the angry young man.*

unwind
Dad always goes for a swim when he wants to ***unwind****.*

release (1) VERB

If you **release** someone or something, you set them free.

discharge
Having been found not guilty, the prisoner was ***discharged****.*

free
Sir Galahad rode up to the tower, determined to ***free*** *the imprisoned damsel.*

liberate
The rebels hoped to ***liberate*** *their country from the evil dictator's rule.*

→ *See* **rescue**

release (2) VERB

If you **release** something, you unfasten it.

loose
Sadira ***loosed*** *her horse into the paddock after she'd groomed him.*

undo
With some effort, the prisoner managed to ***undo*** *his ropes.*

unfasten
Ron struggled to ***unfasten*** *the rusty bolt that was keeping the door shut.*

reliable ADJECTIVE

Reliable people and things can be trusted and depended upon.

dependable
It had been a ***dependable*** *old car, and Mum was sorry to sell it.*

faithful
Wooster's ***faithful*** *butler, Jeeves, was always around to sort things out.*

responsible
Mrs Konchevsky said she needed a ***responsible*** *person to run an errand.*

trustworthy
It is important that a best friend is ***trustworthy****.*

ANTONYM: unreliable

rely VERB

If you **rely** on someone or something, you trust and depend on them.

bank on
I was ***banking on*** *my brother to give me a hand with the washing-up.*

count on
"Can I ***count on*** *your vote?" the councillor asked Mum.*

depend on
She ***depends on*** *her writing to make some money.*

have confidence in
Miss Powell said she ***had confidence in*** *me to captain the team well.*

A B C D E F G H I J K L M N O P Q R S T U V W X Y Z

trust
*I **trusted** my sister with the chocolate, and look what happened!*

remain (1) VERB

If you **remain** in a particular place, you stay there.

linger
*Several people **lingered** outside school, chatting while they waited to be collected.*

stay behind
*Mr Stubbs told us to **stay behind** after the rest of the class had gone.*

stay put (*informal*)
*When the car broke down, we had to get out and **stay put** at the side of the road.*

wait
*"**Wait** here until I come back," William told his brother George.*

ANTONYM: leave

remain (2) VERB

If something remains, it continues to exist.

continue
*"The annual school summer fayre, which we founded, **continued** for many years," said Mr Smith.*

endure
*Strange traditions **endure** almost everywhere in the world.*

persist
*Despite treatment, Orlando's nasty rash **persisted**.*

survive
*After the fire, little of the thatched cottage **survived**.*

LANGUAGE TIP
The **remains** of something are the parts that are left after most of it has been destroyed or used.

remember VERB

If you **remember** someone or something from the past, you still have an idea of them and you are able to think about them.

call to mind
*"You might **call to mind** the last time we had this discussion," Dad said when I asked about an increase in my pocket money.*

recall
*Most people can **recall** their first day at school.*

recollect
*Dad **recollected** that he had cried for his mum when he started school.*

ANTONYM: forget

remind VERB

If someone **reminds** you of something, they help you remember it.

bring to mind
*Mum said that my accident **brought to mind** a time when she had fallen off her bike.*

jog your memory
*"If I forget to repay you, just **jog my memory**," I said to Rosa.*

refresh your memory
*Mr Alpay asked me to **refresh his memory** about last year's sports day.*

remove VERB

If you **remove** something, you take it away.

clear away
*"Please will you **clear away** the tea things?" Mum asked.*

delete
*If you write on a PC, it's easy to **delete** mistakes.*

detach
*The engine was **detached** from the train carriages in the sidings.*

eliminate
*In each round of a knockout competition, the losers are **eliminated**.*

erase
*Once I'd finished the neat version of my composition, I **erased** my pencil notes.*

repair VERB

If you **repair** something that is damaged, you mend it.

fix
*Dad took my watch to the jeweller's to get it **fixed**.*

overhaul
*Before it could work again, the locomotive needed to be completely **overhauled**.*

renovate
*Dan specialises in **renovating** old houses.*

service
*Most cars and machines need to be **serviced** regularly.*

ANTONYM: damage

A B C D E F G H I J K L M N O P Q R S T U V W X Y Z

repay VERB

To **repay** someone is to give back money that is owed.

compensate
The builders had to ***compensate*** *Mr Watson for the damage to his garden.*

pay back
"I can lend you the money if you can ***pay*** *me* ***back*** *by the end of the week," said Jelani.*

recompense
"I'd like to ***recompense*** *you for all your help," the neighbour said.*

refund
If a product is of poor quality, shops have to ***refund*** *your money.*

settle up
"I'll just ***settle up*** *the bill and then we'll go," Dad said, as we packed our bags at the hotel.*

repeat VERB

If you **repeat** something, you say, write or do it again.

redo
My brother had to ***redo*** *his exams as he failed the first time.*

reiterate
Mr Hussein ***reiterated*** *what he'd told us a thousand times before.*

retell
We asked Gran to ***retell*** *the story of getting her first bicycle.*

replace VERB

If someone or something **replaces** someone or something else, they take their place.

substitute
When she wasn't looking, we ***substituted*** *salt for sugar.*

succeed
The prince ***succeeded*** *his mother on the throne when she died.*

take over from
Last term Mrs Mill ***took over from*** *Mr Weir as head teacher.*

take the place of
In Grandad's view, nothing can ***take the place of*** *old steam trains.*

reply (1) VERB

If you **reply** to something, you say or write something as an answer to it.

acknowledge
The prime minister ***acknowledged*** *my letter, but I received no further reply.*

answer
When I rang Marshall's house, his dad ***answered****.*

respond
It was a great service, but the opposing tennis player ***responded*** *with an even faster return.*

retort
When I asked her what she was doing, my sister ***retorted****, "Mind your own business!"*

reply (2) NOUN

A **reply** is what you say or write when you answer someone.

acknowledgment
The council sent no ***acknowledgment*** *to the letter I had written.*

answer
The traveller knocked at the door, but received no ***answer****.*

response
We had a huge ***response*** *to our appeal for old stamps.*

retort
I was only asking the time, but I received a rude ***retort****.*

report (1) NOUN

A **report** is an account of an event or situation.

account
Dad wasn't convinced by my ***account*** *of how the window got broken.*

description
Charles Dickens wrote superb ***descriptions*** *of his characters.*

record
Police have to keep a ***record*** *of every interview they conduct.*

statement
Witnesses are required to make a ***statement*** *of what they saw.*

report (2) VERB

If you **report** that something has happened, you inform someone about it.

recount
*We had to **recount** in our own words the story of Wilbur the pig.*

relate
*On her return, Ulima **related** the whole saga of being in the film.*

state
*The insurance form asks you to **state** what happened.*

represent (1) VERB

If a picture or writing **represents** something, it is intended to show or describe that thing in a particular way.

depict
*My painting **depicted** a spider halfway up a bottle.*

illustrate
*When I'd finished my account, Miss Johanssen asked me to **illustrate** it.*

portray
*The film **portrays** Robin Hood as being a cheerful, heroic type.*

represent (2) VERB

If a sign or symbol **represents** something, it is accepted as meaning that thing.

mean
*The = sign **means** that one thing is equal to another.*

stand for
*The initials UN **stand for** United Nations.*

symbolise
*In badges and logos, a dove is often used to **symbolise** peace.*

reptile NOUN

A **reptile** is one of a group of animals that lay eggs and have cold blood.

➔ Have a look at the **Illustration** page!

rescue (1) VERB

If you **rescue** someone, you save them from a dangerous or unpleasant situation.

free
*They managed to **free** a bird that was caught in some netting.*

liberate
*In a daring raid, the police managed to **liberate** the hostages.*

release
*At last, the driver was **released** from the wreckage of her car.*

save
*A passer-by dived into the sea and **saved** the drowning child.*

rescue (2) VERB

If you **rescue** something, you save it from being lost or destroyed.

recover
*Gold bullion was **recovered** from the wreck of the sunken galleon.*

retrieve
*Investigators managed to **retrieve** the stolen paintings.*

salvage
*Little could be **salvaged** from the blaze.*

resign VERB

If you **resign** from your job, you give it up.

hand in your notice
*As she wanted to set up her own business, Mum **handed in her notice**.*

quit
*"Then I **quit**!" shouted the manager, and stormed out of the dressing room.*

step down
*Due to illness, the manager had to **step down**.*

LANGUAGE TIP
If a king or queen resigns, they are said to **abdicate**.

respect (1) VERB

If you **respect** someone, you admire and like them.

admire
*I **admire** people who can keep calm whatever the circumstances.*

honour
*At a special dinner, the city **honoured** its former mayor.*

value
*Teachers **value** children who are well-behaved and hard-working.*

A B C D E F G H I J K L M N O P Q R S T U V W X Y Z

REPTILES

alligator

gecko

tortoise

lizard

iguana

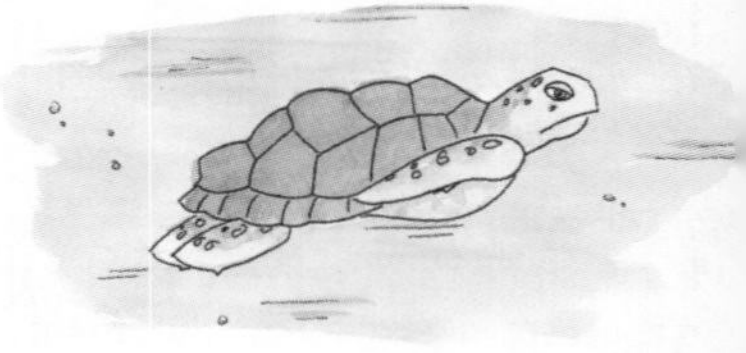

turtle

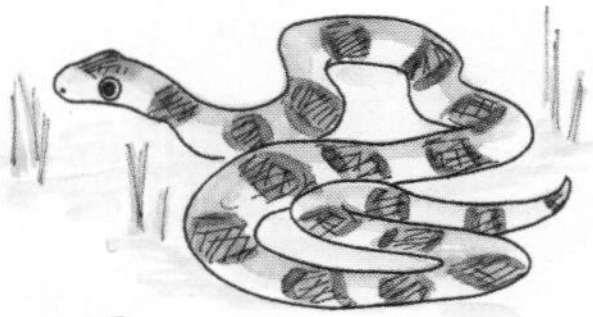

snake

crocodile

Some other types of reptile:

bearded dragon	chameleon	Gila monster	Komodo dragon
monitor lizard	skink	slowworm	terrapin

respect (2) NOUN

Respect is a feeling of admiration for someone's good qualities or achievements.

admiration
*The world had great **admiration** for the African statesman.*

esteem
*The captain was held in high **esteem** by all the members of his crew.*

responsible (1) ADJECTIVE

A **responsible** person is sensible, trustworthy and reliable.

conscientious
*Waseem's report said he was a **conscientious** worker.*

mature
*Shania was a **mature** girl who was obviously going to do well.*

reliable
*The advert asked for a **reliable** delivery person.*

sensible
*You can always rely on my sister to be **sensible** in a crisis.*

trustworthy
*"I need someone **trustworthy** to take this note to the office for me," said Miss Quentin.*

ANTONYM: irresponsible

responsible (2) ADJECTIVE

If you are **responsible** for something, you are the cause of it.

at fault
*It was difficult to tell if anyone was **at fault** for the accident.*

to blame
*I confessed that I was **to blame** for the mess in the kitchen.*

→ *See* **guilty (1)**

rest (1) VERB

If you **rest**, you take a break from what you are doing and relax for a while.

laze
*After all our hard work in the morning, we **lazed** about in the afternoon.*

lounge
*Mum **lounged** on the sofa after work.*

pause
*The secretary **paused** to have a sip of tea.*

relax
*Dad loves to read the paper while **relaxing** in a bath.*

take a breather (*informal*)
*"Why not **take a breather**?" the foreman suggested to his workmen.*

rest (2) NOUN

If you have a **rest**, you do not do anything active for a while.

break
*"Take a **break**," Mum said. "You've earned it."*

nap
*Gramps often has a **nap** in the afternoon.*

relaxation
*After the match, the team was sent away for rest and **relaxation**.*

snooze (*informal*)
*My grandma likes a **snooze** in her chair at any time of day.*

rest (3) NOUN

The **rest** of something is all the parts that are left or have not been mentioned.

balance
*"You can pay a deposit on the bike now and the **balance** later," said the salesman.*

remainder
*When we'd all had a slice of cake, the **remainder** was kept for later.*

restless ADJECTIVE

If you are **restless**, you find it hard to stay still or relaxed because you are bored or impatient.

fidgety
*My little brother gets **fidgety** if he has to sit still for a while.*

jumpy
*As the time for his exam results approached, Zack became very **jumpy**.*

on edge
*Before the game, the whole team was **on edge**.*

unsettled
*Knowing that we were going to the airport in the afternoon, I was **unsettled** all morning.*

ANTONYM: relaxed

a b c d e f g h i j k l m n o p q r s t u v w x y z

result NOUN

The **result** of an action or situation is what happens because of it.

consequence
*Anya's pony was lame, and as a **consequence** had to miss the show.*

effect
*Harry's potion had an instant **effect** on the frog.*

outcome
*All the reporters awaited the **outcome** of the court case.*

return (1) VERB

If you **return** to a place, you go back there.

come back
*My sister enjoys university, but loves **coming back** home.*

reappear
*Seconds after leaving, Mum **reappeared**, having forgotten her keys.*

revisit
*Gran looked forward to **revisiting** her birthplace.*

return (2) VERB

If you **return** something to someone, you give it back to them.

hand back
*After checking my pass, the driver **handed** it **back**.*

refund
*As the new computer was faulty, the store **refunded** Jackson's money.*

restore
*The clock was **restored** to its rightful owner.*

ANTONYM: take

revenge NOUN

Revenge is the act of hurting someone who has hurt you.

retaliation
*My sister kept annoying me so, in **retaliation**, I booby-trapped her bed.*

vengeance
*Sauron sought **vengeance** on those who dared to invade Mordor.*

revolting ADJECTIVE

Something that is **revolting** is horrible and disgusting.

disgusting
*"What a **disgusting** taste!" was all my brother could say about the pie I'd cooked.*

horrible
*There is a **horrible** smell coming from the fridge.*

loathsome
*The **loathsome** creature slimed its way up from the depths.*

nauseating
*I cannot stand the **nauseating** smell of boiled eggs.*

repulsive
*Little Nell could not stand his **repulsive** appearance.*

reward NOUN

A **reward** is something you are given because you have done something good.

bonus
*If Mum's firm has done well, all the employees get a **bonus** at Christmas.*

honour
*For her part in the game, Gina had the **honour** of carrying the trophy.*

prize
*My sister's **prize** was a visit to a television studio to watch a programme being made.*

repayment
*The medal was some **repayment** for all the time and effort the athlete had put in.*

rich ADJECTIVE

Someone who is **rich** has a lot of money or possessions.

affluent
*Mr Higgins lives in a very **affluent** part of town.*

loaded (*slang*)
*"My Uncle Abdul is **loaded**," boasted Sabirah.*

prosperous
***Prosperous** people tend to live in large houses.*

wealthy
*My uncle became **wealthy** after inventing a folding go-kart.*

well-off
*"**Well-off** people often worry too much about money," observed Grandma.*

rid VERB
To **rid** a place of something unpleasant means to succeed in removing it.

clear
*We **cleared** the cellar of all the flood water.*

free
*Spraying with vile-smelling chemicals **freed** the house of woodworm.*

get rid of PHRASE
If you **get rid of** something you do not want, you remove it or destroy it.

delete
*It's a simple matter to **delete** a sentence if you type the story up.*

dispose of
*"How can I **dispose of** the evidence?" the criminal pondered.*

dump
*"It's terrible the way people **dump** rubbish in the countryside," Mrs Cookson complained.*

ride NOUN
A **ride** is a journey on a horse or bicycle or in a vehicle.

drive
*Grandad took us for a **drive** in the country.*

jaunt
*Our **jaunt** into the city centre was great fun.*

journey
*Simon packed a book to read during the coach **journey**.*

trip
*For our prize, we won a **trip** on a real steam train.*

ridiculous ADJECTIVE
Someone or something that is **ridiculous** is very foolish.

absurd
*It's **absurd** to suggest that cars would run more smoothly on square wheels.*

foolish
*"What a **foolish** suggestion!" was Rhys's opinion of my cunning plan.*

ludicrous
*It was **ludicrous** to doubt Lilly's honesty.*

preposterous
*The idea of motorcars would have seemed **preposterous** in Saxon times.*

ANTONYM: sensible

right (1) ADJECTIVE
If something is **right**, it is correct.

accurate
*Weather forecasts are not always **accurate**.*

correct
*"That is the **correct** answer," said the quiz show host.*

true
*"Are these minutes a **true** record of the meeting?" the chairman asked.*

ANTONYMS: incorrect, wrong

right (2) ADJECTIVE
The **right** decision, action or person is the best or most suitable one.

appropriate
*Lightweight clothes are more **appropriate** for summer than winter.*

fitting
*As she had helped cook it, it was only **fitting** that Zaria should get a share of the cake.*

proper
*Grandad showed me the **proper** way to saw wood.*

suitable
*Legolas waited for a **suitable** time to depart.*

right (3) ADVERB
You can use **right** to emphasise the exact time or position of something.

exactly
*Luckily, the taxi arrived **exactly** on time, at eight o'clock.*

precisely
*The parachutist landed **precisely** on the mark.*

ring VERB
When a telephone or bell **rings**, it makes a clear, loud sound.

chime
*The clock on the mantelpiece **chimes** rather musically.*

clang
*On old fire engines, firefighters would **clang** the bell by hand.*

A B C D E F G H I J K L M N O P Q R S T U V W X Y Z

peal
*The bells **pealed** to mark the beginning of the new year.*

tinkle
*The bells on the reindeer **tinkled** as it pulled the sleigh.*

toll
*A single bell **tolled** solemnly as the funeral procession passed by.*

riot (1) NOUN

When there is a **riot**, a crowd of people behave violently in a public place.

commotion
*You could hear the **commotion** from round the corner.*

disturbance
*Police arrested those who had caused the **disturbance**.*

uproar
*One controversial speaker caused **uproar** in the meeting.*

riot (2) VERB

When people **riot**, they behave violently in a public place.

rampage
*Rioters **rampaged** through the streets, breaking windows and shouting.*

revolt
*Asked to pay crippling taxes, the poor peasants **revolted** against the king.*

run wild
*After the match, the supporters of the losing team **ran wild** in the streets.*

rip VERB

If you **rip** something, you tear it.

split
*When the man bent down, his trousers **split**!*

tear
*In fury, Mrs Carr **tore** the comic up.*

rise (1) VERB

If something **rises**, it moves upwards.

ascend
*Over the intercom, the pilot told us we were **ascending** to 30 000 feet.*

climb
*The aeroplane grew smaller as it **climbed**.*

go up
*The hot-air balloon **went up** into the air.*

mount
*As the money came in, the piles of banknotes **mounted**.*

ANTONYM: descend

rise (2) VERB

If prices **rise**, things get more expensive.

go up
*"The cost of houses has **gone up** enormously," the estate agent said.*

increase
*"The cost of fuel has **increased** again," sighed Mum.*

ANTONYM: fall

risk NOUN

Someone or something that is a **risk** is likely to cause harm or have bad results.

danger
*People who drive fast are a **danger** to others.*

gamble
*Taking a **gamble**, the racing driver decided not to stop for new tyres.*

hazard
*That frayed electrical wire is a real **hazard**.*

road NOUN

A **road** is a long stretch of hard ground built between two places so that people can travel along it easily.

LANGUAGE TIP
A road with the same entrance and exit is called a **dead end** or **cul-de-sac**.

roar VERB

If something **roars**, it makes a very loud noise.

bellow
*The buffalo **bellowed** in anger as the hunters approached cautiously.*

howl
*When the moon is full, you can hear the husky dogs **howl** in the icy wastes.*

thunder
*"Do as I say, boy!" **thundered** Squeers at Nicholas Nickleby.*

rob VERB

If someone **robs** a person or place, they steal money or property from them.

burgle
*While Mum's friends were away, their house was **burgled**.*

defraud
*The clerk tried to **defraud** his employers.*

loot
*Marauding Vikings **looted** the treasures of the monasteries.*

steal from
*The robbers had an elaborate plan to disable the burglar alarm and **steal from** the jewellery shop.*

swindle
*Two employees were sacked for **swindling** money from the company.*

LANGUAGE TIP
Someone who robs a person or place is a **burglar**, **robber** or **thief**.

robbery NOUN

Robbery is the action of robbing a person or place.

burglary
*They've been arrested for **burglary**.*

theft
*"**Theft** is a nasty crime. I bet thieves wouldn't like having things stolen!" said Granny.*

rock VERB

When something **rocks**, or you **rock** it, it moves regularly backwards and forwards or from side to side.

sway
*We started **swaying** to the beat of the music.*

swing
*The pendulum of a clock **swings** to and fro.*

rogue NOUN

A **rogue** is a dishonest or mischievous person.

rascal
*Long John Silver was more of a **rascal** than a thoroughly evil pirate.*

scoundrel
*"You **scoundrel**, sir!" bellowed the mayor. "You'll pay for this!"*

villain
*A black-hearted **villain**, Sykes had few friends in the world.*

room (1) NOUN

If there is **room** for something, there is enough space for it.

elbow room
*There was not much **elbow room** in the cockpit.*

space
*"If you arrive early, there'll be plenty of **space** to sit," advised the ticket seller.*

room (2) NOUN

A **room** is a separate section in a building, divided from other rooms by walls.

A room...
at the top of a house is an **attic** or **loft**.
at the bottom of a house is a **cellar** or **basement**.
where several people sleep in a boarding school or hostel is a **dormitory**.
where patients sleep in a hospital is a **ward**.
where patients are operated on in a hospital is an **operating theatre**.
where scientists work is a **laboratory**.

rot VERB

When food, wood or other substances **rot**, or when something rots them, they decay and fall apart.

biodegrade
*Most plastics will not **biodegrade**, which makes them a threat to the environment.*

decay
*When they die, plants and animals **decay**.*

decompose
*The fallen autumn leaves were **decomposing** on the forest floor.*

rotten ADJECTIVE

Something that is **rotten** has decayed.

decayed
*Compost heaps contain **decayed** and decaying plants.*

mouldy
*After being left out for two weeks, the cheese had gone **mouldy**.*

perished
*During the transport strike, tons of vegetables **perished** in their sacks.*

ANTONYM: fresh

A B C D E F G H I J K L M N O P Q R S T U V W X Y Z

rough (1) ADJECTIVE

A **rough** surface is uneven and not smooth.

bumpy
*The rickety bicycle rattled over the **bumpy** cobbled street.*

irregular
*An **irregular** surface is useless for bowling.*

jagged
*Iris trod on the **jagged** edge of a broken bottle and badly cut her foot.*

rocky
*The **rocky** ground was not ideal for pitching our tent.*

stony
*Our car bumped and bounced along the winding **stony** track.*

uneven
*Amir tripped up on the **uneven** footpath.*

ANTONYMS: soft, smooth

rough (2) ADJECTIVE

Something that is **rough** is coarse and hairy.

bristly
*Cutthroat Jake's pirate beard was **bristly** and grizzled.*

bushy
*The old major had a big, **bushy** moustache.*

coarse
*My brother's extreme haircut felt **coarse** when I touched it.*

ANTONYM: smooth

rough (3) ADJECTIVE

If a sea is **rough**, the wind and waves are high.

choppy
*Our boat bounced around in the **choppy** water.*

raging
***Raging** seas smashed into the old pier.*

stormy
***Stormy** weather was forecast.*

turbulent
*The wind howled over the **turbulent** sea.*

wild
*It was a **wild** night, and not a night to be out on the sea.*

ANTONYM: calm

rough (4) ADJECTIVE

Someone who is **rough** treats someone in a harsh or violent way.

brutal
*Prison guards were **brutal** in their punishment of the captive.*

harsh
*Boxers often have to take **harsh** treatment in the ring.*

tough
*Life in the jungle is often **tough**.*

ANTONYMS: gentle, sympathetic

rough (5) ADJECTIVE

Someone who is **rough** has manners that are rude and insensitive.

blunt
*Arthur was known for his **blunt** speaking.*

rude
*The neighbour was known as a **rude**, unpleasant woman.*

ANTONYM: courteous

rough (6) ADJECTIVE

Rough can mean approximate.

approximate
*"Give me the **approximate** time when you'll finish," Mum said.*

vague
*Bhavesh had a **vague** idea of what Mrs Cunningham wanted.*

ANTONYMS: exact, precise

rough (7) ADJECTIVE

A **rough** voice is harsh.

gruff
*A **gruff** voice answered the telephone.*

rasping
*Quilp's **rasping** voice ran through the courtyard.*

ANTONYMS: soothing, soft

rough (8) ADJECTIVE

A **rough** sketch is very basic.

crude
*From a **crude** sketch on an envelope came an award-winning car.*

rough-and-ready
*"This is a **rough-and-ready** plan, but it will do," the builder said.*

ANTONYMS: detailed, precise

roughly ADVERB

Roughly can mean almost or approximately.

about
*"We'll need **about** 20 sausages and 10 bread rolls for the barbecue," Mum told Dad.*

approximately
*"At **approximately** three o'clock, the parade will be in the town centre," the announcement read.*

around
***Around** 300 people came to the wedding.*

ANTONYM: precisely

round ADJECTIVE

Something **round** is shaped like a ball or a circle.

circular
*The round peg goes in the **circular** hole.*

rounded
*The **rounded** nib of the pen helped it to glide smoothly over the page.*

spherical
*Our planet is roughly **spherical** in shape.*

round up VERB

If you **round up** people or animals, you gather them together.

assemble
*Mrs Sneddon **assembled** us all in the playground to see the eclipse.*

collect
*Dad sent me round to the neighbours to **collect** my brother and sister for tea.*

gather
*For shearing, Farmer Gabriel **gathered** his sheep in one large pen.*

herd
*At milking time, cows are **herded** into the farmyard.*

muster
*"In the event of an emergency," the captain announced, "please **muster** on the foredeck."*

row (1) NOUN

A **row** can be an argument.

argument
*Leah could hear a terrific **argument** going on next door.*

disagreement
*Just occasionally, my best friend and I have a real **disagreement**, but we always make up.*

dispute
*A **dispute** about pay caused the workforce to go on strike.*

quarrel
*The two brothers had a **quarrel** about who should inherit the farm.*

squabble
***Squabbles** are always breaking out between my cousins.*

PRONUNCIATION TIP
When it means "an argument", **row** rhymes with "cow".

row (2) NOUN

A **row** can be a lot of noise.

cacophony
*The school band was tuning up – what a **cacophony**!*

din
*Above the **din**, I heard Mrs Ahmed open the classroom door.*

racket
*"What on earth is this **racket** all about?" shouted Mrs Jensen, as she came in.*

PRONUNCIATION TIP
When it means "a lot of noise", **row** rhymes with "cow".

row (3) NOUN

A **row** is several objects or people in a line.

file
*We had to walk in single **file** to the main hall for assembly.*

line
*Several **lines** of cars waited for the ferry.*

queue
*For once, the dinner **queue** was not too long.*

series
*Strip cartoons are formed from a **series** of pictures and captions.*

PRONUNCIATION TIP
When it means "several things in a line", **row** rhymes with "snow".

rubbish (1) NOUN
Rubbish is unwanted things or waste material.

garbage
***Garbage** lay piled up in and around the bin.*

junk
*Dad suggested I help him sort out any **junk** in the garage.*

litter
*"It's amazing how casual some people are about dropping **litter**," observed Haresh.*

refuse
*"I hate it when public **refuse** bins are left to overflow," said Gran.*

scrap
*In the iron foundry, any **scrap** is put back into the furnace.*

trash
*Americans call their waste material "**trash**".*

waste
*In the western world, human **waste** goes into the sewers for treatment.*

LANGUAGE TIP
Trash is a word mainly used in America.

rubbish (2) NOUN
If you talk **rubbish**, you say something foolish.

bunkum (*informal*)
*Dad thought the man was talking **bunkum**.*

drivel
*That book was such **drivel** that I only read one chapter of it.*

hot air (*informal*)
*Everyone knew that Jim was talking **hot air**.*

nonsense
*"It's utter **nonsense** to believe the world is flat!" I told my little brother.*

piffle (*informal*)
*"Don't talk **piffle**, Jeeves!" Wooster exclaimed peevishly.*

twaddle (*informal*)
*Mr Carp told Billy he was talking **twaddle**.*

rub out VERB
If you **rub** something **out**, you delete it.

delete
*With one keystroke, Dad managed to **delete** all his evening's work.*

erase
*If you work in pencil, it's easy to **erase** what you've done.*

remove
*Mr Rafferty suggested that I **remove** "nice" and substitute "pleasant".*

rude ADJECTIVE
Someone who is **rude** is not polite.

abusive
*The player was sent off for being **abusive** to the referee.*

bad-mannered
*It is **bad-mannered** to interrupt people who are talking.*

cheeky
*My brother can be very **cheeky** sometimes.*

ill-mannered
*The **ill-mannered** boy never said "please" or "thank you".*

insolent
*Teachers in our school won't stand for pupils who are **insolent** to them.*

insulting
*If you don't reply to an invitation, it is **insulting** to the host.*

offensive
*Keisha thought that Pauline's remark was **offensive**.*

ANTONYMS: polite, courteous, well-mannered

ruin VERB
If you **ruin** something, you destroy or spoil it completely.

destroy
*Wartime air raids had **destroyed** the city centre.*

devastate
*The hurricane **devastated** a vast area of the coastline.*

spoil
*Adara **spoilt** her book by scribbling on the cover.*

wreck
*"Don't **wreck** your exam chances by staying up late," Dad advised.*

→ *See* **damage (1)**

ruins PLURAL NOUN

Ruins are what is left after something has been severely damaged.

debris
*After the explosion, a huge amount of **debris** remained to be cleared.*

wreckage
***Wreckage** from the aircraft was strewn across the hillside.*

rule VERB

When someone **rules** a country or a group of people, they govern it and are in charge of its affairs.

control
*Mrs Samuels **controls** our class very well.*

govern
*Usually, the party with the most votes is the one that **governs** the country.*

lead
*Some countries are **led** by a prime minister, others by a president.*

reign
*Queen Victoria **reigned** over Britain for most of the 19th century.*

ruler NOUN

A **ruler** is a person who rules a country.

Some types of ruler:

emperor	head of state	king
maharajah	monarch	president
prince	princess	queen
sheikh	sovereign	

run

→ Look at the **Word Power** page!

runny ADJECTIVE

Something that is **runny** is flowing or moving like liquid.

liquid
*The **liquid** chocolate is then poured into moulds to make chocolate Easter bunnies.*

watery
*"This gravy's very **watery**," the diner grumbled.*

ANTONYM: solid

rush VERB

If you **rush** somewhere, or if you are rushed there, you go there quickly.

dash
*I **dashed** to the post office to try and catch the last post.*

hasten
*Sir Bedivere **hastened** to the side of the dying King Arthur.*

hurry
*"We'll have to **hurry** or we'll miss the train," Mum said.*

scurry
*Our hamster Harold **scurried** round and round in his wheel.*

speed
*The police car **sped** towards the scene of the accident.*

→ *See* **run**

A B C D E F G H I J K L M N O P Q R S T U V W X Y Z

run

(1) VERB When you **run**, you move quickly, with both feet leaving the ground at each stride.

run slowly:

jog
*My grandad still goes out **jogging** each day.*

trot
*My brother **trotted** downstairs to answer the door.*

run fast:

bolt
*As soon as I had finished speaking, he **bolted** out of the room.*

dart
*When the vet had finished, the cat **darted** for the door.*

dash
*Craig must have been crazy to **dash** across the road like that.*

gallop
*The horse **galloped** over the finishing line to a loud cheer from the crowd.*

sprint
*On the last lap, Tyrone **sprinted** for the finish.*

tear
*Although my sister **tore** down the road, her friend had disappeared.*

run clumsily:

career
*Out of control, the horse and cart **careered** down the hill.*

lollop *(informal)*
*The dog came **lolloping** up to greet me.*

lumber
*The great carthorse **lumbered** down the road pulling the wagon.*

→ Also have a look at the **Word Power** page for **walk**!

run

(2) VERB If you **run** an activity, or a place such as a school or a shop, you are in charge of it.

administer
*Mum **administers** a team of salespeople.*

be in charge of
*My dad is **in charge of** the store's kitchenware department.*

control
*A lady at a desk **controls** the lighting for the show.*

direct
*As the incident was serious, the chief of police **directed** the rescue.*

manage
*When I grow up, I want to **manage** a factory.*

(3) VERB When a machine **runs**, it is operating.

function
*The ancient laptop **functioned** well enough for the writer to finish the first draft.*

go
*My car isn't **going** very well at the moment.*

operate
*Our washing machine **operates** easily if you know which button to press.*

work
*"I can use a computer," said Dad, "but I'll never understand how one **works**!"*

(4) VERB If a liquid or river **runs** somewhere, it flows there or takes that particular course.

flow
*The waterfall **flowed** noisily over the cliff.*

gush
*Boiling water **gushed** from Dad's leaking car radiator.*

pour
*You could see the sweat **pouring** off the cyclists.*

stream
*The river **streamed** over and around several huge boulders.*

trickle
*The stream **trickled** gently over the rocks.*

A B C D E F G H I J K L M N O P Q R S T U V W X Y Z

Ss

sack VERB

If someone is **sacked**, they are dismissed from their job by their employer.

discharge
*The private was **discharged** from the army for dishonest behaviour.*

dismiss
*A postman or woman might be **dismissed** if they fail to deliver their letters.*

fire (*informal*)
*Dad had to **fire** one of his staff the other day.*

ANTONYM: employ

sad

→ Look at the **Word Power** page!

sadness NOUN

Sadness is a feeling of unhappiness.

dejection
*Her exam results filled Marcia with **dejection**.*

despair
*Losing his family brought Mr Cort to the brink of **despair**.*

grief
*The **grief** shone in Lyra's eyes as she parted from Will for the last time.*

misery
*Deena was a picture of **misery** as she sat in the corner.*

sorrow
*For months after the plane crash, the town was a place of **sorrow**.*

unhappiness
*An air of **unhappiness** filled the old house.*

ANTONYM: happiness

safe (1) ADJECTIVE

If you are **safe**, you are not in any danger.

in safe hands
*We knew that Hammy, our hamster, was **in safe hands** when we left him with our gran.*

out of danger
*We were relieved, after her operation, to hear our aunt was **out of danger**.*

safe and sound
*"The missing walkers have been found **safe and sound**," the journalist reported.*

safe (2) ADJECTIVE

Something that is **safe** does not cause harm or danger.

harmless
*The weedkiller is supposed to be **harmless** to animals.*

nontoxic
*Toys for young children must be made of **nontoxic** materials.*

uncontaminated
*Despite the chemical leak, the river nearby remained **uncontaminated**.*

wholesome
*"This food is **wholesome** and very good for you," said Mum.*

ANTONYM: dangerous

LANGUAGE TIP
A safe vehicle is **roadworthy**. A safe boat or ship is **seaworthy**. A safe plane is **flightworthy**.

safety NOUN

Safety is the state of being safe or protected.

protection
*For **protection** from the sun's rays, Tamara and Kylie had to wear mirrored sunglasses.*

refuge
*The hostel was a place of **refuge** for people in danger.*

security
*For his **security**, the prisoner was ushered through the crowd by armed guards.*

shelter
*The two hobbits sought **shelter** in a vast cave in the side of the mountain.*

same (1) ADJECTIVE

If two things are the **same**, they are like one another.

alike
*The twins were **alike** in several ways.*

identical
*"That's weird! We've got an **identical** vase at home," Lexi said.*

matching
*"A **matching** pair of candlesticks – what am I bid?" the auctioneer began.*

similar
*Although **similar** in looks, Michaela and her sister have very different characters.*

uniform
*"Each can of beans needs to be of **uniform** flavour and quality," explained the factory manager.*

ANTONYM: different

same (2) ADJECTIVE
If something stays the **same**, it is not different from what it was.

consistent
*The umpire was **consistent**: each player received the same treatment.*

unaltered
*Despite her illness, Nora's sense of humour remained **unaltered**.*

unchanged
*After all those years, the house looked **unchanged**.*

unvarying
*With **unvarying** accuracy, the snooker player potted every ball.*

ANTONYMS: inconsistent, varying

LANGUAGE TIP
Words that mean the same as each other are **synonyms**.

save (1) VERB
If you **save** someone or something, you rescue them or help to keep them safe.

come to the rescue
*Fortunately, my sister **came to the rescue** and gave me a lift.*

preserve
*Chris **preserved** leaves by pressing them in blotting paper.*

rescue
*A helicopter **rescued** the injured crewman, taking him to hospital.*

safeguard
*Insurance **safeguards** you if things get lost or damaged.*

salvage
*The tug **salvaged** the abandoned tanker.*

→ *See* **protect**

save (2) VERB
If you **save** something, you keep it so that you can use it later.

hoard
*Fagin carefully **hoarded** the stolen goods.*

put by
*"We've got a little money **put by** for a rainy day," Gran told Mum.*

reserve
*Navdip **reserved** a few sandwiches, in case there were any latecomers to the party.*

ANTONYMS: spend, use

save (3) VERB
If you **save** time, money or effort, you stop it from being wasted.

cut back
*Looking right at me, Dad said we needed to **cut back** on our phone bill.*

economise
*It was difficult for the pop star to **economise**, having once been so rich.*

ANTONYM: waste

say

→ Look at the **Word Power** page!

saying NOUN
A **saying** is a well-known sentence or phrase that tells you something about life.

expression
*"The show must go on" is an **expression** that is familiar to many people.*

motto
*"Dare to be wise" is the **motto** of our school.*

proverb
*Grandad's favourite **proverb** is "A stitch in time saves nine".*

quotation
*My mum was always coming out with **quotations** from Shakespeare.*

scarce ADJECTIVE
If something is **scarce**, there is not very much of it.

few and far between
*On the island, filling stations were **few and far between**.*

in short supply
*Food is **in short supply** all over the country.*

A
B
C
D
E
F
G
H
I
J
K
L
M
N
O
P
Q
R
S
T
U
V
W
X
Y
Z

sad

(1) ADJECTIVE If you are **sad**, you feel unhappy.

blue
*There's no real reason for me to feel so **blue**.*

dejected
*Calum sat, **dejected**, in his room with the lights off.*

depressed
*My friend Anna was **depressed** about moving away.*

despondent
*Having failed to find a job, Jeremy was becoming **despondent**.*

devastated
*Max was **devastated** when he smashed the screen on his new phone.*

distressed
*The **distressed** lady stared at her dented car through her tears.*

down
*I felt very **down** about going back to school.*

downcast
*Georgia was **downcast** after nearly failing her violin exam.*

glum
*Abdel's **glum** face told me immediately what his exam result was.*

low
*Mum was always a bit **low** when Dad had to go away on business.*

melancholy
*It was at this time of day that he felt most **melancholy**.*

miserable
*I was **miserable** when I broke my arm.*

tearful
*There were many **tearful** faces at Mrs Kahn's leaving party.*

unhappy
*The striker was **unhappy** with the way he had played.*

upset
*My aunt was very **upset** about the broken vase.*

sad

(2) ADJECTIVE If something is **sad**, it makes you feel unhappy or upset.

depressing
*I found the film very **depressing**.*

harrowing
*You've had a **harrowing** time this last month.*

heart-breaking
*It was **heart-breaking** to hear what happened to your father.*

heart-rending
*It was **heart-rending** to find out that many of those children were orphans.*

moving
*In a **moving** scene, the old man hugged his long-lost son.*

pitiful
*It was the most **pitiful** sight I had ever seen.*

touching
*It was so **touching** to see how the adults protected the injured cub.*

tragic
*"What **tragic** news to wake up to!" she gasped.*

upsetting
*The report made very **upsetting** reading.*

Try these lively words and phrases!

down in the dumps (*informal*)	*"You look **down in the dumps**," Dad said. "What's wrong?"*
down in the mouth (*informal*)	*She is **down in the mouth** and could do with cheering up.*
gutted (*informal*)	*I was **gutted** that my team lost in the final.*

→ Also have a look at the **Word Power** page for **happy**!

say

(1) VERB If you **say** something, you speak words.

say a lot:

babble
*Little George sat in his pushchair, **babbling** away to himself.*

burble
*As Grandad snoozed, his friend **burbled** on about his childhood.*

chatter
*It feels like Lila never stops **chattering**.*

drone
*Mrs Blake always **drones** on and on about her garden!*

prattle
*I do wish James would stop **prattling** about nothing.*

witter (*informal*)
*They **wittered** on about what they had done at school.*

say angrily:

snap
*"Just do as I say!" my mother **snapped** at my brother and me.*

snarl
*The gangster **snarled**, "You're in for a bit of bother now, son!"*

say hesitantly or slowly:

drawl
*"Y'all are welcome," old Grandpa Walt **drawled** from his chair.*

stammer
*"I d-d-didn't do it!" **stammered** the little girl.*

stutter
*"W-would you l-like a cup of tea?" the office junior **stuttered**.*

say miserably:

groan
*"Not Monday again!" my sister **groaned**, as I sat on her bed.*

moan
*The injured passenger **moaned** something then fell unconscious.*

whimper
*Tearfully, the child **whimpered** that he was completely lost.*

whine
*My kid brother is always **whining** that I never play with him.*

say quietly:

mumble
*"I'm really sorry, miss," he **mumbled**.*

murmur
*People in the crowd **murmured** and a woman came forward.*

mutter
*Harry could hear Ron **muttering** a spell under his breath.*

whisper
*"It's a secret. Can I **whisper**?" Anita asked.*

say

say loudly:

bawl
*Our neighbour is always **bawling** at his children.*

bellow
*"And don't you dare come back!" the farmer **bellowed**.*

call out
*"Is there anyone home?" Mum **called out** as she came in.*

cry
*"Hello!" **cried** Aunty Ruby.*

exclaim
*"Well, what a surprise!" **exclaimed** the man in the blazer.*

shout
*"What are you doing in my room?" she **shouted**. "Get out!"*

yell
*Milly **yelled** that she'd been stung by a wasp.*

say suddenly or rudely:

blurt out
*Neha **blurted out** that she was going to be sick.*

butt in
*"Please don't **butt in**, Harry," Mr Dursley said.*

interject
*"That's certainly not true!" **interjected** Sue.*

interrupt
*"I wish you wouldn't keep **interrupting**, Nadine," Ellie said.*

say strongly or formally:

announce
*Last night my brother **announced** he was joining the navy.*

declare
*The president **declared** anyone who disagreed to be a traitor.*

pronounce
*"I now **pronounce** you husband and wife!" declared the minister.*

state
*He was asked to **state** his name.*

say quickly:

gabble
*"There's no need to **gabble**," Miss Macken said. "Take your time."*

jabber
*The parrot **jabbered** away.*

(2) VERB If you **say** something, you make a remark about something.

comment
*Lots of people **commented** on the photos I posted online.*

mention
*"Did I **mention** that I'm going out on Saturday?" asked Zahin.*

put in
*"Let's stay here," **put in** my aunt.*

remark
*My mum **remarked** on how many birds were in the garden.*

rare
*Golden eagles are mountain birds **rare** in European lands.*

ANTONYM: plentiful

scare VERB

If something **scares** you, it frightens you.

alarm
*"Don't be **alarmed**," the nurse said. "You'll only feel a little prick."*

frighten
*Keep dogs under control so that they do not **frighten** sheep.*

give someone a fright
*I really **gave my sister a fright** with that gorilla mask!*

put the wind up (*informal*)
*Zoltan **put the wind up** me when he pretended to be a ghost.*

shock
*The spate of murders **shocked** the whole city and made people afraid to go out at night.*

startle
*My mum was **startled** when the seagull suddenly swooped on her sandwich.*

terrify
*In wartime, people must be **terrified** when the air-raid sirens sound.*

scary ADJECTIVE (*informal*)

If something is **scary** it is frightening.

alarming
*We found the sudden blast of the foghorn truly **alarming**.*

bloodcurdling
*From another flat in the block came a **bloodcurdling** scream.*

frightening
*The programme was too **frightening** to watch.*

spine-chilling
*Harry goes through many **spine-chilling** tussles with the forces of evil.*

terrifying
*Hanging onto the rope was a **terrifying** ordeal for the fallen climber.*

scatter VERB

If you **scatter** things, you throw or drop a lot of them all over an area.

fling
*The children **flung** the papers in the air in excitement.*

litter
*Clothes were **littered** all over Lewis's bedroom floor.*

sow
*As fast as Grandpa **sowed** his seeds, the birds gobbled them up.*

spread
*"**Spread** the corn evenly," she said, "so that all the chickens get some."*

sprinkle
*Mum carefully **sprinkled** drops of water on the seedlings.*

score NOUN

A **score** is the number of goals, runs or points obtained by the two opponents in a game.

marks
*Mrs Ferguson gave me full **marks** for my maths test.*

result
*"Did you hear the **result** of the big game?" Bruce asked me.*

tally
*The German had notched up an impressive **tally** of grand prix wins.*

total
*After she had marked my answers, Liz told me my **total**.*

scrape VERB

If something **scrapes** something else, it rubs against it harshly.

grate
*As the old car trundled along, its broken exhaust **grated** on the road surface.*

graze
*Iman **grazed** her knee on a wall when she fell off her bike.*

rasp
*Metal **rasped** on metal as Dad filed away at my bike frame.*

scratch
*The cat **scratched** on the door to be let in.*

scratch NOUN

A **scratch** is a small cut or mark in the surface of something.

graze
*He has a slight **graze** on his knee.*

groove
*The woodworker cut decorative **grooves** into the table.*

score
*A vandal had left **scores** in the side of the car.*

scrape
*She had a **scrape** below her right eye.*

scream (1) VERB

If you **scream**, you shout or cry in a loud, high-pitched voice.

bawl
*That spoilt toddler really **bawled** when she was refused sweets!*

cry
*"That's wonderful news!" **cried** her teacher.*

shriek
*You should have heard my sister **shriek** when she saw the toy mouse.*

squeal
*Marsha **squealed** with delight when she saw her birthday present.*

scream (2) NOUN

A **scream** is a loud, high-pitched cry.

cry
*Searching for the lost child, police heard a sudden **cry** from the woods.*

shriek
*The vampire let out a **shriek** and began to crumple – daylight had dawned.*

squeal
*The **squeals** of the hungry piglets could be heard all around the farmyard.*

scruffy ADJECTIVE

Someone or something **scruffy** is dirty and untidy.

bedraggled
*The kitten was a **bedraggled** heap when our neighbour found him.*

ragged
*My football kit was looking pretty **ragged**.*

shabby
*You could tell from her **shabby** coat that times were not too good for the ex-actress.*

tattered
***Tattered** and blackened, the cartoon cat emerged from the explosion.*

tatty
*"That exercise book is too **tatty** for me to mark," Mr Singh said in disgust.*

ANTONYM: smart

search (1) VERB

If you **search** for something, you look for it very thoroughly.

comb
*Police **combed** the area for the missing twins and eventually found them safe and well.*

hunt
*I **hunted** everywhere for my pencil, and finally found it in my pencil case!*

look high and low
*Long John Silver **looked high and low**, but couldn't find the hidden treasure.*

ransack
*Thieves **ransacked** the flat and stole several items of jewellery.*

rummage through
*The investigator **rummaged through** the bin, but found no useful evidence.*

scour
*"I've hidden the clues," Mum said. "I suggest you **scour** the yard."*

LANGUAGE TIP
To search for gold or other valuable minerals is to **prospect**.

search (2) NOUN

A **search** is an attempt to find something or someone.

hunt
*Detectives are continuing the **hunt** for the killer.*

quest
*The pirate's lifelong **quest** for treasure ended in heartbreak.*

LANGUAGE TIP
A **search party** is a group of people who search for a missing person.

seaside NOUN

The **seaside** is a place by the sea, especially where people go on holiday.

beach
*At Mediterranean resorts, the **beaches** are often swarming with people.*

coast
*On the **coast**, the weather was superb, while inland it was cloudy.*

coastline
*"This stretch of **coastline** is the habitat of many wading birds," Uncle Colin told me.*

seashore
Dad and I wandered along the ***seashore*** *looking for driftwood.*

→ Have a look at the **Illustration** page!

second NOUN

A **second** is one of the 60 parts that a minute is divided into.

flash
In a ***flash****, the dog had gobbled the meat I had dropped.*

instant
For an ***instant****, Sam thought the dressing gown on the door was a ghost.*

jiffy (*informal*)
"I'll be back in a ***jiffy****," Colleen promised.*

moment
The ***moment*** *Mum's back was turned, my sister was pulling faces.*

twinkling of an eye
Ratty, in the ***twinkling of an eye****, had the kettle boiling.*

secret ADJECTIVE

Something that is **secret** is known to only a small number of people and hidden from everyone else.

classified
"That information is ***classified****," M said. "I couldn't possibly reveal it."*

confidential
Anything you say to your doctor is ***confidential****.*

private
Some court hearings are kept ***private****, without any press there.*

top-secret
*Moneypenny handed Bond a file marked "****Top-Secret****".*

> **Try these lively words and phrases:**
>
> **cloak-and-dagger**
> *The prisoner was released in a* ***cloak-and-dagger*** *operation.*
>
> **hush-hush** (*informal*)
> *The scientists were working on a very* ***hush-hush*** *project.*

see (1) VERB

If you **see** something, you look at it or notice it with your eyes.

behold (*old-fashioned*)
Ever since Reinhold first ***beheld*** *Everest, he wanted to climb it.*

clap eyes on (*informal*)
"I hadn't ***clapped eyes on*** *my old headmaster for years," Grandpa chortled.*

glimpse
Fiona managed to ***glimpse*** *the film star through the crowds.*

notice
Ken ***noticed*** *that one of his tyres was flat.*

observe
The nurse ***observed*** *a change in my grandad's condition.*

perceive
"I ***perceive****," Holmes said, "that you have recently bought new boots."*

sight
From the east, the lookout ***sighted*** *smoke on the horizon.*

spot
It wasn't hard to ***spot*** *that Mum was expecting a baby.*

watch
From her window, Alisha was able to ***watch*** *the whole of the carnival.*

witness
The passer-by claimed to have ***witnessed*** *three men running from the bank.*

→ *See* **look**

see (2) VERB

If you **see** something, you understand it or realise what it means.

appreciate
"It is difficult to ***appreciate*** *the size of the blue whale," said the naturalist.*

comprehend
"You do not seem to ***comprehend*** *the seriousness of the offence," said the judge.*

follow
It was quite hard to ***follow*** *from the instructions how to put the shelves together.*

get (*informal*)
"I just don't ***get*** *how to do long division," moaned Bharat.*

grasp
After she had explained several times, I finally ***grasped*** *what Daphne was saying.*

THE SEASIDE

Some other words to do with the seaside:

dock	driftwood	estuary	harbour	jetty	mud flats
pebble	promenade	quay	seashore	seaweed	strand line

A
B
C
D
E
F
G
H
I
J
K
L
M
N
O
P
Q
R
S
T
U
V
W
X
Y
Z

realise
*The twins **realised** that they would need help.*

understand
*At last, Steve **understood** what had happened.*

see (3) VERB

If you go to **see** someone, you visit them.

call on
*I often **call on** my grandma on the way home from school.*

look up (*informal*)
*When Dad went to London on business he **looked up** an old school friend.*

visit
*"I've really enjoyed **visiting** you all," said Auntie Megan.*

see (4) VERB

If you **see** to something, you make sure that it is done.

attend to
*Legolas **attended to** the horses, while Frodo saw to the baggage.*

be responsible for
*In our school, Mr Brockbank **is responsible for** music and drama.*

look after
*"Can you **look after** the washing-up while I tidy up?" Mum asked.*

organise
*Kevin and his team **organised** the church fête.*

sort out
*With her courteous, calm approach, Myra was good at **sorting out** angry customers.*

seem VERB

If something **seems** to be the case, it appears to be the case, or you think it is the case.

appear
*"It **appears** that we've run out of honey," Dad remarked at breakfast.*

give the impression of
*At first Mrs Facey **gave the impression of** being very strict, but she's really quite nice.*

look
*"The game **looks** easy, but wait till you try it!" said Holden.*

seize VERB

If you **seize** something, you grab it firmly.

clutch
*The train stopped suddenly. Angela almost fell and had to **clutch** the back of the seat.*

grab
*Rashid **grabbed** his bag and sprinted for the bus.*

grasp
*The old lady **grasped** Katherine's arm and asked for help.*

snatch
*A robber tried to **snatch** her purse, but she held on tightly.*

seldom ADVERB

Something that **seldom** happens, does not happen very often.

hardly ever
*Dad **hardly ever** loses his temper.*

not often
*I'm **not often** late for school because Mum makes sure I leave home on time.*

only once in a while
***Only once in a while** does my sister become a real nuisance.*

rarely
*"**Rarely** has anyone got such high marks," Miss Benjamin said, beaming.*

ANTONYM: often

selfish ADJECTIVE

If you are **selfish**, you care only about yourself, and not about other people.

egotistical
*Film stars are notorious for being demanding and **egotistical**.*

greedy
*It was pretty **greedy** of Salimah to hog all the coloured pencils.*

self-centred
***Self-centred** people generally like to talk about themselves.*

sell VERB

Someone who **sells** things, deals in a particular type of goods to earn money.

deal in
*Jon **dealt in** antique furniture and knows a great deal about the trade.*

peddle
*The old lady scratched a living by **peddling** various household items door-to-door.*

trade in
*Steptoe's Market **trades in** all sorts of second-hand odds and ends.*

send VERB

When you **send** something to someone, you arrange for it to be delivered to them.

dispatch
*"Yes, sir, we **dispatched** your order this morning," came the reply.*

mail
*My auntie in America said she had **mailed** my birthday card.*

post
*School reports are **posted** to our parents at the end of each term.*

sense (1) NOUN

Sense is the ability to think and behave sensibly.

common sense
*Rimon had the **common sense** to tell Mrs Milner what he had seen.*

intelligence
*My brother does such silly things, I sometimes wonder about his level of **intelligence**!*

reason
*The customer almost lost her temper, but finally saw **reason**.*

wisdom
*Aslan was a creature of great knowledge and **wisdom**.*

wit
*Thank goodness Francis had the **wit** to phone for an ambulance!*

sense (2) NOUN

A **sense** of a word is one of its meanings.

connotation
*Even simple words sometimes have more than one **connotation**.*

meaning
*I asked Mr Hammond which **meaning** of the word "sink" he meant.*

sensible ADJECTIVE

If a person or idea is **sensible**, they show good sense and judgment.

practical
*It wouldn't really be **practical** to run a restaurant on Mount Everest.*

prudent
*Mrs Svensson praised us for being **prudent** when we crossed the road.*

rational
*The paramedic was able to remain calm and **rational** in an emergency.*

realistic
*"It is not **realistic** to expect to win every game," Mrs Fern told the team.*

wise
*The **wise** old wizard was always willing to advise others.*

ANTONYMS: foolish, impractical

sensitive (1) ADJECTIVE

If you are **sensitive**, you are easily upset about something.

easily upset
*She is **easily upset** when people won't eat her cooking.*

thin-skinned
*Kim is very **thin-skinned**, and cries easily.*

touchy
*My dad's rather **touchy** about the dent in his car.*

sensitive (2) ADJECTIVE

If something is **sensitive**, it is easily affected or harmed.

delicate
*The dragonfly's wings were far too **delicate** to touch.*

fine
*The baby has to stay out of the sun because of her **fine** skin.*

responsive
*Some flowers are **responsive** to daylight. They close at night.*

separate (1) ADJECTIVE

If something is **separate** from something else, the two things are not connected.

apart
*The new pupil stood slightly **apart** from the others.*

detached
***Detached** houses are not joined to others.*

individual
*I love the **individual** chocolate desserts Mum sometimes buys us as a treat.*

a b c d e f g h i j k l m n o p q r s t u v w x y z

isolated
*Our holiday cottage was **isolated** – not another soul for miles!*

ANTONYMS: connected, together

→ *See* **alone (1)**

PRONUNCIATION TIP
When it is an adjective, **separate** is pronounced **sep**-ar-it.

---

separate (2) VERB

If you **separate** people or things, you cause them to be apart from each other.

detach
*The courageous railwayman managed to **detach** the blazing wagon from the rest of the train.*

disconnect
*Our television would not work as the aerial had been **disconnected**.*

divide
*A curtain **divided** the kitchen area from the rest of the bedsit.*

part
*Dad **parted** the fighting dogs with a bucket of cold water.*

split
*"Why not **split** the chocolate and each have some?" Mum suggested.*

ANTONYM: join

PRONUNCIATION TIP
When it is a verb, **separate** is pronounced **sep**-ar-ate.

---

series NOUN

A **series** is a number of things coming one after the other.

sequence
*The author had written a **sequence** of detective novels.*

string
*For five years, United had a **string** of soccer successes.*

succession
*We'd waited for ages, then a **succession** of buses came at once.*

serious (1) ADJECTIVE

A **serious** problem or situation is very bad and worrying.

critical
*The car engine was in a **critical** state: any longer without oil would have finished it.*

grave
*A sombre announcement came from the palac the king's condition was **grave**, and people should prepare for the worst.*

severe
*X-rays showed that Ken had a **severe** fracture of the ankle.*

serious (2) ADJECTIVE

Serious matters are important and should be thought about carefully.

important
*Sally felt that her best friend's request was too **important** to turn down.*

significant
*Oxygen made a **significant** difference to Hillary's chances of reaching the summit.*

weighty
*"This is a **weighty** matter," said the prime minister, "and is not to be ignored."*

serious (3) ADJECTIVE

If you are **serious** about something, you really mean it.

committed
*"You have to be **committed** to the game if yo want to stay in the team," the coach said.*

determined
*Nisha was quite **determined** when it came to her career.*

sincere
*The millionaire's offer sounded too generous, but he was **sincere** about it.*

serious (4) ADJECTIVE

People who are **serious** are thoughtful, quiet and do not laugh much.

grave
*Uncle Arthur was **grave** and quiet over lunch.*

solemn
*Usually **solemn**, Laith roared with laughter at Petra's joke.*

stern
*Although Mrs Jansen is a **stern** teacher, I enjoy her lessons.*

erve (1) VERB

When someone **serves** customers in a shop, bar or restaurant, they help them and supply them with what they want.

assist
*"May I **assist** you?" said the lady in the cosmetics department.*

attend to
*Naturally enough, the staff **attended to** the people at the front of the queue first.*

wait on
*We were **waited on** by my sister's friend.*

erve (2) VERB

If you **serve** food or drink to people, you give it to them.

distribute
*The kind women **distributed** food to the earthquake victims.*

dole out
*As the prisoners queued, food was **doled out** into their bowls.*

→ *See* **provide**

et (1) NOUN

A **set** is a group of things that go together.

batch
*I burnt the first **batch** of scones, but the second set were delicious.*

collection
*Carter has a superb **collection** of stamps.*

group
*Mrs Crouch hung the paintings in a **group** on the art room wall.*

LANGUAGE TIP
Two things that make a set are called a **pair**.

---

et (2) VERB

If you **set** something, you decide on it.

decide on
*Mum and Dad **decided on** 9.30 as our starting time.*

determine
*It was **determined** that 007 would be the agent's number.*

establish
*Manchester was **established** as the company's headquarters.*

fix
*Qasim and I **fixed** a time to meet up.*

set (3) VERB

To **set** can mean to become firm or hard.

harden
*The cat ran over the cement before it had **hardened**.*

solidify
*The sour milk had **solidified** in a rather unpleasant manner.*

set off; also **set out** VERB

If you **set off** or **set out** on a journey, you start it.

depart
*Frodo and his companion **departed** before anyone else was awake.*

leave
*We **left** for our holidays before I had really woken up.*

settle VERB

If you **settle** something, you decide or arrange it.

agree
*"We need to **agree** a date for the first rehearsal," said Rachel.*

decide
*Have you **decided** where the party's going to be?*

resolve
*The captain is still trying to **resolve** the problem of the stowaway.*

shake VERB

If something **shakes**, it moves from side to side or up and down with small, quick movements.

jolt
*The old jalopy **jolted** along the bumpy roads.*

quiver
*When the dog saw the rabbit, it started **quivering** with excitement.*

shiver
*Such was the cold that the explorers **shivered** constantly.*

shudder
*When it struck the iceberg, the whole vessel **shuddered**.*

tremble
*Mr Brownlow found the orphan on his doorstep, **trembling** with cold.*

vibrate
*On the cobbled French roads, the whole vehicle **vibrated**.*

A B C D E F G H I J K L M N O P Q R S T U V W X Y Z

shape NOUN

The **shape** of someone or something is the form or pattern of their outline.

build
From his shadow, it looked like the man had a burly ***build****.*

figure
My mum has a good ***figure****.*

form
The mythological centaur took the ***form*** *of a horse with the head of a man.*

outline
The designer sketched the ***outline*** *of the car.*

silhouette
The police officer could clearly see the attacker's ***silhouette*** *on the blind.*

→ Have a look at the **Illustration** page!

share (1) VERB

If two people **share** something, they both use it, do it or have it.

distribute
After our service, the harvest produce was ***distributed*** *among old people of the area.*

divide
We ***divided*** *the rest of the cake between us.*

go halves (*informal*)
My brother and I ***went halves*** *on the cost of the bike.*

split
The four of us ***split*** *the sweets between us.*

share (2) NOUN

A **share** of something is a portion of it.

portion
I asked for a small ***portion*** *of pie.*

quota
Each state school receives its ***quota*** *of the country's education money.*

ration
During wartime, food ***rations*** *were very restricted.*

sharp (1) ADJECTIVE

A **sharp** object has an edge or point that is good for cutting or piercing things.

jagged
Jagged *rocks tore a hole in the ship's hull.*

pointed
All that the peasant had with which to defend himself was a ***pointed*** *stick.*

razor-sharp
"Be careful," warned Dad. "That is a ***razor-sharp*** *knife."*

ANTONYM: blunt

sharp (2) ADJECTIVE

Someone who is **sharp** can pick up ideas very quickly.

alert
The ***alert*** *watchman noticed flames coming from the warehouse.*

astute
"It was ***astute*** *of you to see that the swimmer was in trouble," the manager told the lifeguard.*

observant
The wanted man was spotted by an ***observant*** *police officer.*

perceptive
"Michael is a very ***perceptive*** *young man and will go far," said Professor Peabody.*

quick-witted
A ***quick-witted*** *guard punctured the getaway car's tyres.*

ANTONYM: slow

sharp (3) ADJECTIVE

A **sharp** pain is strong and sudden.

acute
Grandad complained of an ***acute*** *pain in his stomach.*

intense
That first night, Crusoe had an ***intense*** *feeling of loneliness.*

sharp (4) ADJECTIVE

A **sharp** picture is well-defined and not blurred.

clear
After the rain, the view of the distant hills was beautifully ***clear****.*

distinct
Dad fiddled with the focus on the projector until the picture was ***distinct****.*

well-defined
The security camera produced ***well-defined*** *pictures of the bank robber.*

ANTONYM: blurred

SHAPES

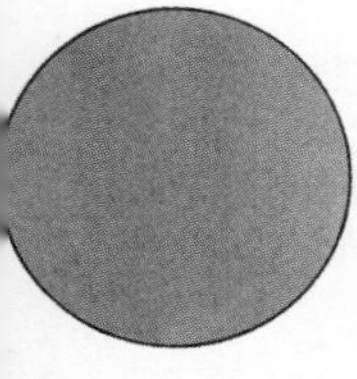
circle

square

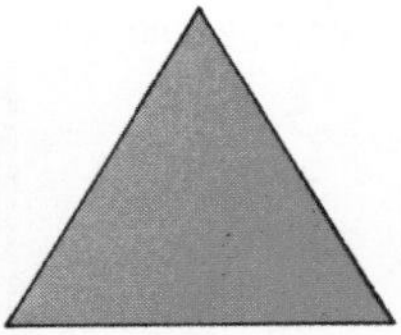
triangle

rectangle

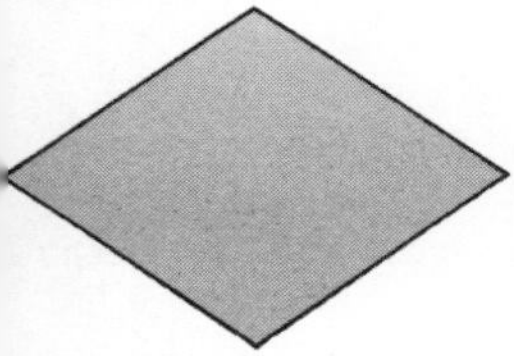
diamond

star

semicircle

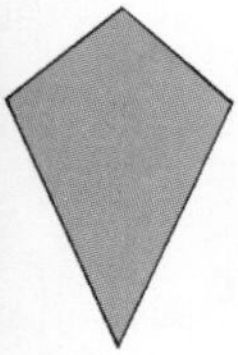
kite

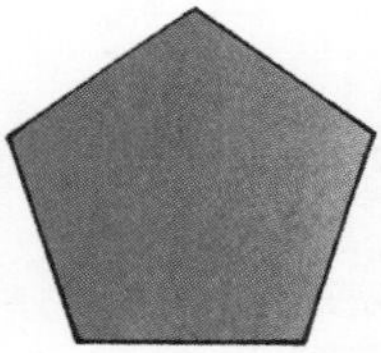
pentagon

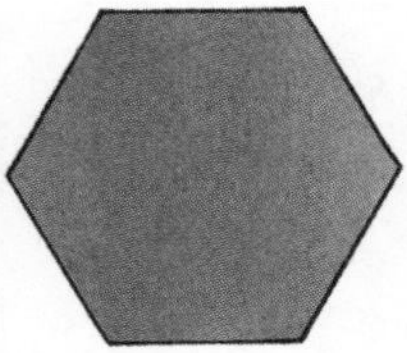
hexagon

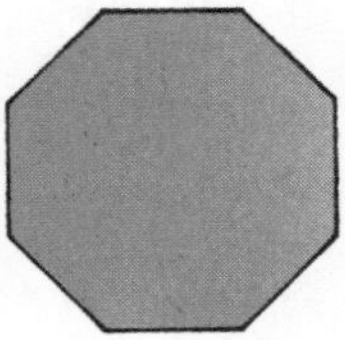
octagon

cuboid

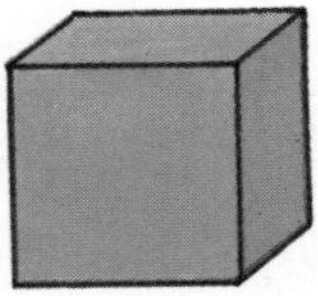
cube

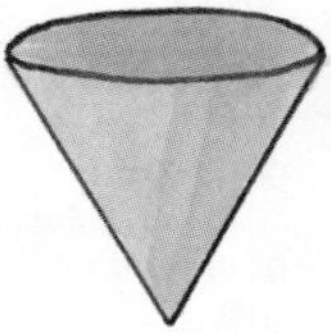
cone

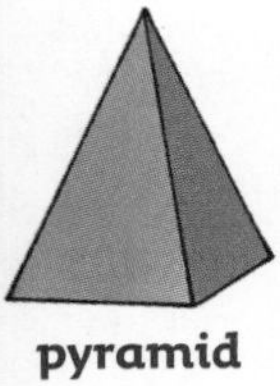
pyramid

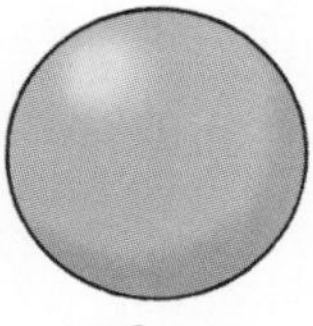
sphere

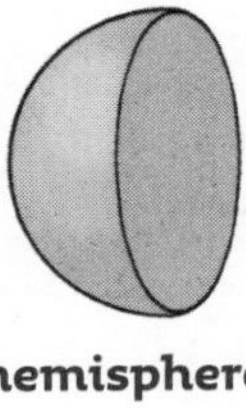
hemisphere

cylinder

A
B
C
D
E
F
G
H
I
J
K
L
M
N
O
P
Q
R
S
T
U
V
W
X
Y
Z

shelter (1) VERB

To **shelter** someone or something means to protect them from bad weather or danger.

protect
*A tree may not **protect** you from a lightning strike in a storm.*

safeguard
*The knight promised the king that he would **safeguard** the princess from danger.*

shield
*The bus shelter **shielded** us from the worst of the rain.*

shelter (2) NOUN

If a place gives **shelter**, it protects you from bad weather or danger.

haven
*A country cottage was the pop star's **haven** from all the publicity.*

protection
*Although small, the umbrella offered some **protection** from the rain.*

refuge
*They took **refuge** from the storm in an old barn.*

sanctuary
*In medieval times, churches offered **sanctuary** to outlaws on the run.*

shine (1) VERB

When something **shines**, it is bright because it gives out or reflects light.

gleam
*Gran's polished brass **gleamed** on the sideboard.*

glint
*Excalibur, the enchanted sword, **glinted** above the lake.*

glisten
*Snow lay everywhere, and the treetops **glistened**.*

glitter
*I made a birthday card for Mum and covered it with little bits of something that **glittered**.*

shimmer
*We watched the ferry set sail across the sea, which was **shimmering** in the sunlight.*

sparkle
*The duchess's diamond **sparkled** in the candlelight.*

LANGUAGE TIP
Something that shines in the dark is **luminous**.

---

shine (2) NOUN

If something has a **shine**, its surface shines.

gloss
*You varnish something to put a **gloss** on it.*

radiance
*A coal fire on a winter's night gives out a lovely **radiance**.*

sheen
*Kalila brushed her pony until its coat had a **sheen**.*

shiny ADJECTIVE

Shiny things are bright and look as if they have been polished.

gleaming
*After I'd finished, Mum's car was **gleaming**.*

glistening
***Glistening** icicles dangled from frozen roofs.*

glossy
*I like to brush my hair until it is **glossy**.*

sleek
*My uncle drew up in a **sleek** new sports car.*

ANTONYM: dull

ship NOUN

A **ship** is a large boat that carries passengers or cargo.

boat
***Boats** range in size from tiny dinghies to supertankers.*

craft
*The estuary was crammed with **craft**.*

vessel
*Before that fateful day, everyone thought the Titanic was an unsinkable **vessel**.*

shiver VERB

When you **shiver**, you tremble slightly because you are cold or scared.

quake
*My aunt **quakes** with fear whenever there's a thunderstorm.*

quiver
*The bomb-disposal expert's hand **quivered** for a moment as he went to cut the wire.*

shake
*Jake sat **shaking** in front of the fire until his cold, wet clothes had dried off.*

shudder
*As we sat at the bus stop in the snow, I started **shuddering** with the cold.*

tremble
*Bonnie **trembled** at the thought of the test coming up.*

shocking ADJECTIVE

Something **shocking** upsets you because it is unpleasant and unexpected.

appalling
*"I think it's **appalling** that they want to demolish that lovely building!" Mum exclaimed.*

dreadful
*When the climber fell so far it was a **dreadful** experience, but she came out of it unscathed.*

horrifying
*It was **horrifying** to think how close we came to having an accident.*

outrageous
*The major considered it **outrageous** not to wear a tie at dinner.*

shoot VERB

To **shoot** can mean to fire a gun.

discharge
*The first mate **discharged** his musket, killing one of the pirates.*

fire
*"Starboard guns – **fire**!" bellowed the captain.*

open fire
*As the battleship swung round, its huge guns **opened fire**.*

shop NOUN

A **shop** is a place where things are sold.

LANGUAGE TIP
A shopping centre, if it is pedestrianised (no cars allowed), is called a **mall** or a **precinct**.

shopping NOUN

Your **shopping** is the goods you have bought in a shop.

goods
*The notice read, "Customers may collect large **goods** from the rear of the store".*

purchases
*People put their **purchases** in baskets or trolleys when they go round supermarkets.*

short (1) ADJECTIVE

Something **short** does not last very long.

brief
*After a **brief** pause to clear her throat, Mrs McQueen began to speak.*

fleeting
*The birdwatcher caught a **fleeting** glimpse of the eagle.*

momentary
*At the end of the concert there was a **momentary** silence, followed by applause.*

short-lived
*The singer's success was **short-lived** – after one hit he faded from the limelight.*

short-term
*String provided a **short-term** solution for our car's dangling exhaust pipe.*

temporary
*There was a **temporary** delay while the train driver ate his sandwiches.*

ANTONYM: long

short (2) ADJECTIVE

Someone or something **short** is small in height, length or distance.

dumpy
*She looked at her **dumpy** figure in the mirror.*

little
*A **little** distance ahead the road divided and we weren't sure which way to go.*

low
*There was a **low** outbuilding round the back of the house.*

small
*"It's only a **small** hill – you will all get up it," Mr Barraclough encouraged everyone.*

squat
*The cottage we stayed in on holiday was a **squat** little place with windows in the roof.*

wee
*At the foot of the mountain, beside the loch, stood a **wee** house.*

ANTONYMS: tall, long

LANGUAGE TIP
The word **wee** is used mainly in Scotland.

short (3) ADJECTIVE

If something is in **short** supply, you do not have enough of it.

limited
*As a result of the ban, water was **limited** and had to be rationed.*

scarce
*During the war, food was very **scarce** and people became hungry.*

ANTONYM: abundant

short (4) ADJECTIVE

A **short** piece of writing is not very long.

brief
*"Write a **brief** description of your house," Mr Coopland told us.*

concise
*Entries in a dictionary should be **concise** and not too long-winded.*

succinct
*Mum wrote a **succinct** letter to the council about parking on our street.*

ANTONYM: lengthy

shortage NOUN

If there is a **shortage** of something, there is not enough of it.

deficiency
*A **deficiency** of vitamin C gave 18th-century sailors a disease called scurvy.*

lack
*Owing to a **lack** of support, the show has been cancelled.*

scarcity
*The **scarcity** of houses led to a rise in prices.*

shortfall
*There is a 5000-person **shortfall** in recruitment for the army.*

LANGUAGE TIP

A shortage of food is a **famine**. A shortage of water is a **drought**.

---

shot (1) NOUN

A **shot** is the sound of a gun being fired.

blast
*One **blast** of the colonel's shotgun scared the tiger away.*

report
*The **report** of a gun was heard deep in the jungle.*

shot (2) NOUN (*informal*)

If you have a **shot** at doing something, you try to do it.

attempt
*Before 1953, there were many unsuccessful **attempts** to climb Everest.*

crack (*informal*)
*"I'll have a **crack** at the mission, sir!" the lieutenant said.*

effort
*The American golfer resolved to have one last **effort** for the title.*

try
*"I'm going to have a **try** at the painting competition," I told Mum and Dad.*

shout (1) VERB

If you **shout** something, you say it very loudly.

bawl
*The sergeant major **bawled** at everyone, including his wife.*

bellow
*"Don't go!" **bellowed** Bilbo. "I'm trapped!"*

call
*I could hear someone **calling** my name but I couldn't see anyone.*

yell
*As a toddler, I used to **yell** every time I had my hair cut.*

ANTONYM: whisper

shout (2) VERB

If you **shout** at someone, you speak angrily to them.

rant
*Striding up and down, the corporal **ranted** at his platoon.*

rave
*The prisoner paced in his cell, **raving** and tearing his hair.*

roar
*From the other side of the field, we could hear Mr Philpot **roaring** in anger.*

show (1) VERB

If you **show** someone how to do something, you demonstrate it to them.

demonstrate
*"Allow me to **demonstrate**, madam," said the salesman.*

instruct
Mr Klein ***instructed*** *us on how to give first aid.*

teach
Miranda's friend ***taught*** *her how to ride.*

show (2) VERB
If you **show** something, you let someone see it.

display
Our school's sports trophies are ***displayed*** *in a cabinet.*

exhibit
Mrs Sherringham arranged for us to ***exhibit*** *our art in the local town hall.*

present
In court, one lawyer ***presents*** *the case for the prosecution, another for the defence.*

show (3) VERB
If you **show** something to someone, you prove it.

demonstrate
Brunel ***demonstrated*** *the power of the screw propeller.*

prove
"This display will ***prove*** *my amazing powers!" announced the magician.*

show (4) VERB
If a picture **shows** someone or something, it represents or depicts them.

depict
The Mona Lisa ***depicts*** *a young lady with a curious smile.*

illustrate
I drew a diagram to ***illustrate*** *the water cycle.*

portray
Painters like Monet ***portrayed*** *everything in terms of colour and light.*

represent
In Van Gogh's picture, the orange circle ***represents*** *the rising moon.*

show (5) VERB
If you **show** someone to a room or seat, you lead them there.

direct
"Please could you ***direct*** *me to the airport?" the tourist asked.*

escort
At the theatre, an usher ***escorted*** *us to our seats.*

guide
An elderly lady ***guided*** *us round the museum.*

show (6) NOUN
A **show** is a display or exhibition.

display
Our year group put on a gymnastics ***display****.*

exhibition
I decided to enter some of my photographs in the ***exhibition****.*

presentation
Our class ***presentation*** *of the term's work was a great success.*

show (7) NOUN
A **show** is a form of entertainment at the theatre or on television.

concert
Everyone enjoyed the ***concert*** *given by the school orchestra.*

presentation
Before the film started, there were trailers for future ***presentations****.*

production
For our Christmas ***production****, we are going to do 'Oliver'.*

show off VERB (*informal*)
If someone is **showing off**, they are trying to impress people.

boast
Quasim ***boasted*** *about his new trainers.*

brag
Verrucca kept ***bragging*** *that her parents were wealthy.*

crow
If someone wins at sport, they do not need to ***crow*** *about it.*

flaunt
Our next-door neighbour is very wealthy, but doesn't like to ***flaunt*** *it.*

gloat
Dursley was always ***gloating*** *about Harry's situation.*

swagger
My cousin ***swaggered*** *around in his new soccer kit.*

shrill ADJECTIVE
A **shrill** sound is loud and high-pitched, like a whistle.

high-pitched
The sound was so ***high-pitched*** *he had to clap his hands over his ears.*

piercing
*Johnny let out a **piercing** cry when the animal bit him.*

screeching
*The children knew that there was an owl outside. It kept them awake with its **screeching** call.*

sharp
*The signal was to be a **sharp** blast on the captain's whistle.*

shrink VERB

If something **shrinks**, it becomes smaller.

contract
*When you cook spinach, it **contracts** to half the size.*

diminish
*With each step we took, the distance between us and home **diminished**.*

dwindle
*As the days passed, the shipwreck survivors' supplies gradually **dwindled**.*

shrivel
*When grapes are dried, they **shrivel** to become currants and raisins.*

wither
*Without water, the plant had **withered** and died.*

ANTONYM: grow

shut VERB

If you **shut** something, you close it.

close
*Mum asked me to **close** the drawer before someone banged into it.*

fasten
*"**Fasten** the gate so the dogs don't escape," my sister called.*

lock
***Locked** out of her house, Sonya sat on the steps and waited for her mum to get home.*

push to
*"Please **push** the door **to** on your way out," Mrs Dharawal requested.*

seal
*I **sealed** my sandwich box firmly, to make sure the sandwiches stayed fresh.*

ANTONYM: open

shut up VERB (*informal*)

If you tell someone to **shut up**, you want them to stop talking.

hush
*"**Hush**, I thought I heard a noise," Nadine said urgently.*

keep quiet
*"Please **keep quiet** in the library", the notice read.*

pipe down (*informal*)
*I wish my little brother would **pipe down** sometimes. He's always talking!*

shy ADJECTIVE

A **shy** person is quiet and uncomfortable in the company of other people.

bashful
*With her head down and a **bashful** expression, my little sister began to sing her song.*

reserved
*The new girl was quite **reserved**, so everyone tried to make her feel welcome.*

self-conscious
*"I'm not normally **self-conscious**, but I hate wearing fancy dress," said Chane.*

timid
*"Excuse me, but am I in the right room?" the **timid** newcomer enquired.*

ANTONYM: confident

sick (1) ADJECTIVE

If you are **sick**, you are ill.

in poor health
*Grandad had been **in poor health** for some time, but is now on the road to recovery.*

poorly
*As Petra felt **poorly**, she asked to go home early.*

under the weather (*informal*)
*"I'm sorry to hear your mum's **under the weather**," Mrs Roberts said.*

unwell
*Because the opera singer felt **unwell**, his part was taken by an understudy.*

ANTONYM: well

sick (2) ADJECTIVE

If you feel **sick**, you feel as if you are going to vomit.

ill
*After my third slice of cake I started to feel **ill**, so I declined a fourth.*

nauseous
*The smell coming from the factory was enough to make anyone feel **nauseous**.*

queasy
*"Please can I sit in the front? I always feel **queasy** when I sit in the back," complained my sister.*

sick of ADJECTIVE

If you are **sick of** doing something, you think you have been doing it for too long.

bored with
*After a few minutes, I become **bored with** computer games.*

fed up with
***Fed up with** the constant thud of music, Dad finally came and asked us to turn it down.*

tired of
*Duncan was **tired of** his sister bossing him around.*

side (1) NOUN

The **sides** of something are its different surfaces or edges.

The side of...

an army is called a **flank**.
a dice is called a **face**.
a page is called a **margin**.
a river is called a **bank** or **shore**.
a road is called a **curb** or **verge**.
a table is called an **edge**.

side (2) NOUN

The two **sides** in a war, argument, game or relationship are the two people or groups involved.

camp
*"You cannot switch **camps** halfway through," Miss Parvinder warned before the debate.*

faction
*There was much disagreement between different **factions** in the government.*

party
*Dad supports a different political **party** from Mum.*

team
*My favourite soccer **team** comes from Manchester, but it's not United!*

sign (1) NOUN

A **sign** is a board or notice with words, a picture or a symbol on it, giving information or a warning.

notice
*The estate agent came round and put up a "For Sale" **notice** outside our house.*

placard
*The protesters marched through the streets with their **placards** held high.*

poster
*For our class show, we made a **poster** for the school board.*

sign (2) NOUN

A **sign** is a mark or other piece of evidence that tells you something.

clue
*Police brought in dogs to hunt for **clues** about the crime.*

hint
*The pains in his chest were a **hint** that he should take it easy.*

indication
*A red traffic light is an **indication** that drivers should stop.*

warning
*There had been no **warning** that the earthquake was going to hit the town.*

sign (3) NOUN

A **sign** is a mark or symbol that always has a particular meaning.

emblem
*Certain **emblems** are used to hallmark silver.*

symbol
*The cross is an important **symbol** of Christianity.*

signal (1) NOUN

A **signal** is a gesture, sound or action that is meant to give a message to someone.

gesture
*With a sweeping **gesture**, the conductor thanked the orchestra.*

indication
*Mrs Scowcroft's pointing finger was an **indication** that I was in big trouble.*

A B C D E F G H I J K L M N O P Q R S T U V W X Y Z

sign
Some people think that seeing a magpie is a ***sign*** *of bad luck.*

LANGUAGE TIP
The hand signals that deaf people use to communicate with are called **sign language**.

➔ Have a look at the **Illustration** page!

signal (2) VERB

If you **signal**, you make a gesture, sound or action that is meant to give a message to someone.

gesticulate
The police officer ***gesticulated*** *angrily at the driver to stop.*

gesture
Mrs Ameobi silently ***gestured*** *to us to listen carefully.*

motion
Dad ***motioned*** *for me to come towards him quietly, so as not to disturb the baby.*

wave
My idiotic friend Byron kept ***waving*** *to people he didn't know.*

silence NOUN

When there is **silence**, there is no sound.

hush
As the eclipse's shadow moved across the sun, a ***hush*** *fell on the land.*

peace
The ***peace*** *of the hillside was shattered by the deafening noise of a jet fighter.*

quiet
City people are often disturbed by the ***quiet*** *of the countryside.*

stillness
Somewhere in the ***stillness*** *of the ancient monastery, a low bell began to toll.*

silent (1) ADJECTIVE

If a place is **silent**, there is no sound.

hushed
The lights went down and the theatre was ***hushed****, waiting for the show to begin.*

quiet
"A ***quiet*** *atmosphere is essential when you're trying to write," Mrs Angel insisted.*

soundless
The night was ***soundless****: the sheep lay asleep and the stars shone brightly.*

still
Apart from the soft burble of the stream, all in the valley was ***still****.*

ANTONYM: noisy

silent (2) ADJECTIVE

If you are **silent**, you are not saying anything.

dumb
Struck ***dumb*** *with surprise, Charlie watched the ground disappear beneath him.*

lost for words
For once, Mrs St John was ***lost for words*** *at her leaving party.*

mute
The audience was ***mute*** *with admiration after the marvellous performance by the singer.*

noiseless
With ***noiseless*** *steps, Barney crept to the edge of the dump.*

speechless
Dad was ***speechless*** *with rage at the sight of his wrecked greenhouse.*

tongue-tied
When it came to present the bouquet, my sister was ***tongue-tied****.*

silly (1) ADJECTIVE

Something that is **silly** is foolish.

absurd
"Humans on Mars! Don't be ***absurd****," Grandad muttered.*

daft
When my brother won the raffle, he just stood there with a ***daft*** *grin on his face.*

idiotic
Although Tyree's idea was an ***idiotic*** *one, I went along with it.*

ridiculous
My uncle tells ***ridiculous*** *tales about kippers swimming and haggis flying.*

ANTONYM: sensible

silly (2) ADJECTIVE

Someone who is **silly** is childish.

daft
Although it is ***daft*** *to laugh when others are being serious, I sometimes can't help it!*

immature
"I want no more ***immature*** *behaviour in this classroom!" exclaimed Mr Ince.*

SIGNALS

buoy

bell

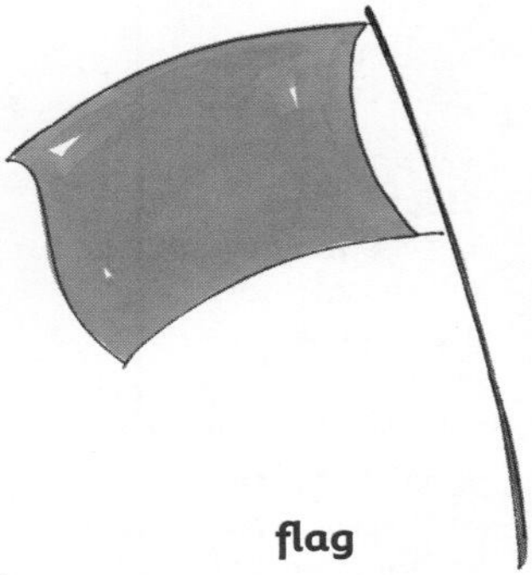

flag

flare

road sign

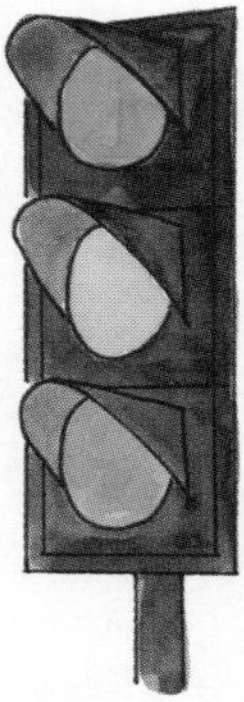

traffic light

whistle

Some other types of signal:

alarm	beacon	beeper	bicycle bell	car horn
foghorn	hooter	pager	siren	smoke

A B C D E F G H I J K L M N O P Q R S T U V W X Y Z

irresponsible
*"Playing with matches is an **irresponsible** thing to do," Mum told me severely.*

ANTONYM: sensible

simple ADJECTIVE

Something that is **simple** is easy to understand or do.

clear
*The instructions were **clear**, but somehow we still messed it up!*

elementary
*Sherlock Holmes believed that detective work was **elementary** for anybody.*

straightforward
*Fortunately, Gran's operation was a **straightforward** one.*

uncomplicated
*Boiling is an **uncomplicated** way to cook an egg.*

understandable
*It was an **understandable** mistake for anyone to make.*

ANTONYM: complicated

single ADJECTIVE

A **single** thing is only one and not more.

individual
*In the cloakroom we each have **individual** pegs.*

separate
*On holiday, we all had **separate** rooms.*

sole
*My brother's **sole** reason for being nice to me was to borrow my bike.*

solitary
*I couldn't find a **solitary** book on the subject that we'd been told to read about.*

ANTONYM: multiple

LANGUAGE TIP
If there is only a single one of something in the world, it is **unique**.

sit VERB

When you **sit**, you rest your bottom on something such as a chair or the floor.

be seated
*"Please **be seated**," Ratty said to Mole.*

perch
*There were no chairs left, so I **perched** on the radiator.*

settle
*Grandad **settled** in an armchair, and promptly fell asleep.*

ANTONYM: stand

situation (1) NOUN

A **situation** is what is happening in a particular place at a particular time.

case
*Dale was usually at home but, in this **case**, was nowhere to be found.*

circumstances
*The running track was wet, so in the **circumstances** my time was a good one.*

plight
*With sharks all around, the swimmer found himself in a terrible **plight**.*

position
*The prime minister said that the current economic **position** was a good one.*

state of affairs
*"I'm afraid this **state of affairs** will not do," our head teacher warned us.*

situation (2) NOUN

The **situation** of a town or a building is its surroundings and its position.

location
*The **location** of the ranch was outside town.*

setting
*What a **setting** for a picnic: white sand, turquoise sea and waving palm trees!*

site
*Being close to the railway station, the **site** for the new hotel was ideal.*

size (1) NOUN

The **size** of something is how big it is.

dimensions
*We had to know the fridge's **dimensions** to see if it would fit our kitchen.*

proportions
*In the tropics, plants grow to huge **proportions**.*

size (2) NOUN

The **size** of something can mean the fact that it is very large.

immensity
*As the mountaineers looked up at Everest, they realised the **immensity** of the task.*

magnitude
*Believe it or not, most stars have a far greater **magnitude** than our sun.*

vastness
*Crusoe marvelled at the **vastness** of the ocean around his island.*

skill NOUN

Skill is the knowledge and ability that enable you to do something well.

expertise
*When I was doing my homework, Mum's **expertise** with a computer came in useful.*

knack
*There's a **knack** to blowing bubbles.*

proficiency
*After three years of classes, my auntie had acquired some **proficiency** at painting.*

talent
*Sabra had a **talent** for acting, but was she tough enough to make it a career?*

technique
*Driving a racing car requires a different **technique** from driving a normal car.*

skin (1) NOUN

Skin is the natural covering of a person or animal.

coat
*Before the cat show, we brushed Tibbles' **coat** to make her shiny.*

hide
*The **hides** of cattle are tanned to make leather.*

skin (2) NOUN

Skin is the outer covering of a fruit or vegetable.

peel
*Orange **peel** is not always easy to remove.*

rind
*Mum added finely chopped lemon **rind** to the cake mixture.*

skip VERB

When you **skip**, you step forward and hop, first with one foot and then the other.

bounce
*She jumped up in delight and **bounced** over to greet him.*

caper
*The jester made jokes and **capered** before the king.*

dance
*To their delight, a butterfly **danced** lightly amongst the grass in front of them.*

hop
*She **hopped** over the rope as they spun it faster and faster.*

leap
*He tried to catch her, but she **leaped** away, laughing wildly.*

sleep (1) VERB

When you **sleep**, you close your eyes and your whole body rests.

doze
*Despite our music, Claire **dozed** in her rocking chair.*

kip (*informal*)
*When we were on holiday we all **kipped** after lunch as it was too hot to play outside.*

slumber
*Goldilocks still **slumbered** as the bears approached their house.*

snooze
*The pier was full of people **snoozing** in deckchairs.*

take a nap
*"If you're tired, **take a nap**," my mum suggested.*

LANGUAGE TIP
Animals that **hibernate** spend the winter in a state like a deep sleep.

---

sleep (2) NOUN

A **sleep** is when you close your eyes and your whole body rests.

doze
*"I think I'll have a **doze**," Grandad said, from the depths of his armchair.*

kip (*informal*)
*"If you want a **kip**, that's okay by me," my sister said.*

nap
*Sneezewort was taking a **nap** when the doorbell rang.*

rest
*Before he set out, Mole felt a short **rest** was called for.*

A B C D E F G H I J K L M N O P Q R S T U V W X Y Z

siesta
*Because of the heat, many Mediterranean people have an afternoon **siesta**.*

slumber
*The prince awoke from his **slumber** to find a frog on his pillow.*

snooze
*It was amazing that the driver could have a **snooze** just before the race.*

sleepy ADJECTIVE

If you are **sleepy**, you are tired and feel like sleeping.

drowsy
*After the meal he felt pleasantly **drowsy**.*

tired
*After playing out for three hours, I felt **tired**.*

ANTONYM: wide-awake

slide VERB

When something **slides**, it moves smoothly over or against something else.

glide
*Good skaters **glide** gracefully over the ice.*

skid
*To prevent **skidding** on icy roads, the council spreads salt and grit on them.*

skim
*The stone I threw **skimmed** gracefully across the water.*

slip
*The toddler's feet **slipped** from under him and he fell on his bottom.*

slither
*The colourful rock snake **slithered** slowly over the ground.*

slight ADJECTIVE

Something that is **slight** is small in amount or degree.

insignificant
*"Don't trouble me with **insignificant** details," the prime minister snapped.*

minor
*Mr Iversen's arthritis was only a **minor** inconvenience for him on the walk.*

small
*Just a **small** amount of some spices can make a big difference to the flavour of a dish.*

trivial
*It didn't seem worth bothering Dad with such a **trivial** matter.*

slim ADJECTIVE

A **slim** person has very little fat.

slender
*My sister has always been quite **slender**.*

trim
*After some weeks at her keep-fit class, Mum was pleased at how **trim** she looked.*

slip (1) VERB

If you **slip**, you accidentally lose your balance.

lose your footing
*Having **lost his footing**, the climber dangled from his rope.*

skate
*On the wet floor, my feet **skated** from under me and I landed on my behind.*

skid
*As Kaila came running round the corner she **skidded** on the grass.*

slide
*When the snow hardened, we could **slide** in the playground.*

slither
*We **slithered** our way down the muddy slope.*

slip (2) VERB

If you **slip** somewhere, you go there quickly and quietly.

sneak
*They **sneaked** out of the house while their parents were watching TV.*

steal
*At the dead of night, Ron and Hermione **stole** down the stairs.*

tiptoe
*Mum spotted me **tiptoeing** into the kitchen.*

slippery ADJECTIVE

Something that is **slippery** is smooth, wet or greasy. It is difficult to keep hold of or to walk on.

greasy
*The door handle was so **greasy** he couldn't turn it.*

icy
*Be careful driving as it's very **icy** today.*

oily
*Uncle Manfred's car skidded on an **oily** patch in the road.*

slimy
*Mark tried to hold the soap but it was too wet and **slimy**.*

sloppy (1) ADJECTIVE

Sloppy work is careless or badly done.

messy
*Mr Carr knew Martin's essay would be **messy**.*

slapdash
*"This is **slapdash** stuff, Zara!" Mrs Kureshi barked. "Do it again."*

slipshod
*I was in such a hurry that my maths homework was pretty **slipshod**.*

untidy
*Mum despaired about my brother's **untidy** appearance.*

ANTONYM: careful

sloppy (2) ADJECTIVE

Someone or something that is **sloppy** is sentimental.

romantic
*For Dad, the bunch of flowers was quite a **romantic** gesture.*

slushy (*informal*)
*"I hate those **slushy** films with people kissing in them," Ben said.*

slow ADJECTIVE

Someone or something that is **slow** is moving, happening or doing something with very little speed.

leisurely
*We had a **leisurely** day by the sea, sometimes swimming, sometimes just lazing.*

ponderous
*His steps were heavy and **ponderous** as he came slowly towards us.*

sluggish
*My brother is **sluggish** when it comes to getting ready in the morning.*

unhurried
*Moving at her own **unhurried** pace, the waitress laid the tables.*

ANTONYM: fast

slow down VERB

If something **slows down**, or something slows it down, it moves or happens more slowly.

decelerate
*The jet ski **decelerated** and gently swished up onto the beach.*

reduce speed
*Police warn motorists to **reduce speed** in foggy conditions.*

ANTONYM: accelerate

slowly ADVERB

If something happens **slowly**, it happens with very little speed.

at a snail's pace
*Either side of the roadworks, traffic moved **at a snail's pace**.*

by degrees
***By degrees**, the huge bridge girder was shifted into place.*

gradually
*Despite his lead, the runner realised that the pack was **gradually** gaining.*

unhurriedly
***Unhurriedly**, Mum unfastened the punctured wheel, carefully putting the nuts aside.*

ANTONYM: rapidly

sly ADJECTIVE

Someone who is **sly** is good at tricking people in a not very nice way.

crafty
*You have to watch him because he's a **crafty** little boy.*

cunning
*She seems charming, but actually she can be quite **cunning**.*

devious
*They are **devious** when it comes to getting their own way.*

smack VERB

If you **smack** someone, you hit them with your open hand.

slap
*She had the urge to **slap** her annoying little brother.*

spank
*In the olden days, **spanking** children was common.*

a b c d e f g h i j k l m n o p q r s t u v w x y z

A B C D E F G H I J K L M N O P Q R S T U V W X Y Z

small

→ Look at the **Word Power** page!

smart (1) ADJECTIVE

A **smart** person is clean and neatly dressed.

elegant
*Dad looked **elegant** in his dinner suit, dress shirt and bow tie.*

neat
*With the kitchen scissors, my sister helped to make my hair **neat**.*

stylish
*Mr Nemeth was wearing a **stylish** new suit.*

ANTONYM: scruffy

smart (2) ADJECTIVE

A **smart** person is clever.

bright
*Katie was **bright** and hoped to go to university.*

quick-witted
*"You have to be **quick-witted** to appear on quiz shows," observed Grandpa.*

sharp
*A **sharp** lookout spotted the lifeboat.*

smash (1) VERB

If you **smash** something, you break it into a lot of pieces by hitting it or dropping it.

demolish
*Out of control, the truck **demolished** a garage and came to rest in a garden.*

destroy
*Our roof was **destroyed** when the oak tree blew down.*

shatter
*A loose stone flew up and **shattered** our car windscreen.*

smash (2) VERB

To **smash** against something means to hit it with great force.

collide
*In the storm, the ferry **collided** with the pier.*

hammer
*The crane swung round and its great iron ball **hammered** into the building's wall.*

ram
*Propelled by the might of 20 Romans, the huge pole **rammed** into the city gates.*

smell (1) NOUN

A pleasant **smell** is a nice odour or scent.

aroma
*The **aroma** of roasting coffee beans drifted into the street.*

fragrance
*"Why not try our new **fragrance**?" urged the perfume saleswoman.*

perfume
*Scented candles give off a pleasant **perfume**.*

scent
*In the rose garden, the **scent** was almost overpowering.*

smell (2) NOUN

An unpleasant **smell** is an odour or scent that is not nice.

odour
*Will's trainers give off a dreadful **odour**, particularly when he's been running.*

pong (*informal*)
*Some people's feet can give off quite a **pong** when they get wet.*

reek
*The **reek** of cigarette smoke filled the small café we stopped at.*

stench
*The **stench** of the flooded sewers was overpowering.*

stink
*Rotten eggs create a powerful **stink**.*

whiff
*There was a real **whiff** of gas somewhere outside our house.*

LANGUAGE TIP

Pong is an informal word used in Britain and Australia.

smell (3) VERB

If you **smell** something, you notice it with your nose.

scent
*The dogs **scented** a deer nearby and started to bark.*

sniff
*Dad strode out of the hotel door to **sniff** the seaside air.*

small

(1) ADJECTIVE Something **small** is not large in size.

little
*"We're organizing a **little** party for Granny," Mum announced.*

microscopic
*A **microscopic** amount of blood was found on her jacket.*

miniature
*There is also a **miniature** railway which you can ride on.*

minuscule
*He gave a **minuscule** shake of his head.*

minute
*He asked for **minute** details of what had happened.*

teeny weeny *(informal)*
*There was a **teeny weeny** spider in the corner of the room.*

tiny
*From the top of the hill, the cars looked **tiny**.*

(2) ADJECTIVE A **small** person is not large in size.

diminutive
*The giant missed the **diminutive** figure of Jack below his knees.*

petite
*Our neighbour is a **petite** woman.*

slight
*In spite of her **slight** build, the gymnast was very strong.*

(3) ADJECTIVE Something **small** is not large in amount.

meagre
*Copperfield struggled to live on his **meagre** allowance.*

negligible
*In the desert, the annual rainfall is **negligible**.*

paltry
*"Sir, that is a **paltry** sum of money!" Mr Bumble snorted.*

poor
*The wages for a waitress are very **poor**.*

(4) ADJECTIVE Something **small** is not large in importance.

insignificant
*"It's too **insignificant** an issue to argue about," said my friend.*

petty
*"Don't worry me with **petty** matters," said the headteacher, dismissively.*

trifling
*To a millionaire, a thousand pounds is a **trifling** sum.*

unimportant
*Tabloids often put seemingly **unimportant** stories on the front cover.*

→ Also have a look at the **Word Power** page for **big**!

A B C D E F G H I J K L M N O P Q R S T U V W X Y Z

smell (4) VERB

If someone or something **smells** in an unpleasant way, they do not smell very nice.

reek
*My sister **reeked** of Mum's perfume – she'd put on far too much.*

stink
*The car **stank** of petrol after he had overfilled the tank.*

> **Try these lively words and phrases:**
>
> **hum**
> *Dad's socks **hum** a bit, don't they?*
>
> **stink to high heaven**
> *The canal **stinks to high heaven** in the summer.*

smelly ADJECTIVE

Someone or something **smelly** has a strong and unpleasant smell.

evil-smelling
*The witch moved towards the children, holding an **evil-smelling** potion.*

foul-smelling
*Many sewers are less **foul-smelling** than you would think.*

stinking
*I tipped the **stinking** leftovers of the cauliflower cheese into the bin outside.*

smile VERB

When you **smile**, the corners of your mouth move outwards and slightly upwards, because you are pleased or amused.

beam
*Mr Linderoth **beamed** and presented Ganesh with the trophy.*

grin
*Rudy **grinned** as he thought of the trick he had played on Melvin.*

smirk
*"There's nothing to **smirk** about, Laurel," snapped Mrs Dublin.*

ANTONYM: frown

smooth (1) ADJECTIVE

A **smooth** surface has no roughness and no holes in it.

even
*When I had rubbed the surface down, it was **even** enough to paint.*

glassy
*The **glassy** lake reflected the mountains that surrounded it.*

polished
*The **polished** pebbles had been worn down by the sea.*

ANTONYM: rough

smooth (2) ADJECTIVE

Smooth hair or fabric is soft to the touch.

glossy
*Mum's hair always looks very **glossy** when she's been to the hairdresser.*

silky
*After the dog had been in the sea, her coat felt **silky**.*

sleek
*The owner stroked the **sleek** neck of the winning racehorse.*

velvety
*I ran my hand across the **velvety** material.*

→ *See* **shiny**

snack NOUN

A **snack** is a small, quick meal.

bite
*Gran suggested we had a **bite** before our journey.*

nibbles (*informal*)
*Although there was no sit-down meal, **nibbles** were provided.*

refreshments
*At the fête, **refreshments** included hot dogs and burgers.*

snatch VERB

If you **snatch** something, you take it quickly and suddenly.

grab
*The boy **grabbed** an apple from the cart as he ran past.*

grasp
*The prince suddenly **grasped** her hand. "Please help me," he said.*

seize
*Robin Hood **seized** a stick and fought the Sheriff of Nottingham's men.*

sneak VERB
If you **sneak** somewhere, you go there quietly, trying not to be seen or heard.

creep
*Hermione **crept** into the cellar, her heart pounding.*

slink
*The puppy **slunk** away, knowing he'd been naughty.*

slip
*Dressed in black from head to toe, the spy **slipped** past the watchman.*

steal
*Gollum tried to **steal** away from the cave, but he was spotted.*

tiptoe
*As his father snored, Aldo **tiptoed** silently past the door.*

sneaky ADJECTIVE
Someone who is **sneaky** is dishonest or deceitful.

crafty
*My Uncle Fred is a very **crafty** card player.*

deceitful
*Verrucca was a **deceitful** girl who was always telling lies.*

devious
*Kameko was upset by Tamara's **devious** plot to keep the party secret from her.*

dishonest
*Only a **dishonest** person would not hand in a purse they found.*

sly
*The **sly** old witch offered the princess a poisonous apple.*

soft (1) ADJECTIVE
If something is **soft**, it is not hard, stiff or firm.

spongy
*The ball wouldn't bounce on the wet, **spongy** earth of the lawn.*

squashy
*To be at their best, melons should not be too **squashy**.*

supple
*The expensive shoes were made from lovely **supple** leather.*

ANTONYMS: hard, firm

soft (2) ADJECTIVE
If fabric or hair is **soft**, it is nice to touch.

downy
*The hotel bedrooms all have **downy** soft beds with crisp white sheets.*

fleecy
*My waterproof jacket has a **fleecy** lining cold weather.*

furry
*I love hugging Mum when she's wearing her **furry** sweater.*

silky
*Show dogs receive hours of brushing on their **silky** coats.*

velvety
*The tissues were supposed to feel **velvety**, but they didn't to me.*

ANTONYM: coarse

soft (3) ADJECTIVE
If a breeze is **soft**, it is gentle.

gentle
*What had been merely a **gentle** breeze turned into a strong wind.*

light
*A **light** wind billowed the sails and set Columbus on his way.*

soft (4) ADJECTIVE
If lighting is **soft**, it is dim.

dim
*In the **dim** light of the vault, Ron made out two piercing eyes.*

subdued
*A dimmer switch allows you to adjust your lights from bright to **subdued**.*

ANTONYM: bright

soft (5) ADJECTIVE
If a sound is **soft**, it is quiet and gentle.

faint
*From our cottage, we could hear the **faint** wash of the sea on the shore.*

gentle
*From my bedroom I could hear Mum's **gentle** singing in the baby's room.*

muted
*The **muted** sound of conversation came from beyond the heavy oak door.*

soothing
*Soon the hypnotist's **soothing** voice had Kieron in a trance.*

whispering
*The children could hear **whispering** voices coming from behind the closed door.*

ANTONYMS: loud, harsh

soldier NOUN

A **soldier** is a person in an army.

A soldier who...
is new is a **recruit**.
is on guard is a **sentry**.
is based on a ship is a **marine**.
will fight for any country in return for money is a **mercenary**.

solve VERB

If you **solve** a problem or a question, you find a solution or answer to it.

answer
*I sometimes have trouble **answering** the clues in crosswords.*

crack
*Through luck, hard work and sheer brilliance, the Enigma code was **cracked**.*

decipher
***Deciphering** ancient writing on cave walls was Claudia's speciality.*

explain
*The puzzle of the statue's missing jewel was hard to **explain**.*

get to the bottom of
*At last we **got to the bottom of** the mystery.*

work out
*Jiro struggled to **work out** where he made the mistake.*

some ADJECTIVE

You use **some** to refer to a quantity or number when you are not stating the exact quantity or number.

a couple of
*It only takes me **a couple of** minutes to get ready.*

a few
*"Why don't you invite **a few** friends?" Mum suggested.*

a number of
***A number of** tourists got off the bus.*

a quantity of
*Police announced that **a quantity of** diamonds had gone missing.*

one or two
*The charity had expected **one or two** volunteers, but was flooded with offers.*

sometimes ADVERB

Something that happens **sometimes**, happens occasionally, rather than always or never.

at times
***At times**, our dad can get rather irritable.*

every now and then
*Mrs Saha takes us for a class walk **every now and then**.*

from time to time
***From time to time**, we see old Mr Ormerod totter down to the shops.*

now and then
***Now and then**, you'll hear a cuckoo.*

once in a while
***Once in a while**, Mole would long for his cosy home.*

ANTONYMS: always, never

soon ADVERB

If something is going to happen **soon**, it will happen in a very short time.

before long
*When I woke it was bright but, **before long**, the rain had started.*

in a little while
*I kept prodding away at the hole, and **in a little while** I could see daylight.*

presently
*Baldmoney wandered through the trees, **presently** coming to a clearing.*

shortly
*"Another programme will follow **shortly**," the radio announcer informed us.*

ANTONYM: later

sore ADJECTIVE

If part of your body is **sore**, it causes you pain and is uncomfortable.

inflamed
*Dad's **inflamed** knee meant no squash for him.*

painful
*My toe was really **painful** where my clumsy brother had stood on it.*

raw
*Where her boots had rubbed, Meredith's foot was **raw**.*

tender
*Weeks after the kettle accident, Lamar's hand was still **tender**.*

sorry (1) ADJECTIVE

If you are **sorry** about something you have done, you feel sadness or regret because of it.

apologetic
*"It's no use being **apologetic** unless you regret what you've done," said Mr Frost.*

ashamed
*Euan was **ashamed** at having stolen the ruler.*

remorseful
*Tyla was genuinely **remorseful**.*

repentant
*From Hassan's mournful face, his teacher could tell he was truly **repentant**.*

ANTONYM: unashamed

sorry (2) ADJECTIVE

If you are **sorry** for someone else, you feel sympathy towards them.

compassionate
*When Gran died, everybody at Mum's work was **compassionate**.*

sympathetic
*Mr Forlan was **sympathetic** when I explained my difficulty.*

ANTONYM: unsympathetic

sort (1) VERB

If you **sort** things, you arrange them into different groups.

categorise
*Movies are **categorised** according to their suitability for different ages.*

classify
*Mattie **classified** her fossil finds according to geological period.*

grade
*Gravel is **graded** by size as it falls through a series of metal meshes.*

organise
*Mr Morrison told the captains to **organise** us into teams.*

put in order
*Before delivering them, Akil had to **put** the newspapers **in order**.*

sort (2) NOUN

Different **sorts** of something are different types of it.

category
*Books are divided into two main **categories**: fiction and non-fiction.*

class
*The prize bull won every **class** it was entered for.*

group
*Weathermen classify clouds into several different **groups**.*

kind
*It was hard to tell what **kind** of plane it was from so far away.*

type
*My big sister said the film star wasn't her **type** of actor.*

A sort of...

animal is known as a **species**.
book or film is known as a **genre**.
car is known as a **make**.
dog is known as a **breed**.
plant is known as a **variety**.

sort out VERB

If you **sort out** a problem or misunderstanding, you find a solution to it.

clear up
*With a simple explanation, Mrs Earnshaw **cleared up** our misunderstanding.*

deal with
*Dad **dealt with** all the arrangements for the family holiday.*

solve
*Mum **solved** the problem of how to fit all the suitcases into the car.*

sound NOUN

A **sound** is something that you hear.

Sounds a dog makes:

bark	growl	howl	snarl
whimper	whine	yap	

Sounds a cat makes:

mew	miaow	purr	spit	yowl

Sounds an insect makes:

buzz	hum	murmur

a b c d e f g h i j k l m n o p q r s t u v w x y z

Sounds a horse makes:
neigh snort whinny

Some other sounds animals and birds make:

A bull **bellows**.

A cow **lows** or **moos**.

A crow **caws**.

A donkey **brays**.

An elephant **trumpets**.

A frog **croaks**.

A kookaburra **laughs**.

A lion **roars**.

A monkey **chatters**.

A mouse **squeaks**.

An owl **hoots** or **screeches**.

A pig **grunts** or **snuffles**.

A gull **mews** or **screams**.

A sheep **bleats**.

sour ADJECTIVE

If something is **sour**, it has a sharp, acid taste like lemons or vinegar.

acidic
*I don't like the taste of fresh grapefruit – it's too **acidic** for me.*

bitter
***Bitter** medicines often have sweetener added to them.*

sharp
*Lemons taste too **sharp** for most people to eat them whole.*

tart
*The lemon cake was quite **tart**.*

vinegary
*"That salad dressing is too **vinegary** for me," complained Granny.*

LANGUAGE TIP
When milk turns sour it **curdles**.

space (1) NOUN

Space is the area that is empty or available in a place, building or container.

capacity
*The adverts boasted about the **capacity** of the people carrier.*

elbow room
*At the wedding reception, there was little **elbow room** at the tables.*

room
*As there wasn't enough **room** in the flat, we moved to a house.*

volume
*Most of the box's **volume** was taken up by polystyrene packaging.*

space (2) NOUN

Space is the area beyond the earth's atmosphere surrounding the stars and planets.

➔ Have a look at the **Illustration** page!

space (3) NOUN

A **space** is a gap between two things.

blank
*"If you're not sure of the answer, leave a **blank**," said Mr Kelly.*

gap
*Through the **gap** between the door and its frame wafted the smell of fresh bread.*

opening
*The cat squeezed through the tiny **opening** between the fence posts.*

spare ADJECTIVE

Something that is **spare** is extra, or kept to be used when it is needed.

extra
*Kemal said he could work a few **extra** hours.*

free
*I chipped in that I had some **free** time on Tuesday afternoon.*

surplus
*Dad told us to work off our **surplus** energy by chopping firewood.*

sparkle VERB

If something **sparkles**, it shines with a lot of small bright points of light.

dance
*Julia's eyes **danced** with mischief.*

glint
*When they opened the treasure chest, jewels **glinted** in the light.*

glisten
*The sea was calm, **glistening** in the rays of the sun.*

glitter
*The expensive diamond ring **glittered** on the jeweller's table.*

shimmer
*Her dress **shimmered** with hundreds of tiny sequins.*

SPACE

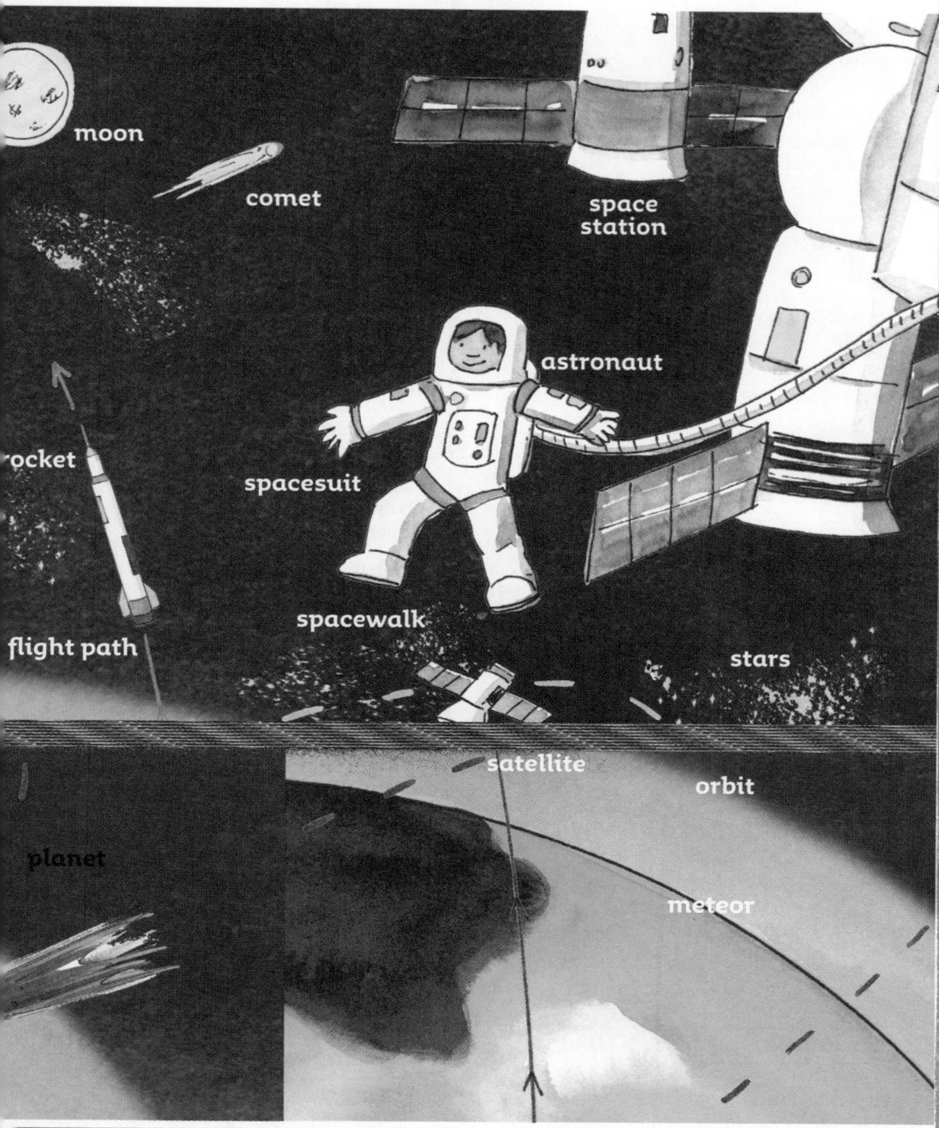

Some other words to do with space:

asteroid	black hole	blast off	capsule
control centre	galaxy	launch pad	landing
spacecraft	sun	supernova	touchdown

twinkle
*Stars **twinkled** in the cloudless sky.*

speak VERB

When you **speak** to someone, you use your voice to say words.

communicate
*The factory was so noisy, it was hard for the workers to **communicate** with each other.*

express
*The head teacher **expressed** her thanks to the parents for their support.*

say
*"Once we enter the woods, you must not **say** a word," warned Gandalf.*

talk
*"Doesn't that professor **talk** with a strange voice?" Jane muttered.*

utter
*"Don't **utter** a word once we get inside," warned the captain.*

special ADJECTIVE

Someone or something **special** is different from other people or things, often in a way that makes them more important or better than others.

exceptional
*I overheard Mr Lescott say that Hiroshi has an **exceptional** talent.*

important
*"Don't hang up. This is **important**!" urged the reporter.*

momentous
*The queen's visit was a **momentous** occasion for the school.*

out of the ordinary
*"It's **out of the ordinary** to see otters here," the wildlife expert said.*

unique
*The salesman said it was a **unique** opportunity to buy at that price.*

ANTONYM: ordinary

speed (1) NOUN

Speed is the rate at which something moves or happens.

haste
*In her **haste** to catch the bus, my sister forgot her sports kit.*

pace
*Poor old Dad couldn't keep up with the **pace** of our volleyball game.*

rapidity
*I noticed the tide coming in with alarming **rapidity**.*

rate
*Cars come off the production line at a **rate** of dozens per day.*

swiftness
*We were impressed by the **swiftness** of the postal service.*

velocity
*A bullet reaches a **velocity** of around 1000 miles per hour.*

→ *See* **hurry (2)**

speed (2) VERB

If you **speed** somewhere, you move or travel there quickly.

go like the wind
*When we found the injured climber, Mick **went like the wind** to get help.*

race
*The huge wave **raced** towards the shore with enormous speed.*

tear
*The greyhound **tore** round the racetrack at top speed.*

zoom (*informal*)
*As soon as the traffic lights turned green, the motorbike **zoomed** off.*

→ *See* **hurry (1)**

spend (1) VERB

When you **spend** money, you buy things with it.

fork out (*slang*)
*The celebrity **forked out** a fortune on designer clothes and shoes.*

pay out
*I **paid out** quite a lot for my new bike, but it was worth it.*

splash out
*With my birthday money, I **splashed out** on an expensive computer game.*

LANGUAGE TIP
If you spend money wastefully, you **fritter** it **away** or **squander** it.

spend (2) VERB

If you **spend** time or energy, you use it.

devote
*After Grandad retired, he **devoted** all his energy to gardening.*

pass
*Waiting for the ferry, we **passed** our time playing a silly game called "Bunnies".*

while away
*The old woman **whiled away** the winter hours spinning wool.*

ANTONYM: waste

spill VERB

If you **spill** something such as a liquid, you let it flow out of a container by mistake.

scatter
*Matt dropped the bucket and **scattered** seed everywhere.*

slop
*Careful! You're **slopping** milk all over the clean tablecloth.*

tip
*The baby picked up his plate and **tipped** cereal down his jumper.*

upset
*Alison waved an arm and **upset** the jug of fruit juice.*

spin VERB

If someone or something **spins**, it turns quickly around a central point.

pirouette
*As the ballerina **pirouetted**, the music whirled and soared.*

revolve
*The water flowed down the chute and the ancient mill wheel began to **revolve**.*

rotate
*A car's wheels **rotate** extremely fast.*

twist
*I **twisted** round to see who was kicking me.*

whirl
*As we **whirled** round, the rest of the fair became a blur of lights and jangly music.*

spite NOUN

Spite is the desire to deliberately hurt or upset somebody.

bitterness
*Full of **bitterness**, Miss Prinn plotted to destroy the man who had left her at the altar.*

hate
*The prisoner was full of **hate** for his jailers.*

ill-feeling
*You could tell there was **ill-feeling** between the two brothers.*

in spite of PHRASE

In spite of is used to begin a statement that makes the rest of what you are saying seem surprising.

despite
*Our school fête was a great success **despite** the appalling weather.*

regardless of
***Regardless of** the danger, the medic crawled out to rescue the wounded soldier.*

split VERB

If something **splits**, or if you **split** it, it divides into two or more parts.

come apart
*"The handle s-s-sort of **came apart** in my h-h-hand," I stammered.*

crack
*The road ahead was flooded because a water pipe had **cracked**.*

separate
*The two halves of the egg **separated**, and I dropped the yolk into the mixture.*

splinter
*As the vessel struck the timber pier, it **splintered**.*

tear
*You could see the agony on the sprinter's face when she **tore** a muscle.*

split up VERB

If a couple **split up**, they begin to live apart.

break up
*Katie was more than upset that her parents had **broken up**.*

part
*My brother and his girlfriend **parted** after only going out for three weeks.*

separate
*After **separating** for some months, the couple were reunited.*

LANGUAGE TIP
If a married couple split up permanently and legally, they get a **divorce**.

---

spoil (1) VERB

To **spoil** something means to damage it or stop it being successful or satisfactory.

damage
*Centuries of wind and weather had **damaged** the cathedral stonework.*

deface
*My friend **defaced** the poster by giving the woman a moustache.*

destroy
*The protester toppled the statue in an attempt to **destroy** it.*

harm
*We should use chemicals that do not **harm** the environment.*

mess up (*informal*)
*"It would really **mess** things **up** if I failed my exams," said my worried brother.*

ruin
*Dad **ruined** Mum's white shirt by putting it in the wash with my red sweater.*

wreck
*My painting was completely **wrecked** when I knocked over the water jar.*

spoil (2) VERB

To **spoil** children means to give them everything they want, making them selfish.

cosset
*I enjoy going to stay with Grandma and Grandpa, as they **cosset** me.*

mollycoddle
*Our neighbours **mollycoddled** their son Timmy and now he's a total pain.*

pamper
*The **pampered** kitten had all it could ever wish for.*

overindulge
*"You must not **overindulge** your cat," the vet warned Mrs Peacock. "It's not healthy."*

ANTONYM: deprive

spooky ADJECTIVE

Something that is **spooky** is frightening and creepy.

bloodcurdling
*All at once, a **bloodcurdling** scream rent the cold night air.*

eerie
*From deep within the cave came an **eerie** howling noise.*

ghostly
*Along the battlements walked the **ghostly** shape of a Viking warrior.*

mysterious
*A murder had been committed, but where was the body? Highly **mysterious**!*

spine-chilling
*In a **spine-chilling** moment, a hand shot towards my face out of the darkness.*

spot (1) NOUN

A **spot** is a small, round coloured area on a surface.

blemish
*My lovely cousin hasn't got a single **blemish** on her smooth skin.*

blotch
*Mrs Naylor was less than pleased with the ink **blotch** on my maths work.*

mark
*Because there was a **mark** on one of them, Mum bought the shoes cheaply.*

smudge
*"What's that **smudge** on your exercise book?" I asked Dirran.*

speck
*There was a **speck** of mud on the carpet after I'd walked through with dirty shoes.*

spot (2) NOUN

A **spot** is a particular place.

location
*"The exact **location** where the stars are getting married is a secret," said the reporter.*

position
*The **position** for the foundation stone was right by the hospital entrance.*

site
*Mountains would make an impractical **site** for an airport.*

spot (3) VERB

If you **spot** something, you suddenly see it.

catch sight of
*On holiday, we **caught sight of** three dolphins*

notice
*"Did you **notice** what she was wearing?" my sister enquired.*

observe
*From her hideout, the police officer **observed** the suspect leaving home.*

spray (1) VERB

If you **spray** a liquid over something, you cover it with drops of the liquid.

shower
*Sally **showered** me with fizzy lemonade.*

splash
*As the car drove past, it **splashed** a pedestrian with muddy water.*

A B C D E F G H I J K L M N O P Q R S T U V W X Y Z

sprinkle
*Uncle Leo has bought a device that **sprinkles** the lawn with water every few hours.*

squirt
*I took revenge by **squirting** my sister with the hose pipe.*

spray (2) NOUN

Spray is many small drops of liquid splashed or forced into the air.

fountain
*When the water main burst, a **fountain** shot into the air.*

mist
*At Niagara, the falling water creates a constant **mist** below.*

shower
*The sprinkler came on and sent a **shower** of water over the lawn.*

spread VERB

If you **spread** a substance on a surface, you put a thin layer of it on the surface.

daub
*Many old houses were built by **daubing** clay and muck over interwoven wood.*

smear
*My baby brother **smeared** chocolate all over his face.*

sprinkle VERB

If you **sprinkle** a liquid or powder over something, you scatter it over it.

pepper
*To scare the intruders, the farmer **peppered** the air with shotgun pellets.*

shower
*The winning driver **showered** the two runners-up with champagne.*

splash
*When you are hot, **splashing** cold water on your face can help to cool you down.*

spray
*"If you **spray** me with that hose, I will find a way to get you back," my brother warned.*

squash VERB

If you **squash** something, you press it so that it becomes flat or loses its shape.

compress
*At the landfill site, huge bulldozers **compressed** the waste in the hole.*

crush
*I saw a programme where an old car was **crushed** into a tiny cube.*

flatten
*The best way to **flatten** cans for recycling is to take both ends off.*

trample
*In some places, grapes are still **trampled** under foot to get the juice out.*

squeeze VERB

If you **squeeze** something somewhere, you force it into a small space.

cram
*Eight of us were **crammed** into one go-kart as it roared down the hill.*

jam
*Harshita couldn't **jam** any more clothes into her suitcase.*

pack
*They had tried to **pack** more people into the hall than there was room for.*

squash
*On the plane, I was **squashed** between a couple from Texas.*

stuff
*Store detectives caught the man trying to **stuff** the CD in his pocket.*

wedge
*Dad managed to **wedge** a piece of wood under the table leg to make it steady.*

squirt VERB

If a liquid **squirts**, or you **squirt** it, it comes out of a narrow opening in a thin, fast stream.

gush
*Water **gushed** from the burst pipe.*

spurt
*Oil came **spurting** out of the oil well.*

→ *See* **spray (1)**

stagger VERB

If someone **staggers**, they walk unsteadily.

lurch
*The bear **lurched** forward, then fell.*

reel
*The man **reeled** a little as he walked out on deck with his friends.*

totter
*When Tristan broke his leg, he had to **totter** round on crutches for weeks.*

A B C D E F G H I J K L M N O P Q R S T U V W X Y Z

stand VERB

If you cannot **stand** someone or something, you do not like them at all.

endure
*Dad told Steph he couldn't **endure** the music any longer.*

suffer
*Mum is not one to **suffer** fools gladly.*

tolerate
*"I cannot **tolerate** sloppy work," a red-faced Mrs Taggart shouted.*

stand for VERB

If something **stands for** something, it represents or means that.

represent
*On maps, a cross **represents** a church.*

symbolise
*The star of David is an emblem which **symbolises** Judaism.*

star NOUN

A **star** is a famous actor, sports player or musician.

celebrity
*"Minor **celebrities** are always trying to be seen on television," observed Craig.*

personality
*Many show-business **personalities** raise money for charities.*

stare VERB

If you **stare**, you look at something for a long time.

gawp
*Passers-by stopped to **gawp** at the amazing display in the shop window.*

gaze
*I **gazed** at Mum's trendy new hairstyle.*

look
*He **looked** at her with open hostility.*

→ *See* **watch**

start (1) VERB

If you **start** something, or something **starts**, you begin it or it begins.

commence
***Commencing** at nine o'clock, school lasts until late afternoon.*

get going
*The workers **got going** with the new road.*

get under way
*No sooner had the match **got under way**, than a player was injured.*

ANTONYM: finish

To start...
a computer is to **boot up**.
a motorbike is to **kick-start** it.
again is to **resume** or **restart**.

start (2) VERB

If you **start** a new business or other venture, you create it.

create
*From a small record shop, the couple **created** a huge music empire.*

found
*"This company was **founded** by Joshua Fothergill in 1879," said the guide proudly.*

initiate
*The airline **initiated** a new service flying to New Zealand.*

launch
*"The company is due to **launch** a new soft drink," the spokeswoman said.*

start (3) NOUN

The **start** of something is the point or time at which it begins.

beginning
*A sore throat is often the **beginning** of a cold, in my experience.*

birth
*Blues music had its **birth** in the southern states of the USA.*

dawn
*The **dawn** of the motorcar era was at the end of the 19th century.*

outset
*From the **outset**, you could see that Goran was going to be a great tennis player.*

state VERB

If you **state** something, you say it clearly and formally.

announce
*Hugh **announced** he intended to be a champion tennis player one day.*

assert
*Rachel **asserted** it was her right to be in charge of the garden project.*

declare
*Sophie **declared** she would never speak to her friend again.*

say
*"It's my turn," **said** Indigo, "and that's all there is to it."*

stay VERB

If you **stay** in one place, you do not move away from it.

hang around (*informal*)
*The postman **hung around** for a minute or two, but no one answered the door.*

linger
*Unwilling to go away, the dog **lingered**, waiting for some food.*

loiter
*"Get to class and stop **loitering** in the playground," Mr Foxe told the stragglers.*

remain
*After the meeting ended, we **remained** behind to help put the chairs away.*

settle
*In the 18th and 19th centuries, many immigrants **settled** in America.*

wait
*"**Wait** there until I come back," Dad said to us as he dashed off.*

steady ADJECTIVE

Something that is **steady** is firm and not moving about.

firm
*"In tennis, it's important to have a **firm** grip on your racket," the coach explained.*

secure
*Dad made sure that the ladder was **secure** before he climbed up to the window.*

stable
*Tightrope walkers carry a huge pole to help keep them **stable**.*

ANTONYM: unsteady

steal VERB

If someone **steals** something, they take it without permission and without meaning to return it.

nick (*informal*)
*"Don't **nick** my biscuits while I'm out of the room," I warned Dilip.*

pinch
*The naughty boys **pinched** some apples from Mr MacDonald's tree.*

swipe
*Someone **swiped** Jay's coat, which he'd left hanging in the cloakroom.*

walk off with
*Someone had **walked off with** my ruler.*

To steal...

by assault is called **mugging**.

during a riot is called **looting**.

from a home is called **burglary** or **housebreaking**.

from a shop is called **shoplifting**.

from coaches in the olden days is called **highway robbery**.

from company money is called **embezzlement** or **fraud**.

from ships is called **piracy**.

game is called **poaching**.

small items is called **pilfering**.

someone else's writing is called **plagiarism**.

steep ADJECTIVE

A **steep** slope rises sharply and is difficult to go up.

precipitous
*From the crag high above, a **precipitous** slope stretched down to the lake.*

sheer
*Below the climber was a **sheer** drop of a thousand metres.*

vertical
*Part of the theme-park ride was a **vertical** drop into total darkness.*

ANTONYM: gradual

step (1) NOUN

A **step** is the movement of lifting your foot and putting it down again when you are walking, running or dancing.

footstep
*Mr Parnaby's **footsteps** echoed on the tiled floor of the corridor.*

pace
*Nervously, the volunteer took a **pace** forward from the line.*

stride
*We had to measure how many giant **strides** it took us to cross the field.*

A B C D E F G H I J K L M N O P Q R S T U V W X Y Z

step (2) NOUN

A **step** is one of a series of actions that you take in order to achieve something.

move
*"Working hard at school is the best **move** that anyone can make," advised the pop star.*

phase
*"In summer, the final **phase** of our building work will begin," the head teacher announced.*

stage
*"The next **stage** will be to transfer pupils into the new classrooms," Mr Knight continued.*

stick (1) VERB

If you **stick** one thing to another, you attach it with glue or tape.

cement
*Plastic pipes are often **cemented** together with a special adhesive.*

fasten
*The secretary **fastened** the cheque to the letter before putting it in the envelope.*

glue
*My silly sister managed to **glue** her book to the desk.*

paste
*"Now **paste** your labels inside your books," Miss Sinclair instructed.*

tape
*I **taped** a small first-aid kit to the frame of my bike.*

stick (2) VERB

If something **sticks** to something else, it becomes fixed to it.

adhere
*Static electricity can make bits of paper **adhere** to your clothing.*

cling
*"The transparent film **clings** to the dish you wrap it round," Mum explained.*

stick (3) VERB

If you **stick** a long or pointed object into something, you push it in.

poke
*The inquisitive child **poked** her finger into the jelly.*

stab
*He **stabbed** the page with his finger.*

thrust
*The karate teacher **thrust** his hand forward with a loud shout.*

stick out VERB

If something **sticks out**, it projects from something else.

jut out
*Medieval houses **jutted out** over narrow streets.*

project
*The jib of the crane **projected** over the building site.*

protrude
*My cousin has an upper lip which **protrudes** over her lower lip.*

stick up for VERB (*informal*)

If you **stick up for** someone or something, you support or defend them.

side with
*Just for a change, I **sided with** my brother in this argument.*

stand up for
*It is important to **stand up for** what you believe in.*

sticky ADJECTIVE

If something is **sticky**, it is covered with a substance that can stick to other things.

adhesive
*"Attach the cardboard with **adhesive** tape," the television presenter explained.*

glutinous
*What should have been a trifle had turned into a **glutinous** mess.*

gooey (*informal*)
*Meringues are **gooey** to start with, crisp when baked.*

tacky
*"Don't touch that paint! It's still **tacky**," the decorator shouted.*

stiff ADJECTIVE

Something that is **stiff** is firm and not easily bent.

firm
*As the sand seemed **firm**, we decided we could safely walk on it.*

hard
*The concrete had set rock **hard**.*

inflexible
*Poles used in the pole vault event were once **inflexible**.*

rigid
*Once we'd got the framework **rigid**, we could put the rest of the tent up.*

solid
*The pond had turned to **solid** ice overnight.*

taut
*The fisherman pulled his rod up until the line was **taut** with the weight of the fish.*

ANTONYM: flexible

still ADJECTIVE

If someone or something is **still**, they stay in the same position without moving.

calm
*The sea was totally **calm**, with hardly a ripple.*

inert
*The sleeping baby lay **inert** in her cot.*

motionless
***Motionless** in the water, the Marie Celeste showed no sign of life.*

stationary
*My dodgem was **stationary** when my brother's bumper car crashed into it from behind.*

stop (1) VERB

If you **stop** doing something, you no longer do it.

call it a day (*informal*)
*It was late and, after writing for some hours, John decided to **call it a day**.*

cease
*Suddenly all the soldiers **ceased** firing. The war was over.*

finish
*"Are you never going to **finish** in there?" Mum called through the bathroom door.*

halt
*"Squad, **halt**!" the sergeant major bellowed.*

leave off
*Each morning she would begin exactly where she had **left off**.*

quit
*To stay healthy, my big sister decided to **quit** smoking.*

stop for a while:

break
*The film crew and cast **broke** for lunch.*

pause
*After **pausing** to take a swig of water, Mrs Scholes continued.*

stop gradually:

peter out
*The flow of sand in the hourglass **petered out**, and the time was up.*

run down
*Much to our relief, the wind-up musical box began to **run down**.*

stop suddenly:

break off
*The star **broke off** the interview to take a phone call.*

cut short
*Play in the tennis match was **cut short** owing to a downpour.*

interrupt
*A sudden flash of lightning **interrupted** my thoughts.*

stop (2) VERB

If you **stop** someone from doing something, you prevent them from doing it.

hinder
*Protesters did their best to **hinder** the new road development.*

obstruct
*Crowds **obstructed** the workers' buses by standing in the road.*

prevent
*By sitting in the trees, people **prevented** them from being cut down.*

restrain
*Police were called in to **restrain** the campaigners.*

stop (3) VERB

If something **stops**, it comes to an end.

cease
*After three days the rain finally **ceased**.*

conclude
*Shows often **conclude** with all the actors taking a bow.*

end
*The concert **ended** with a firework show.*

finish
*Our school day **finishes** at around four o'clock.*

store (1) NOUN

A **store** is a supply of something that is kept until it is needed.

hoard
*No one knew about Gollum's secret **hoard** of shiny rings.*

reserve
*The government keeps a **reserve** of fuel for emergency situations.*

A
B
C
D
E
F
G
H
I
J
K
L
M
N
O
P
Q
R
S
T
U
V
W
X
Y
Z

stock
*Unfortunately, the shop's **stock** of washing powder had run out.*

supply
***Supplies** of grain were running low.*

store (2) VERB

When you **store** something somewhere, you keep it there until it is needed.

hoard
*Ebenezer **hoarded** his money as a squirrel hoards nuts.*

stash
*The burglar **stashed** the stolen jewels under a floorboard until he could sell them.*

stock
*Mum and Dad's shop **stocks** all sorts of paint.*

stockpile
*During the fuel crisis, the government **stockpiled** coal.*

A place where you store...
food for a home is a **larder** or **pantry**.
goods is a **warehouse** or **depot**.
grain is a **granary**.
valuables is a **safe**, **strongroom** or **bank vault**.

storm NOUN

A **storm** is a period of bad weather, when there is heavy rain, a strong wind, and often thunder and lightning.

Some types of rainstorm:

cloudburst	deluge
downpour	thunderstorm

Some types of snowstorm:

blizzard	whiteout

Some types of windstorm:

cyclone	gale	hurricane
tornado	twister	typhoon

stormy ADJECTIVE

If the weather is **stormy**, storms are happening.

raging
*Down its slipway, the lifeboat plunged into the **raging** sea.*

squally
*It was a **squally** shower, here one minute and gone the next.*

tempestuous
*The cave provided the travellers with some shelter from the **tempestuous** night.*

turbulent
*The weather was **turbulent**, with gusts of wind reaching 90 miles an hour.*

wild
*A **wild**, wet wind blew off the moor, rattling the windows of the old stone farmhouse.*

story NOUN

A **story** is a telling of events, real or imaginary, spoken or written.

account
*Gasping for breath, the rescued seaman gave an **account** of what had happened.*

anecdote
*Mrs Giggs was always telling us **anecdotes** from her early life.*

chronicle (*old-fashioned*)
*Monks laboured for many years to write a **chronicle** of their times.*

legend
*Ulysses and Theseus were figures in ancient Greek **legend**.*

narrative
*The fast-moving **narrative** of the book kept me gripped for hours.*

novel
*My brother and I prefer reading **novels** to watching television.*

tale
*The Suitcase Kid is a **tale** about a child whose parents have divorced.*

yarn
*Uncle Tim is good at telling **yarns**.*

LANGUAGE TIP
The general name for imaginary stories is **fiction**.

strange (1) ADJECTIVE

Someone or something **strange** is unusual or unexpected.

bizarre
*The fire-eater on the unicycle made a **bizarre** spectacle.*

curious
*How **curious** – a light in the abandoned mill in the middle of the night!*

extraordinary
*The northern lights are an **extraordinary** and beautiful phenomenon.*

odd
*Beachcombers find many **odd** things along the shoreline.*

peculiar
*I had a **peculiar** feeling that someone was watching me.*

unusual
*Although one often hears a cuckoo, it's **unusual** to see them.*

weird
*The children felt there was something **weird** about Madam Doubtfire.*

ANTONYMS: normal, ordinary

strange (2) ADJECTIVE

Something **strange** cannot be explained.

baffling
*Even for Sherlock Holmes, it was a particularly **baffling** case.*

inexplicable
*For some **inexplicable** reason, my dad was standing on his head.*

mysterious
*A **mysterious** newcomer rode into the frontier town of Cactus Creek.*

mystifying
*It was impossible to decipher the **mystifying** code.*

stranger NOUN

A **stranger** is someone you have never met before.

alien
*When the family first moved abroad they felt like **aliens**, but they soon settled down.*

foreigner
*Some countries are more welcoming to **foreigners** than others.*

newcomer
*The **newcomers** received a friendly reception in the town.*

outsider
*I hated being made to feel like an **outsider**.*

stray VERB

If people or animals **stray**, they wander away.

be lost
*Our cat **was lost** for a week when we moved house.*

go astray
*Someone left the gate open and all the sheep **went astray**.*

straggle
*A few of the children **straggled** out into the garden.*

wander
*Samantha didn't notice she had **wandered** away from her brothers.*

stream (1) NOUN

A **stream** is a small river.

brook
*A **brook** flowed through the village.*

creek
*At low tide, the **creek** turned into a trickle.*

stream (2) NOUN

A **stream** is a steady flow of something.

current
*"Be careful of the strong **current** in the estuary," the canoeing instructor warned.*

jet
*As the pump started, a **jet** of water shot out of the hose.*

surge
*The dam broke, sending a huge **surge** of water down the valley.*

torrent
*When our bath overflowed, a **torrent** of water ran down the stairs.*

strength NOUN

Strength is how strong or powerful someone or something is.

brawn
*The muscleman's impressive **brawn** made him a huge hit in martial-arts films.*

might
*The rugby team's combined **might** made them formidable opponents.*

power
*Hydraulic machines like diggers have tremendous **power**.*

stamina
*Marathon runners need lots of **stamina**.*

ANTONYM: weakness

stress NOUN

Stress is worry and nervous tension.

pressure
*Dad was feeling the **pressure** of his work.*

strain
*It was quite a **strain** for Mum to look after Grandad when he was ill.*

A B C D E F G H I J K L M N O P Q R S T U V W X Y Z

worry
*The **worry** of losing her job gave Athena sleepless nights.*

stretch VERB

If you **stretch** something soft or elastic, you pull it to make it longer or bigger.

extend
*The firefighter **extended** the hose by pulling it off the reel.*

lengthen
*Angela **lengthened** the dough with a rolling pin.*

strict ADJECTIVE

Someone who is **strict** controls other people very firmly.

firm
*Mr Meaks is a **firm** teacher but is always fair.*

harsh
***Harsh** punishment awaited anyone who disagreed with the emperor.*

severe
*For misbehaving, Kuldeep got a very **severe** warning from Mrs Greer.*

stern
*The warder's **stern** look was enough to scare even the toughest prisoner.*

ANTONYM: lenient

strong (1) ADJECTIVE

Someone who is **strong** has a lot of physical power.

brawny
*My sister's boyfriend is **brawny** and likes going to the gym.*

muscular
*With training, the puny weakling was transformed into a **muscular** hulk.*

powerful
*It took a **powerful** punch to floor the heavyweight champion.*

sturdy
***Sturdy** volunteers helped lift the boxes of supplies into the trucks.*

ANTONYM: weak

strong (2) ADJECTIVE

Strong objects are able to withstand rough treatment, and are not easily damaged.

durable
*Most plastic objects are fairly **durable**.*

hard-wearing
***Hard-wearing** boots are essential for hiking.*

heavy-duty
*The farmer had a **heavy-duty** coat for going out into the fields in winter.*

robust
*Children's toys have to be **robust** to survive.*

sturdy
*Dad built us a **sturdy** table for the patio.*

tough
*"Your school shoes need to be **tough** for all the wear they get," said Mum.*

ANTONYM: fragile

strong (3) ADJECTIVE

Strong feelings are great or intense.

deep
*Dad's cousin Colin has a **deep** love of wildlife.*

fervent
*Malik is a **fervent** supporter of the local basketball team.*

intense
*Mrs Murphy has an **intense** dislike for careless work.*

struggle VERB

If you **struggle** to do something, you try hard to do it but find it difficult.

exert yourself
*Sayyid had to **exert himself** to be nice to his cousin.*

make every effort
*Lois **made every effort** to get in the team, but it didn't work.*

strain
*They **strained** to lift the sack, but it was too heavy.*

stubborn ADJECTIVE

Someone who is **stubborn** is determined not to change the way they think or how they do things.

determined
*My brother is a **determined** character. He doesn't often change his mind.*

obstinate
*Always **obstinate**, Violet Elizabeth threatened to scream if she didn't get her way.*

persistent
*Keith was very **persistent** about wanting to do ballet.*

pig-headed
***Pig-headed** people will never admit that they're wrong.*

ANTONYM: weak

study (1) VERB

If you **study** a subject, you spend time learning about it.

learn
*Alex went to France for the summer to **learn** the language.*

read up on
*Holly had been **reading up on** how to look after guinea pigs.*

swot (*informal*)
*Matt said he was going to have to **swot** for his exams.*

study (2) VERB

If you **study** something, you look at it carefully.

examine
*Kimberly **examined** her new science book with interest.*

investigate
*Sherlock Holmes liked to **investigate** unusual cases.*

look into
*The head teacher said she would **look into** the problem.*

research
*Botanists are always **researching** plant diseases and trying to find cures.*

stuff (1) NOUN

You can refer to a group of things as **stuff**.

belongings
*"Fetch your **belongings** and we'll go" Mum said.*

bits and pieces
*The **bits and pieces** from my model were spread over the table.*

equipment
*Divers have to check their **equipment** very carefully before they go in the water.*

gear
*All the sports **gear** at our school goes in a special shed.*

paraphernalia
*It's amazing the amount of **paraphernalia** kayakers need.*

stuff (2) VERB

If you **stuff** something somewhere, you push it there quickly and carelessly.

cram
*Azalea **crammed** her mouth full of strawberries.*

force
*Dad **forced** his shoes into the trunk, then sat on the lid.*

jam
*I **jammed** my feet into the shoes, but they were definitely too small.*

stuffy ADJECTIVE

If a place is **stuffy**, there is not enough fresh air in it.

close
*They could hardly breathe because the air was so **close**.*

heavy
*The air was **heavy** with smoke, so the children stayed inside.*

muggy
*The **muggy** day made them all feel limp and listless.*

stale
*The air in the dragon's cave was **stale** and smelled of burning toast.*

stifling
*Great-grandma's room is always **stifling**, but that's how she likes it.*

warm
*It was so **warm** we had to fling open all the windows.*

stupid ADJECTIVE

Someone or something that is **stupid** is not sensible or wise.

daft
*My **daft** brother is always getting into trouble.*

foolish
*Gramps said he'd done many **foolish** things as a young man.*

idiotic
*"That's an **idiotic** idea," Claire said rather scathingly to Andy.*

ignorant
*An **ignorant** woman barged past me in the queue for the cinema.*

a b c d e f g h i j k l m n o p q r s t u v w x y z

irresponsible
*It's **irresponsible** to wander off without telling your parents.*

silly
*"What a **silly** thing to do," I thought to myself.*

ANTONYMS: sensible, wise

subject NOUN

The **subject** of a book, programme or conversation is the thing or person it is about.

issue
*"Don't change the subject. The **issue** we're discussing is your homework," Mum said.*

matter
*"We will discuss the **matter** at the next staff meeting," the head teacher told Mr Benn.*

question
*The **question** our class had to debate was: "Should we have homework at the weekend?"*

topic
*The importance of multiplication tables is a **topic** often mentioned in classrooms.*

successful ADJECTIVE

If you are **successful** in something, you achieve what you want to do.

prosperous
*After early setbacks, Madhur was now a **prosperous** banker.*

triumphant
***Triumphant** after his victories, Caesar waved to the cheering Roman crowds.*

victorious
*Despite being **victorious** yet again, Nelson was mortally wounded.*

ANTONYM: unsuccessful

sudden ADJECTIVE

Something that is **sudden** happens quickly and unexpectedly.

abrupt
*When his cheating was exposed, the card player made an **abrupt** departure.*

hasty
*"It's foolish to make **hasty** decisions, if you have time to think," advised Mrs Duff.*

unexpected
*The **unexpected** arrival of the pop star caused a great commotion.*

suddenly ADVERB

Something that happens **suddenly** happens quickly and unexpectedly.

on the spur of the moment
***On the spur of the moment**, Mum decided to take us to the seaside.*

out of the blue (*informal*)
*The lottery win came **out of the blue**.*

without warning
***Without warning**, lightning struck the roof.*

suggest VERB

When you **suggest** something, you offer it as an idea.

advise
*The hairdresser **advised** Mum on what style would suit her.*

make a suggestion
*"If I might **make a suggestion**...," Mr Faisal put in.*

propose
*Dad **proposed** that we went camping for our holidays.*

recommend
*"Many machine manufacturers **recommend** this soap powder", said the advert.*

suit VERB

If an arrangement **suits** you, it is convenient and suitable for you.

be acceptable to
*Miss Davies hoped the camp arrangements **were acceptable to** all parents.*

be convenient
*"Would the 20th **be convenient** for our next meeting?" the chairwoman asked.*

please
*"We aim to **please** our customers," the shop manager beamed.*

satisfy
*Dad wasn't sure if the dinner he'd cooked would **satisfy** all the family.*

suitable (1) ADJECTIVE

If something is **suitable**, it is right or acceptable for a certain occasion, time or place.

appropriate
*We were expected to wear **appropriate** clothes for a formal occasion.*

apt
*As the pilot was buried, it was **apt** that a plane should fly overhead.*

fitting
*It was a **fitting** end to a successful presentation.*

proper
*"Make sure you put **proper** shoes on," Mum shouted up.*

ANTONYM: inappropriate

suitable (2) ADJECTIVE

If something is **suitable**, it is right or acceptable for a certain person.

acceptable
*Mum and Dad hoped their offer for the house would be **acceptable**.*

convenient
*"Would Friday be **convenient** for delivery?" the furniture man enquired.*

satisfactory
*We hoped to find a **satisfactory** spot for a picnic.*

ANTONYM: unsuitable

sunny ADJECTIVE

When it is **sunny**, the sun is shining.

bright
*Out to sea, the sky was **bright** and blue, but inland it was cloudy and dark.*

clear
*After the shower, it was so **clear** you could see for miles.*

fine
*Although **fine** weather was forecast, it rained heavily all day.*

summery
*The arrival of the swallows accompanied the **summery** weather.*

sunlit
*From the island beach, I gazed at **sunlit** cliffs across the water.*

ANTONYMS: cloudy, overcast

sunset NOUN

Sunset is the time when the sun goes down.

dusk
*As **dusk** crept over the city, lights began to twinkle in the darkness.*

nightfall
***Nightfall** came and the birds fell silent in the great wood.*

sundown
*With **sundown** came the fort's final bugle call of the day.*

twilight
*At **twilight**, the bats begin to flutter in the gathering darkness.*

support (1) VERB

If something **supports** an object, it is underneath it and holding it up.

prop up
*To **prop** it **up**, scaffolding surrounded the leaning tower.*

reinforce
*Metal bars are used to **reinforce** the concrete in buildings.*

strengthen
*Steel girders are often used to help to **strengthen** skyscrapers.*

support (2) VERB

If you **support** someone, you give them money, help or encouragement.

assist
*Volunteers went along to **assist** the caterers supplying food and drink at the end of the marathon.*

back
*Our mayor **backed** the club's plan for a new sports field.*

encourage
*"Please come along to the match to **encourage** our cricket team," the head teacher said in assembly.*

stand by
*When the bullies tried to fight Kirk, several of us **stood by** him.*

stick up for (*informal*)
*"I'll **stick up for** you if you ask Dad for a raise in our pocket money," my little brother told me.*

suppose VERB

If you **suppose** that something is so, you think that it is likely.

assume
*Holmes **assumed** that Watson would accompany him to Baskerville Hall.*

expect
*Everyone **expected** our assembly to be good, and it was.*

imagine
*"I **imagine** you get very hot in here," Mum said to the checkout lady.*

A B C D E F G H I J K L M N O P Q R S T U V W X Y Z

presume
Mr Higgins ***presumed*** *that Winnie was ill, but I knew she wasn't.*

sure (1) ADJECTIVE

If you are **sure** about something, you know you are right.

certain
"Are you ***certain*** *this is the way?" Dad asked, doubtfully.*

confident
Lyra was ***confident*** *she could find an answer to the mystery.*

convinced
Mrs Dyer was ***convinced*** *that Jonah was telling the truth.*

positive
"I am ***positive*** *I left it here somewhere," muttered the professor.*

ANTONYM: unsure

sure (2) ADJECTIVE

If something is **sure** to happen, it will definitely happen.

bound
"I knew you were ***bound*** *to break it," he muttered angrily.*

certain
According to the trainer, the horse was ***certain*** *to win.*

guaranteed
"I tell you," said Kapil, "United are ***guaranteed*** *to win the cup."*

ANTONYM: doubtful

surprise (1) NOUN

Surprise is the feeling caused when something unexpected happens.

alarm
My brother called out in ***alarm*** *during the night, but it was just a dream.*

amazement
You could see the ***amazement*** *on people's faces as the clown popped up out of the cake.*

astonishment
We watched the show in ***astonishment****.*

dismay
To their ***dismay****, the children saw their ball go flying over the wall.*

incredulity
The audience watched the magician's trick with ***incredulity****.*

shock
It was a great ***shock*** *to discover that our rabbi[t] was going to have babies.*

wonder
The crowds gazed in ***wonder*** *as the magnificent fireworks exploded overhead.*

surprise (2) NOUN

A **surprise** is an unexpected event.

blow
It was a big ***blow*** *to Felicity when she failed her exams.*

bombshell (*informal*)
The president's resignation came as a ***bombshell*** *to the world.*

revelation
What a ***revelation*** *– a teacher who was a wrestler in his spare time!*

shock
The singer got quite a ***shock*** *when she was told that she had won the competition.*

Try these lively words and phrases:

bolt from the blue
Leon's shock news was a ***bolt from the blue****.*

turn-up for the books
The little team's victory was a real ***turn-up for the books****.*

surprise (3) VERB

If something **surprises** you, it gives you a feeling of surprise.

alarm
Our cat was ***alarmed*** *by the thunder and lightning.*

amaze
The shy new girl ***amazed*** *us by singing beautifully.*

astonish
Jaidev ***astonished*** *his team-mates by scoring six times.*

astound
Everyone was ***astounded*** *at the tightrope walker's skill.*

leave open-mouthed
The sheer rudeness of the waitress ***left*** *us* ***open-mouthed****.*

shock
The death of Gran's friend ***shocked*** *her deeply.*

stagger
*"I'm **staggered** to hear how badly we've done in the cricket," Dad complained.*

startle
*The deer was **startled** by the sound of voices and bounded into the woods.*

stun
*Shakira was **stunned** to hear that she'd been picked for the team.*

surprise (4) VERB

If you **surprise** someone, they see you suddenly and unexpectedly.

burst in on
*Police **burst in on** the thieves just as they had opened the safe.*

catch off guard
*Mum and I were **caught off guard** by the tide coming in so quickly.*

catch red-handed
*"If we lie in wait, we'll **catch** them **red-handed**,"said the sergeant.*

catch unawares
*Dad **caught** me **unawares** with his camera as I was pulling a face.*

surprised ADJECTIVE

If you are **surprised**, you have a feeling of surprise.

amazed
*I was truly **amazed** that the magician managed to escape.*

astonished
*I was **astonished** to discover that the lovely actress was 70 years old.*

astounded
*Everyone was **astounded** by the result at the end of the competition.*

open-mouthed
*We were **open-mouthed** with amazement as the gymnast flew through the air.*

taken aback
*Julianne was **taken aback** to meet her teacher on the beach.*

thunderstruck
*Anika was totally **thunderstruck** when she won a holiday in South America!*

suspicious (1) ADJECTIVE

If you are **suspicious** of someone, you do not trust them.

doubtful
*Dad was **doubtful** about the second-hand car salesman.*

sceptical
*We were all highly **sceptical** of the salesman's glib talk.*

suspicious (2) ADJECTIVE

If something is **suspicious**, it causes suspicion.

doubtful
*There was something **doubtful** about the woman's appearance.*

dubious
*The low price of the Swiss watch made it highly **dubious**.*

fishy (*informal*)
*"There's something **fishy** about that van," the inspector said.*

shady (*informal*)
*With his moustache, trilby hat and turned-up collar, the man looked a **shady** customer.*

swap; also swop VERB

If you **swap** one thing for another, you replace the first thing with the second.

exchange
*The tourists **exchanged** the rest of their dollars for euros.*

replace
*Mum said it was time to **replace** our fridge with a newer one.*

substitute
*For security, a decoy van was **substituted** for the one carrying the gold.*

switch
*Police foiled the swindlers by **switching** the real notes for fake ones.*

trade
*Crafty Elian offered to **trade** his computer game for two of mine.*

swell VERB

If something **swells**, it becomes larger and rounder than usual.

bloat
*He ate such a big sandwich that his stomach **bloated** uncomfortably.*

bulge
*The ogre's belly **bulged** over his belt.*

get bigger
*Mr Jones measured the pumpkins every day, willing them to **get bigger**.*

grow
*Before his horrified eyes, the toad **grew** to an enormous size.*

SWORDS

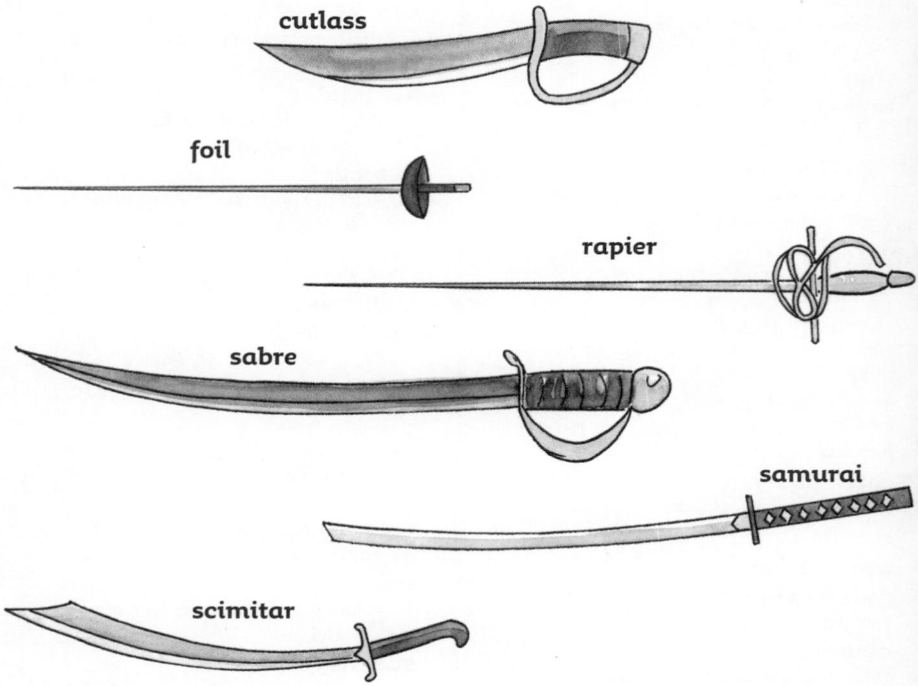

swindle NOUN

A **swindle** is a trick in which someone is cheated out of money or property.

fraud
*Several people were jailed for their part in the insurance **fraud**.*

racket
*"I'm sure that market trader is involved in some sort of **racket**," thought the constable.*

rip-off (*informal*)
*"That ghost train was a real **rip-off**," Adrienne said in disgust.*

scam (*informal*)
*The con men's **scam** was to trick people into buying useless watches.*

switch VERB

If you **switch** one thing for another, you replace the first thing with the second.

replace
*The magician **replaced** his wand with a bunch of flowers.*

substitute
*To thwart thieves, the duchess **substituted** fake jewels for the real ones.*

swap
*Nasir wanted to **swap** his bike for my computer.*

sword NOUN

A **sword** is a weapon consisting of a very long blade with a short handle.

→ Have a look at the **Illustration** above!

Tt

take (1) VERB

If you **take** someone or something to a place, you get them there.

carry
*We **carried** the heavy rock to the far corner of the garden.*

convey
*Mrs Merson asked me to **convey** her thanks to my mother for her help.*

transport
*Huge tankers are used to **transport** the oil.*

take (2) VERB

If you **take** someone to a place, you lead them there.

escort
*Warders **escorted** the prisoner back to her cell.*

guide
*The curator **guided** us round the museum.*

lead
*The trail of paw prints **led** us to the badger's sett in the woods.*

usher
*The cinema attendant **ushered** us to our seats.*

take (3) VERB

When you **take** one number from another, you subtract it.

deduct
*The shop owner **deducted** some money from my pay for the sandwich I had for lunch.*

remove
*Miss Singh asked us to **remove** ten apples and count how many were left.*

subtract
*Lesley **subtracted** four from ten and managed to get seven!*

take (4) VERB

You can use **take** to mean need or require.

call for
*"This mission **calls for** agents with courage," they were warned.*

demand
*Most exams **demand** a great deal of effort.*

need
*The job **needed** total concentration.*

require
*My cut **required** five stitches.*

talent NOUN

Talent is the natural ability a person has to do something well.

ability
*Charlotte was featured on TV because of her musical **ability**.*

aptitude
*Kerena has an **aptitude** for working with little children.*

flair
*Jeremy showed a **flair** for drawing when he was very young.*

genius
*Ms Kent's **genius** as a teacher makes her lessons exciting.*

gift
*My grandad has a **gift** for making people feel confident.*

knack
*"It takes a special **knack** to build these model kits," Simon said.*

skill
*The children admired the conjuror's **skill**.*

talk (1) VERB

When you **talk**, you say things to someone.

chat
*Mum was **chatting** on the phone for hours!*

chatter
*Mr Mustaffa told us to stop **chattering** and start working.*

gossip
*Our neighbours **gossip** away over the wall.*

hold a conversation
*It's hard to **hold a conversation** when my brother plays his loud music.*

speak
*"Can you **speak** clearly, please," Dad shouted into his mobile.*

→ *See* **say**

talk (2) NOUN

A **talk** is a conversation, discussion or speech.

a b c d e f g h i j k l m n o p q r s t u v w x y z

address
The prime minister gave an ***address*** *to a roomful of business people.*

chat
"Let's have a ***chat*** *about it tomorrow," Mum suggested.*

conversation
The twins held a secret ***conversation*** *behind the shed.*

debate
Our class took part in a ***debate*** *on school uniforms.*

discussion
After a ***discussion****, we were asked to write our ideas down.*

lecture
The scientist gave a ***lecture*** *on astrophysics.*

speech
As chairman of the PTA, Dad was asked to give a ***speech****.*

talkative ADJECTIVE

If you are **talkative**, you talk a lot.

chatty
Our new neighbour seemed very ***chatty****.*

communicative
The shy newcomer was not very ***communicative****.*

long-winded
My uncle is rather ***long-winded*** *in the stories he tells.*

tall ADJECTIVE

If someone or something is **tall**, they are more than average height.

gangly
The ***gangly*** *giraffe could reach leaves high on the tree.*

lanky
Lanky *people have a better chance at basketball.*

soaring
Soaring *mountains towered in front of us.*

towering
Towering *skyscrapers dominated the New York skyline.*

ANTONYM: short

tame ADJECTIVE

A **tame** animal is not afraid of humans and will not hurt them.

docile
Some cats can be a bit vicious, but Sam's is really ***docile****.*

domesticated
Domesticated *animals help humans in lots of ways.*

gentle
Most pets are ***gentle*** *and easy to handle.*

obedient
However ***obedient*** *that dog seems, it's still dangerous.*

ANTONYM: wild

tangle (1) NOUN

A **tangle** is a mass of things that are twisted together and difficult to separate.

confusion
I finally found the right cable in the ***confusion*** *of wires.*

jumble
The towels had been left in a ***jumble*** *on the changing-room floor.*

knot
In the charmer's basket was a ***knot*** *of writhing snakes.*

muddle
The skipping-ropes are always in a ***muddle****.*

tangle (2) VERB

If you **tangle** something, you twist it into knots.

entangle
Why is it that phone wires always ***entangle*** *themselves?*

knot
After so long lost in the jungle, Karen's hair had ***knotted*** *and become greasy.*

twist
Somehow the cables had ***twisted*** *together and Dad couldn't find the ends.*

ANTONYM: untangle

tap VERB

If you **tap** something, you hit it lightly and quickly.

drum
Heavy rain ***drummed*** *on the greenhouse roof.*

knock
Who was ***knocking*** *at the door so late at night?*

A B C D E F G H I J K L M N O P Q R S T U V W X Y Z

rap
*Mrs Pennant **rapped** on the desk to get our attention.*

strike
*The giant hammer **struck** the bell and the sound boomed out over the city.*

target NOUN

A **target** is a result that you are trying to achieve.

aim
*Their **aim** was to raise £1000 for charity.*

ambition
*Adhira's **ambition** is to become a florist.*

goal
*My brother's **goal** is to join the air force.*

objective
*The **objective** of the meeting was to choose a new class president.*

taste (1) VERB

If you **taste** food or drink, you have a small amount to see what it is like.

nibble
*Emma **nibbled** a piece of dry toast.*

sample
*In the supermarket, Mum and I **sampled** some cheese before we bought it.*

sip
*I **sipped** the ginger beer, but it tasted strong.*

taste (2) NOUN

The **taste** of something is its flavour.

LANGUAGE TIP
If something has no strong taste, it is **bland** or **plain**.

The taste of...

candyfloss could be described as **sugary**.
chilli could be described as **hot** and **fiery**.
curry could be described as **hot** and **spicy**.
honey could be described as **sweet** and **syrupy**.
ice cream could be described as **sweet** and **creamy**.
lemons could be described as **acidic**, **sharp** or **sour**.
oranges could be described as **tangy**.
sausages could be described as **meaty**.
strong coffee could be described as **bitter**.

tasty ADJECTIVE

Something that is **tasty** has a pleasant flavour.

appetising
*The school cook had laid on a really **appetising** spread.*

delectable
*"That meal was **delectable**," I told Gran.*

delicious
*Instead of the usual bland taste, the burger was really **delicious**.*

mouthwatering
*On the buffet table were all sorts of **mouthwatering** treats.*

scrumptious (*informal*)
*Will makes the most **scrumptious** cheese on toast.*

ANTONYM: tasteless

teach VERB

If someone **teaches** you, they help you learn about something or show you how to do it.

coach
*Our neighbour **coaches** my soccer team on a Wednesday evening.*

educate
*A school's job is to **educate** its pupils.*

instruct
*The sergeant **instructed** the squad in how to use a rifle.*

train
*Mrs Hadji **trained** the team for the area athletics competition.*

teacher NOUN

A **teacher** is someone who teaches at a school or college.

coach
*A sports **coach** has to know how to get the best out of his or her team.*

instructor
*The driving **instructor** was very patient.*

professor
*University **professors** do research and writing as well as teaching.*

schoolteacher
*My uncle is a **schoolteacher** in Canada.*

tutor
*My parents hired a personal **tutor** to help my brother with maths.*

A B C D E F G H I J K L M N O P Q R S T U V W X Y Z

team NOUN

A **team** is a group of people who play together against another group in a sport or game.

line-up *(informal)*
With their new players, the Reds had a powerful ***line-up****.*

outfit *(informal)*
"I'll turn that bunch of scruffs into the finest ***outfit*** *in the area," barked the PE teacher.*

side
Our ***side*** *was bound to win after all the training we'd had.*

squad
My older brother is a prop in the school rugby ***squad****.*

tear (1) VERB

If you **tear** something, you damage it by pulling so that a hole or rip appears in it.

ladder
Mum caught her tights on a nail and ***laddered*** *them.*

rip
Trying to climb an oak tree, I ***ripped*** *my jeans.*

shred
In the office there is a machine that ***shreds*** *documents into tiny strips.*

split
Our large uncle managed to ***split*** *his trousers when he bent down.*

PRONUNCIATION TIP
For this meaning, **tear** rhymes with "hair".

tear (2) VERB

To **tear** can mean to go somewhere in a hurry.

charge
Joel ***charged*** *through the door after his brother.*

dart
Ingrid ***darted*** *across the deserted street.*

fly
I love ***flying*** *down the hill on my bike.*

race
We always ***race*** *home from school so that we don't miss our favourite TV programme.*

shoot
The leading runner ***shot*** *over the finishing line well ahead of the others.*

speed
The cyclist accelerated and ***sped*** *past the others.*

zoom
With a screech of tyres the racing cars ***zoomed*** *over the starting line.*

PRONUNCIATION TIP
For this meaning, **tear** rhymes with "hair".

tease VERB

If somebody **teases** you, they deliberately make fun of you or embarrass you.

mock
We secretly ***mocked*** *the teacher for his strange voice.*

poke fun at
We can ***poke fun at*** *my dad without him minding too much.*

ridicule
Kitty was asking to be ***ridiculed*** *by always arriving so late.*

taunt
The bully ***taunted*** *the small boy until he burst into tears.*

torment
My sister's friends delight in ***tormenting*** *me.*

telephone VERB

If you **telephone** someone, you speak to them using a telephone.

call
The advert invited you to ***call*** *the firm for a free sample.*

phone
Mum ***phoned*** *us when she arrived at the airport.*

ring
Mumtaz left a message asking me to ***ring*** *him when I got home.*

→ *See* **contact**

tell (1) VERB

If you **tell** something to someone, you let them know about it.

communicate
Through the window, Jude tried to ***communicate*** *his news using sign language.*

inform
If a pupil is ill, the parents have to ***inform*** *the school immediately.*

notify
*When her purse was stolen, Mum had to **notify** the police.*

point out
*Mr Delap **pointed out** that we were only a week away from our tests.*

tell (2) VERB

If you **tell** someone something loudly or officially, you announce it.

announce
***Announcing** her retirement, the player said she would miss tennis.*

proclaim
*The emperor **proclaimed** the betrothal of his daughter.*

tell (3) VERB

If you **tell** someone something that they didn't know, you reveal it to them.

confess
*Finally, the suspect **confessed** that she had committed the crime.*

reveal
*The newspaper **revealed** that the singer was leaving the group.*

tell (4) VERB

If you **tell** someone to do something, you order them to do it.

command
*Lorek **commanded** his warriors to advance on the fortress.*

direct
*The fire officer **directed** workers to leave the building.*

instruct
*Passengers were **instructed** to go on deck and wait by the lifeboats.*

order
*"I'm **ordering** you to do that now!" yelled the sergeant.*

tell (5) VERB

If you **tell** something like a story or report, you narrate it.

narrate
*The story we read for homework was **narrated** in the first person.*

recount
*An old sailor **recounted** his adventures in the navy.*

relate
*When she got home, Cristabel **related** all that she had seen.*

report
*Lookouts **reported** that they had seen smoke on the horizon.*

tell (6) VERB

If you **tell** things apart, you judge one thing from another.

differentiate
*Janet found it difficult to **differentiate** between plants and weeds.*

distinguish
*Even tiny babies can **distinguish** their mother from other people.*

tell off VERB

If you **tell** someone **off**, you speak to them strongly because they have done something wrong.

lecture
*Mum **lectured** me about coming in late again on a school night.*

reprimand
*My brother was **reprimanded** for forgetting his sports kit.*

scold
*Granny used to be **scolded** for not learning her multiplication tables.*

temper NOUN

A **temper** is an angry mood.

fury
*My little brother stamped his foot in **fury** when I wouldn't play with him.*

rage
*The emperor's **rage** knew no limits, and often resulted in trouble.*

tantrum
*The crowd booed when the tennis star threw a **tantrum**.*

lose your temper PHRASE

If you **lose your temper**, you become angry.

throw a tantrum
*Have you ever seen a toddler **throw a tantrum**? What a sound!*

throw a wobbly (*informal*)
*I couldn't see why Dad **threw a wobbly**. It was an old clock, after all.*

ANTONYM: keep calm

A B C D E F G H I J K L M N O P Q R S T U V W X Y Z

tempt VERB

If you **tempt** someone, you try to persuade them to do something by offering them something they want.

entice
*The wolf-grandmother **enticed** the children into the cottage.*

lure
*We tried to **lure** the fox by leaving meat near the chicken run.*

persuade
*Mum **persuaded** us to go shoe shopping.*

ANTONYM: discourage

tempting ADJECTIVE

If something is **tempting**, it is attractive and difficult to resist.

enticing
*The buffet included an **enticing** array of cakes and biscuits.*

inviting
*On a hot summer's day, the sea is particularly **inviting**.*

ANTONYM: uninviting

tender ADJECTIVE

Someone who is **tender** shows gentle and caring feelings.

gentle
*My uncle's a **gentle** person who would never hurt anyone.*

kind
*Julia has a **kind** mother who comforts her when she's upset.*

loving
*Elliott gave his aunt a **loving** hug each time they met.*

soft-hearted
*Mum is always **soft-hearted** when it comes to small animals.*

terrible (1) ADJECTIVE

Something that is **terrible** is serious and unpleasant.

awful
*Most people make **awful** mistakes at one time or another.*

frightful
*It was a **frightful** accident for us to witness.*

horrific
*The crash scene made a **horrific** sight.*

shocking
*The player was sent off for a **shocking** tackle.*

terrible (2) ADJECTIVE

Something that is **terrible** is of very bad or of poor quality.

appalling
*"This is **appalling** work," Mrs Berger barked. "Do it again!"*

awful
*My maths homework was **awful**.*

dreadful
*I had never seen such a **dreadful** movie!*

terrific ADJECTIVE

Something that is **terrific** is very pleasing or impressive.

excellent
*Our family had an **excellent** holiday in Austria.*

fantastic
*"What a **fantastic** goal!" the commentator screamed.*

magnificent
*The **magnificent** portrait seemed almost to look at you.*

marvellous
*From our block, there is a **marvellous** view over the city.*

superb
*My grandad complimented the chef on a **superb** meal.*

test (1) VERB

When you **test** something, you try it to find out what it is, what condition it is in, or how well it works.

analyse
*To find the cause of the disease, scientists **analysed** the food we had eaten.*

check
*Men in special suits **checked** the building for contamination.*

evaluate
*The reporter was given a brand-new car to **evaluate** and report on.*

test (2) VERB

To **test** someone means to ask questions to find out how much they know.

assess
*To **assess** our knowledge, Mrs Holland asked us a barrage of questions.*

evaluate
*"I'm now going to **evaluate** how much you've learnt in this lesson," she said.*

examine
*The class was **examined** on the term's work in maths.*

test (3) NOUN

A **test** is a deliberate action or experiment to find out whether something works or how well it works.

analysis
*An **analysis** of the water detected traces of pollution.*

check
*Mum's car went in for a safety **check**.*

evaluation
*We have to do an **evaluation** of a book we've read.*

experiment
*Scientists conducted an **experiment** with mice in a maze.*

inspection
*Every school has to have an **inspection** every now and then.*

theft NOUN

Theft is the crime of stealing.

burglary
***Burglary** involves entering someone else's premises.*

robbery
*After the **robbery**, the getaway car wouldn't start.*

shoplifting
*The amount of **shoplifting** in the store had gone down since the security guard had started.*

thick ADJECTIVE

Something **thick** has a large distance between its two sides.

broad
*A weightlifter's shoulders are usually **broad**.*

bulky
*The courier delivered a **bulky** package.*

chunky
*Dad cut me off a **chunky** slice of bread.*

ANTONYM: thin

thief NOUN

A **thief** is a person who steals.

burglar
*The **burglar** fell while climbing down the drainpipe.*

mugger
*Police are clamping down on **muggers** in the city streets.*

pickpocket
*The Artful Dodger was Fagin's chief **pickpocket**.*

robber
*A band of **robbers** terrorised the western town.*

shoplifter
*Stores warn **shoplifters** that they will be taken to court.*

thin (1) ADJECTIVE

Something that is **thin** is much narrower than it is long.

narrow
*We squeezed through the **narrow** gap in the fence.*

slender
*Willow trees have **slender** branches that droop down in a very attractive way.*

slim
*The joke book was a **slim** volume.*

thin (2) ADJECTIVE

A **thin** person or animal has very little fat on their body.

bony
*The starving animal was **bony** and in very poor condition.*

gaunt
*My sister looked **gaunt** when she got home from her trip.*

skinny
*People said the tennis player was **skinny**, but she seemed fit enough.*

undernourished
*Sadly, there are far too many **undernourished** people in the world.*

ANTONYM: fat

thin (3) ADJECTIVE

Thin fabric is made from fine materials.

delicate
*Ancient fabrics are very **delicate** and tend to crumble when handled roughly.*

fine
*The curtains were made of a **fine** net.*

flimsy
*Abbie's jacket was too **flimsy** to keep out the cold.*

ANTONYM: thick

thin (4) ADJECTIVE

Thin liquids contain a lot of water and flow easily.

diluted
*If you use **diluted** paint, you will need to apply at least two coats.*

runny
*I like my egg yolk **runny**, not hard.*

watery
*The hostages were given **watery** soup and a piece of bread.*

ANTONYM: thick

thing NOUN

A **thing** is an object, rather than a plant, animal or person.

article
*In the game you had to guess the **article** from its description.*

item
*"I have several **items** of lost property here," our form teacher announced.*

object
*Madaleine found some strange **objects** in the box from the attic.*

things PLURAL NOUN

Things are your clothes and possessions.

belongings
*On camp, Mrs Butt told me to tidy my **belongings**.*

gear
*We had to carry some of the **gear**.*

paraphernalia
*A parent delivered all the heavy **paraphernalia**.*

possessions
*She was in the USA, but Nancy's **possessions** were being shipped to China.*

stuff
*We'd forgotten about lots of the **stuff** we'd stored in the loft.*

think (1) VERB

When you **think** about ideas or problems, you use your mind to sort them out.

consider
*"Have you ever **considered** being a nurse?" Mrs Kemp asked me.*

contemplate
*Mum needed somewhere quiet in order to **contemplate**.*

ponder
*Will **pondered** for a while, and then decided on his course of action.*

reflect
*I was **reflecting** whether to walk to school or catch a bus.*

think (2) VERB

If you **think** something, you believe it is true.

accept
*Mrs Johnson **accepted** that Tania was telling her the truth.*

believe
*Keon **believed** that he could pass his exams.*

reckon
*The spy **reckoned** someone was tailing him.*

think up VERB

If you **think** something **up**, you invent it.

create
*Between them, the two women **created** a range of comic characters.*

invent
*Two Hungarian brothers called Biro **invented** the ballpoint pen.*

thirsty ADJECTIVE

If you are **thirsty**, you feel as if you need to drink something.

dehydrated
*If it's hot and you've a headache, you're probably **dehydrated**.*

parched
*In the blazing heat of the desert, the cowboy was really **parched**.*

thought (1) NOUN

A **thought** is an idea or opinion.

concept
*The **concept** of the jet engine was completely new in 1930.*

idea
*"What a clever **idea**!" Mr Prutton exclaimed when I made my suggestion.*

notion
*I had a **notion** that the car in front would turn left.*

opinion
*Grandad was never shy about sharing his **opinions**.*

view
*Mrs Fortune asked me for my **view** on the story.*

thought (2) NOUN

Thought is the activity of thinking.

consideration
*"It sounds like a great idea. I'll give it my **consideration**," said Svetlana's boss.*

contemplation
*Mr Finnegan stared out of the window for ages, lost in **contemplation**.*

meditation
*Silent **meditation** helps people to relax.*

reflection
*After some **reflection**, I've changed my mind about what to do.*

thoughtful (1) ADJECTIVE

A **thoughtful** person thinks of what other people want or need and tries to be kind to them.

caring
*Most nurses are very **caring** people who take pleasure in helping others.*

considerate
*It was **considerate** of the gentleman to hold the door open for me.*

kind
*Mum told me that my present was a **kind** gesture.*

ANTONYM: thoughtless

thoughtful (2) ADJECTIVE

If you are **thoughtful**, you are quiet and serious, because you are thinking of something.

lost in thought
*As he sat on the swings, Wesley was **lost in thought**.*

pensive
*"You look **pensive**," Gran said. "What's the matter?"*

threaten VERB

If you **threaten** someone, you tell them you intend to harm them in some way.

bully
*A boy in Class 6 tried to **bully** me into giving him sweets.*

intimidate
*Because of her size, the girl reckoned she could **intimidate** me.*

menace
*The secret police **menaced** people they thought might be traitors.*

thrill NOUN

A **thrill** is a sudden feeling of great excitement, pleasure or fear.

buzz (*informal*)
*Dad said he received a real **buzz** from his flying lessons.*

kick (*informal*)
*Dennis got a **kick** out of playing jokes on people.*

pleasure
*Listening to beautiful music provides a simple **pleasure**.*

throw VERB

When you **throw** something, you let it go with a quick movement of your arm, so that it moves through the air.

chuck (*informal*)
*My mate Robbie **chucked** my sweater over the railings.*

fling
*Lateefa **flung** her bread roll at me, and that was the start of the food fight.*

heave
*The shot-putter **heaved** the iron ball as far as she could.*

hurl
*Javelins are the spears that athletes **hurl** as far as they can.*

sling
*Samuel took off his jacket and **slung** it onto the back seat of the car.*

toss
*The kilted Scotsman **tossed** the huge pole up and over the fence.*

throw away VERB

If you **throw away** something that you do not want, you get rid of it, usually by putting it in the rubbish bin.

discard
*"Don't **discard** your drinks cans – recycle them!" read the sign.*

dispose of
*The criminal's problem was how to **dispose of** the evidence.*

A B C D E F G H I J K L M N O P Q R S T U V W X Y Z

dump
*"Why do some people **dump** rubbish in the countryside?" she sighed.*

jettison
*To avoid landing in the sea, the balloonist had to **jettison** everything except the fuel.*

thump VERB

If you **thump** someone or something, you hit them hard with your fist.

clout (*informal*)
*Billy Carter often got **clouted** by his bullying brother.*

pound
*The boxer **pounded** the punchbag as if he meant business.*

punch
*After being **punched** by the lurking baddie, Bond lay dazed on the ground.*

wallop
*Grandad says he often used to get **walloped** at school.*

tidy (1) ADJECTIVE

Something that is **tidy** is neat and arranged in an orderly way.

neat
*A **neat** row of cottages lined the street.*

shipshape (*informal*)
*Mr Barmby told us he wanted our dormitory **shipshape**.*

spick-and-span (*informal*)
*Everything was **spick-and-span** for the sergeant's inspection.*

tidy (2) VERB

If you **tidy** a place, you make it neat by putting things in their proper place.

clear up
*We were ordered to **clear up** the mess we'd made in the kitchen.*

put in order
*Once things were **put in order**, we could go out to play.*

spruce up
*Dad decided to **spruce up** the garage, and tried to rope me in to help.*

tie VERB

If you **tie** one thing to another, you fasten it using cord of some kind.

attach
*The tiny terrier was **attached** to the post by a piece of string.*

bind
*As the bat handle was cracked, Nasser **bound** it with tape.*

knot
*There are various ways to **knot** a tie, but I can never remember any of them.*

secure
*Moira **secured** her bike to the lamppost with a chain and lock.*

LANGUAGE TIP
If you tie up a boat, you **moor** it. If you tie up a horse, you **tether** it.

---

tight (1) ADJECTIVE

If clothes are **tight**, they fit you very closely.

close-fitting
*I thought my sister looked smart in her **close-fitting** suit.*

snug
*My new jeans were a **snug** fit, but not easy to put on.*

ANTONYM: loose

tight (2) ADJECTIVE

If a space is **tight**, there is little spare space.

confined
*A dungeon cell is usually a very **confined** space.*

constricted
*Because of a parked van, access to the street was **constricted**.*

cramped
*The cabin was **cramped**, with bunks, a washbasin and little else.*

restricted
*Space on deck was **restricted** as more tourists poured onto the boat.*

ANTONYM: spacious

tight (3) ADJECTIVE

If something is **tight**, it is not slack or relaxed.

firm
*"Make sure you have a **firm** grasp of the rail when the ride starts," the man advised.*

secure
*The police officer had the thief in a **secure** grip.*

taut
*As soon as the towrope was **taut**, the car lurched forward.*

tilt VERB
If you **tilt** an object, or if it **tilts**, it is moved so that one end or side is higher than the other.

incline
*No sooner had we stood the tall clock up, than it started to **incline** forwards.*

lean
*The old tower in Pisa has gradually **leant** more and more over the years.*

list
*The stricken liner was **listing** heavily in the water.*

slant
*The roof **slanted** at 45 degrees.*

slope
*Our street **sloped** down to the river.*

tip
*Amisha pushed off with her feet and **tipped** the seesaw so that she was up in the air.*

time (1) NOUN
Time is a particular period in history.

age
*The 19th century was the **age** of steam power.*

days
*Gran remembers the **days** of steam trains.*

era
*The **era** of the great ocean liners ended as jet airliners entered service.*

period
*The **period** after the Second World War saw great shortages in Europe.*

time (2) NOUN
A **time** is a particular point when something happens.

moment
*This was the **moment** when Tim could have won the game.*

occasion
*For many people, weddings are big **occasions**.*

point
*At that **point**, the angry lady got up and walked out of the meeting.*

stage
*The next **stage** of the project was for the roof to be put on.*

time (3) NOUN
A **time** is a particular period when something happens.

period
*During the holiday **period**, Dion helped his mother in the shop.*

season
*Autumn is the **season** for apple picking.*

spell
*Granny had a **spell** in hospital recently.*

stretch
*Dad thought a **stretch** of grounding was a suitable punishment for me.*

term
*The gangster was sent down for a long **term** in jail.*

while
*Fraser decided to go out for a short **while**.*

tiny ADJECTIVE
Something **tiny** is extremely small.

microscopic
*I got a **microscopic** bit of sand in my eye, but it really hurt!*

miniature
*These days, **miniature** cameras can produce high-quality pictures.*

minute
*The cameras hidden in cricket stumps are **minute**.*

ANTONYM: huge

tip (1) NOUN
The **tip** of something long and narrow is the end of it.

end
*The **end** of the cat's tail began to twitch in annoyance.*

peak
*Mist covered the **peak** of the mountain, so they decided not to go up.*

point
*Georgia likes to keep a sharp **point** on her pencils.*

top
*The **top** of an iceberg is always much smaller than the part below the water line.*

A B C D E F G H I J K L M N O P Q R S T U V W X Y Z

tip (2) VERB

If you **tip** an object, you move it so that it is no longer straight.

lean
*Robert **leaned** his chair back and almost lost his balance.*

overturn
*The boat **overturned** and they all fell into the water.*

spill
*Nina **spilled** her juice all over the table and chair.*

tilt
*If you **tilt** that jug any further you'll lose the lot.*

tired (1) ADJECTIVE

If you are **tired**, you have less energy or enthusiasm than normal.

drained
*After her day's work, Mum looked **drained**.*

exhausted
*Frodo felt **exhausted** and looked around for somewhere to rest.*

weakened
***Weakened** by fever, the explorer remained in the hut.*

weary
*The **weary** hare lay down under a tree.*

worn out
*By the end of term, poor Mrs Etherington was **worn out**.*

> **Try these lively words and phrases:**
>
> **shattered**
> *He was **shattered** and too tired to concentrate on schoolwork.*
>
> **dead on your feet** (*informal*)
> *Mandy's **dead on her feet** because she has two jobs.*

ANTONYM: energetic

tired (2) ADJECTIVE

If you are **tired**, you feel as if you want to sleep.

drowsy
*Still **drowsy**, Dimitri rose and blundered to the bathroom.*

sleepy
*Grandad often feels **sleepy** after lunch and dozes off in his armchair.*

ANTONYM: wide-awake

together (1) ADVERB

If people do something **together**, they do it with each other.

collectively
***Collectively**, schools in our area raised enough money to train a guide dog.*

hand in hand
*The owl and the pussycat danced **hand in hand** by the edge of the sand.*

jointly
*Our new library was funded **jointly** by the school and the PTA.*

shoulder to shoulder
***Shoulder to shoulder**, the soldiers fought off the attacking hordes.*

side by side
*The whole class worked **side by side** to dig the garden.*

together (2) ADVERB

If things happen **together**, they happen at the same time.

all at once
*I waited for an hour, then three buses came **all at once**.*

in unison
*When the head teacher came into the room, we all stood up **in unison**.*

simultaneously
*Guns fired a salute. **Simultaneously**, the fly-past jets roared overhead.*

tool NOUN

A **tool** is any hand-held piece of equipment that you use to help you do a particular task, such as cutting or measuring.

implement
*Garden **implements** include spades and forks.*

instrument
*A barometer is an **instrument** for measuring air pressure.*

utensil
*Dad likes to have all the correct kitchen **utensils** when he's cooking.*

→ Have a look at the **Illustration** page!

TOOLS FOR CUTTING

cleaver

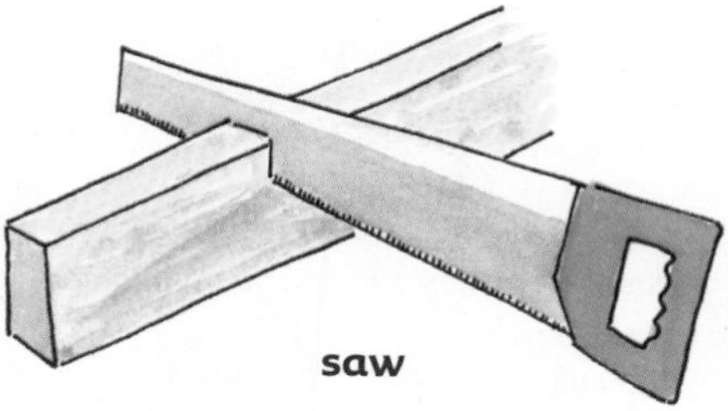

saw

axe

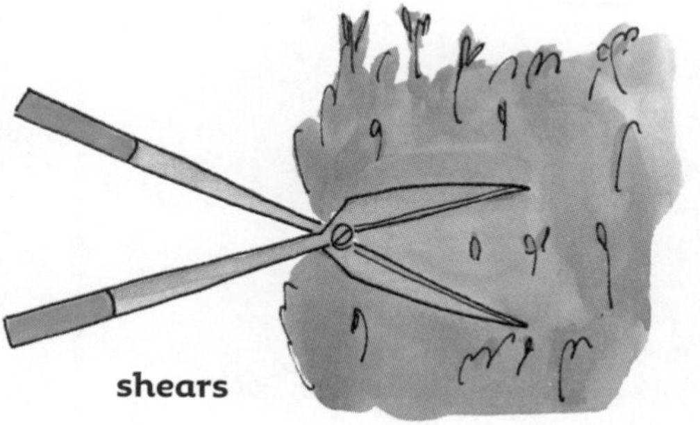

shears

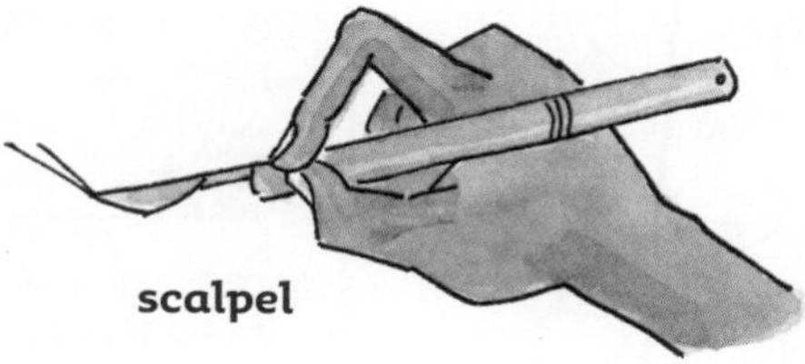

scalpel

mower

chisel

Some other types of cutting tool:

carving knife	clippers	craft knife	guillotine
knife	razor	scissors	secateurs

A B C D E F G H I J K L M N O P Q R S T U V W X Y Z

top (1) NOUN

The **top** is the highest point, part or surface of something.

crest
*Surfers aim to ride in on the **crest** of a wave.*

height
*At the **height** of her fame, the singer decided to retire.*

peak
*Athletes try to stay in the **peak** of condition.*

summit
*On the mountain **summit**, the climbers gazed around them in wonder.*

ANTONYM: bottom

top (2) ADJECTIVE

A **top** person or thing is the chief person or thing of a particular type.

foremost
*Dr Zenden is the **foremost** cancer specialist.*

greatest
*Pele was perhaps the world's **greatest** soccer player.*

leading
*"We are the **leading** supplier of double-glazed windows," boasted the advert.*

total ADJECTIVE

Total can mean complete.

absolute
*I felt an **absolute** idiot in fancy dress.*

complete
*Reports came in that the mission had been a **complete** success.*

out-and-out
*There was no doubt that Goldfinger was an **out-and-out** villain.*

sheer
***Sheer** determination got the runner to the finishing line in first place.*

thorough
*My baby brother can be a **thorough** nuisance at times.*

utter
*"Don't talk such **utter** nonsense," Mum said.*

touch VERB

If you **touch** something, you put your fingers or hand on it.

feel
*In the dark, I **felt** something rough and hard at eye level.*

finger
*The jeweller **fingered** the ring, all the while staring at it.*

handle
*The vet **handled** the poorly kitten very gently.*

tough (1) ADJECTIVE

Something that is **tough** is strong and difficult to break or damage.

durable
*We have a set of **durable** plates for picnics.*

hard-wearing
*Road surfaces need to be **hard-wearing**.*

resilient
*The **resilient** little car lasted another year.*

robust
*It's a good job my baby sister's toys are **robust**, as she's not very gentle with them!*

sturdy
*The tree house was **sturdy** enough to hold four of us at once.*

tough (2) ADJECTIVE

Food that is **tough** is difficult to cut and chew.

chewy
*The meat was so **chewy** I had to leave it.*

gristly
*Occasionally, sausages can be **gristly** and hard to chew.*

leathery
*I struggled to eat a **leathery** piece of turkey.*

ANTONYM: tender

tough (3) ADJECTIVE

A **tough** task or way of life is difficult or full of hardship.

arduous
*The climbing party faced an **arduous** trek through the foothills.*

demanding
*Marathon races are very **demanding**, physically and mentally.*

gruelling
*New recruits endured a **gruelling** month of exercise and discipline.*

ANTONYM: easy

tragedy NOUN

A **tragedy** is a very sad or disastrous event or situation, especially one in which people are killed.

calamity
*What a **calamity**! The falling chandelier smashed the wedding cake.*

catastrophe
*The earthquake was the third **catastrophe** to strike the country that year.*

disaster
***Disaster** struck when the road bridge collapsed during rush hour.*

misfortune
*Losing your passport when on holiday is a serious **misfortune**.*

train (1) VERB

If you **train**, you prepare for a sports match or race by doing exercises.

exercise
*Most professional athletes **exercise** daily.*

practise
*The swimming team **practises** three mornings a week before school.*

work out
*My brother **works out** in the gym through the week and plays rugby at the weekend.*

train (2) VERB

If you **train** someone, you help them prepare for a sports match or race.

coach
*Mr Boateng **coached** the school soccer team.*

drill
*The soldiers were **drilled** until they could have paraded in their sleep.*

instruct
*Emma **instructs** trainee nurses.*

traitor NOUN

A **traitor** is someone who betrays their country or the group that they belong to.

spy
*The two **spies** were jailed for selling secrets.*

turncoat
*When he joined a rival team, fans accused the player of being a **turncoat**.*

trap VERB

If you **trap** someone or something, you catch them using a trap.

capture
*Bandits **captured** the stagecoach in the canyon.*

corner
*With dogs on one side and men on the other, the fox was **cornered**.*

ensnare
***Ensnared** in barbed wire, the prisoner was forced to surrender.*

travel VERB

If you **travel**, you go from one place to another.

journey
*The messenger **journeyed** through the night.*

voyage
*In 1492, Columbus **voyaged** to the New World.*

LANGUAGE TIP
When birds travel to follow the seasons they **migrate**.

treasure VERB

If you **treasure** something, you look after it carefully because it is important to you.

cherish
*The previous owners had **cherished** the house.*

prize
*The painting was one that the gallery's curator **prized** most.*

value
*Melinda really **values** her friendship with Hadia.*

treat VERB

If you **treat** someone or something in a particular way, you behave that way towards them.

deal with
*I admired the way my mum **dealt with** awkward customers.*

handle
*My brother Mark always knows how to **handle** difficult people.*

tree NOUN

A **tree** is a large plant with a hard trunk, branches and leaves.

LANGUAGE TIP
Young trees are called **saplings**.

Trees that...

have needles and cones are **coniferous** trees or **conifers**.

stay green all year round are **evergreen**.

lose their leaves in winter are **deciduous**.

Some types of coniferous tree:

cedar	fir	juniper
pine	redwood	yew

a b c d e f g h i j k l m n o p q r s t u v w x y z

A B C D E F G H I J K L M N O P Q R S T U V W X Y Z

Some types of deciduous tree:

ash	beech	birch
elm	eucalyptus	hazel
horse chestnut	maple	oak
poplar	sweet chestnut	teak
walnut	willow	

tremble VERB
If you **tremble**, you shake slightly, usually because you are frightened or cold.

quake
*Millie was **quaking** when she went in to see the head teacher.*

quiver
*The poor wet dog **quivered** in its kennel.*

shiver
*It's strange how you **shiver** when you go from cold air to warm air.*

tremendous (1) ADJECTIVE
Something that is **tremendous** is large or impressive.

almighty
*Suddenly, there was an **almighty** explosion.*

colossal
*A **colossal** iceberg loomed out of the mist ahead of the ship.*

enormous
*Then, with an **enormous** crunch, the two ships collided.*

huge
*One ship had a **huge** mass of tangled metal where its bow should have been.*

terrific
*There was a **terrific** gash in the side of the other ship.*

tremendous (2) ADJECTIVE
Something **tremendous** is very good or pleasing.

excellent
*The Shakespeare play we saw was **excellent**.*

great
*I thought the actor playing Hamlet was **great**.*

marvellous
*The rest of the cast were **marvellous** too.*

sensational
*The author's books have been a **sensational** success.*

wonderful
*It's **wonderful** to think of so many children enjoying books.*

trick (1) VERB
If someone **tricks** you, they deceive you.

bamboozle *(informal)*
*The quickness of the magician's fingers **bamboozled** me.*

con *(informal)*
*Gran was **conned** by two men pretending to be from the electricity company.*

deceive
*The shot **deceived** the goalkeeper by dipping in the air.*

dupe
*The trickster tried to **dupe** the tourist into buying Tower Bridge.*

fool
*"You certainly had me **fooled**!" I said to Skye as she took the wig off.*

trick (2) NOUN
A **trick** is an action done to deceive someone.

con *(informal)*
*The holiday villas in Spain turned out to be a total **con**.*

deception
*We were all taken in by the talented magician's cunning **deception**.*

hoax
*My sister made a **hoax** phone call pretending to be my teacher.*

practical joke
*My **practical joke** backfired when I got covered in flour myself.*

prank
*Gran says that she was always playing **pranks** as a child.*

trickle VERB
When a liquid **trickles** somewhere, it flows slowly in a thin stream.

dribble
*Water only **dribbled** from the tap. Where was the burst pipe?*

drip
*"What's that **dripping** from the fridge?" Mum asked.*

leak
*Water had **leaked** into all the cupboards below the sink.*

ooze
*Something slimy and smelly was **oozing** from the tank.*

seep
*Over the years, rain had **seeped** in through the roof.*

ANTONYM: gush

tricky ADJECTIVE

Someone or something **tricky** is difficult to do or deal with.

awkward
*It was an **awkward** situation – to risk trouble or keep quiet?*

complicated
*I don't reckon maths is as **complicated** as people sometimes think.*

delicate
***Delicate** matters need to be handled tactfully.*

difficult
*Raymond found the exam question very **difficult** to answer.*

trip (1) NOUN

A **trip** is a journey made to a place.

excursion
*Two coaches arrived to take us on the **excursion**.*

jaunt
*Mum and I went on a shopping **jaunt** to spend my birthday money.*

journey
*By train, the **journey** was relaxing and speedy.*

outing
*This year our class **outing** was to the seaside, where there was also a funfair.*

visit
*Before the **visit**, we did research on medieval castles.*

voyage
*In 1912, the Titanic sank on her maiden **voyage**.*

trip (2) VERB

If you **trip**, or **trip over**, you catch your foot on something and fall over.

lose your footing
*The sailor **lost his footing** as he was climbing the mast, and fell into the sea.*

stumble
*Gran **stumbled** over a lump of stone in the path.*

→ *See* **fall (1)**

trouble (1) NOUN

Trouble is a difficulty or problem.

bother
*"Changing goods is no **bother**, madam," the shopkeeper insisted.*

difficulty
*Swimming out to sea, Zeke soon got into **difficulty**.*

dire straits
*We were in **dire straits** when the car broke down in the middle of nowhere.*

hot water (*informal*)
*"You'll get into **hot water**, my young lady," Gran warned.*

misfortune
*It was Benjie's **misfortune** to run into his teacher when he was supposed to be ill.*

problem
*Mum had no **problem** in changing the car tyre.*

trouble (2) NOUN

If there is **trouble**, people are arguing or fighting.

commotion
*"What's all the **commotion**?" snapped Mrs Charlton, entering the room.*

disturbance
*Some **disturbance** at the event caused the police to arrive.*

unrest
*Before the revolution, there had been **unrest** in the capital for some time.*

trouble (3) VERB

If you **trouble** someone, you worry or bother them.

disturb
*Grandad didn't like being **disturbed** during his nap.*

inconvenience
*My brother didn't want to **inconvenience** Dad, but he did need a lift.*

pester
*"Stop **pestering** me!" I snapped. "The answer's still 'no'."*

→ *See* **annoy**

A B C D E F G H I J K L M N O P Q R S T U V W X Y Z

trouble (4) VERB

If something **troubles** you, it worries or bothers you.

concern
*The doctor was **concerned** about Grandad's health.*

distress
*We were all **distressed** to hear of our neighbour's accident.*

upset
*It **upsets** me to think of the time our rabbit had to be put down.*

worry
*"Try not to let the exam **worry** you," my auntie said.*

true (1) ADJECTIVE

A **true** story or statement is based on facts and is not invented.

accurate
*The notes were an **accurate** record of the conversation.*

correct
*"Is it **correct** that some people eat snails?" I asked.*

factual
*"What I need is **factual** writing, not a story," Miss Wilcox emphasised.*

ANTONYM: false

true (2) ADJECTIVE

If something is **true**, it is real and genuine.

authentic
*To think Grandad owned an **authentic** vintage car!*

genuine
*The signature was definitely **genuine**, and not a forgery.*

real
*The jewels were not fake but **real**.*

ANTONYM: fake

trust VERB

If you **trust** someone, you believe they are honest and reliable, and will treat you fairly.

believe in
*I **believed in** what Ganesh was telling me.*

depend on
*You can always **depend on** Linda to help you.*

have faith in
*With our big match coming up, Miss Clemence **had faith in** us to win.*

put your trust in
*The hobbits were forced to **put their trust in** the wizard.*

rely on
*"Can I **rely on** you to keep a secret?" Ian asked.*

ANTONYM: distrust

try (1) VERB

If you **try** to do something, you make an effort to do it.

attempt
*The athlete **attempted** a jump higher than she'd ever achieved before.*

do your best
*Mrs Tessem said she was relying on us to **do our best** in the test.*

endeavour
*"You must **endeavour** to be honest at all times," Grandad advised.*

strive
*By frantic baling, the crew **strove** to keep the boat afloat.*

Try these lively words and phrases:

give something a whirl
*Why not **give** coding **a whirl**?*

have a crack (informal)
*The runner said she would love to **have a crack** at the world record.*

have a go (informal)
*Bilbo had never ridden before, but he was willing to **have a go**.*

try (2) VERB

If you **try** something, you use it, taste it or experiment with it to see how good or suitable it is.

evaluate
*Mum was sent a sample of a new perfume to **evaluate**.*

put to the test
*Sir Lancelot **put** the sword **to the test** in battle.*

sample
*While it was still hot, I **sampled** the cake that Dad had baked.*

test
*Having **tested** the van, the mechanic was satisfied.*

try (3) NOUN
A **try** is an attempt to do something.

attempt
*Before success in 1953, many **attempts** had been made to climb Everest.*

bash *(informal)*
*"Go on! Have a **bash** at the rope slide," my brother urged.*

effort
*With his final **effort**, the jumper managed to clear the bar.*

shot *(informal)*
*Mary had another **shot** at starting the car.*

turn VERB
When you **turn**, you move so that you are facing or going in a different direction.

pivot
***Pivoting** on his left leg, Frank blasted the ball with his right.*

revolve
*The head teacher **revolved** in his swivel chair to see who had come in.*

rotate
*Our door key **rotates** clockwise to open, anticlockwise to lock.*

spin
***Spinning** round, Yardan caught us creeping up on him.*

swivel
*Mrs Gupta **swivelled** her chair round to face the class.*

twirl
*The dancers **twirled** in a blaze of colour.*

twist
***Twisting** this way and that, Della managed to avoid the obstacles.*

whirl
*"For the falcon to swoop, you **whirl** the meat around your head," demonstrated the falconer.*

turn down VERB
If you **turn down** an offer or request, you refuse or reject it.

decline
*Sadly, I had to **decline** Fola's party invitation.*

refuse
*The council **refused** an application to build a factory by the river.*

reject
*When he applied for art college, my brother was **rejected**.*

ANTONYM: accept

turn into VERB
When something **turns into** something else, it becomes something different.

be transformed into
*Through cleaning, our car **was transformed into** a respectable vehicle.*

become
*With a puff of the lamp, Aladdin **became** a wealthy nobleman.*

convert into
*A futon **converts** from a sofa **into** a bed.*

metamorphose into
*Caterpillars **metamorphose into** butterflies.*

mutate into
*Sometimes I wish my brother would **mutate into** a nicer creature!*

turn over VERB
If you **turn** something **over**, or it **turns over**, it moves so that the top part faces downwards.

capsize
*As the wind caught the dinghy, it **capsized**.*

flip over
*The magician **flipped over** a card, then another and another.*

overturn
*When cars skid badly, they sometimes **overturn**.*

turn up VERB
If someone or something **turns up**, they arrive or appear somewhere.

appear
*Just as we'd given her up, Samirah **appeared**, out of breath.*

arrive
*We **arrived** just in time for the show.*

attend
*My parents like to **attend** school meetings if they can.*

show up *(informal)*
*"Trust Brad to **show up** late," someone whispered in my ear.*

a b c d e f g h i j k l m n o p q r s t u v w x y z

A B C D E F G H I J K L M N O P Q R S T U V W X Y Z

twist (1) VERB

When you **twist** something, you turn the two ends in opposite directions.

coil
__Coiling__ itself round the pole, the snake made for the hole in the ceiling.

wind
"By __winding__ the thread round, it becomes far stronger," Granny explained.

twist (2) VERB

If you **twist** something, you move or bend it into a strange shape.

bend
As part of her act, the woman used to __bend__ iron bars.

buckle
Under the impact of collision, the front of the truck __buckled__.

distort
The heat of the furnace __distorts__ the shape of the glass.

mangle
It's a miracle the girl escaped from the __mangled__ wreckage.

warp
All Dad's old vinyl records __warped__ in the sun.

twist (3) VERB

If you **twist** part of your body, you injure it by turning it too sharply or in an odd direction.

sprain
Bindiya __sprained__ her ankle when she fell while playing tennis.

wrench
Dad was in pain after he __wrenched__ his knee.

type NOUN

If something is the same **type** as something else, they belong to the same group and have many things in common.

category
I would put our head teacher in the "strict" __category__.

class
The "Pacific" was an old __class__ of steam locomotive.

kind
A jackal is a __kind__ of wild dog that can be found in Africa.

sort
Zina is the __sort__ of person you like as soon as you meet her.

variety
Of the many __varieties__ of roses, Mum likes climbers best.

A type of...

animal is known as a **species**.

book or film is known as a **genre**.

car is known as a **make**.

dog is known as a **breed**.

plant is known as a **variety**.

typical ADJECTIVE

Something that is **typical** of a person or animal is usual and what is to be expected of them.

average
We are just an __average__ family in an __average__ house on an __average__ street.

characteristic
__Characteristic__ of Mr Hendrie was a tendency to crack jokes.

normal
A __normal__ day in our house might seem pretty crazy to you!

standard
To obtain a passport, you have to follow the __standard__ procedure.

usual
It was __usual__ for our neighbour to leave at around eight o'clock.

Uu

ugly ADJECTIVE

Someone or something that is **ugly** is very unattractive or unpleasant.

hideous
*The monster had a **hideous** face, misshapen and warty.*

repulsive
*With such a **repulsive** appearance, the creature was bound to scare people.*

unattractive
*Everyone else disagreed, but Dad thought the pop star was **unattractive**.*

unsightly
*That disused shop is an **unsightly** feature of the high street.*

ANTONYM: beautiful

unbelievable (1) ADJECTIVE

Something that is **unbelievable** is so unlikely that it is hard to believe.

far-fetched
*Sam is always telling **far-fetched** stories.*

implausible
*Hadira's excuse was completely **implausible**.*

preposterous
*"What you say is absolutely **preposterous**!" spluttered the professor.*

unbelievable (2) ADJECTIVE

Something that is **unbelievable** is very surprising or wonderful.

astonishing
*The sunset over the bay made an **astonishing** sight.*

incredible
*With an **incredible** effort, the lifeboat man plucked the sailor from the sea.*

uncertain ADJECTIVE

If you are **uncertain** about something, you are not sure about it.

doubtful
*"It is **doubtful** whether we'll be able to go to the party," Mum said.*

dubious
*We were a bit **dubious** about the idea at first, but it turned out well.*

hesitant
*I was **hesitant** about going in the water because I am not a strong swimmer.*

undecided
*Ghita was **undecided** about her future plans.*

unsure
*Mrs Coulter was **unsure** where Lyra had gone.*

uncomfortable ADJECTIVE

If you feel **uncomfortable** in a situation, you feel worried or nervous.

awkward
*Dressed in a chicken costume, Seamus felt **awkward**.*

embarrassed
*I felt totally **embarrassed** when Mum started loudly talking about me.*

ill at ease
*You could see by Anthony's fidgeting that he was **ill at ease**.*

uneasy
***Uneasy** because of the silence, Petra watched and waited.*

ANTONYM: relaxed

unconscious ADJECTIVE

If someone is **unconscious**, they are unable to see, feel or hear anything that is going on.

in a coma
*After the accident, the teenager remained **in a coma** for several weeks.*

knocked out
*A jab of anaesthetic, and the cat was soon **knocked out** for his operation.*

out cold (*informal*)
*When the ball hit her on the head, Trisha was **out cold** for some minutes.*

stunned
*Louis was momentarily **stunned**, having hit his head on the beam.*

ANTONYM: conscious

LANGUAGE TIP
If you are made unconscious for an operation, you are **anaesthetised**.

A B C D E F G H I J K L M N O P Q R S T U V W X Y Z

uncover VERB

If you **uncover** something, you take the cover off it.

expose
*Lisa lifted the stone to **expose** a huge insect habitat.*

reveal
*Two days' digging **revealed** a superb Roman mosaic.*

unveil
*The duchess pulled the cord to **unveil** the new statue.*

unwrap
*"Aren't you going to **unwrap** your present?" Dad enquired.*

ANTONYM: cover

under PREPOSITION

If something is **under** something else, it is below or beneath it.

below
***Below** the surface of the water swam many brightly coloured fish.*

beneath
***Beneath** the trees, the daffodils bloomed.*

underneath
*Dad ran a garage business **underneath** some railway arches.*

understand VERB

If you **understand** what someone says or what you read, you know what it means.

appreciate
*Poor Gran was too ill to **appreciate** what was going on.*

follow
*"I don't **follow**," said Dad, looking mystified.*

grasp
*I found the idea of decimals quite easy to **grasp**.*

realise
*"Did you **realise** that you were speaking to the new head teacher?" Crispin asked.*

take in
*It was a while before Femi could **take in** what was happening.*

Try these lively words and phrases:

catch on
*Wait a minute! I'm beginning to **catch on**.*

get the picture
*Luca doesn't explain things very well, but you **get the picture**.*

undo VERB

If you **undo** something like a knot, you loosen or unfasten it.

unbutton
*To listen to my breathing, the doctor asked me to **unbutton** my shirt.*

unfasten
*He **unfastened** the strap of his watch and put it on the table.*

untie
*Damini eventually **untied** the knot.*

unzip
*We **unzipped** the tent and pulled back the flap to reveal a beautiful morning.*

→ *See* **open (1)**

unfair ADJECTIVE

Something that is **unfair** does not seem right, reasonable or fair.

biased
*Viewers phoned in to complain that the programme was **biased**.*

prejudiced
*Some people are **prejudiced** when they discuss anybody who is different.*

unjust
*The verdict was **unjust**: an innocent woman was going to jail.*

ANTONYM: fair

unhappy ADJECTIVE

An **unhappy** person is sad and miserable.

depressed
*Niles was quite **depressed** when he didn't get a part in the play.*

down
*My sister was **down** about her exam results.*

gloomy
*The outlook for any country in the grip of recession is **gloomy**.*

miserable
In the pouring rain, we had a thoroughly ***miserable*** *day out.*

sad
I felt ***sad*** *to leave our little house.*

ANTONYM: happy

unkind ADJECTIVE

Someone who is **unkind** is unpleasant and rather cruel.

cruel
It was ***cruel*** *to keep the dog tied up outside all day.*

harsh
People in Victorian times were generally more ***harsh*** *when dealing out punishment.*

malicious
Some ***malicious*** *person had started spreading some very nasty rumours.*

mean
It was ***mean*** *of Josh to say those things.*

nasty
The ***nasty*** *little girl kicked and scratched.*

spiteful
My sister is sometimes ***spiteful*** *to me when I annoy her.*

unpleasant
Mrs Rae was rather ***unpleasant*** *in a couple of her comments in my report.*

unsympathetic
Mr Bumble was ***unsympathetic*** *to Oliver's request for more food.*

unknown (1) ADJECTIVE

If someone or something is **unknown**, they are not familiar or famous.

humble
The actor had started out as a ***humble*** *waiter and was now world-famous.*

obscure
My brother went to see some ***obscure*** *pop group in concert.*

unfamiliar
There were several ***unfamiliar*** *names on the list of people attending the premiere.*

unsung
There are many ***unsung*** *heroes in our history.*

unknown (2) ADJECTIVE

If someone's name or identity is **unknown**, people do not know who they are.

anonymous
A large sum of money was given by an ***anonymous*** *donor.*

nameless
"Someone, who shall be ***nameless****, has broken a window," Mrs Sherwood said.*

unidentified
An ***unidentified*** *witness claims to have seen what happened at the scene of the accident.*

unnamed
"Reports say that a man, as yet ***unnamed****, was injured early today," said the newsreader.*

unlucky ADJECTIVE

If you are **unlucky**, you are unfortunate and have bad luck.

hapless
Watched by the hawk, the ***hapless*** *vole came out into the sunshine.*

ill-fated
Through the night, the ***ill-fated*** *vessel steamed towards the iceberg.*

jinxed
Playing City, United seemed to be ***jinxed****, as they always lost.*

luckless
The ***luckless*** *skier once more picked herself up from the snow.*

unfortunate
Kardai had an ***unfortunate*** *accident, coming off his bike.*

wretched
They are working to help the ***wretched*** *children caught up in the conflict.*

unnecessary ADJECTIVE

Something that is **unnecessary** is not necessary.

needless
The jockey was fined for ***needless*** *use of the whip during the race.*

nonessential
The members of the expedition were told to leave behind ***nonessential*** *items.*

superfluous
"We can do without your ***superfluous*** *comments," Mrs Malik said acidly.*

uncalled-for
The waiter's rudeness was ***uncalled-for****.*

ANTONYM: necessary

A B C D E F G H I J K L M N O P Q R S T U V W X Y Z

unpleasant (1) ADJECTIVE
An **unpleasant** person is unfriendly or rude.

disagreeable
*Justin may be clever, but he's quite a **disagreeable** man.*

horrid
*She was a **horrid** person, who never said a kind word to anyone.*

nasty
***Nasty** comments like that are totally unnecessary and harmful.*

obnoxious
*"What an **obnoxious** bloke he is," my sister remarked.*

→ *See* **bad-tempered**

unpleasant (2) ADJECTIVE
Something **unpleasant** is not enjoyable and may make you uncomfortable or upset.

disagreeable
*I found the roller-coaster ride an altogether **disagreeable** experience.*

horrible
*"Some tourist resorts are **horrible** places," commented Gran.*

repulsive
*The evil old miser leered at us in a **repulsive** manner.*

revolting
*"I can't eat this stuff – it's **revolting**!" I protested.*

unsuccessful ADJECTIVE
If you are **unsuccessful**, you do not succeed in what you are trying to do.

fruitless
*Our search proved **fruitless**. Tibbles the cat was nowhere to be found.*

futile
*Mum made a **futile** attempt to find her missing ring in the dark.*

vain
*She waved her hand in a **vain** attempt to get his attention.*

ANTONYM: successful

unsuitable ADJECTIVE
Things that are **unsuitable** are not right or suitable for a particular purpose.

inappropriate
*Young children often come out with **inappropriate** comments.*

out of place
*Tim's words were **out of place** at a wedding.*

unsuited
***Unsuited** to life behind a desk, my big brother joined the air force.*

wrong
*The purple curtains looked **wrong** in a green room.*

ANTONYM: suitable

untidy (1) ADJECTIVE
If a place is **untidy**, it is not tidy.

chaotic
*Furniture had been knocked over and the room was **chaotic**.*

cluttered
*Kyle's bedroom is more **cluttered** than mine.*

higgledy-piggledy (*informal*)
*Everything in Karen's room is completely **higgledy-piggledy**.*

jumbled
*When my sister borrows my CDs, she always leaves them **jumbled**.*

messy
*My brother's room is always **messy**.*

untidy (2) ADJECTIVE
If a person's work is **untidy**, it is not neat and well-arranged.

careless
*"This work is **careless**. Do it again," Miss Pearson ordered.*

messy
*Due to a leaking Biro, Gary's work was **messy**.*

slipshod
***Slipshod** presentation is something Mr Stone won't tolerate.*

slovenly
*"**Slovenly** work will get lower marks than tidy work," said Mrs Cameron.*

untidy (3) ADJECTIVE
If a person looks **untidy**, they do not look smart.

bedraggled
*Rehan looked **bedraggled** after walking ten miles in the rain.*

scruffy
*Dad complained that my brother looked **scruffy**.*

unkempt
***Unkempt** hair needs washing and combing.*

ntrue ADJECTIVE

Something that is **untrue** is not true.

false
*The suspect's alibi proved to be **false**.*

inaccurate
*Dan gave an **inaccurate** version of the event.*

incorrect
*It is **incorrect** to say that the moon is made of blue cheese.*

misleading
*Tabloid newspapers sometimes give **misleading** information.*

wrong
*"I'm afraid what you say is **wrong**," Mrs Mohanty said.*

nusual ADJECTIVE

Something that is **unusual** is not usual and does not happen very often.

abnormal
*A lorry with an **abnormal** load needed a police escort.*

exceptional
*With **exceptional** skill, the skier negotiated the slalom at top speed.*

extraordinary
*How **extraordinary** to hear birds sing at night.*

freak
*A **freak** whirlwind destroyed the barn.*

odd
*It was **odd** to see her so far away from home.*

rare
*"First editions of Shakespeare plays are very **rare** indeed," said the bookseller.*

remarkable
*The New York skyline is a **remarkable** sight.*

strange
*Camels are **strange** in being able to survive for long periods without water.*

upset (1) ADJECTIVE

If someone is **upset**, they are unhappy and disappointed.

disappointed
*Dev was **disappointed** with his exam results.*

dismayed
*We were **dismayed** to find that the train had gone a minute before.*

distressed
*The little boy was **distressed** that he had lost his mother.*

saddened
*We were **saddened** by the death of our neighbour.*

tearful
*Will bid a **tearful** farewell to the girl he had grown so fond of.*

upset (2) VERB

If someone or something **upsets** you, it makes you feel worried or unhappy.

bother
*It took more than a few flies to **bother** Diane.*

dismay
*Mum **dismayed** us when she cut our pocket money.*

distress
*"You mustn't **distress** yourself," I said to the worried old lady.*

faze
*Thunder, fireworks – nothing **fazed** her.*

hurt
*Aba was **hurt** to not be invited to the party.*

trouble
*My Gran was **troubled** by a pain in her back.*

worry
*The delay didn't **worry** the pilot, but the lack of fuel did.*

upside down ADJECTIVE

If something is **upside down**, it is the wrong way up.

inverted
*Leave the bottle **inverted** to get all the sauce out.*

on its head
*The situation was turned **on its head** when the other team scored twice.*

topsy-turvy
*The house was all **topsy-turvy**, with the bedrooms downstairs and the kitchen upstairs.*

use (1) VERB

If you **use** something, you do something with it that helps you to do a job or sort out a problem.

apply
*Doctor Foster **applied** his scientific knowledge to build a rocket.*

employ
*The tennis player had to **employ** all her shots to win the match.*

make use of
*We **made use of** scrap parts to build a go-kart.*

operate
*The disabled lady **operated** her wheelchair with two fingers.*

utilise
*According to the internet, it is possible to **utilise** a tin can to mend a car exhaust pipe.*

LANGUAGE TIP
To use a sword or an axe is to **wield** it.

PRONUNCIATION TIP
When it is a verb, **use** is pronounced **yooz**.

use (2) NOUN

A **use** is the purpose or value of something.

point
*I couldn't see the **point** of our homework.*

purpose
*The **purpose** of seat belts is to stop you hitting the windscreen or the seat in front in a crash.*

value
*"I cannot see the **value** of a video mobile phone," complained Grandad.*

PRONUNCIATION TIP
When it is a noun, **use** is pronounced **yooss**.

useful ADJECTIVE

If something is **useful**, you can use it to help you in some way.

beneficial
*Just a little extra teaching proved very **beneficial** for Jo's maths.*

effective
*CDs can be very **effective** in learning a foreign language.*

helpful
*We hope this thesaurus proves **helpful** to young writers!*

valuable
*The three men gave **valuable** assistance to the police.*

worthwhile
*"Go to an orchestral concert. You'll find it a **worthwhile** experience," advised Mr Kinsella.*

ANTONYM: useless

useless (1) ADJECTIVE

Something that is **useless** is no good for anything.

ineffective
*The tiny hammer was completely **ineffective**.*

of no use
*Wetsuits are **of no use** in the desert.*

unusable
*My mobile phone was **unusable** after I'd dropped it in the bath.*

useless (2) ADJECTIVE

If a course of action is **useless**, it will not achieve what is wanted.

futile
*It is **futile** to take a phone as there is no signal*

hopeless
*For Scott, it was a **hopeless** situation: the food was gone and the blizzard still raged.*

impractical
*A camera tripod is **impractical** when you are following animals on the move.*

pointless
*It seemed **pointless** to take my best clothes to camp.*

usual ADJECTIVE

Something that is **usual** is expected and happens often.

everyday
*Arguments are an **everyday** occurrence in some households.*

normal
*It was **normal** for Mrs Quashie to go for a walk twice a day.*

regular
*The fisherman took a **regular** trip to check his lobster pots.*

usually ADVERB

If something **usually** happens, it is expected and happens often.

as a rule
***As a rule**, old Mrs Grant doesn't go out of doors much.*

normally
*Mum **normally** makes my breakfast, but at weekends I make my own.*

traditionally
***Traditionally**, there is a carnival in September.*

Vv

vague ADJECTIVE

Things that are **vague** are not definite or clear.

dim
*When he woke, Marty had only a **dim** memory of the frightening dream.*

general
*He gave a **general** outline of the project and left us to work out the details.*

hazy
*Mrs Jefferson could give only a **hazy** description of the burglar.*

woolly
*His account of the holiday in Spain was rather **woolly**.*

vain ADJECTIVE

A **vain** person is too proud of how they look or what they can do.

boastful
*Spencer didn't mind sounding **boastful** about his adventures.*

conceited
*I don't want Emma for a friend. She's far too **conceited**.*

proud
*He's too **proud** to admit that he might be wrong.*

valuable ADJECTIVE

Something that is **valuable** is of great worth or very important.

costly
*Diamonds are more **costly** than pearls.*

expensive
*Millionaires tend to travel in **expensive** cars.*

precious
*The ring may have been powerful, but to Gollum it was **precious**.*

priceless
*"Our gallery is full of **priceless** works," the curator told us.*

treasured
*Great Gran's chair is a **treasured** possession in our family.*

ANTONYM: worthless

LANGUAGE TIP
Invaluable means very valuable. It is not the opposite of valuable.

value NOUN

Value is the importance or usefulness of something.

advantage
*Nailah could see the future **advantage** of working hard at school.*

benefit
*Mrs Oakley's help with my maths was of great **benefit**.*

merit
*The **merits** of sport are that it's enjoyable, keeps you fit and keeps you busy.*

usefulness
*There is no doubting the **usefulness** of computers.*

vanish VERB

If something **vanishes**, it disappears or does not exist any more.

disappear
*In a puff of smoke, the magician **disappeared**.*

evaporate
*When water boils, it **evaporates** into the air.*

fade
*As the sun **faded** from sight, lights twinkled in the harbour town.*

ANTONYM: appear

variety (1) NOUN

A **variety** of things is a number of different kinds.

assortment
*There was an **assortment** of biscuits still in the tin.*

collection
*The family had a huge **collection** of books on shelves around the room.*

mixture
*I like to have a **mixture** of chocolates.*

range
*The shop sold a **range** of shampoos.*

a b c d e f g h i j k l m n o p q r s t u v w x y z

A B C D E F G H I J K L M N O P Q R S T U V W X Y Z

variety (2) NOUN

A **variety** is a particular type of something.

class
*There are several different **classes** of butterfly here.*

kind
*She couldn't decide what **kind** of rose to plant by the gate.*

sort
*We've got lots of different apples. Which **sort** do you like best?*

type
*How quickly a plant grows depends on what **type** it is.*

various ADJECTIVE

Various can be used to mean several different types of something.

assorted
*I love those tins of **assorted** biscuits.*

miscellaneous
*The magazine included articles on **miscellaneous** topics.*

version NOUN

A **version** of something is a form of it in which some details are different from other forms.

account
*Esther's **account** of the holiday was very different from Charlie's.*

description
*Everyone gave a different **description** of the accident.*

story
*The teacher didn't know whose **story** she should believe.*

very ADVERB

Very is used before words to emphasise them.

absolutely
*Mrs Chakrabarti said she was **absolutely** delighted with my work.*

enormously
*My baby brother was **enormously** proud to be the team's mascot.*

exceedingly
*After the storm, I was **exceedingly** glad to get back home.*

extremely
*The three of them are working **extremely** well together.*

greatly
*Beethoven's music is **greatly** loved by many.*

highly
*A soldier's boots must be **highly** polished.*

most
*"We were **most** grateful for your help," the letter read.*

really
*The tourists were **really** impressed by the sights of London.*

terribly
*"May I say how **terribly** honoured I am," began the prince.*

terrifically
*Drag racers are **terrifically** powerful cars.*

truly
*The fireworks display was **truly** magnificent.*

vicious (1) ADJECTIVE

If an action is **vicious**, it is cruel and violent.

barbaric
*The police said the man had suffered a **barbaric** attack.*

brutal
*The army launched a **brutal** attack on the enemy.*

cruel
*The prisoner would always remember the **cruel** look in the jailer's eye.*

savage
*The lion launched a **savage** attack and brought the wildebeest down.*

violent
*Gangsters use **violent** methods to get what they want.*

vicious (2) ADJECTIVE

If what someone says is **vicious**, it is cruel and spiteful.

cruel
*His father's **cruel** words stayed with Timon for a lifetime.*

malicious
*Some people enjoy sharing **malicious** gossip.*

spiteful
*We all have to learn how to cope with **spiteful** remarks.*

victory NOUN

A **victory** is a success in a battle or competition.

success
*Supporters cheered the team for its **success** in the match.*

triumph
*The slaying of the fearsome dragon was a **triumph** for the knight.*

win
*The swimming team had never been beaten and was confident it would have another **win**.*

view (1) NOUN

A **view** is everything you can see from a particular place.

outlook
*Grandad's bungalow had a lovely **outlook** over the sea.*

panorama
*From the top of the hill, a wonderful **panorama** stretched away before us.*

scene
*Our classroom was a very busy **scene**.*

view (2) NOUN

A **view** is a belief or opinion.

belief
*"It's my **belief** that big corporations have too much power," said the protester.*

opinion
*Jim and I had differing **opinions** on school.*

point of view
*From my **point of view**, school was not always fun, but very necessary.*

viewpoint
*Jim's **viewpoint** is that school was great fun, in spite of all the lessons.*

violence NOUN

Violence is behaviour that is intended to hurt or kill.

bloodshed
***Bloodshed** was common in the realm of the evil emperor.*

brutality
*"This was a crime of enormous **brutality**," the police spokesman said.*

brute force
*Guards used **brute force** to break down the door.*

savagery
*The **savagery** of the massacre was beyond all description.*

terrorism
*Sadly, some people resort to **terrorism** to try to get their way.*

violent (1) ADJECTIVE

Someone who is **violent** behaves in a way that is intended to hurt or kill.

bloodthirsty
***Bloodthirsty** Vikings roared through the village waving axes and flaming torches.*

brutal
*The **brutal** murderer was arrested by a team of undercover police officers.*

murderous
*With a **murderous** look in his eye, the pirate leapt aboard.*

vicious
***Vicious** criminals tend to be jailed for a long time.*

ANTONYM: gentle

violent (2) ADJECTIVE

A **violent** force is very strong and does harm or damage.

devastating
*The **devastating** power of the tornado swept away all in its path.*

powerful
*Each **powerful** blow of the battering ram set the gate shivering.*

raging
*The small boat was tossed hither and thither in the **raging** sea.*

wild
*"February is a time of **wild** weather in these parts," the farmer told us.*

visit VERB

If you **visit** someone, you go to see them and spend time with them.

call on
*Gran **called on** Mum to say hello and see how we all were.*

drop in on (*informal*)
*"Do **drop in on** me when you're passing," the old lady said.*

look up (*informal*)
*When we took a trip to London we **looked up** some old friends.*

pay a visit to
*We **paid a visit to** the Houses of Parliament.*

Ww

wait (1) VERB

If you **wait**, you spend time in a place or situation, usually doing little or nothing, before something happens.

hang around (*informal*)
*We had to **hang around** for ages at the bus stop before the bus came.*

hold on (*informal*)
*"Would you **hold on**, please," the voice on the phone said.*

linger
*After class, Chipo **lingered** outside to talk to Miss Pennington.*

pause
*We **paused** in our walk to get our breath back.*

remain
*The doctor has said that Grandpa will have to **remain** in hospital for the time being.*

stay
*Dad told us to **stay** where we were while he bought the tickets.*

wait (2) NOUN

A **wait** is a period of time before something happens.

delay
*A voice from the loudspeaker apologised for the **delay** in the train's arrival.*

hold-up
*Apparently, the **hold-up** at the crossroads was caused by faulty traffic lights.*

interval
*After a brief **interval**, the orchestra was ready and the conductor came on stage.*

pause
*There was a **pause** when the cricket match stopped because of the rain.*

wake VERB

When you **wake**, or something **wakes** you, you become conscious again after being asleep.

awake
*The campers **awoke** to find a goat nibbling their tent.*

awaken
*The sound of thunder **awakened** the dog, which started barking.*

come to
*When Marisa **came to**, all the others had got up and gone.*

rouse
*The farmer was **roused** at dawn by the crowing of the cockerel.*

stir
*It was early and few people were **stirring**.*

walk

→ Look at the **Word Power** page!

wander VERB

If you **wander** in a place, you walk around in a casual way.

drift
*A group of my sister's friends **drifted** into an amusement arcade.*

meander
*We **meandered** here and there along the beach, picking up pebbles.*

mooch
*My brother **mooched** off to be by himself.*

ramble
*We **rambled** through the woods, looking for edible mushrooms to pick.*

roam
*My parents had **roamed** all over the fair trying to find us.*

stroll
*After lunch, the family **strolled** down by the river.*

want VERB

If you **want** something, you feel that you would like to have it or do it.

crave
*With all this loud music, Tom **craved** a bit of peace and quiet.*

desire
*"What do you **desire**, O Master?" the Genie of the Lamp enquired.*

walk

VERB When you **walk**, you move along by putting one foot in front of the other on the ground.

walk normally:

go on foot
It was only a short distance to the park, so we ***went on foot****.*

walk slowly:

amble
We ***ambled*** *along the shore, looking for shells and driftwood.*

dawdle
We ***dawdled*** *to school without a care in the world.*

saunter
She ***sauntered*** *out to buy a paper.*

stroll
Couples ***strolled*** *along in the sunshine.*

walk steadily:

march
The army ***marched*** *rapidly towards Hastings.*

pace
I was ***pacing*** *up and down, waiting for the postman to arrive.*

plod
All day we ***plodded*** *through field after field.*

trek
Scott and his men were forced to ***trek*** *across the polar ice.*

walk reluctantly:

traipse
Zoe ***traipsed*** *miserably around the shops after her mum.*

troop
After the game, the players ***trooped*** *into the changing room.*

trudge
Joely ***trudged*** *along, head down.*

walk purposefully:

stride
Mr Radebe ***strode*** *into the room and slammed the door.*

walk loudly:

stamp
Leon ***stamped*** *from room to room looking for his keys.*

stomp
Angrily, he ***stomped*** *out the door.*

thunder
Nicola ***thundered*** *up the stairs.*

walk quietly:

tiptoe
Being very careful not to wake the baby, we ***tiptoed*** *into the room.*

→ Also have a look at the **Word Power** page for **run**!

fancy
*"I **fancy** a burger with plenty of sauce," my brother fantasised.*

hanker after
*On a Friday night, Dad always **hankers after** an Indian takeaway for dinner.*

long for
*During the long, cold winter, Amanda **longed for** the warmth of summer.*

wish for
*Abha dearly **wished for** someone to play with.*

war NOUN

War is a period of fighting between countries or states, where weapons are used and many people may be killed.

battle
*The famous 1066 **battle** was fought several miles away from Hastings.*

combat
*Troops go into **combat** to defend their country.*

conflict
*The **conflict** between the two sides lasted for several years.*

fighting
*The **fighting** ceased when the armistice was signed.*

warfare
***Warfare** is a very unpleasant business.*

ANTONYM: peace

warm ADJECTIVE

Something that is **warm** has some heat, but not enough to be hot.

lukewarm
*"Waiter, this tea is **lukewarm**!" the customer complained.*

tepid
*As the washer had been on, my bath water was only **tepid**.*

ANTONYM: cool

warn VERB

If you **warn** someone, you tell them that they may be in danger or trouble.

alert
*Michael, having seen the stricken yacht, managed to **alert** the coastguard.*

forewarn
*The witches **forewarned** the king of his downfall.*

raise the alarm
*When she saw smoke pouring from the window, Raziya **raised the alarm**.*

→ *See* **advise**

warning NOUN

A **warning** is something done to warn somebody of a possible danger or problem.

alarm
*As soon as the **alarm** went, firefighters were dashing for their machines.*

alert
*Notice of the **alert** went out, and maximum security was introduced.*

caution
*Police issued a **caution** to my brother for riding his bike dangerously.*

notice
*All the houses in the neighbourhood were given **notice** about the new road.*

premonition
*Fiona had a **premonition** that something bad was going to happen.*

→ *See* **sign (1)**

wash VERB

If you **wash** something, you clean it with water and soap.

bathe
*When I grazed my knee, Dad **bathed** it and put a dressing on.*

cleanse
*Finally I **cleansed** the kitchen floor with disinfectant.*

LANGUAGE TIP
If you wash your hair, you **shampoo** it. If you wash clothes, you **launder** them.

waste (1) VERB

If you **waste** time, money or energy, you use too much of it on something that is not important or you do not need.

blow (*informal*)
*Having won all that money, the gambler **blew** it on more gambling.*

fritter away
*It's a shame to see people **fritter away** their money on nothing.*

squander
*United **squandered** all their chances to win.*

throw away
*"This is your big chance," Mum said. "Don't **throw** it **away**."*

waste (2) NOUN

Waste is rubbish or other material that is no longer wanted, or that is left over.

garbage
*The **garbage** from the restaurant goes into big bins round the back.*

leftovers
*The **leftovers** from a meal can be used to make other dishes.*

remnants
*Achal and I managed to scoff the **remnants** of the adults' party food.*

rubbish
*"Make sure you pick up all your **rubbish**," said Mr Brahmin after our class picnic.*

scrap
*Much **scrap**, whether it's paper, plastic or metal, can be recycled.*

sewage
*In cities, **sewage** has to travel a long way through sewers before it can be treated.*

trash
*Our **trash** is collected weekly, and it is my job to put the bin out every Wednesday.*

LANGUAGE TIP
Trash is a word mainly used in America.

watch VERB

If you **watch** something, you look at it for some time and pay attention to what is happening.

concentrate on
*Mrs Richards told us to **concentrate on** the board.*

gaze at
*My sister spends hours **gazing at** herself in the mirror.*

observe
*The ornithologist sat quietly in the hide to **observe** the birds on the lake.*

pay attention
*"Now **pay attention**, you men!" the major rapped.*

stare at
*The outlaw and the sheriff **stared at** each other across the dusty street.*

view
*"You will be able to **view** the play very well from these seats," the usher told us.*

watch out VERB

If you **watch out** for something or someone, you keep alert to see if they are near you.

be on the alert
*It pays to **be on the alert** for any sign of danger.*

be on your guard
*"**Be on your guard**," the colonel warned. "There are enemy spies about."*

beware
*A sign said, "**Beware** of falling boulders". Were we supposed to catch them?*

keep your eyes open
*The captain told his crew to **keep their eyes open** for enemy submarines.*

look out
*Mrs O'Brien suggested we **look out** for deer.*

water NOUN

Water is a clear liquid that all living things need in order to live.

Some sounds water makes:
A brook **gurgles**.
Rain **patters** or **splashes**.
A river **rages**.
A spring **bubbles**.
A tap **drips**.
A waterfall **thunders**.

wave (1) VERB

If you **wave** your hand, you move it from side to side.

beckon
*Zaria **beckoned** me over to her house.*

gesture
*With a flapping movement, the police officer **gestured** for Dad to pull in.*

signal
*A crewman on the ferry **signalled** us to park where he indicated.*

wave (2) VERB

If you **wave** something, or if it **waves**, it moves from side to side.

brandish
*In triumph, the victorious soldier **brandished** the enemy flag.*

a b c d e f g h i j k l m n o p q r s t u v w x y z

A B C D E F G H I J K L M N O P Q R S T U V W X Y Z

flap
*The flag was **flapping** in the wind.*

flourish
*The musketeer **flourished** his sword, then held it aloft.*

flutter
*At the marina, boat pennants on the masts **fluttered** in the wind.*

shake
*Granny took the tablecloth outside and **shook** it to get the crumbs off.*

way (1) NOUN

The **way** of doing something is how you do it.

approach
*I liked Mrs Melville's **approach** to school – very firm, but good fun too.*

manner
*My gran has an odd **manner** of reading a book, very close to her face.*

means
*Hitchhiking is one **means** of getting from A to B very cheaply.*

method
*Mr Moahnty explained the **method** of doing the experiment.*

procedure
*There is a particular **procedure** for poaching eggs properly.*

technique
*The **technique** of shooting at soccer involves keeping your head down.*

way (2) NOUN

The **way** to a place is how you get there.

direction
*"Which **direction** is the town centre, please?" asked the visitor.*

journey
*The **journey** to Mordor was a long and dangerous one for a hobbit.*

route
*Our **route** took us through beautiful scenery.*

weak (1) ADJECTIVE

If someone is **weak**, they do not have much strength or energy.

delicate
*Mum said she was feeling rather **delicate** after her dose of flu.*

faint
*Kaila felt quite **faint** when she got to the end of her running race.*

feeble
*Grandad was very **feeble** when he came out of hospital.*

frail
***Frail** old people are at risk from broken bones if they fall.*

weak (2) ADJECTIVE

Something that is **weak** is likely to break or fail.

flimsy
*The **flimsy** fence soon fell down.*

fragile
*Mum's china teapot was **fragile**, as I found out when I dropped it.*

rickety
*I sat down gently in the **rickety** old chair.*

unsafe
*I told Violet the bridge was **unsafe**, but she wouldn't listen.*

weather NOUN

Weather is the conditions of sunshine, rain, wind or snow at a particular time in a particular place.

LANGUAGE TIP
The study of weather and climate is **meteorology**.

→ *See* **cold** and **hot** and **rain (1)** and **storm** and **wind (1)**

weight NOUN

Weight is the heaviness of something.

burden
*The **burden** of a head teacher's responsibility is considerable.*

load
*In a suspension bridge, the **load** is carried by the piers at either end.*

pressure
*To save his colleagues, the miner bore the **pressure** of the rock on his shoulders.*

weird ADJECTIVE

Something that is **weird** seems strange and peculiar.

curious
*They were on the way to school when a **curious** thing happened.*

extraordinary
*Suddenly an **extraordinary** bird appeared in the garden.*

funny
*"That's **funny**," said Mum. "I made twelve cakes. Now there are only ten."*

odd
*They heard an **odd** creaking sound coming from the cellar, and looked at each other in alarm.*

peculiar
*The stone was covered in **peculiar** marks, like ancient writing.*

strange
*Today a **strange** notice appeared in the sweetshop window.*

unusual
*The woman was wearing an **unusual** hat.*

well (1) ADJECTIVE

If you are **well**, you are healthy.

able-bodied
*The gym can be used by both **able-bodied** and disabled people.*

fit
*Mum and Dad have joined a gym to get **fit**.*

healthy
*"If you want to stay **healthy**, eat proper food and take exercise," advised the nurse.*

in good health
*Our neighbour was **in good health** for a lady of nearly 80.*

ANTONYM: ill

get well PHRASE

If someone **gets well**, they recover after an illness.

convalesce
*The wounded sailor was sent to **convalesce** at a special home.*

recover
*Children tend to **recover** from injury more quickly than adults.*

well (2) ADVERB

If you do something **well**, you do it to a high standard.

admirably
*Ulan coped **admirably** when his mum was poorly.*

brilliantly
*My eldest brother did **brilliantly** at university, and is now a scientist.*

expertly
*He twirled the spaghetti **expertly** around his fork.*

splendidly
*Mum and Dad said we acted **splendidly** in the school play.*

successfully
*The harvest **successfully** in, it was time to relax for Farmer Palfrey.*

superbly
*Dad played **superbly** to win the tennis shield.*

wonderfully
*The choir sang **wonderfully** in the concert.*

ANTONYM: badly

wet (1) ADJECTIVE

Something that is **wet** is covered or soaked with water or another liquid.

slightly wet:

clammy
*My forehead was **clammy**. Had I got the fever?*

damp
*A **damp** cloth is very effective for dusting.*

moist
*Those little **moist** wipes in a packet are good for car journeys.*

very wet:

drenched
*After two hours in the rain, everybody was **drenched**.*

dripping wet
*Running only a few metres in the storm left us **dripping wet**.*

saturated
*When something is **saturated**, it can hold no more liquid.*

soaked
*By the time the boat trip ended, we were **soaked**.*

soggy
*Although the pitch was **soggy**, the game went ahead.*

spongy
*On top of the moor, the ground was **spongy** and full of water.*

waterlogged
*As the pitch was **waterlogged**, there was no chance of playing.*

A B C D E F G H I J K L M N O P Q R S T U V W X Y Z

wringing (*informal*)
*All my clothes were **wringing** when I finally got in out of the rain.*

> **Try these lively words and phrases:**
>
> **like a drowned rat**
> *I got completely soaked and ended up **like a drowned rat**.*
>
> **soaked to the skin**
> *By the time he got home he was cold and **soaked to the skin**.*

ANTONYM: dry

wet (2) VERB

If you **wet** something, you make it wet.

drench
*My rotten brother **drenched** us with the hose pipe.*

saturate
*The mechanic's overalls were **saturated** with oil.*

soak
*After a hike, it's great to **soak** your feet in warm water.*

whole ADJECTIVE

A **whole** thing is all of that thing.

complete
*The **Complete** Works of Shakespeare is a very large book indeed.*

entire
*On our holiday we spent the **entire** time down on the beach.*

full
*A guide gave us the **full** tour of the old house, telling us all about its history.*

unabbreviated
*The **unabbreviated** version of a word or phrase is often easier to understand.*

wicked (1) ADJECTIVE

A **wicked** person is very bad.

cruel
*Several Roman emperors were **cruel** in their punishments.*

evil
*A pair of **evil** eyes peered out from the slit in the door.*

villainous
*The twins were **villainous** to the core.*

wicked (2) ADJECTIVE

A **wicked** deed is very bad.

devilish
*With **devilish** cunning, Blofeld masterminded his scheme for world domination.*

diabolical
*In the Middle Ages, some **diabolical** tortures were employed.*

malicious
*Someone had been making **malicious** phone calls.*

vicious
*With a **vicious** thrust of her sword, the pirate queen cut the rope holding him.*

vile
*Blackmail is a **vile** crime.*

ANTONYM: good

wide ADJECTIVE

Something **wide** measures a large distance from one side to another.

broad
*Paris is famous for its **broad** avenues.*

extensive
*We went for a walk along the **extensive** beach close to the cottage.*

large
*The **large** caravan took up more than one berth in the campsite.*

wild (1) ADJECTIVE

Wild animals and plants live in natural surroundings and are not looked after by people.

undomesticated
*"Animals in the reserve are completely **undomesticated**," the guide told us.*

untamed
*The **untamed** jungle is full of wildlife.*

ANTONYM: tame

wild (2) ADJECTIVE

Wild land is natural and uncultivated.

uncultivated
*Further up the slopes, fields give way to **uncultivated** moorland.*

unspoilt
*The **unspoilt** beaches of northern Scotland are wonderful.*

ANTONYM: cultivated

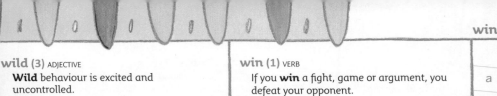

wild (3) ADJECTIVE

Wild behaviour is excited and uncontrolled.

frantic
*Keanu was going **frantic**, trying to attract my attention.*

hysterical
*The **hysterical** crowd tried to approach the singer as he left the stage.*

out of control
*Completely **out of control**, the mob smashed windows and looted stores.*

riotous
*Fortunately, **riotous** behaviour is rare in most countries.*

uncontrollable
*My sister had an **uncontrollable** urge to start leaping and yelling.*

wild (4) ADJECTIVE

Wild weather is stormy.

blustery
***Blustery** weather is not the best time to go for a sail.*

howling
*A **howling** gale swept in from the Atlantic Ocean.*

raging
***Raging** seas lashed against the harbour wall.*

violent
***Violent** squalls ripped past the shops along the seafront.*

willing ADJECTIVE

If you are **willing**, you are glad and ready to do what is wanted or needed.

agreeable
*Elina's mum was **agreeable** to my staying the night.*

cooperative
*Our neighbours were very **cooperative** about sharing the cost of mending the fence.*

game
*Jon is always **game** to go for a bike ride.*

prepared
*When Gran was ill, many people were **prepared** to take meals to her.*

ready
*Mrs Tarnat was **ready** to go through my work any time I asked her to.*

ANTONYM: unwilling

→ *See* **keen**

win (1) VERB

If you **win** a fight, game or argument, you defeat your opponent.

be victorious
*The Greeks **were victorious** over the Persians at the Battle of Marathon.*

succeed
*In conquering Britain, Claudius **succeeded** where Julius Caesar had failed.*

triumph
*City **triumphed** over United in the final.*

ANTONYM: lose

win (2) VERB

If you **win** something, you succeed in obtaining it.

accomplish
*Our team **accomplished** victory in the general-knowledge quiz.*

achieve
*Safiya **achieved** the highest marks in the test.*

attain
*Willem Jansz **attained** a place in history as the first European to see Australia.*

gain
*Mrs Bramble had **gained** a reputation as an excellent teacher.*

ANTONYM: fail

LANGUAGE TIP
To win several times in succession is to be on a **winning streak**.

win (3) NOUN

A **win** is a victory in a game or contest.

conquest
*The Norman **conquest** of England began in 1066.*

success
*The Rovers' **success** was down to the hard work they had put in.*

triumph
*The driver celebrated his **triumph** with champagne.*

victory
*Admiral Nelson died as news came of his **victory** at Trafalgar.*

ANTONYM: defeat

a b c d e f g h i j k l m n o p q r s t u v w x y z

wind (1) NOUN

Wind is a current of air that moves across the land and sea.

a gentle wind:

breeze
*A slight **breeze** rippled the silvery surface of the great lake.*

draught
*"Please shut the door – there's a **draught**," my father said.*

a violent wind:

cyclone
*Everyone was being warned about the approaching **cyclone**.*

gale
*A **gale** roared down the valley, whipping the autumn leaves off the trees.*

hurricane
*When the **hurricane** struck, whole roofs danced crazily in the sky.*

tornado
*The grey coil snaked up to the dense black cloud – a **tornado** was coming!*

typhoon
*A **typhoon** scattered the junks in the Chinese harbour.*

a sudden, unexpected wind:

gust
*The sudden **gust** sent the kite soaring high up into the clear blue sky.*

squall
*No sooner had the **squall** shaken up the leaves, than it was over.*

PRONUNCIATION TIP
When it means "a current of air", **wind** rhymes with "tinned".

wind (2) VERB

If something **winds**, it twists and turns.

coil
*Slowly, the snake **coiled** itself round the prey, and squeezed.*

loop
*The cowboy **looped** the lasso round the pommel of his saddle.*

roll
*The cashier **rolled** the wrapping paper into a tube to make it easier for me to carry.*

twist
*A clematis plant **twists** itself round other plants.*

turn
*The snake **turned** back on itself, making a loop.*

PRONUNCIATION TIP
When it means "twisting and turning", **wind** rhymes with "mind".

wind (3) VERB

If a road or river **winds**, it is not straight, but twists and turns.

bend
*The road **bends** several times in the next few miles.*

curve
***Curving** their way down the valley, the railway lines gleamed in the sun.*

meander
*The river **meandered** towards the sea.*

snake
*A commuter train **snaked** round the bend towards the station.*

twist
*The river **twisted** through the bottom of the valley.*

zigzag
*From the top of the cliff, a path **zigzagged** its way down to the sea.*

PRONUNCIATION TIP
When it means "not straight", **wind** rhymes with "mind".

windy ADJECTIVE

If it is **windy**, there is a lot of wind.

blowy
*It was **blowy**, and the dust swirled in the deserted streets.*

blustery
*In the estuary, sailing boats leant away from the **blustery** wind.*

breezy
*We had our picnic on the **breezy** cliff top overlooking the small harbour.*

squally
***Squally** showers blow up quickly, then die away again just as suddenly.*

windswept
*The **windswept** beach was deserted on a winter's afternoon.*

ANTONYM: calm

winner NOUN

A **winner** is someone who wins something.

champ *(informal)*
No one could box more than three rounds with the ***champ****.*

champion
To become ***champion****, drivers have to win more races than anyone else.*

conqueror
On her way to the title, she was the ***conqueror*** *of several former champions.*

victor
The Duke of Wellington was the ***victor*** *at the Battle of Waterloo.*

ANTONYM: loser

wipe VERB

If you **wipe** something, you rub its surface lightly to remove dirt or liquid.

dry
I quickly ***dried*** *the table with a tissue to get rid of the spilt milk.*

dust
There was no time to ***dust*** *the sideboard before the visitors arrived.*

mop
We had to ***mop*** *the kitchen floor after we'd tramped through in our football boots.*

polish
Dad ***polished*** *his favourite shoes ready for the interview.*

rub
"You'll have to ***rub*** *a bit harder than that," said Mum.*

wise ADJECTIVE

Someone who is **wise** can use their experience and knowledge to make sensible decisions and judgments.

perceptive
It was ***perceptive*** *of Helena to notice that Nuri was upset.*

prudent
Dan was very ***prudent****, and saved up his pocket money to buy the game he wanted.*

sensible
Mrs Nolan praised Faraji for making such a ***sensible*** *decision.*

shrewd
Dad is a ***shrewd*** *man when it comes to buying antiques.*

ANTONYM: foolish

wish VERB

If you **wish** for something, you desire or want it.

crave
Although my sister ***craved*** *chocolate, she was determined not to have any.*

hanker after
My friend Abiba ***hankered after*** *a new bike.*

long for
I ***longed for*** *the school holidays to arrive.*

yearn for
Grandad ***yearned for*** *the long-lost wartime days to return.*

wither VERB

If a plant **withers**, it shrivels up and dies.

droop
Dad rushed out to water the flowers because they were ***drooping****.*

dry up
All my seedlings ***dried up*** *in the sun.*

shrink
In the drought, the runner beans ***shrank*** *to half their normal size.*

shrivel
The leaves on the tree ***shrivelled*** *instead of turning a glorious red.*

wilt
She gave the wrong food to the houseplant and it soon began to ***wilt****.*

wobble VERB

If something **wobbles**, it shakes or moves from side to side because it is loose or unsteady.

quake
The ground ***quaked*** *as a tank rumbled past.*

rock
Believe it or not, all tall buildings ***rock*** *slightly in the wind.*

sway
As the wind blew, the tall pine tree ***swayed*** *gently.*

teeter
She watched the cup ***teeter*** *on the edge of the table before it fell.*

totter
My baby sister ***tottered****, bandy-legged, towards the door.*

wobbly ADJECTIVE

Something **wobbly** is shaking or moving from side to side because it is loose or unsteady.

A
B
C
D
E
F
G
H
I
J
K
L
M
N
O
P
Q
R
S
T
U
V
W
X
Y
Z

rickety
*Our shed is so **rickety** we daren't even hammer nails in to mend it.*

unbalanced
*For a moment the yacht was **unbalanced**, and tipped alarmingly.*

unstable
*Made **unstable** by the inrush of water, the ferry turned on its side.*

unsteady
***Unsteady** on his feet, the old man grabbed a nearby rail.*

ANTONYM: steady

woman NOUN

A **woman** is an adult, female human being.

ANTONYM: man

A woman...
who is engaged is someone's **fiancée**.
on her wedding day is a **bride**.
who is married is a **wife**.
whose spouse has died is a **widow**.
who has children is a **mother**.

wonder VERB

If you **wonder** about something, you think about it and try to guess or understand more about it.

ask yourself
*I often **ask myself** who might be out there in space.*

ponder
*Habika sat in the yard and **pondered** what she should do.*

puzzle
*We **puzzled** over why Tommy should have gone home so suddenly.*

wonderful ADJECTIVE

Someone or something **wonderful** is marvellous or impressive.

amazing
*It's **amazing** that a tortoise can live for over 150 years.*

awesome (*informal*)
*The snow-capped mountain is an **awesome** sight.*

fantastic (*informal*)
*I'm told that the northern lights create a **fantastic** display.*

impressive
*The Sydney Harbour Bridge is an **impressive** structure.*

incredible
*From our hotel there was an **incredible** view over the valley.*

magnificent
*From below, the white summit of Everest looked **magnificent** in the dawn.*

marvellous
*White-water rafting is a **marvellous** experience.*

phenomenal
*To win five gold medals is a **phenomenal** achievement.*

remarkable
*"It is quite **remarkable** what chimpanzees can do," said the zookeeper.*

sensational
*"That new musical is **sensational**," Mrs Gupta told Mum.*

terrific (*informal*)
*We had a **terrific** time at Haresh's party.*

word NOUN

A **word** is a single unit of language in speech or writing which has a meaning.

expression
*"Damsel" and "maiden" are old-fashioned **expressions** for "girl".*

term
*The words "bairn" and "wee" are just two of many Scottish dialect **terms**.*

The words...
that describe a picture are known as the **caption**.
that you use are expressed in your **language**.
that you know form your **vocabulary**.
of a book are known as the **text**.
of a play come from a **script**.
of a conversation are known as **dialogue**.
of a film come from a **script**.
of a song are its **lyrics**.

work (1) VERB

When you **work**, you spend time and energy doing something useful.

labour
*Malika and I **laboured** away, building our tree house.*

slave
*After we'd been **slaving** for two hours, Mum brought us a drink.*

slog away (*informal*)
*In the meantime, my sister was **slogging away** at her exam work.*

sweat (*slang*)
*A gang of labourers **sweated** and strained to raise the giant stone.*

toil
*We **toiled** in the sun and got very thirsty.*

Try these lively words and phrases:

keep your nose to the grindstone
*If you **keep your nose to the grindstone**, you will be a success.*

put your shoulder to the wheel
*It's difficult to **put your shoulder to the wheel** again after a holiday.*

work like a Trojan
*Sally **works like a Trojan**, but she never seems to get tired.*

work your fingers to the bone
*The farmers **worked their fingers to the bone** growing potatoes and apples.*

ANTONYM: relax

LANGUAGE TIP
To work with someone is to **cooperate** or **collaborate** with them.

work (2) VERB

People who **work** have a job which they are paid to do.

be employed
*Mum **is employed** at a firm of engineers.*

earn a living
*Grandad **earns his living** as a bricklayer.*

ANTONYM: be unemployed

work (3) VERB

If something **works**, it does what it is supposed to do.

function
*These days, most new cars **function** smoothly and reliably.*

operate
*On many bikes, the gears **operate** from a switch on the handlebars.*

work (4) NOUN

Work is the type of job someone has.

career
*I am hoping for a **career** as a journalist.*

employment
*Dad's first **employment** was as a waiter.*

job
*"What **job** does your dad do?" Ted asked.*

occupation
*My cousin's previous **occupation** was as a police officer.*

profession
*Teaching can be a rewarding **profession**.*

trade
*The building **trade** is sometimes busy, sometimes slack.*

work (5) NOUN

Work is tasks that have to be done.

assignment
*The journalist's **assignment** took her overseas.*

chore
*We all have a different **chore** to do around the house each week.*

duty
*"It is the **duty** of the monitor to check that everyone is ready," said Mrs Harley.*

task
*Dev was given the **task** of collecting in everyone's homework.*

yakka (*informal*)
*A decade of hard **yakka** on the land made Gramps old before his time.*

LANGUAGE TIP
Yakka is an informal word used in Australia and New Zealand. The work that you produce is your **output**, **production** or **performance**.

work out PHRASE

If you **work out** an answer to a problem, you solve it.

calculate
*I **calculated** it would take someone 23 years to walk to the moon (if they could!).*

figure out
*Philip finally **figured out** the way to fit the car wheel.*

A
B
C
D
E
F
G
H
I
J
K
L
M
N
O
P
Q
R
S
T
U
V
W
X
Y
Z

solve
*Gran and Dad used to enjoy **solving** crossword puzzles.*

worker NOUN

A **worker** is someone who does a regular paid job.

craftsman
*The carpenter was a skilled **craftsman**.*

employee
*Dad's firm has 700 **employees** working there.*

labourer
*The **labourers** stopped for lunch at one o'clock.*

workman
*Several **workmen** came to install the heating system.*

LANGUAGE TIP

The workers of one organisation can be called the **employees**, **staff** or the **workforce**.

---

world NOUN

The **world** is the planet we live on.

earth
*The **earth** is precious but, sadly, many humans do their best to spoil it.*

globe
*All over the **globe**, life can be found in every form imaginable.*

planet
*Our **planet** orbits the sun once every year.*

worn out (1) ADJECTIVE

Something that is **worn out** is damaged or worn so much that it is no longer useful.

decrepit
*We teased Mr Hogg about his **decrepit** car.*

run down
*Many of the warehouses along the canal are **run down**.*

useless
*Keisha threw away the **useless** pen.*

worn out (2) ADJECTIVE

Someone who is **worn out** is extremely tired.

exhausted
*At the end of term, Mrs Hibbert looked **exhausted**.*

shattered (*informal*)
*After the long car journey, we were all **shattered**.*

tired out
***Tired out** after a day's digging, Gramps slumped in the chair.*

weary
*By the time the walkers reached the inn, they were certainly **weary**.*

worried ADJECTIVE

If you are **worried**, you are unhappy and anxious about a problem, or about something unpleasant that might happen.

anxious
*I told Mum not to be **anxious** when I was away at camp.*

concerned
*Everyone was **concerned** about the recent spate of burglaries.*

distressed
*Jim gets **distressed** when anyone lets off fireworks nearby.*

troubled
*The old couple were **troubled** by their lack of money for heating.*

uneasy
*Since the break-in next door, Mum felt **uneasy** about going on holiday.*

worry (1) VERB

If you **worry**, you feel anxious about a problem, or about something unpleasant that might happen.

brood
*Isha refused to tell me why he was **brooding**.*

feel uneasy
*Gran **felt uneasy**, knowing that our family was away.*

fret
*"I do wish you wouldn't **fret** about something so trivial," Dad said.*

worry (2) VERB

If you **worry** someone with a problem, you disturb or bother them by telling them about it.

bother
*I didn't like to **bother** Richard, but I desperately needed a hand.*

harass
*The young reporter **harassed** her editor until she was given a better job.*

hassle (*informal*)
*"Don't **hassle** me," Dad said. "I'll mend your bike tomorrow."*

trouble
*Although she didn't want to **trouble** folk, Mrs Staunton really did need daily help.*

worry (3) NOUN

A **worry** is a person or thing that causes you to feel anxious or uneasy.

headache (*informal*)
*Finding supply teachers can be a real **headache** for schools.*

trouble
*Mum and her neighbours often share their **troubles** over a cup of coffee.*

worthwhile ADJECTIVE

If something is **worthwhile**, it is important enough to spend time or effort doing it.

beneficial
*Mountain air is very **beneficial** for people with lung problems.*

helpful
*Talib found extra tuition in literacy very **helpful**.*

useful
*The television programme gave several **useful** tips on decorating.*

valuable
*"Your help with my project has been very **valuable**," Mum told us.*

worth it
*Although very tiring, the trek up to the volcano was **worth it**.*

ANTONYM: worthless

wrap VERB

If you **wrap** something, you fold cloth or paper around it.

bundle
*Dick Whittington **bundled** his few belongings together and set out for the city.*

cloak
*That summer's morning, the valley was **cloaked** in mist.*

enclose
*A card was **enclosed** in the package containing my birthday present.*

envelop
*The whole affair was **enveloped** in mystery.*

surround
*With luck, the computer would be safe, **surrounded** by soft packaging.*

wreck VERB

To **wreck** something means to break, destroy or spoil it completely.

demolish
*A runaway truck **demolished** a bus shelter and a lamppost.*

devastate
*The city had been **devastated** by a bombing.*

ruin
*"You've **ruined** my painting, you oaf!" cried the artist.*

write off (*informal*)
*My big brother managed to **write off** his car by crashing it against a tree.*

ANTONYM: create

wriggle VERB

If a person or animal **wriggles**, they twist and turn their body in a lively and excited way.

squirm
*It was haircut time, and my baby brother **squirmed** in the chair.*

worm
*In Victorian times, children had to **worm** their way up chimneys to clean them.*

writhe
*Clutching her injured leg, the woman **writhed** in agony.*

write VERB

When you **write**, you use a pen or pencil to form letters, words or numbers on a surface.

To write...

badly is to **scrawl** or **scribble**.

emails or letters to someone is to **correspond** with them.

what people are saying is to **transcribe**, to **record** or to **take minutes**.

a rough version of something is to **draft** it.

a message on a document or on a surface is to **inscribe** it.

writer NOUN

A **writer** is a person who writes as a job.

author
*My favourite **author** came to talk to us at school today.*

creator
*The **creator** of the character Fungus the Bogeyman is Raymond Briggs.*

A person who...

writes about other people's lives is a **biographer**.

writes novels is a **novelist**.

writes for a newspaper is a **correspondent**, **journalist** or **reporter**.

writes plays is a **playwright** or **dramatist**.

writes poetry is a **poet**.

writes music is a **composer**.

wrong (1) ADJECTIVE

If something is **wrong**, it is not correct, accurate or truthful.

false
*The judge accused the witness of making a **false** statement.*

inaccurate
*Tabloid newspapers are often accused of printing **inaccurate** reports.*

incorrect
*"That's an **incorrect** answer," the quiz-show host said pompously.*

mistaken
*I was **mistaken**: the book was written by Tolkien, not C.S. Lewis.*

untrue
*It's **untrue** to say that new ideas are always better than old ones.*

ANTONYMS: accurate, correct, right

wrong (2) ADJECTIVE

If something is **wrong**, it is bad or immoral.

dishonest
*It is **dishonest** to tell lies or to twist the truth.*

illegal
*Dropping litter is **illegal** in most countries, and in any case it is a bad habit.*

immoral
*Many people think that testing cosmetics on animals is **immoral**.*

Try these lively words and phrases:

barking up the wrong tree
*When they got the results of the experiment, the scientists realised they were **barking up the wrong tree**.*

wide of the mark (*informal*)
*That answer isn't as **wide of the mark** as it seems.*

wrong (3) ADJECTIVE

If someone is **wrong**, they are mistaken or have wrongly judged.

at fault
*The truck driver was **at fault** for driving too fast.*

in error
*My calculation was **in error** by twenty pence.*

mistaken
*"I was **mistaken** about that man," my auntie said. "I thought he was that chap off the telly."*

to blame
*My sister felt she was **to blame** for the broken glasses.*

YOUNG ANIMALS

chick (chicken)

kit (rabbit)

cub (bear)

lamb (sheep)

puppy (dog)

joey (kangaroo)

Some other types of young animal:

calf (cow)	cygnet (swan)	duckling (duck)	fawn (deer)
foal (horse)	gosling (goose)	kid (goat)	kitten (cat)
leveret (hare)	owlet (owl)	piglet (pig)	pup (seal)

A B C D E F G H I J K L M N O P Q R S T U V W X Y Z

Yy

yell VERB

If you **yell**, you shout loudly, usually because you are angry, excited or in pain.

bawl

*My brother **bawled** up the stairs that dinner was ready.*

bellow

*The sergeant **bellowed** orders at the cadets.*

cry out

*I **cried out** in pain when I stubbed my toe.*

shout

*Zaki and Zina were **shouting** about whose turn it was to do the washing-up.*

yellow ADJECTIVE

If something is **yellow**, it has the colour of buttercups, egg yolks or lemons.

Shades of yellow:

amber	canary yellow	gold
lemon	mustard	saffron

young ADJECTIVE

A **young** person, animal or plant has not lived very long and is not yet mature.

➔ Have a look at the **Illustration** page!

Zz

zero NOUN

You can use **zero** to mean none at all.

nil

*They knew their chances of Dad taking them to the cinema were **nil** unless they promised to behave.*

none at all

*Old Mother Hubbard looked for food in her cupboard, but there was **none at all**.*

nothing

*There was **nothing** Jackie could find to wear for the evening out.*

zigzag VERB

If something **zigzags**, it goes in a line that keeps changing direction sharply.

bend

*Rory tried to draw a straight line, but it **bent** all over the place.*

twist

*The road **twisted** dangerously and the taxi driver found it hard to control the car.*

wind

*A narrow sheep track **wound** across the field.*

Writing Wizard

Before you start your story

We're going to be giving you a few hints and tips, which will help you to write brilliant stories.

What is my style?

Think about how you wear different styles of clothes for different occasions, for example school, going out or relaxing at home with friends. Writing is just the same – you use different styles for different types of writing. For example, you would write a scary mystery in a very different style to a funny diary, and a dramatic poem would be very different to an adventure story. Have a go at writing in as many different styles as you can!

Who are my readers?

Think about how you talk to different people in different ways, for example your friends, your family and your teachers. Writing is just the same – you write differently for different readers. Thinking about your readers while you write will help you to find the right style of writing for them.

Plan, plan, plan!

Before you start writing, you must make a plan! When you're travelling somewhere new, you use a map. When you're writing, you use your plan as a map. It helps you to understand where you are going and how to get there. Keep your plan with you while you're writing so you don't wander off and get lost! Have a look at the next page to see what your plan might look like.

Story plan

STORY TITLE:

What is my style?	**Who are my readers?**

CHARACTERS:

Who are the people in your story and what part do they play?

SETTING:

Where and **when** does your story take place?

BEGINNING:

Set the scene by introducing the characters and the setting. How are you going to hook readers and make them want to read on?

MIDDLE:

What's the main event of your story? How are you going to get from the beginning to the end without getting lost?

END:

How are you going to make your ending as strong as your opening?

Writing an exciting story

You will have met some very interesting people and been to some fascinating places in the stories you've read. Use the techniques we will show you on the next few pages to make your own writing come alive!

Creating brilliant people

You have the power to make anyone you want! So, who are you going to create? Make sure that they are brilliant and believable. Get to know your main characters really well by asking yourself questions like these.

How old is the character?

What do they look like – are they tall, sporty, fashionable, have freckles?

What's their personality like – are they kind, adventurous selfish, shy?

Using all your senses to describe places

Describing something using all your senses is incredibly powerful. It's particularly useful when describing settings. Think of a place in a story you are writing or have written recently and describe it using the questions below

What can you **feel**?

What can you **hear**?

What can you **smell**?

Use all five senses if you can!

What can you **see**?

What can you **taste**?

Describing feelings

A good writer understands how their characters are feeling and can describe those emotions. This is called *empathy*. Try these techniques to convey feelings to your readers.

- Think about point of view. You could use a narrator to tell the story from his or her own point of view. This makes it easy to describe emotions. For example:
  I felt ashamed and I didn't know what to do.
- Use actions to show emotions. For example, to show that someone is angry:
  She slammed the door loudly and stamped down the stairs.
- Use body language to show emotions. For example, to show that someone is scared:
  He shivered and wrapped his arms around himself as the footsteps got closer.

Using interesting adjectives and adverbs

This thesaurus is bursting with amazing adjectives and awesome adverbs. The Word Power pages are particularly brilliant!

Don't use words that are just 'good'... Use words that are 'splendid' or 'magnificent', 'tremendous' or 'wonderful'!

Don't just write 'well'... Write 'brilliantly' or 'fantastically', 'fabulously' or 'amazingly'!

Using special writing techniques

Read Text A and then read Text B.

Text A	Text B
The waves hit the beach. The wind blew through the trees. Rain ran down the window.	The waves crashed and smashed onto the beach. The wind howled through the trees like a pack of hungry wolves. The raindrops were rivers, which rapidly ran down the window.

As you can see, Text B is much more interesting to read. The writer has used four different writing techniques to make the text sound more exciting. Try using techniques like those shown below in your writing to keep your reader interested.

- ***simile:*** a way of comparing two things or people using 'like' or 'as': '*like a pack of hungry wolves*'.
- ***metaphor:*** a way of comparing two things or people by saying that one thing 'is' something else: '*The raindrops were rivers*'.
- ***alliteration:*** using words that start with the same letter close together in the same sentence: '*The raindrops were rivers, which rapidly ran down the window*'.
- ***onomatopoeia:*** using words that mimic the sound of the thing they describe: '*crashed*', '*smashed*' and '*howled*'.

Jsing a variety of long and short sentences

Read Text A and then read Text B.

Text A	Text B
I opened the door. I stood in the doorway. I could see a boy in the shadows. He was hiding. He was still. I moved slowly. I didn't want to frighten him.	I opened the door. As I stood in the doorway, I could see a boy hiding in the shadows; he was still. I moved slowly because I didn't want to frighten him.

Text B is more effective because the writer uses a mixture of short and long sentences and different kinds of punctuation, which makes it more interesting to read.

Using a variety of openers

Vary the way that you start your sentences to make your writing more interesting.

For example, you could use:

- a description opener: A huge, terrifying beast ...
- an adverb opener: Slowly, he turned around ...
- an '-ing' opener: Panting, she ran faster ...
- a 'where' opener: At the end of the road stood a ...

After you have written your story

It's easy to make mistakes when you're in the middle of writing an exciting story, so always read it through at the end. If possible, read it aloud, so that you will be able to hear any mistakes and correct them.

The following points are also a useful checklist when you have finished your story:

- **Does your story make sense?**

Make sure that your plot and structure are clear.

Don't forget your beginning, middle and end!

- **Have you used correct sentences?**

Remember to use full stops and capital letters!

This will make your writing easier to read and your readers will know where one sentence ends and the next begins.

- **Have you checked your spelling?**

Check any words you are unsure of. If in doubt, look up the word in a dictionary!

- **Have you used the correct punctuation?**

You must use the correct punctuation symbols to show your readers what is a sentence, a question, an exclamation or speech.

- **Have you used paragraphs?**

Don't forget to break your writing into paragraphs because these make it much clearer for your readers.

- **Have you used the correct grammar?**

Check that you've used the correct tense – stick to either past or present.

You're ready to start on your own story-writing adventures now. Always be imaginative and be brave. Happy writing!